Beef, Brahmins, and Broken Men

Beef, Brahmins, and Broken Men

An Annotated Critical Selection

from
The Untouchables

B.R. Ambedkar

Edited and annotated by Alex George and S. Anand

Introduction by Kancha Ilaiah Shepherd

Columbia University Press
New York

Columbia University Press
Publishers Since 1893
New York Chichester, West Sussex
cup.columbia.edu

Beef, Brahmins, and Broken Men: An Annotated Critical Selection from The Untouchables
First published by Navayana Publishing Pvt Ltd
ISBN 9788189059915
Annotations and this edition © 2020 Navayana Publishing Pvt Ltd
All rights reserved

The Untouchables: Who Were They and Why They Became Untouchables? was first published in 1948 by Amrit Book Depot, Delhi

Library of Congress Cataloging-in-Publication Data

Names: Ambedkar, B. R. (Bhimrao Ramji), 1891–1956 author. | George, Alex, editor. | Anand, S. (Journalist), editor. | Ilaiah, K. (Kancha), 1952– author of introduction.
Title: Beef, brahmins, and broken men : an annotated critical selection from the Untouchables, who were they and why they became untouchables? / B.R. Ambedkar ; edited and annotated by Alex George and S. Anand ; introduction by Kancha Ilaiah Shepherd.
Other titles: Untouchables. Selections. Annotated critical selection from the Untouchables, who were they and why they became untouchables?
Description: Shahpur Jat, New Delhi : Navayana ; [New York] : Columbia University Press, 2019 | Includes bibliographical references and index.
Identifiers: LCCN 2019036120 (print) | LCCN 2019036121 (ebook) | ISBN 9780231195843 (cloth) | ISBN 9780231195850 (paperback) | ISBN 9780231551519 (ebook)
Classification: LCC DS422.C3 A742 2019 (print) | LCC DS422.C3 (ebook) | DDC 305.5/688095475—dc23
LC record available at https://lccn.loc.gov/2019036120
LC ebook record available at https://lccn.loc.gov/2019036121

Not for sale in South Asia

[Ambedkar's dedication, 1948]

Inscribed to the memory of

NANDNAR

RAVIDAS

CHOKHAMELA

THREE RENOWNED SAINTS WHO WERE BORN AMONG THE UNTOUCHABLES AND WHO BY THEIR PIETY AND VIRTUE WON THE ESTEEM OF ALL

Contents

Introduction
    No Democracy Without Beef: Ambedkar, Identity
    and Nationhood
    Kancha Ilaiah Shepherd   11

Fool's Errand: A Note on the Notes to and Selection from
    Ambedkar's *The Untouchables*
    S. Anand and Alex George   65

      From B.R Ambedkar's *The Untouchables: Who Were
      They and Why They Became Untouchables?*

Preface   87

      Part IV: New theories of the origin of Untouchability.

Chapter IX: Contempt for Buddhists
as the root of Untouchability   112

Chapter X: Beef-eating as the root of Untouchability   146

      Part V: The new theories and some hard questions

Chapter XI: Did the Hindus never eat beef?   153

Chapter XII: Why did non-Brahmins give up
beef-eating?   183

Chapter XIII: What made the Brahmins become vegetarians?	199
Chapter XIV: Why should beef-eating make Broken Men Untouchable?	255
Part VI: Untouchability and the date of its birth	
Chapter XV: The Impure and the Untouchables	278
Chapter XVI: When did Broken Men become Untouchables?	323
The Broken Men theory: Beginnings of a Reading Alex George and S. Anand	351
References	375
Acknowledgments	399
Index	400

Beef, Brahmins, and Broken Men

No democracy without beef: Ambedkar, Identity and Nationhood

Kancha Ilaiah Shepherd

> We would have felt proud if the Vice Chancellor has told that we were suspended because we organized Ambedkar Vardhanthi, Babri Masjid demolition day and Beef festival in the last week. Anyways, this is not the first. Assertion of Dalits has been met with these kind of cunning suppression all over India—It's Christmas month, resurrection is more than likely in this season.
>
> —Rohith Vemula, 18 December 2015, Facebook post

In April 2012, a beef-themed food festival was organized by the Dalit students of Osmania University in Hyderabad. This was a good two years before the Bharatiya Janata Party (BJP) took control of the Indian parliament with Narendra Modi as prime minister with the brazenly stated religious agenda called Hindutva that is at odds with the Constitution, and seven years before it renewed its pincer-like hold on state and society in May 2019. The festival was part of B.R. Ambedkar's 121st birth anniversary celebrations, in which Dalit, Shudra, Adivasi and Muslim students, teachers and other social and political activists participated. Beef biryani was served in plenty, and the 'pure vegetarian' nationalism propagated by the right-wing

Brahmanic forces was collectively challenged. The public and celebratory consumption of beef was and is projected as anti-Indian by the right wing. A food item turned into an object of stigma and shame was being reclaimed as a symbol of pride, as a right. The purpose of the Osmania University beef festival was equally to declare that those opposed to beef were anti-human. About fifty members of Akhil Bharatiya Vidyarthi Parishad (ABVP), the students' wing of the BJP, stormed the venue and attacked the organizers and beef-eaters. The BJP was not a significant player in the southern state in 2012 and yet they could will their way to gratuitous violence. Five people were injured in the scuffle that ensued.

'Beef stalls', as they are called, have been successfully put up at the annual cultural festivals of all three major universities in Hyderabad, the city where I have lived and taught most of my professional life. In April 2011, the English and Foreign Languages University in the city saw fights break out over a beef festival in celebration of Ambedkar's birth anniversary by the Dalit Adivasi Bahujan Minority Students' Association (DABMSA) and the Telangana Students' Association (TSA). This festival was also attacked by the ABVP. A news report said:

> According to members of DABMSA and TSA, the ABVP activists barged into the campus kitchen, threw down the vessels in which the beef was cooked, and desecrated the food. The next day, beef supporters initiated a "food bandh" on campus, closing down the messes, canteens and stores and demanding inclusion of beef in the menu. They said that no food would be available on campus if their demands were not met (Thomas 2011).

The third major university in the city, the Central University of Hyderabad (HCU), gained global attention four years later, not for its achievements in the humanities or the sciences, but when Rohith Vemula, a PhD scholar in Science, Technology and Society Studies, committed suicide by hanging himself in January 2016. Over the past decade, HCU too had seen Dalit-Bahujan[1] students come up with stalls that served beef biryani, known locally as Kalyani biryani. The Kalyani variation of the meat-and-rice dish, that Hyderabad is reputed for, has an antiquity of some three hundred years. It is known for its distinctive flavouring of cubes of beef with tomato, cumin and coriander. It is no coincidence that Rohith Vemula was part of the Ambedkar Students' Association (ASA) that organized a beef festival. The date chosen was 6 December. It marks both Ambedkar's death anniversary and the day the Babri Masjid (a sixteenth-century mosque in Faizabad district, Uttar Pradesh) was demolished by coordinated right-wing militia under the aegis of Hindutva forces in 1992.

The epigraph to this introductory essay makes it clear why Rohith Vemula was forced to his death by a state that had declared war on young Dalit men and women who had dared to organize 'beef parties' and question the whims of the state (see *#Caste Is Not a Rumour: The Online Diary of Rohith Vemula* [2017], a compilation of his key Facebook posts from 2008 to January 2016).

Rohith and four other Dalit students—Vijay Kumar P., Seshu Chemudugunta, Sunkanna Velpula, and Dontha Prashanth, all members of the Ambedkar Students' Association—were suspended for allegedly assaulting an ABVP student leader on campus. Bandaru Dattatreya, a BJP member of parliament, and then Union Human Resource Development Minister Smriti Irani (whose portfolio included education) were proactively involved in suspending the 'anti-national' Dalit students. After being forced out of their hostel rooms and being denied access to libraries, the five Dalit students pitched a makeshift tent—a veliwada in Telugu—on campus, in the university shopping complex. It was made of life-size vinyl-printed posters of anti-caste thinkers, poets and activists from across the subcontinent—Buddha, Kabir, Gurram Jashuva, Ambedkar, Kanshi Ram, Savitribai Phule, Jotiba Phule, Ayyankali and Periyar.

On 17 January 2016, Vemula left behind a powerful suicide note entitled "My birth is my fatal accident", indicting the university authorities and the world at large, and took his own life in a friend's room. He hanged himself with the ASA banner. In the wake of protests and demands for justice for Rohith that spread across India and the international community of scholars and intellectuals, Kailash Vijayvargiya, a senior BJP leader in Delhi, had this to say: 'One who protested against the execution of terrorists, one who said he feels like sin whenever he sees saffron colour, *one who publicly announced to organise a beef party* ... cannot be a weak youth, who would have committed suicide' (*Hindustan Times*, 31 January 2016, emphasis added).

Rohith was part of a movement among students from diverse caste and minority backgrounds who across campuses in India have been conducting the kind of caste-aware and anti-caste politics that generations before them had not even thought of. Following the Ambedkar centenary celebrations and the implementation of the Mandal Commission recommendations (that offered quotas for members of the Backward Classes in education and jobs in the public sector to redress caste discrimination), both in the year 1990, the confidence of students belonging to Dalit, Adivasi and other Shudra communities rose.[2] Around the same time, the emergence of Kanshi Ram and Mayawati of the Bahujan Samaj Party empowered such politics. Dalit students have often formed alliances with other social, religious and sexual minorities, allowing for a spectrum of solidarities to emerge. Surely, there were left and radical left student movements in the country all along, but none of them ever gave thought to the beef question or to what was served on their plates in mess halls as 'standard' food over the decades. Since the late 1980s and 1990s, student bodies named after anti-caste icons such as Ambedkar, Periyar and Phule established themselves across campuses and questioned the Brahmanic status quo. The Ambedkar Students' Association in HCU, for instance, was formed in 1993. Such Ambedkarite politics and its critique of what was seen as Brahmanical food culture (and often curricula) gave impetus to the beef festivals. The pressure created by such Dalit initiatives also led to Ambedkar being taken seriously as a thinker and philosopher to be taught in universities. Beef festivals, despite the skirmishes with the authorities that their existence entailed, came to be a fixture in Hyderabad since 2006. The scholar Sambaiah Gundimeda, an alumnus of HCU, offers us a history of 'beef stalls':

> The Dalit Students Union, a few months before the *Sukoon* Festival in 2006, challenged this hegemony. They argued that the food in the stalls did not represent the cultural diversity of the university community, comprising students, teaching and non-teaching staff of the university, and was simply another manifestation of the hegemony of the upper castes and their culture. The university, as a public institution, it was further argued, should not allow its public space to be colonized by a particular culture. Instead, it should ensure that space is shared equally by every culture of the university community. In short, the cultural festival of the university should represent the many cultures of Indian society. As a

step towards equality in representation, the Dalit Students Union demanded that it should be allowed to set up a beef stall in the *Sukoon* festival. It was argued that beef constitutes an important part of the food habits of dalits and is thus part and parcel of dalit culture. Besides, such food culture is equally shared by Muslims and a few others from caste Hindu cultural backgrounds. The administration, the executive body of the university, was 'irritated', to quote one of the Dalit Students Union delegates, by this request and instantly denied permission for the stall on the grounds that 'consumption of beef... (in the campus) creates caste and communal tensions' (Gundimeda 2009, 130).

In 2012, the same year as Osmania University's first ever beef festival, Jawaharlal Nehru University tried to catch up and sought to play host to a historical first in the national capital: a beef and pork festival planned by a group called The New Materialists (who were careful to choose a non-sectarian name for themselves). I was to speak at the event called "Why Beef and Pork Food Festival in JNU?" held on the JNU campus on 17 August 2012.

A statement issued by The New Materialists made its argument forcefully:

> When we asked many of the so-called comrades about the celebration of beef and pork festival, they said that celebrating beef and pork festival is a sentimental issue. They advised us to cook beef or pork in our rooms and they promised to join us. So cooking beef and pork in room is not sentimental but openly celebrating is problematic for them. Because the public sphere belongs only to the hegemonic culture that is brahminism. In India, the public space is not yet public i.e. not for Muslims, Buddhists, Christians or any

Join Public Meeting on

WHY BEEF AND PORK FOOD FESTIVAL IN JNU?

Speakers
- Prof. **Kancha Ilaiah**, Author of "Why Am I not a Hindu", MAN Urdu University, Hyderabad.
- Prof. **A.K. Ramakrishnan**, JNU
- Prof. **S.N. Malakar**, JNU
- Dr. **Vivek Kumar**, JNU
- Dr. **Y.S. Alone**, JNU
- Ms. **Vani Subramaniam**, Film Maker
- Ms. **Sheeba Aslam Fehmi**, Columnist writer

17th August, Sutluj Mess
9.30 pm

THE NEW MATERIALISTS

other religion but only for Hinduism. The public space in India is private space for Hindu brahminical forces and thus nobody else can enter into this 'public space'. All the beef shops in India in many of the cities including Hyderabad are pushed into interior areas. Now the democratic space in India is shrinking and JNU as an institution is not an exception to it (The New Materialists 2012).

However, a functionary of the Vishwa Hindu Parishad approached the Delhi High Court, and it ruled that the festival should not be allowed, citing the Delhi Agricultural Cattle Preservation Act, 1994 (Chandran 2012a, 2012b). Often the Rashtriya Swayamsevak Sangh, the BJP and its many affiliates (known as the Sangh parivar or family) are blamed for the militant politicization of Hinduism, but few acknowledge or realize that a cow slaughter ban has been in place in Delhi since 1994, instated by a BJP government, which continued when the Congress party came to power and held power in the state for fifteen years. In many Congress-ruled states the ban has been in place since the 1950s. Although this law—like most laws in India—was not forcefully implemented, in 2017 the zealous Modi regime extended the ban to bulls and bullocks too. In effect, the BJP declared all beef-eaters to be 'anti-nationals'. It comes as no surprise that communities that do not put their hand to the plough—Brahmin, Kshatriya and Vaishya, of Jain and Hindu belief—sit in judgment about the cultural practices of labouring castes.

Most beef sellers in Delhi and other places where cow meat is proscribed are forced to claim that they are selling 'buff', or buffalo meat. Consumption of beef, or its proscription, does not seem to agitate or excite the secular-liberal elite either. The vociferous defenders of A.K. Ramanujan's essay "Three hundred Ramayanas" (Ramanujan 1991) or Wendy Doniger's *The Hindus: An Alternative History* (2010)—both of which got into trouble with the Hindu right and were banned—would never sign a we-love-beef petition. Consequently, when I participated in a television debate on an English language channel, the left-wing Brahmin historian from JNU, Mridula Mukherjee, best known for being the co-author with Bipan Chandra of the influential textbook *India's Struggle for Independence* (2000), argued that the beef question was one of 'nationalist sentiment', and asked why anyone would organize such 'anti-national' festivals in university campuses. A beef festival today is a breach of peace.

These beef festivals, or even the attempts to organize them, have fostered a pan-Indian movement among Dalit/Bahujan/Adivasi and other minoritized groups to assert their food rights, often at risk to life and limb. Poems and songs around beef were composed; pamphlets were issued. Literary texts by Dalits, Shudras and Adivasis were re-examined to look at how food culture, especially beef, figures in the lives of people.

Even after the mass conversion to Buddhism initiated by Ambedkar in 1956—in which he led half a million Dalits away from Hinduism and caste—beef has remained a staple in many Dalit households in Maharashtra. The 2009 Pune University Women Studies Centre project, *Isn't This Plate Indian: Dalit Histories and Memories of Food*, anchored by the feminist scholar Sharmila Rege, bears testimony to this (see Rege et al. 2009). As part of their master's course, students interviewed several Dalit men and women and documented their food practices and unique recipes. Daya Pawar's autobiography *Baluta* (1978), translated from Marathi in 2015, describes the significance of chaanya—strips of smoked beef roasted until they turn crisp. Cow's flesh is cut into long strips and hung on ropes and sun-dried for two to three days. It is then cut into smaller pieces, called chaanya, which can last a few months. Such practices are spread across the subcontinent with variations in the style of curing and preparation—what binds all is the love of meat. A range of tribals and lower Shudra communities eating fresh and dry beef is commonplace. Yet, the rest of the world has been made to believe that Brahmin–Bania-led Gandhian vegetarianism is standard Indian food culture.

A Marathi book of 2015, Shahu Patole's *Anna He Apoornabrahma* (Food is an Incomplete Creation), documents rare meat recipes from the Dalit households of Maharashtra. The author in an interview says:

> In old days, you could not afford to buy live animals and slaughter them. As a rule, these two communities (Mahars

and Mangs in Marathwada) had to clear away carcasses of animals, and they would eat the flesh. If there was a festival, or if there was a sacrifice of an animal, that was the only time you got live or halal meat. And we ate what we had to eat, because that was what was available… Let's take the subject of *chaturmaas* [a four-month holy period according to the Hindu calendar when fasts are observed]. Whom does this period place restrictions on? Those who do not engage in any strenuous physical activities. If a farmer or a labourer does nothing for four months, then they might also follow the ritual. So these traditions exist only for those people who do not earn their living through physical work. For those who do, even religion does not place any restrictions (Karkare 2016).

The new cultural assertion over beef has spawned powerful poetry and music as well. Here's an excerpt from "Goddu Mamsam" (Beef) by Digumarthi Suresh Kumar in Telugu in Naren Bedide's translation:

> When its udders were squeezed and milked
> You didn't feel any pain at all
> When it was stitched into a chappal you stamped underfoot
>   and walked
> You didn't feel hurt at all
> When it rang as a drum at your marriage and your funeral
> You didn't suffer any blows
> When it sated my hunger, it became your goddess? (2011)

Another bardic poet from Tamil Nadu, N.D. Rajkumar, who performs his poems set to ragas, sounds as forceful in Anushiya Ramaswamy's translation:

> Here, lay the cow
> Down in the middle of

The living room
Gut it, slice, and dice

O, Women, I have come
The God of the Forest
Give us this day
A feast of flesh (2010, 43)

Naliganti Sharath, a powerful poet and one of the principal organizers of the beef festival in Osmania University (who added Cobbler to his name after I added Shepherd), penned the 'Beef Anthem' that ends:

Buddha, Socrates, Plato, Aristotle,
Jesus, Mohammed, Marx, Ambedkar,
Newton, Einstein, Stephen Hawking,
Martin Luther, Malcolm X,
Lincoln, Lenin, Stalin, Guevara
Bob Marley, Bob Dylan,
Mike Tyson, Serena Williams,
Paul Robeson, Michael Jackson,
All the legends, all beef-eaters
Beef is the secret of life (2012)

In Chennai, popular movie director Pa. Ranjith who has pioneered Dalit themes and protagonists in mainstream cinema (with blockbusters like *Madras* [2014], *Kabali* [2016], *Kaala* [2018]) started the unabashedly Ambedkarite Neelam Cultural Centre that provides a platform for young Dalit rappers. Under the banner of The Casteless Collective, their 'Beef Song' launched in 2018 has become very popular.

While the harming and lynching of Dalits and Muslims—for either consuming or possessing beef, for slaughtering a cow past its prime, for skinning its carcass, or for merely transporting cows—has made headlines in recent years, the Dalit-led efforts to assert beef-eating with pride have not made as much news. In 2017, the union government issued a notification to tighten the regulation of the cattle trade across the country. The new rules on transporting cattle made communities that have nurtured our cattle economy over centuries look like enemies of the cow. They were dubbed as 'cow smugglers' by the forces of Hindutva. Students of the Indian Institute of Technology (IIT) in Madras, under the banner of the Ambedkar–Periyar Study Circle, protested this move with a beef festival in which several non-Dalit students took part. Even though beef is not proscribed in the state of Tamil Nadu, this again led to violence between student groups. As a consequence, December 2018 saw the segregation of vegetarian and non-vegetarian students in the hostel mess in IIT Madras.

Beef and its Indian trajectory

It is against this backdrop that we must today engage with what B.R. Ambedkar has said about the place of the cow and consumption of beef in his important but much-neglected 1948 work of historical investigation, *The Untouchables: Who Were They and Why They Became Untouchable?* The sidelining of Ambedkar and particularly this work in academic and intellectual circles, both in India and around the world, is symptomatic of the fact that most visible academicians and intellectuals of India or of Indian origin tend to be Brahmins or from the Brahmanical classes who show no interest in beef and the politics surrounding it. While the vegetarian, cow-loving Gandhi of the trading Bania caste was packaged and projected as an anti-colonial icon, the equality-loving, caste-hating Ambedkar was treated like an Untouchable by the elite.

Published against a landscape of everyday violence and fear that has escalated since 2014, this annotated edition of selections from *The Untouchables*, with a specific focus on the cow and the implications of eating beef reflected in its new title, will go a long way in busting several myths around the consumption of beef and the rather modern love for the cow that the non-labouring Hindu castes espouse. Communities that have never grazed cows have constructed theories of the cow's sacredness. This elaborate annotative exercise also looks at how and why this subversive and radical work of scholarship was neglected by so-called Marxist and liberal scholars for decades, which has brought us to the ugly present.

Ambedkar's argument, some of which is in agreement with the scholarship of Indologists before him, is as follows: around the fourth century of the Common Era, Brahmanism countered Buddhism's democratic and egalitarian appeal by appropriating its message of ahimsa; the cow became the central figure in this appropriation. Whereas earlier cows were sacrificed because they were sacred, now the sacredness became an excuse for their protection. However, because there were people who lived outside the village, as Broken Men, and who had the duties of collecting cow carcasses and eating their meat, they became figures of scorn. Their degraded position, compounded by their poverty, forced them to consume leftover meat, resulting in the creation of a new form of discrimination: Untouchability.

According to Ambedkar, these 'Broken Men' were Buddhists, not as practising bhikkus, but as people whose local idols, yakshas, yakshis, had been incorporated into the Buddhist pantheon by travelling monks. Although a majority of castes ate meat, it was the compounded effect of the above factors, chief among which was the continued consumption of cow carcasses even when the rest of the culture had moved away from it, that resulted in their ostracism and the birth of a new category of oppression. This perhaps can explain why the different castes that eat pig, sheep, goat, chicken or fowl did not form solidarity with them.

Ambedkar's work was published at a time when the debate around the cow had come to assume an exclusively Hindu–Muslim angle. However, Ambedkar sought to turn the focus firmly on the caste aspect and the pre-colonial, pre-Islamic past. He focused his study on old Brahmanical texts and the scholarship around them. His is an effort at paying the Brahmins back in their own coin and proving how their current-day arguments about the cow do not measure up to what their own texts say. However, he does not engage with the lived experiences of beef-eating among Dalits, Adivasis and Shudra communities. Nor does Ambedkar stop to examine the role of the buffalo in the Indian meat and dairy economy.

I shall not concern myself here with examining Ambedkar's hypothesis since this task has been undertaken at some length in the annotations and the adjunct essay on the Broken Men Theory. Besides, the links between Untouchability and beef-eating are more than clear. With an eye on history and Ambedkar's theory, my concern is with the unfolding present and how any proscription against beef by a modern, secular state strikes at the very heart of the health and livelihood of the poorest Indians while at the same time criminalizing large swathes of the population. The ban on consumption of beef and the curbs on trading in cattle today are nothing but the state practising a severe form of Untouchability with the collusion of the courts of law. Dalits, Muslims, Adivasis—or for that matter all who consume beef irrespective of identity—face a threat to life today. It is thus imperative to interrogate how this has come to be.

While working on *The Untouchables*, Ambedkar was also heading the Drafting Committee of the Indian Constitution; a document that, sadly, does not reflect his concerns on the question of the cow. In the years leading up to the so-called freedom struggle, both the Hindu right and influential figures like Gandhi harped on the cow's special place in the Hindu order of things. Akshaya Mukul (2015) has shown in his recent work how the reformist Arya Samaj (founded in 1875 by Swami Dayanand Saraswati), the Hindu Mahasabha (founded in 1915) and the Gita Press (established in 1923) drummed up caste-Hindu hysteria around the cow, especially as a means to browbeat Muslims. Mukul also chronicles the efforts of the mercantile Marwaris in funding what came to be known as the gau-raksha (cow protection) movement. Gandhi, whose ashrams and movements were funded by wealthy Marwari businessmen, preferred the less militant term go-seva, service of the cow, and in 1941 he established the Goseva Sangh with help from his patron, the industrialist Jamnalal Bajaj. Although Gandhi did not push for a law proscribing the slaughter of the cow, he argued that Muslims should voluntarily give up eating the cow. He once wrote: 'My religion teaches me that I should by personal conduct instill into the minds of those who might hold different views, the conviction that cow-killing is a sin and that, therefore, it ought to be abandoned' (1925, 21). Gandhi believed vegetarianism to be morally and nutritionally superior and he strongly advocated that the Untouchable castes give up meat-eating altogether. Yet he never asked the Brahmins and Banias to graze cows or try their hand at leather-work or agriculture. (His gestural politics was limited to cleaning toilets and also asking the scavenging castes to take pride in their work without expecting anything in return.) Generations of social scientists were influenced by his thinking, but scholars from Dalit-Bahujan backgrounds are now forcefully challenging this logic. For instance, Christina Sathyamala (2018) critiqued the 'structural violence of Hindu vegetarianism':

> Though Gandhi was averse to all flesh-eating, his upper-caste Hindu sensibility was particularly outraged at the consumption of beef, and it was the 'untouchable' caste groups which became the target for his reformist propaganda as they were the ones who openly consumed the flesh of cow. It was left to Ambedkar, born of this 'untouchable' caste group, to show how it was that the food hierarchy among the Hindus, specifically beef consumption, provided the material basis of the unjust caste system (Sathyamala 2018, 4).

While modernists like Nehru and Ambedkar were not for a religious ban on cow slaughter in the Constitution, they were under enormous pressure from the Hindu right in the wake of the Partition and the subsequent riots. Oddly enough, neither Nehru as prime minister nor Ambedkar intervened or said anything of significance on the cow protection debates in the Constituent Assembly.

From the time of debates in the Constituent Assembly to the televised shouting matches of today, it has been difficult to define and legalize the sacrality of the cow. The speeches by Syed Muhammad Sa'adulla and Frank Anthony, among others, pressing for clarity regarding the 'cow question' in the Constitution are cited and reproduced today. Gandhi, on his part, in 1947 tells a prayer gathering in Delhi of a 'wave sweeping the country', and that 'he was being flooded with telegrams demanding that cow slaughter be stopped. He was urged to persuade [prime minister] Jawaharlal Nehru and [home minister] Sardar Patel to enact cow protection laws' (De 2019, 255–6). During the Constituent Assembly debates, members representing the mercantile Marwari community interests joined hands with Brahmins—Seth Govind Das, Pandit Thakur Das Bhargava, Shibban Lal Saxena, Ram Sahai and Raghu Vira were most vocal in demanding a law to prevent the slaughter of the cow and wanted this enshrined as a 'fundamental right'. This had earlier been dismissed by Ambedkar, in his capacity as chairman of the Drafting Committee of the Constitution, stating that fundamental rights dealt only with human beings and not animals.

Thanks to Ambedkar, India did not become the only nation in the world to offer a 'fundamental right' to an animal. The concern for cows was however introduced into the Constitution in ambiguous language under the Directive Principles of State Policy. The provision under Article 48 entitled "Organisation of agriculture and animal husbandry" reads: 'The State shall endeavour to organise agriculture and animal husbandry on modern and scientific lines and shall, in particular, take steps for preserving and improving breeds, and prohibiting the slaughter of cows and calves and other milch and draught cattle.' On his part, Ambedkar ensured that Article 48 eschews religious language. While as a fundamental right it would have been enforceable, its inclusion as a directive principle makes it a non-justiciable though enabling provision. That is, each state in the federally bound Union of India is free to legislate on this matter. This is why we may relatively easily procure beef in Kerala, Tamil Nadu or the North-eastern states but not in Delhi, Madhya Pradesh or Gujarat.

It is not that the 'secularism' of the Congress is something one can count on, for after 1950, the Congress party-led states of Bihar, Uttar Pradesh, Rajasthan and Madhya Pradesh were the first to enact laws banning cow-slaughter. Since the so-called anti-colonial period, the Hindu right has been comfortably accommodated within the Congress. The BJP of today merely panders to a right-wing, caste-loving Untouchable-hating Hindutva-influenced public that is inherent to Hinduism, a tendency encouraged by everyone from Congress Gandhians to communist and socialist Brahmins. For instance, in the 2018 assembly election, after the BJP government in Madhya Pradesh was ousted, the new Congress government emphasized its commitment to cow protection and cow shelters. On 30 January 2019, Gandhi's death anniversary, the Congress chief minister of the state announced that one thousand gaushalas (cow shelters) will be set up in Madhya Pradesh in four months to accommodate nearly one lakh stray cows and progeny. By March of the same year, he had laid the foundation for thirty-six such gaushalas in Vidisha, making it clear that the party intended to fulfil its promise within the declared time period.

The violence of the non-violent

Let us now turn to some macabre yet defining moments in recent history. In what's marketed as 'vibrant' Gujarat, after present-day prime minister Narendra Modi, who belongs to the Bania caste of Modh Ghanchi but claims Other Backward Class status, had ruled as chief minister for three terms (2001–2014), members of a 'gauraksha samiti'—self-anointed cow-protection committees tacitly supported by the ruling BJP and schooled in the ideology of the RSS—entered the house of Balubhai Sarvaiya, a Dalit, in the village of Mota Samadhiyala on 11 July 2016. They assaulted seven persons: Sarvaiya, his wife Kuvarben, sons Vasram and

Ramesh, two relatives Ashok and Bechar, and a neighbour, Devarshi Banu, who had come to their rescue. Their alleged crime was that they had slaughtered a cow and were skinning it; later investigations proved that the cow was already dead. Dalit-Untouchables are expected to dispose of the carcass of a dead cow anyway. The mob then picked up Ramesh, Vasram, Ashok and Bechar, stripped and tied them to the rear of a car and dragged them half-naked to the town Una, twenty-five kilometres away, where they were again flogged in front of a police station. The mob was so confident that the proceedings were recorded with phone cameras and posted on social media, ostensibly to inspire others. The video went viral but before it could inspire right-wing mobs to do likewise, it spread indignation among Dalits and protests erupted across India.

While the BJP and its many Hindutva affiliates are sometimes compelled to account for assaults on Dalits—given that Dalits are deemed to be Hindus, even if of a lesser order—similar assaults on Muslims are brazenly justified. In September 2015, 52-year-old Mohammad Akhlaq of Bisara village in Dadri, on the outskirts of Delhi, was brutally attacked and killed by a mob led by local BJP leaders. His 22-year-old son Danish was left severely injured. Rather than acting against the criminals, the police filed a First Information Report against the victims for the consumption of beef. Meat found in Akhlaq's refrigerator was subjected to forensic tests and was claimed to be that of a cow. The RSS-run journal *Panchajanya* justified the lynching with a cover story "Vedas order killing of the sinner who kills a cow" (*Panchajanya*, 21 October 2015). Earlier, in 2014, in an address on state-owned national broadcaster Doordarshan on the eve of the Hindu festival Vijayadashami, the chief of the RSS, Mohan Bhagwat, said: 'We feel it necessary to put a ban on meat exports, beef in particular and cow smuggling in the immediate future [cited in Saba Naqvi 2014].'

As of February 2019, India Spend, a policy research think-tank, reported that of the 123 instances of cow-related violence between 2010 and 2018, 98 per cent occurred after the BJP came to power in 2014. Muslims account for 56 per cent of the victims of such violence and for 78 per cent of those killed because of it (Saldanha 2019). That Dalits account for around 10 per cent of these victims should not detract us from the fact that many of the Muslims in India are converts from erstwhile oppressed castes, and the xenophobic hatred of the Hindutva forces against Muslims is compounded by their general hatred for the productive castes. Parallel to these developments, as constitutional historian Rohit De says: 'The last decade has seen new laws regulating the slaughter of cows enacted in Maharashtra, Karnataka, Haryana, and Rajasthan. There have been writ petitions before the high courts of Delhi, Madras, and Bombay as well as the Supreme Court of India either asserting or challenging the bans on cow slaughter' (2019, 249–50).

While a false image of India as a land of vegetarianism and nonviolence has been created across the globe, the truth is the opposite. Even government studies, such as the annual National Family Health Survey, have shown that up to 70 per cent of Indians eat meat—negatively labelled in India as 'non-vegetarian' food. Nutritionist and scholar Veena Shatrugna has consistently argued that the so-called standard Indian vegetarian fare of lentils-vegetable-rice-ghee-curd was made normative, starting in the 1960s, due to state-led policy efforts, often helmed by Brahmins and vegetarians. The former deputy director of the National Institute of Nutrition says:

The RDA (recommended dietary allowance) was calculated in laboratories by well-meaning, nationalist scientists and economists. Eminent people like C. Gopalan, V.M. Dandekar, Nilakanth Rath and M.S. Swaminathan. When you do nutrition in a lab, cost becomes a major factor. These were all upper class, upper caste—Brahmins, for the most part—who used their own preference for vegetarian diets to offer simple, scalable solutions to provide "adequate" calories to the vast numbers of the poor of the country. They did not understand the food culture of the poor people who ate a variety of meats from mutton to pork, rabbits, tortoises, beef, and birds, apart from a whole lot of fruits, berries, tubers and eggs (Jishnu 2015).

Combined with this was the so-called Green Revolution of the 1970s, where capitalism was imposed on a feudal agrarian system in the name of redressing the prevailing food crisis. This introduced machine-intensive monocultures of cash crops that came to decide the food on our plates in public institutions. This 'pure vegetarian' Gandhian brigade has no solution for the dire scarcity of food, caused in no small part by the beef and meat bans, in a country with a current population of over one billion. It is no exaggeration to claim that if everyone adopted vegetarianism, the nation would collapse. While Shatrugna speaks in her professional capacity, the Hindi writer and critic Anita Bharti, in an interview with Sharanya Deepak, speaks from personal experience:

> "I don't understand this word [essentials]. Rice, turmeric, jaggery—who thinks about, who can afford and eat these? My husband is from an upper-caste Kshatriya family, and I remember the first time I went to eat at his house," she said. "*Roti, sabzi, dal, dahi, achar* (bread, vegetables, lentils, yoghurt,

pickles) and salad all for one meal, whereas in my house, we ate *roti*, and one dish, that's all we needed." She added, "The upper-caste minimum is our maximum" (Bharti 2016).

Yet it is not the mere consumption of meat that leads to violence. The cow—not the black buffalo—is at the heart of the matter. And it is the notional association of beef-eating with Untouchability that lies at the root of the problem. From Gandhi to former president Rajendra Prasad (a Kayastha by caste) to Narendra Modi, including judges in the Supreme Court (see Gundimeda and Ashwin 2018), countering bigots with facts and reason does not get us far. If reason were to govern our lives, caste itself could have been wished away. Like Ambedkar says in *Annihilation of Caste*, caste accords with neither reason nor morality; it merely seeks hierarchy, one way or another:

> How are you going to break up caste, if people are not free to consider whether it accords with reason? How are you going to break up caste, if people are not free to consider whether it accords with morality (2014 [1936], 303)?

It is a fact—clear as daylight to even Brahmin scholars before and after Ambedkar (from P.V. Kane 1941 to D.N. Jha 2001)—that the Vedic Brahmins did eat beef and slaughtered cows, and to them no Untouchability applied. Since caste can never be held accountable to morality or even notional equality, the modern association of beef-eating with Untouchability is as such irrational. And if eating beef is a marker of Untouchability, giving it up does not remove the taint either. This argument was made by Periyar way back in 1926 in a speech he delivered at the village Siravayal in Karaikudi district:

> [...] they find fault with you [Paraiars], that foul smell comes from your body, that you do not take bath, do not wash

clothes, that you eat beef, that you drink alcohol and preach that you must give up all these. […] it is not an honest act to say that your eating beef and drinking alcohol is the reason for your being 'paraiar'. In fact, those who eat beef and drink alcohol are ruling the world today. Besides if you eat beef, the fault is not yours. As you have not been allowed to earn, eat well, walk in the streets, freely move about to go and work and earn accordingly, you are obliged to eat with your limited resources to have more to eat whatever can be had for that money. […] My conclusion is that this is a dishonest, irresponsible reason for keeping you in a degraded condition rather than a real cause. I am not objecting that beef and alcohol should be given up. But when some say that if you give up these your caste will have a higher status, then I object to that dishonest uttering. I will not ask you to give up beef or alcohol just to raise your caste to a high level. For that, there is no need for you to do either. […] giving up what is consumed by all has nothing to do with becoming a higher caste. So if any one says avoiding beef and alcohol is good to become a higher caste I say it is a lie (Periyar 2015).

Among the Scheduled Caste communities and Dalit individuals, there are many who do not eat beef and yet face Untouchability. The solution to this, as I have been arguing for some time now, is Dalitization—the philosophical and material opposite of what Brahmanical sociologists like M.N. Srinivas, Andre Beteille and their acolytes have described as Sanskritization (the desire for upward mobility by imitating a superior caste, with the Brahmins at the apex, despite their being a social and cultural minority).

Dalitization as democratization

Dalitization is not simply about eating beef but about changing one's attitude to questions of dignity, food culture and labour. It is a move toward equality. Dalitization is about the democratisation of society by disregarding the false divisions of the sacred and the profane, of the high and the low. Dalitization is surely not about forcing anyone to eat beef or any meat; it is about challenging those who question the right of others (often Dalits and Muslims) to eat beef or any food of their choice; it is about challenging the false and unnatural consensus around vegetarianism imposed unjustly and violently. The act of serving and partaking of beef (or pork) in public in India is quite like the Ambedkar-led act of drawing water from the Chavadar Lake in Mahad in 1927. Echoing what Ambedkar had said at Mahad—'We are not going to the Chavadar Tank to merely drink its water. We are going to the Tank to assert that we too are human beings like others. It must be clear that this meeting has been called to set up the norm of equality'—the Dalit and non-Dalit students behind beef festivals on campuses are saying that by serving and eating beef they are not merely quelling hunger, but asserting that they too are human beings, the food they love to eat is just as equally food. Each beef festival is a meeting to set up the norm of equality.

Ambedkar, in a speech at the Round Table Conference in 1932, speaks of the caste system being an 'ascending scale of reverence and a descending scale of contempt'. The contempt, in essence, is for work that involves both the body and the mind, physical and intellectual labour. Consequently, graded hierarchy leaves those who deal with the disposal of dead cattle and their skinning and tanning as the lowliest of castes. Meanwhile, so-called upper castes claim greatness for themselves for what is ostensibly the thoughtless repetition of useless tasks: the Brahmin chants his slokas unconcerned by

their meaninglessness; the Kshatriya kills enemy after enemy without stopping to think why; the Vaishya is preoccupied with counting the money he amasses. These castes are deemed more productive than the labourers who creatively work the land, who use their tools to fashion new objects, who solve problems and engineer the world so that its harshness can be survived.

Another of Ambedkar's dictums explained in *Annihilation of Caste* (2014) is that caste as a system is not just 'a division of labour but a division of labourers'. It therefore follows that while the disposal of a carcass became the occupation of one caste (Mahar), another caste (Chambhar) is expected to skin the dead animal, tan the hide, and make useable goods of it. Hierarchies within Untouchable castes become possible only because of their being scaffolded to a larger System of Castes (as Ambedkar was wont to say, using capitals for emphasis) sustained by Brahmanic ideology. The more closely a person works with organic matter—be it earth, fabric, wood or animal skin—the lower she is placed in the descending scale of contempt. With no irony, castes that are forced to do the work of cleaning—including attending to basic human needs such as shaving, washing clothes, and scavenging—are considered ritually impure. While exit from the matrix of caste does not come about by merely giving up a 'traditional' occupation, at the same time annihilation of caste is not possible without breaking the caste–occupation nexus.

While Ambedkar was right in asking all Untouchables to stop doing the pro bono 'duty' of disposing off dead cattle and eating carrion and surviving on rotting leftovers thrown at them from a distance—in Gujarat a young Dalit leader Jignesh Mewani issued a similar call in wake of Una in 2016—it is not as if desisting from such occupations rids one of the stigma of Untouchability. To stop eating beef is neither practical nor economically viable. Indeed, there's a big difference between eating beef out of choice and being forced to eat it out of lack of choice like Untouchables have done over centuries. Their traditional duty—projected often as right—as part of the caste order, was to dispose of carcasses and in the process claim every part of the dead cow (or buffalo). On the other hand, the upper-caste vegetarianism is not a food culture based on individual choice either; it is merely a habit enforced in childhood. Besides, no Dalit community ever forces anyone else to consume beef. Conventionally, those designated as Untouchable, impoverished and exploited as they are, did not get to eat a cow after having slaughtered it in its prime; as a rule they had the 'right' to a cow only after it had died of old age or disease. The meat is therefore often stringy, not juicy, and yet they made the most of it.

The meat of our fellow mammal is as much a metaphor of convenience today as Ambedkar diagnosed it to be in 1948. He argued that many Hindu ritualistic beliefs like Brahmanical idolatry, vegetarianism and devotion to the cow came into practice only as the stronghold of Brahmanism was threatened by the popularity of Buddhism, and thus what was 'sacred' needed to be constantly performed, uttered, and upheld—but always in ways that were oblique. As Ambedkar, following Durkheim, explains in *The Untouchables*:

> The interdiction on contact rests upon the principle that the profane should never touch the sacred. Contact may be established in a variety of ways other than touch. A look is a means of contact. That is why the sight of sacred things is forbidden to the profane in certain cases. For instance, women are not allowed to see certain things which are regarded as sacred. The word (i.e., the breath which forms

part of man and which spreads outside him) is another means of contact. That is why the profane is forbidden to address the sacred things or to utter them (p. 253–4 in this edition).

An interdiction cannot, however, stop people from eating what they will and must eat. Besides, if one of the theoretical premises of democracy is equality—and India's claim is it is the most populous democracy on earth—then equality must begin with food and the right to eat what one likes, wants and needs. What one eats cannot and must not be legislated about, unless it involves partaking of endangered species (a pastime of the very rich) or eating one's own species (an aberration). Yet one often hears stories of how many non-Dalits, Shudras and even higher castes happily tuck into beef across India—ostensibly for its taste—but would not admit to doing so in public. It is not as if the beef stalls of Hyderabad and other mainland Indian cities that I have been to are frequented exclusively by Dalits and Muslims. Others do queue up on the sly.

Just like Veena Shatrugna tells us of the consequences of Brahmin male domination in the field of sciences that decided on key, life-affecting factors like 'recommended dietary allowance' (that exclude eggs), it is again mostly the Brahmanical scholars who have dominated the social sciences and have made decisions on what is to be studied and how. Surely we have had several anthropologists and sociologists doing immersive studies by living with weavers, potters, various Adivasis, slum-dwellers and so on (often without partaking of regular food with them). But the life-worlds of these labouring communities are reflected neither in what's taught in schools, colleges and universities nor in the food served in the mess halls—be it in the Jawaharlal Nehru University in Delhi or Osmania University in Hyderabad. The well-funded liberal arts universities mushrooming across

India (Ashoka, Jindal, Shiv Nadar, Azim Premji, FLAME), where the wards of the rich pay up to a million rupees a year to get into reservation-free 'islands of excellence', offer no room for debate on these issues in their curricula or mess halls.

There's little doubt that the so-called secular-liberal intellectual in India, often a high caste person, is squeamish about beef. They may, if at all, eat it in the protected environs of a star hotel paying a heavy price, or when they travel abroad, but they do not countenance beef being served as part of one of the conferences or seminars organized in university premises.

Except in Kerala, where almost everyone save for some Brahmins eats beef, even the Indian left, which remains Brahmin-dominated, does not really push the beef question even in places like Chennai or Hyderabad where the sale of beef is not banned. In fact, in West Bengal, a communist stronghold for decades (where Muslims account for 27 per cent of the population and Scheduled Castes 23 per cent), a Communist Party of India (Marxist) leader and former Kolkata mayor, Bikash Ranjan Bhattacharya, was severely reprimanded by a cross-section of Left Front leaders for participating in a 'beef-eating event' in 2015 held after the murder of Akhlaq. *The Hindu* reported on 7 November 2015:

> "During the meeting, CPI's State Secretariat member Swapan Banerjee said that Mr. Bhattacharya should not have participated in the beef-eating event as it may create negative impression on a section of the society," a senior Left Front leader told *The Hindu*. He also said the CPI leadership expressed its displeasure over the "media hype" created by the organiser's [sic] of the event. "Mr. Banerjee wondered what Mr. Bhattacharya was trying to prove by taking part in that protest. He said that food habits are

one's personal matter. He could have eaten beef at home," the Front leader added. According to Front insiders, senior Forward Bloc leader Hafiz Alam Sairani also criticized Mr. Bhattacharya's actions. "Left Front chairman Biman Basu also agreed that it would have been better if Mr. Bhattacharya did not take part in the event," sources said.

An incident from my days in the left-based civil liberties movements in Andhra Pradesh comes to mind. When I was part of the Andhra Pradesh Civil Liberties Committee, I suggested that they serve beef at their annual conference in 1995. This was unprecedented. The Brahmin leaders fell silent. The exclusion of beef had apparently happened almost naturally over the years. One fellow-Shudra member of the group, Burra Ramulu, said that he could arrange beef to be served at the Warangal conference, and he did. I recall most Brahmin delegates avoided the beef-eating except for the writer and lawyer K. Balagopal.

What is the way out? It is neither practical for whole swathes of a population to stop doing labour that enriches and sustains the lives of millions, nor would they be able to wholly Sankritise themselves and, over generations, turn into Brahmins. Ambedkar, in a speech in the Constituent Assembly on 4 November 1948, was right in condemning the Indian village as a 'sink of localism, a den of ignorance, narrow-mindedness and communalism'. He even advocated that Dalits, who have no nostalgia for any mythic golden age, must try and migrate to cities, get an education and Westernise themselves to escape caste. Good, modern education in the English medium may be a way out of Sanskritization and Hinduisation but that, in most cases, is an unequal desire with vegetarian Brahmin and Bania children dominating this field.

Conversion to Buddhism, Ambedkar had hoped, would

offer the ultimate exit from caste. But we have seen over the decades that thronging to the cities does not quite end the workings of caste nor does conversion since Dalit Christians and 'Pasmanda' Muslims (as low-caste Muslims are known in parts of North India) continue to face caste discrimination. Often in cities the low-end jobs are reserved for Dalits, poor Muslims and other poorer backward castes or Shudras, irrespective of whether they are Buddhists who have given up beef-eating or not.

Caste as a system survives by devising new ways of keeping people fenced in and fenced out. In this light, the call for Dalitization is not just rhetoric but a call for reason: it does not mean a mere reversal by embracing what Brahmanical thought denigrates, but it is about taking reasonable pride in items of food and forms of labour that would earn respect, status and wealth in any other society. We must learn to recognize that there's more art in a well-made shoe, in a fried strip of salted beef, in an expertly wrought clay pot and in a sheaf of freshly harvested grain than in a single meaning-defying verse from the *Rig Veda* or of contemporary poets who in 2015 returned state-issued awards to protest the killings in the name of the cow and Hindutva. This is why in Telugu we often say to someone who is idling: *pani-paata leda*? Which means, don't you have any work-and-song to go about? For the working castes, work and song go together; ethnologists and anthropologists have laboured enough in fields of their own making to prove this.

While in the Sanskritization thesis, the figure of the Brahmin is imagined as the norm, and the obscure, inaccessible and exclusionary Sanskrit language is projected as an aspirational ideal, for Dalitization, we must take the beef-eating labouring

Untouchable figure as our new universal. If everyone who claims to be secular and enlightened in India adopts this approach and ceases to see beef as the food of only Dalits and Muslims, it will be a bigger blow to caste-fixated Hindutva than conversion to Buddhism or any religion can be. It also removes the onus from the Dalits and oppressed castes, who are often asked to adjust, to try and 'fit in', and puts it on the privileged castes—the ones who benefit from this system, the ones who need to desist from their casteist ways and the ones who actually should be asked to change their behaviour. This also means beef, as a source of rich protein, needs to be embraced by everyone. If vegetarianism has been forced down our throats for centuries, it is time we reclaimed beefarianism. It is time we let go of Brahmanism or the ideology of caste that has concocted a theory of starving the labouring castes while the Brahmins and Vaishyas stay away from the actual work of production and labour, espousing a spirituality that assumes an anti-life ethic.

The buffalo, from Harappa to now

If history is what we need to keep looking back at for validation, we may well turn to the Harappan era that begins at about 7000 BCE. Recent advances in archaeology, linguistics, genetics (Reich 2018) and history (Joseph 2018) have proven how the buffalo in India was both domesticated and consumed in the Harappan period. It has also emerged that the Harappans had little to do with those who came later and called themselves Aryan and spoke Sanskrit. The Harappans, themselves migrants from Zagros (western Iran), mingled and interacted with people whom historians are designating as the First Indians of pre-history, who in turn were Out-of-Africa migrants. Science and history now tell us in one voice that all of us who call India home—Dalit, Shudra, Brahmin, Tribal, Aryan and Dravidian, Ancestral North Indian or Ancestral South Indian, Hun, Turk, Austroasiatic and Mongol—came out of Africa. All of us ate many things to survive; our food cultures evolved both scientifically and organically over time. Beef has been very much an 'Indian' food since the beginnings of what we call civilization in the subcontinent.

It is also a fact that today buffaloes in India produce more milk than cows, and that their thicker milk contains not only more fat (7.5 per cent against 3.5 per cent in cows) but a higher percentage of Vitamin A (9 per cent for buffalo milk against 7 per cent for cow) and calcium (41 per cent against 27 per cent), among other positives. While cows account for 45 per cent of milk production in India, not all these cows are indigenous. Over half of this yield comes from cross-bred animals containing genetic material of 'Western' breeds such as Holstein Friesian, Jersey and Brown Swiss. Indigenous breeds, considered worship-worthy by the non-productive Brahmanic castes, while accounting for 45 per cent of India's milch population, produce just about a fifth of its milk. A senior Indian journalist reporting on agriculture for over two decades has this to say:

> For an indication of where farmers' rational choices are leading to, one needn't look beyond Gokul and Vrindavan—the holy sites of Lord Krishna's childhood life centred around cows, milk, butter and *gopis* [young herding women Krishna was promiscuous with in mythic stories]. According to the 2007 Livestock Census, Mathura district, of which they are part, had a total cattle population of 141,326, whereas its buffalo numbers were five times higher, at 722,854 (Damodaran 2012)

So the so-called 'cow belt' (a term for the regions UP and

Bihar, also called Aryavrata) has actually become a buffalo belt. A Ministry of Agriculture report of 2016 proffers this: 'The percentage share of buffalo milk production estimate in total milk production estimate in Uttar Pradesh was 69.54 per cent during 2014–15' (Ministry of Agriculture and Farmers Welfare 2016). Since keeping a cow and transporting or slaughtering it has been made impossible through legal means, the BJP and the Congress may competitively and unwittingly be ensuring that the farming communities soon give up on the native cows and take to only the hardy and unholy buffaloes.

Besides its contribution to the dairy economy, the buffalo enriches our lives even after its slaughter or death: by 2013, India emerged as the largest exporter of buffalo beef, known in the trade as carabeef, beating Australia and Brazil with 1.56 million tonnes. As of 2018, according to the United Nations' Food and Agriculture Organisation (FAO), India has the largest cattle inventory in the world (34 per cent) and is followed by Brazil and China. The United States comes fourth. In the leather industry, too, the buffalo leads—of total leather exports from India, 40 per cent of buffalo and 30 per cent of goat rawhide skins are used for leather. Across India—which has 20 per cent of the world's cattle and buffalo and 11 per cent of the world's goat and sheep populations—the buffalo is a much-loved animal. Though not all Dalit-Bahujans can afford a buffalo, they graze it, love it, eat it, and are intimately familiar with its cultural and economic value.

It comes as no surprise that since the Harappan period several cultural practices have survived the imposition of the tyrannical caste system by the Aryan Brahmins for over two thousand five hundred years. Offering an overview across disciplines, Joseph writes that the items that twenty-first century

Indians use which can be traced back to the Harappan era can make for an endless list: from precision-made burnt bricks made of uniform height to width to length ratio of 1:2:4, to seals depicting veneration for the peepul (bo) tree and seals where buffaloes are shown being both venerated and speared, seals with yogic-looking figures wearing a horned buffalo headdress, seals with the serpent and possibly the phallic symbol, to the 'handi' or cooking pot with a ridge to avoid direct heat on the hand, and more—all of these 'have been derived not from the earliest Vedas, but from the pre-Aryan population' (Joseph 2018, 144). The Harappan civilisation spread across one million square kilometres, a third of what constitutes India today, has left a deep impact on how we now live and on what we eat.

While the cow was made central to the Vedic worldview—as an object of both sacrifice and food of the Brahmins—the black buffalo was ignored. In fact, latter-day Hinduism turned the buffalo into a demonic asura character called Mahisha or Mahishasura (*mahisha* is the word for buffalo in Sanskrit). The goddess Durga murders the buffalo-headed demon Mahisha and assumes the name Mahishasura-mardini, the woman who kills the Mahisha. This ritual murder of a figure of Shudra-Untouchable-indigenous origin, shown often as a denier of caste laws, is one among many acts of murder in Brahmanic narratives. In several parts of South India, Mahishasura's ritual killing is re-enacted, and Dalits are forced to do the slaughtering as archived by the Kannada Dalit writer Aravinda Malagatti in his autobiography *Government Brahmana* (1994, 2007). Such killings are celebrated by a large section of Hindus as festivals—such as the Durga puja and its many variants in the East and North of India. In 2011 and 2014, when Bahujan and Dalit groups sought to celebrate a Mahishasura festival in Delhi as a counter to high-caste celebrations of Durga puja, the police attempted to hunt down and arrest the organizers, including Pramod Ranjan, the managing editor of *Forward Press* (*Round Table India* 2014).

Consider this. 'This animal [the buffalo] has not been given its due place in the livestock sector. Paradoxically, it is discriminated against merely on account of its dark colour. This is clear apartheid against buffalo in relation to its other cousins.' Do not assume that I am citing from my own 2004 work, *Buffalo Nationalism*. This is from the FAO's India report, published the same year as my book. The report further says: 'The buffalo, if reared properly in hygienic environments, would provide food security and rural employment to the small and marginal farmer. This would be possible only if its by-products are exploited ingenuously for benefit of mankind. Buffalo produces good quality of milk and meat. Its meat is lean, low in cholesterol and has excellent blending quality for production of corn beef, hot dogs and sausages.'

One of the most useful animals in India has been shown no respect in the theory and practice of Hinduism; politicized Hindutva merely cashes in on this sentiment. In India, we find several books, old and new, on the cow but rarely one on the buffalo. That the buffalo is black is the simple and racist reason. It comes as no surprise that this animal does not find any protection under the BJP's rule, though it shall continue to contribute to the economy. Neither Gandhi nor the Hindutva forces that assassinated Gandhi consider the slaughter of a buffalo (or a goat) as violence. This skewed idea of nonviolence, which sacralises the cow while demonising the buffalo, is both racist and casteist. Such hypocrisy—of projecting the ideology of caste onto animals that know nothing of caste—is unique to the Brahmanic mindset.

With the largest population of the world's buffaloes and cows, India leads global milk production and is the third largest exporter of beef according to a 2017 joint report of the FAO and the Organisation for Economic Cooperation and Development (OECD). The report says India was expected to maintain 'its position as the third largest beef exporter, accounting for 16 per cent of global exports in 2026' (OECD-FAO 2017). Why is so much beef exported and who are involved in this business? Reports from the US in 2015 said that beef has overtaken basmati rice as India's largest agricultural food export in sheer value (Iyengar 2015). Who is benefiting from this huge export market for cow and buffalo beef from India? Certainly not the Muslims and Dalits who are accused of cow smuggling.

One of the largest slaughter houses and biggest beef exporter in India, Al Kabeer Exporters Pvt. Ltd., occupies 400 acres on the outskirts of Hyderabad. This major modernized establishment is jointly owned by Satish Saberwal, a high-caste Punjabi Khatri, along with Ghulamuddin Shaikh, his partner. Al Kabeer reported business worth Rs 6500 million in 2016. Another major Indian beef exporter, Al Noor Export, is headquartered in Delhi, and owned by a family of Suds, who again are non–beef-eating Punjabi Khatri by caste. Al Noor's slaughter house is located in Sher Nagar village in Muzaffarnagar district of UP. The names of their companies are misleadingly Islamic since they cater largely to the Arab world's needs. In fact, a business newspaper reported in 2007 that Al Kabeer is branded 'Samurai' in Japan, 'Falcon Foods' in the UK and 'Tayebat Al Emarat' in the UAE (Chamikutty 2007).

At the same time, according OECD's 2017 data on meat consumption, India ranks among the lowest annual per capita consumers of beef and veal at 0.5 kg compared to Ethiopia's

2.3 kg, Vietnam's 9.3 kg and the United States' 25.9 kg (OECD 2019). In India, 44 per cent of children are malnourished (that is, 48.2 million). Of these, 45 per cent have stunted growth and another 20 per cent are too thin. And beef is recognized as a source of rich protein and is way cheaper and healthier than the much-promoted broiler chicken, which many studies have revealed is high on steroids and antibiotics. In 2010, beef retailed in Hyderabad at Rs 80 a kilo; by 2014, the price shot up to Rs 140 and, after a Hindutva-driven state clamped down on beef, it retails now at Rs 180 or more. In Indian cities today, where vegetables like okra can cost up to Rs 120 a kilo, beef is a far more nourishing option, serving more heads.

One often encounters in India and across the world two ethical issues when it comes to eating meat—environmental concerns and the ethics of killing animals. Often, to counter Dalit and Shudra-led initiatives to reclaim meat and beef, we are told we must heed the compassion of the Buddha, who by most accounts ate a meal of pork even on his deathbed. Universally, human beings have evolved by eating all kinds of meat. Agriculture comes much later—the taste for burnt meat is almost a primal instinct. Yet it is a scientific fact that livestock accounts for about 14.5 per cent of global greenhouse gas emissions, according to the FAO. Last year, it was reported that ruminants such as cattle, buffalo, sheep and goats produce nitrous oxide, carbon dioxide and crucially methane through belching. But unlike in the West or even Latin American nations, in India most cattle are not factory farmed; poultry is. India's dairy industry was pegged at Rs 5.5 trillion in 2015 and engages 73 million small and marginal dairy farmers. Renowned Indian environmentalist Sunita Narain has argued how environmentalism does not mean vegetarianism:

Indian farmers still practice cow-buffalo-goat economy that is of small scale. In fact, this economy has been sustainable for the fact that it is in the hands of small farm owners. Animals are their insurance policy; their ways of managing bad times, made worse today because of climate change-induced variables and extreme weather... the strident and often violent call for cow protection has led to the total breakdown of this economy of the poor. Cattle are now abandoned. They have become a menace, marauding fields and destroying crops. Remember Indian farmers do not fence their fields; they cannot afford it and actually this is good for soil and water conservation. Now this is not going to work (Narain 2019).

Cows can live up to twenty-five to thirty years but they are considered productive only till they can be milked—from the age of three to ten or twelve at best. The so-called cow-worshipping Hindutva forces also dispose of aged cows since they are a mere drain on resources. The reason most foreigners in India are bemused by the many cows on the streets, ambling aimlessly on main thoroughfares in peak traffic and foraging from overflowing garbage dumps, is because most people abandon their non-productive cows and render them homeless. The BJP is not even sincere about saving these cows. The media regularly reports the death by starvation of large numbers of cows in cow shelters across North India, especially in Uttar Pradesh, ruled by its saffron-clad, Modi protégé chief minister, Yogi Adityanath. You rarely see stray buffaloes since people see nothing divine in this black animal and are happy to send it to a slaughter house after it has ceased to produce milk, thereby earning a good sum in the process.

Despite these indisputable facts, the highest courts of the

land have taken a sentimental and religious view of the matter, impacting the lives and livelihoods of millions of persons involved in the cattle economy. Gundimeda and Ashwin (2018) analyse two important verdicts on cow slaughter in independent India—*Mohammed Hanif Quareshi and others v. State of Bihar* in 1958 and *Mirzapur Moti Kureshi Kassab Jamat and others v. State of Gujarat* of 2005. The authors demonstrate how the Indian Supreme Court has legitimized majoritarian sentiments in the law by conceding valuable ground to cow worshippers. In both cases, Muslim butchers had moved the courts to challenge 'the total ban on cow slaughter under three Fundamental Rights, respectively Article 14 (right to equality), 19(1)(g) (right to practice any profession and carry on any occupation) and 25 (right to freedom of religion). They argued that the total ban imposed by the three states (which were Bihar, Uttar Pradesh and Madhya Pradesh) placed Article 48 as a Directive Principle of State Policy above the Fundamental Rights (Gundimeda and Ashwin 2018, 164). The subsequent miscarriages of justice are accounted for by the authors:

> The State Legislature of Gujarat had introduced the Bombay Animal Preservation (Gujarat Amendment) Act of 1994, enlarging the prohibition of slaughtering bulls and bullocks below the age of 16 years to a total ban on slaughter of cows and their progeny. As the Gujarat Act infringed the long-held Supreme Court position, its constitutional validity was challenged before the Gujarat High Court, which promptly struck down the impugned legislation, arguing that the 1994 Act imposed an unreasonable restriction on Fundamental Rights and was ultra vires the Constitution. This was probably a strategic refusal, allowing the state of Gujarat to appeal to the Supreme Court by a Special Leave Petition. A

Supreme Court Bench of seven judges, led by Chief Justice Lahoti, re-examined the issue and in the final verdict, six judges upheld the validity of the impugned amendment. The Court eschewed not just established principles of constitutional interpretation but overruled the earlier settled jurisprudence on the slaughter of bulls and bullocks in Hanif Quareshi case. Unmistakably, this judgment was pro-Hindutva, and against Dalits/OBC, Adivasis, Muslim and Christian minorities…. He [Chief Justice R.C. Lahoti] also rendered the Fundamental Rights subservient to the Directive Principles, an interpretation, as Jaising et al. (2016) argue, that was 'both disingenuous and dangerous and precisely what the constitution-makers wanted to guard against' (167).

The bench headed by then Chief Justice Lahoti made some astounding statements. Statements that are akin to the claims of a minister in the Modi government that Indians devised plastic surgery, test tube babies and the airplane more than five thousand years ago in some mythic past.

[T]he value of dung is much more than even the famous 'Kohinoor' diamond. An old bullock gives 5 tonnes of dung and 343 pounds of urine in a year which can help in the manufacture of 20 cartloads of composed manure. This would be sufficient for manure need of 4 acres of land for crop production. The right to life is a fundamental right and it can be basically protected only with proper food and feeding and cheap and nutritious food grains required for feeding can be grown with the help of dung. Thus the most fundamental thing to the fundamental right of living for the human being is bovine dung (Gundimeda and Ashwin 2018, 170).

Gundimeda and Ashwin tell us how the Chief Justice was merely (re)citing the claims made by right-wing, cow-worshipping pamphleteers. Consequently, the Indian state has been proactive about creating gau-shalas, shelters for abandoned and stray cows.

Contrast this with what the state has done to address the issue of mass malnutrition among the country's children. The introduction of the midday meal scheme, inaugurated in the Madras Presidency in 1925 during the colonial period, was revived in Tamil Nadu by chief minister M.G. Ramachandran in 1982. By the 1990s, twelve states followed suit since India, as part of its commitment to the UN Convention on the Rights of the Child (1990), had to address the issue. The midday meal programme was modelled on the 1946 US scheme, the National School Lunch Act. By 2001, the Supreme Court directed the universalisation of this programme. Now, the National Food Security Act of 2013 covers this scheme and seeks to redress the nutritional needs of over 120 million children. Eggs and milk were made part of the diet to address malnutrition. But after the Modi-led BJP government has come to power, only five of the nineteen states governed by the BJP or its allies provide eggs to children. In 2015, Chief Minister Vasundhara Raje of Rajasthan declared that there was no question of offering eggs in the midday meal scheme and in food distributed at anganwadi centres (there are 1.4 million such centres meant to provide rural child care). 'We respect religious sentiments of the people. We will not distribute eggs or any other [edible] item that hurts anyone's religious feelings,' said Raje. If they can be so squeamish about eggs, the struggle to put beef on the table is going to be long and arduous.

The caste system's inferiorizing of those who deal with

cattle (dead or alive) and leatherwork has resulted not just in intolerance but also in the lack of evolution of diversity in red-meat products produced in India. According to FAO reports, hardly one per cent of the total meat produced in India is used for processing. Contrast what you may buy from an Indian retail store compared to Germany's wide range of sausages (Bratwurst, Blutwurst, Bregenwurst, Liverwurst) and salamis (dry-cured, aged from chorizo to pepperoni). Consider the range of knives and precision instruments used for cutting meat in the Western world. In African nations, all manner of liver pâté (seasoned meat) is tinned and sold—from zebra to ostrich to wildebeest. Think of the range of cheeses in France. This comes from not just love for food but from respect for communities that deal with animals. In India, many of the inferiorized castes have wonderful ways of salting and preserving meat (and fish). When these communities are despised and rendered resourceless, how will their skills and techniques be valorized and commodified?

Oddly but not surprisingly, Italy, known for its Parmesan cheese, today employs more than 45,000 migrants from India across four thousand farms, to make cheese. Most of the migrants are from Punjab. They earn €15–20 an hour, depending on skill; some make €3,000 a month and enjoy a good standard of living. However, India, despite being the largest producer of milk in the world, has barely developed its cheese industry. One of the most important ingredients that led to the development of different varieties of cheese across the world is rennin—the inner lining of a calf's stomach, which acts as the starting agent in the coagulation of milk. With the taboos on cow-slaughter and the scant respect for people who graze cattle, care for them, and also eat them, the development of such culinary culture was arrested. For the most part, Indian markets are flooded with processed cheeses that do not require rennin.

The allied leather industry is another large contributor to the economy. India is the world's second largest producer of footwear and leather garments, and the industry employs over 2.5 million workers. But the mechanization of the industry hasn't changed the caste nature of the work. A 2017 study, conducted by Roseanne Hoefe for the India Committee of The Netherlands, covering Uttar Pradesh (Agra in particular), West Bengal (Kolkata) and Tamil Nadu, which together account for ninety per cent of India's leather production, found that Dalits make up eighty per cent of the workforce in both Agra and Tamil Nadu. In the 1960s, governmental policy focussed on promoting small-scale production centres. This contributed to creating a class of upper-caste owners with an underlying class of Muslim and Dalit workers. But since liberalization, a move has been made towards export-oriented large manufacturing companies, rendering large swathes of Dalits unemployed, undermining traditional leather work, and reducing the workforce into factory employees. In Agra, small-scale units continue to thrive, but most of them remain unrecorded, which makes the flouting of employment norms easy. The leather industry also generates large amounts of pollutants and effluents, the most direct victims of which are the workers themselves. Working in hazardous conditions, often without any protective gear, the workers are prone to fever, eye inflammation, skin diseases, lung cancer, body, joint and muscle pain, musculo-skeletal injuries, asthma and eczema. Furthermore, most of the workers are employed on contract basis, which means, in addition to the loss of job security, the workers also cannot claim redress from their employers in case of injuries. This casualization has also weakened hitherto strong trade unions, allowing the employers to pay the workers significantly below the minimum wage. Most recognized unions are controlled by managements. The low salaries in this industry can be tied to the caste nature of working with leather, which is often looked down upon (Hoefe 2017). An average leather worker makes about half the pay of a worker in the electronics or textile industries.

While societies across the world have seen wholesale discrimination against communities, no person of colour in America or Europe or even in apartheid South Africa has been ostracized or killed on the basis of the food they consume. The segregation has often been on colour lines and directed at the extraction of surplus through cheap or unpaid labour (slavery). Across the world, despite other markers of difference, food brings people together and helps establish cultural common ground—not so in India. Surely there are ideas of the sacred and the profane and of food taboos in both organized and tribalistic religions, but none of this leads to either Untouchability or lynching. If an elite engineering institute like IIT Madras believes in separate dining spaces for vegetarians and meat-eaters in 2018, the kind of hell rural India is can only be imagined.

Such violence and murderous action based on the consumption of food or the trading of cow ought to have led to an international scandal but this has not happened. The reason is that intellectuals and scholars from India, instead of taking the lead in standing up to such violence, have come to believe that food habits and practices such as Untouchability are a part of Hindu 'tradition' and 'culture'. Cultural diversity and respecting 'Hindu' sentiments are offered as pathetic excuses for sidestepping the issue of a fundamental right to food of one's choice. While the BJP-led violence against Muslims and Dalits saw the so-called liberal–secular intellectuals come up with the 'Not in My Name' campaign in 2017, and 2015 saw writers, poets and filmmakers outraged by Akhlaq's murder (and the assassinations of intellectuals critical of the government) return state awards in order to shame the Modi government, hardly one of these intellectuals expressed support to or showed up at the beef festivals organized by Dalit and marginalized people in the recent past.

We do not know whether Ambedkar, a very private person, relished beef or not. Given his community's stereotypical association with the meat, he likely stayed off it while in India. He may have eaten it during his days in the US and Europe. In contrast, Gandhi issued daily bulletins about what he ate and what he expected others to eat. His positions on the cow and Untouchables eating beef merely helped the Hindutva forces to use violence against eaters of beef and enforce vegetarianism on everyone.

The onus now, however, must be on non-Dalits taking the initiative in serving and eating beef, and thus secularizing it. This annotated edition offers enough evidence that Shudra communities did eat the flesh of the cow in history but gave it up after it became associated with Untouchability. In post-independence India, even Dalit leaders of Kanshi Ram's stature stayed shy of such civilisational questions and merely focussed on wresting political power; the need to build social and political coalitions for electoral politics makes a politician wary of an initiative like a beef festival. While the BJP or the Congress can blatantly push for a cow-protection agenda, even Mayawati as chief minister cannot promote beef-eating as a counter. It does not work as realpolitik. Electoral politics will not be able to challenge spiritual fascism; the moral onus of this is on non-Dalits and civil society.

As a non-Dalit Shudra intellectual, I belong to a small minority of non-Dalits participating in the Dalit-led beef festivals. Today, people across castes who believe in the secularisation of food habits need to step up. In 2001, defying the Indian state, Dalits took the caste issue to the United Nations' World Conference against Racism in Durban. *Beef, Brahmins and Broken Men* likewise seeks to take an important issue to a worldwide audience. It is both an invitation to engage with Ambedkar's writings on the beef question and to deepen democracy in India.

There is no bigger spiritual experience than equality, to experience equality is to be truly alive, and beef gives life.

Notes

1 By Dalit-Bahujan, I mean the Dalit Untouchables (officially Scheduled Castes at 17 per cent of the population), the Backward and Other Backward Classes formerly categorized as Shudra (55 per cent), and the indigenous population of Tribals (8 per cent), together comprising seventy per cent, and thus constituting a staggering oppressed majority. The conceptual term 'Bahujan' is attributed to Gautama Buddha, who used it in the credo 'bahujana hitaya, bahujana sukhaya' that emphasized the welfare of the majority or of everyone. It was Jotirao Phule (1827–1890), an intellectual and political forebear of Ambedkar, who used Bahujan with the valency it has today. The term entered contemporary popular discourse when Kanshi Ram founded the Bahujan Samaj Party in 1984. Well before the BSP, Kanshi Ram in 1978 established the Backward and Minority Communities Employees Federation (BAMCEF). I had theorized this category in my 1996 work, *Why I am Not a Hindu: A Sudra Critique of Hindutva Philosophy, Culture and Political Economy.*

2 Till 1990, it was only the Schedules Castes and the Schedules Tribes (as Dalits and Adivasis are termed in state parlance) who together comprise 22.5 per cent of the population, who could avail of reservation in the education and job sectors. In 1990, the Mandal Commission extended 27 per cent to the Backward Classes and Other Backward Classes, as erstwhile Shudra communities (who comprise nearly fifty per cent of the population) are officially known. This led to massive protests by the entitled castes. Though often the lesser educated BC and OBC castes are at loggerheads with the better educated but more impoverished Dalits in rural India, the implementation of the Mandal Commission in some ways brought them together

since the very idea of affirmative action had come under attack from reactionary forces in society led by a largely Brahmin-controlled media. Often the Dalits and Shudras, when they came together under the theoretical framework of Dalit-Bahujan, heralded a coalition of solidarities. This mode of conducting politics is often reflected in the names of student organizations such as the Dalit Adivasi Bahujan Minority Students' Association (DABMSA) mentioned earlier.

References

Ambedkar, B.R. 1990. *The Untouchables: Who Were They and Why They Became Untouchable?* In *BAWS 7*. Bombay: Education Department, Government of Maharashtra. (Orig. publ. 1948.)

———. 2014 [1936]. *Annihilation of Caste: The Annotated Critical Edition*. New Delhi: Navayana.

Adcock, Cassie. 2010. "Sacred Cows and Secular History: Cow Protection Debates in Colonial North India". *Comparative Studies of South Asia, Africa and the Middle East*. Vol. 30, No. 2. Durham: Duke University Press.

Beals, Gregory and Erik Messori. 2018. "The Indians Saving Italy's Traditional Cheese Industry". https://www.aljazeera.com/indepth/inpictures/indians-saving-italy-traditional-cheese-industry-181219153130114.html. 27 December. Accessed 17 April 2019.

Bharti, Anita. 2018. Interview with Sharanya Deepak. "There is No Dalit Cuisine". *Popula*. 20 November. https://popula.com/2018/11/20/there-is-no-dalit-cuisine/ Accessed 17 April 2019.

Chamikutty, Preethi. 2007. "The growth of Al Kabeer". 3 October. https://economictimes.indiatimes.com/the-growth-of-al-kabeer/articleshow/2423616.cms. Accessed 3 June 2019.

Chandra, Bipan & Mridula Mukherjee. 2000. *India's Struggle for Independence*. New Delhi: Penguin.

Chandran, Ravi. 2012a. "Exactly whose sentiments are hurt by beef and pork?". *Round Table India*. http://roundtableindia.co.in/index.php?option=com_content&view=article&id=5764:exactly-whose-sentiments-are-hurt-by-beef-and-pork-&catid=119:feature&Itemid=132 Accessed 14 April 2019.

———. 2012b. "Exactly whose sentiments are hurt by beef and pork? Part 2". *Round Table India*. http://roundtableindia.co.in/index.php?option=com_content&view=article&id=5781:exactly-whose-sentiments-are-hurt-by-beef-and-pork-part-2&catid=119&Itemid=132 Accessed 14 April 2019.

Damodaran, Harish. 2012. "Cow Belt or Buffalo Nation?" 18 April. https://www.thehindubusinessline.com/opinion/columns/harish-damodaran/cow-belt-or-buffalo-nation/article22985221.ece. Accessed 19 April 2019.

De, Rohit. 2019. "Cows and Constitutionalism". *Modern Asian Studies*. Vol. 53, No. 1. Cambridge: Cambridge University Press. 240–77.

Doniger, Wendy. 2010. *The Hindus: An Alternative History*. Oxford: Oxford University Press.

Gandhi, M.K. 1925. "Presidential Address at Cow-Protection Conference, Belgaum." *Young India*. 29 January. Repr. CWMG. Vol. 30, No. 21. New Delhi: Publications Division Government of India.

Gundimeda, Sambaiah. 2009. "Democratization of the Public Sphere: The Beef Stall Case in Hyderabad's Sukoon Festival". *South Asia Research*. Vol. 29, No. 2. New Delhi: SAGE. 127–49.

Gundimeda, Sambaiah & V. Ashwin. 2018. "Cow Protection in India". *South Asia Research*. Vol. 38, No. 2. New Delhi: SAGE. 156–76.

Hoefe, Rosanne. 2017. *Do leather workers matter? Violating Labour Rights and Environmental Norms in India's Leather Production: A report by*

ICN—March 2017. Utrecht: India Committee of the Netherlands.

Henry, Nikhila (ed.). 2016. *#Caste Is Not a Rumour: The Online Diary of Rohith Vemula.* New Delhi: Juggernaut Books.

The Hindu. 2015. "CPI(M) leader slammed for participating in 'beef' event". 7 November. https://www.thehindu.com/news/cities/kolkata/cpim-leader-slammed-for-participating-in-beef-event/article7852855.ece

Hindustan Times,. 2016. "BJP leader Kailash Vijayvargiya casts doubt over Rohith Vemula's death". https://www.hindustantimes.com/india/bjp-leader-kailash-vijayvargiya-casts-doubt-over-rohith-vemula-s-death/story-SaORnjl7Fxgb3VSrPlnPXL.html. 31 January. Accessed 15 May 2019.

Ilaiah, Kancha. 1996. *Why I am Not a Hindu: A Sudra Critique of Hindutva Philosophy, Culture and Political Economy.* Calcutta: Samya.

———. 2012. *Buffalo Nationalism: A Critique of Spiritual Fascism.* Calcutta: Samya.

Iyengar, Rishi. 2015. "India Stays World's Top Beef Exporter despite New Bans on Slaughtering Cows". 24 April. *Time.* http://time.com/3833931/india-beef-exports-rise-ban-buffalo-meat/. Accessed 20 April 2019.

Jadeja, Gopika. 2018: "'We will build an over bridge': Gujarati Dalit poetry and the politics of cow protection." *Contemporary South Asia.* Vol. 26. Abingdon: Routledge. 305–20.

Jishnu, Latha. 2015. "Meaty tales of vegetarian India". *Down to Earth.* 11 June. https://www.downtoearth.org.in/coverage/meaty-tales-of-vegetarian-india-47830. Accessed 14 April 2019.

Joseph, Tony. 2018. *Early Indians: The Story of Our Ancestors and Where We Came From.* New Delhi: Juggernaut.

Karkare, Aakash. 2016. "Why an ex-journalist chose to document his Dalit culture in a food book". https://scroll.in/magazine/820140/why-an-ex-journalist-chose-to-document-his-dalit-culture-in-a-food-book. 15 November. Accessed 22 April 2019.

Kumar, Digumarthi Suresh. 2011. (). "Beef". Translated by Naren Bedide. *Round Table India*. http://roundtableindia.co.in/lit-blogs/?tag=digumarthi-suresh-kumar

Mandal, Sudipto. 2016. "Rohith Vemula: An unfinished portrait". https://www.hindustantimes.com/static/rohith-vemula-an-unfinished-portrait/. Accessed 20 April 2019.

Ministry of Agriculture and Farmers Welfare. 2016. "Buffalo Milk Production Estimates in India during 2014–15". https://community.data.gov.in/buffalo-milk-production-estimates-in-india-during-2014-15/. Accessed 15 May 2019.

Mukul, Akshaya. 2015. *Gita Press and the Making of Hindu India*. New Delhi: Harper Collins.

Naqvi, Saba. 2014. "Prime Cuts". *Outlook*. 20 October. https://www.outlookindia.com/magazine/story/prime-cuts/292209. Accessed 19 April 2019.

Narain, Sunita. 2019. "India's Cow Crisis Part 3: Brutal to kill India's ancient uber economy". *Down to Earth*. 19 February. https://www.downtoearth.org.in/news/agriculture/india-s-cow-crisis-part-3-brutal-to-kill-india-s-ancient-uber-economy-62752. Accessed 12 April 2019.

OECD. 2019. Meat consumption (indicator). doi: 10.1787/fa290fd0-en. Accessed on 04 June 2019.

OECD-FAO Agricultural Outlook 2017–2026. 2017. *OECD-FAO Agricultural Outlook*. Paris: OECD Publishing. https://dx.doi.org/10.1787/agr_outlook-2017-en. Accessed 10 April 2019.

Panchajanya. 2015. "Vedas order killing of the sinner who kills a cow". 21 October.

Patole, Shahu. 2015. *Anna He Apoornabrahma*. Aurangabad: Janshakti Wachal Chalwal.

Pawar, Daya. 2015. *Baluta*. Translated by Jerry Pinto. New Delhi: Speaking Tiger. (Orig. Marathi, 1978. Mumbai: Granthali)

Periyar, E.V. Ramasami. 2015. "Untouchability." Translated by T.

Marx. http://periyarwritings.org/index.php/english/caste/31720-untouchability. Accessed on 12 June 2019.

Rajkumar, N. D. 2010. *Give Us This Day A Feast of Flesh*. Translated by Anushiya Ramaswamy. New Delhi: Navayana.

Ramanujan, A. K. 1991. "Three Hundred Ramayanas: Five Examples and Three Thoughts on Translation", in *Many Ramayanas: The Diversity of a Narrative Tradition in South Asia*. Edited by Paula Richman. Berkeley: University of California Press. 22–48.

Ranjhan, S.K. 2004. *Indian Meat Industry Perspective*. Food and Agriculture Organization of the United Nations (FAO). Rome, Italy http://www.fao.org/3/agrippa/665_en-12.htm. Accessed 2 October 2012.

Reich, David. 2018. *Who We Are and How We Got Here*. New Delhi: Oxford University Press.

Rege, Sharmila, Deepa Tak, Sangita Thosar & Tina Aranha. 2009. *Isn't This Plate Indian?: Dalit Histories and Memories of Food*. Pune: Krantijyoti Savitribai Phule Women's Center.

Round Table India. 2014. "Police goons raid Forward Press, Hindutva goons attack Mahishasur festival". 10 October. http://roundtableindia.co.in/index.php?option=com_content&view=article&id=7690:police-goons-raid-forward-press-hindutva-goons-attack-mahishasur-festival&catid=119:feature&Item id=132. Accessed 19 April 2019.

Saldanha, Alison. 2019. "Incomes Shrink As Cow-Related Violence Scuttles Beef, Leather Exports: New Report". *IndiaSpend*. February 19. https://www.indiaspend.com/incomes-shrink-as-cow-related-violence-scuttles-beef-leather-exports-new-report/

Sathyamala, Christina. 2018. "Meat-eating in India: Whose food, whose politics, and whose rights? Policy Futures in Education", in *Policy Futures in Education*.

Sharath, Naliganti. 2012. "Osmania University student Naligandi sarth's beef anthem". *Dalit Camera,* 16 April. https://www.youtube.com/watch?v=vFZBOZRL3Uc&pbjreload=10

Srinivas, M.N. 2002a. "A Note on Sanskritisation and Westernisation". In *Collected Essays*. New Delhi: Oxford University Press. 201–21.

———. 2002b. "The Changing Position of Indian Women". In *Collected Essays*. New Delhi: Oxford University Press. 279–301.

The Casteless Collective. 2018. "Beef song". https://www.youtube.com/watch?v=2Z_as486hxI. Accessed 14 April 2019.

The New Materialists. 2012. "Why Beef and Pork Food Festival at JNU?". *RoundTableIndia*, 16 August. https://roundtableindia.co.in/index.php?option=com_content&view=article&id=5577:why-beef-and-pork-food-festival-at-jnu&catid=129:events-and-activism&Itemid=195. Accessed 14 April 2019.

Thomas, Suresh P. 2011. "The Beef War Logs". *Fountain Ink*. 15 November. https://fountainink.in/reportage/the-beef-war-logs. Accessed 20 March 2019.

Vemula, Rohith. 2017. *#Caste Is Not a Rumour: The Online Diary of Rohith Vemula*. Ed. Nikhila Henry. New Delhi: Juggernaut Books.

Vemula, Rohith. 2016. "My birth is my fatal accident: Full text of Dalit student Rohith's suicide letter". *The Indian Express*, January 19. https://indianexpress.com/article/india/india-news-india/dalit-student-suicide-full-text-of-suicide-letter-hyderabad/. Accessed 20 May 2019.

Fool's Errand
A Note on the Notes to and Selection from Ambedkar's *The Untouchables*

S. Anand and Alex George

> *'Gaay ki poonch tum rakho, hume hamari zameen do'*
> 'You hold the tail of the cow/ just give us our land now'
> —Slogan coined by Jignesh Mewani at Azadi Kooch
> (Freedom March), in July 2017, a year after the Una
> violence against Dalits over a dead cow in Gujarat

> It may well turn out that this attempt of mine is only an illustration of the proverbial fool rushing in where the angels dare not tread. But I take refuge in the belief that even the fool has a duty to perform, namely, to do his bit if the angel has gone to sleep or is unwilling to proclaim the truth.
>
> —B.R. Ambedkar in *The Shudras* (1946)

B.R. Ambedkar's *The Untouchables: Who Were They and Why They Became Untouchables?*—the sequel to his 1946 work, *The Shudras: Who they were and How they came to be the Fourth Varna of the Indo-Aryan Society*—was first published in October 1948 by Amrit Book Co., Delhi. It is an investigation into the origins of Untouchability, self-declared as 'a pioneer attempt in the exploration of a field so completely neglected by everybody'.

The long history of Brahmanism, and the persistence of its colonizing efforts and effect, is predicated on the naturalisation of caste and Untouchability. Harking back to the Buddhist tradition of anti-metaphysical thinking—that asserted the this-worldliness and materiality of all perceivable phenomena—Ambedkar refutes these pretensions. Not content with the mere naming of Untouchability as immoral, Ambedkar begins from the premise that its very existence is 'most unnatural'. At the outset, he acknowledges that:

> If any non-Brahmin were to make such an attempt the Brahmin scholars would engage in a conspiracy of silence, take no notice of him, condemn him outright on some flimsy grounds or dub his work useless. As a writer engaged in the exposition of the Brahmanic literature I have been a victim of such mean tricks (90).

Given the general apathy of historians and other learned men and women towards Ambedkar, it is as if he was foretelling the fate of his work. As you will see in this heavily annotated selection, the handful of university historians and scholars who have deigned to engage with *The Untouchables* (or *The Shudras* or *Riddles in Hinduism*) tend to be dismissive of Ambedkar. The book's principal arguments—constructed using available textual evidence from within Brahmanic sources and by invoking comparable parallels from other parts of the world—are that those labelled Untouchables in the subcontinent were originally Buddhists defeated by a resurgent Brahmanism, hence called Broken Men, and their practice of beef-eating, especially when they were excommunicated and forced into the disposal of and consumption of the meat of the dead cow, resulted in their being stigmatized and cast out of the main village. The

Mahar caste, to which Ambedkar belonged, was expected to perform duties for the village as part of the baluta system, free work for which they received 'payment' such as the right to the dead cow's carcass, and hence its flesh and skin. While some educated Mahar leaders initiated a reform movement just ahead of Ambedkar's time and sought to give up beef-eating to seek inclusion into an antipathetic Hinduism, Ambedkar historicizes the issue of Untouchability (Rao 2009) and is vehement in his disavowal of Hinduism. In the very first paragraph of *The Untouchables*, he declares:

> The Hindu Civilization… could hardly be called civilization. It is a diabolical contrivance to suppress and enslave humanity. Its proper name would be infamy.

This raises the hackles of scholars who in the guise of being bipartisan and objective will not brook such a partisan declaration of intent. In a nation whose intellectual class has been predominantly Brahmin, as Ambedkar notes of his time—and most universities in India still have less than three per cent of Dalits or Adivasis on their faculty against the constitutionally stipulated 22.5 per cent reflective of the demographic reality—the chances of Ambedkar getting a fair hearing outside of 'unlearned' Dalit circles have been remote. Caste and Untouchability 'studies' (quite like the studies of multifarious aspects of Hinduism) have also seen a preponderance of Western interest, often tinged with a seemingly benign yet typically noble premise such as: 'As social scientists, it is our aim to try to understand the phenomenon, and the present book is precisely an attempt to tackle some of the general features of untouchability' (Deliège 1999, ix). Our endeavour, which decidedly resists university discourse, is a recoil against the untouchability Ambedkar has been habitually subjected to.

The Untouchables was published when Ambedkar was in the thick of things as the first Law Minister of independent India as well as Chairman of the Drafting Committee of the Constitution. Within a month of its publication, he submitted the draft constitution to the Constituent Assembly in November 1948. Overseeing a Constitution that outlawed Untouchability if not caste, Ambedkar did not think his task was over. He was well aware that the Constitution, however enlightened a document, could not effect a change in the thinking of most Hindus if they continued to control the state apparatus. Besides, there was much unhappiness over this covenant in which he tried to safeguard the interests of the minorities in a Hindu-majority–driven society. Writes Keer in his biography:

> It was not that all the members were pleased with the form of the Constitution. There were a few dissenting voices. A member said that the Constitution was worthless as the Provinces were reduced to the status of Municipalities. Another bewailed that the Constitution-maker had discarded the idea of decentralization favoured by Gandhi. *Yet a third one felt sorry that the Constitution did not provide for a ban on cow-slaughter* (Keer 1954, 409–10, emphasis added).

In an otherwise Ambedkarite constitution, the Gandhians did manage to sneak in the cow. Article 48 of the Directive Principles of State Policy states that the government shall 'in particular, take steps for ... prohibiting the slaughter of cows and calves and other milch and draught cattle'. It is this caveat that has come to haunt anyone associated with beef-eating and the slaughtering and disposal of a dead cow in contemporary India. Gandhi called the cow 'a poem of pity' and held that 'the central fact of Hinduism is cow protection. Cow protection to me is one of the most wonderful phenomena in human evolution' (*Young India*, 6 October 1921, quoted in Gandhi 1987, 33–4). While he condemned violence against Muslims in the name of cow-protection, he wanted to convince Muslims to give up sacrificing or eating the cow, for he, like other irrational Hindus, saw the divine in the bovine. History and facts are summarily cast out; an ahistoric 'cultural truth' is proffered as sacral. About the existential relationship of Untouchables with the cow, Gandhi had nothing to say, though he opined, in 1936, that 'some of the untouchables are worse than cows in understanding. I mean they can no more distinguish between the relative merits of Islam and Hinduism and Christianity than a cow.' Despite scores of such bizarre intuitive 'truths' delivered from a self-mounted perch, Gandhi has enjoyed the attention and respect, love and adulation of a range of scholars who otherwise have displayed little patience with or interest in Ambedkar beyond the token respects they are forced to pay in recent times because of *politics*.

Not driven by mere feelings but reason, Ambedkar conducted several parallel exercises in passionate scholarship to dispel and expose such ingrained prejudices and myths even as he worked on the Constitution. His long-time secretary and typist, Nanak Chand Rattu, in his memoir says that since 1950 Ambedkar was under tremendous financial stress and in a hurry to publish as many of his books as he could, given the political setbacks he faced (he lost the 1951 Lok Sabha election from North Bombay and also a by-election he contested in 1952 from Bhandara constituency) and his failing health (he suffered from acute diabetes since 1947). Rattu (1997, 59) lists the following manuscripts Ambedkar was working on: (i) Buddha and His

Dhamma, (ii) Buddha and Karl Marx, (iii) Revolution and Counter-revolution in Ancient India, (iv) Riddles in Hinduism, (v) Riddle of Rama and Krishna (vi) Riddle of Trimurti and (vii) Riddle of Woman. All, including his opus *The Buddha and His Dhamma*, came to be published posthumously.

While this annotated critical selection from *The Untouchables* comes in the wake of similar work at Navayana on *Annihilation of Caste* (2014) and *Riddles in Hinduism* (2016), the increasing violence against Muslims and Dalits in the name of cow-protection that India has witnessed since the coming to power of the right-wing Bharatiya Janata Party in 2014 gave our project an urgency that has governed the selections we have made here. We have chosen only those portions of *The Untouchables* that dwell upon the connection between beef-eating and Untouchability—that is from Chapter IX to the last Chapter XVI, comprising two-thirds of the book. Ambedkar divides the book into six sections spread across sixteen chapters. The first three sections (chapters I to VIII) provide an overview of Untouchability among Hindus and non-Hindus, outline the comparable cases of outcasteness among the near-forgotten Fuidhirs in Ireland and the Alltudes in Wales in pre-historic Britain (for all of whom he applies the term Broken Men), seek to understand the logic behind separate settlements for such outcastes and crucially argue against the racial theories that sought to explain the origin and proliferation of caste and Untouchability:

> If anthropometry is a science which can be depended upon to determine the race of a people, then the result obtained by the application of anthropometry to the various strata of Hindu society disprove that the Untouchables belong to a race different from the Aryans and the Dravidians. The

measurements establish that the Brahmin and the Untouchables belong to the same race. From this it follows that if the Brahmins are Aryans the Untouchables are also Aryans. If the Brahmins are Dravidians the Untouchables are also Dravidians. If the Brahmins are Nagas, the Untouchables are also Nagas... The racial theory of the origin of Untouchability must, therefore, be abandoned (Ambedkar 1990a, 302–4).

Here, Ambedkar was challenging the view that caste was a result of a series of invasions—first by the Dravidians over the Nagas, and then by the Aryans over the Dravidians. Ambedkar, amongst others, argued that this was a Western construction which Indian scholars and ideologues—under the aegis of a colonial hegemon—were only happy to adopt. The narrative was one of a master race (the Aryans) and their inferior subjects, and it was propagated in order to emphasise Western supremacy by virtue of descent. Indeed, in doing so, there came to be an 'Aryan brotherhood' at the highest levels of the state machinery, wherein the British coloniser would invoke common Aryan descent to ennoble the Brahmin, albeit while keeping him colonized, and claim superiority and dominance over the rest of the subcontinental population (the lower castes and classes). Dorothy Figueira (2015) provides ample evidence of how this identity called 'Aryan' was developed and mobilized in the West in order to spur colonial ambitions and claim cultural superiority. Gandhi adopted a similar tack in South Africa to argue how whites and high-caste Indians share an Aryan ancestry (Desai and Vahed 2015). In tandem with the colonial machinery that reaffirmed one's caste identity, a static society of socially degraded people confined to their position, incapable of breaking their bonds, came to be. In breaking with this elitism, Ambedkar presented a nuanced picture. In *Who Were the Shudras* (1946), he rejected racial difference as the origin of caste by rigorously invalidating various theories of invasions in the subcontinent. Further, he cites sociologist G.S. Ghurye's study of nasal indices across castes and regions, which reveal no racial difference underlying the stratifications of caste difference that have come to exist. Following this, in *The Untouchables*, through interpretive and linguistic analyses, he presents evidence supporting the fact that the existence of the three races—Aryans, Dravidians and Nagas—is a myth. He also argued along the same lines in 1936, in *Annihilation of Caste*:

> ...the caste system came into being long after the different races of India had commingled in blood and culture. To hold that distinctions of castes are really distinctions of race, and to treat different castes as though they were so many different races, is a gross perversion of facts. What racial affinity is there between the Brahmin of the Punjab and the Brahmin of Madras? What racial affinity is there between the untouchable of Bengal and the untouchable of Madras? What racial difference is there between the Brahmin of the Punjab and the Chamar of the Punjab? What racial difference is there between the Brahmin of Madras and the Pariah of Madras? The Brahmin of the Punjab is racially of the same stock as the Chamar of the Punjab, and the Brahmin of Madras is of the same race as the Pariah of Madras. The caste system does not demarcate racial division. The caste system is a social division of people of the same race (Ambedkar 2014, 237–8).

Ambedkar's intellectual forebear, the radical thinker Jotiba Phule (1827–90) and his contemporary 'Periyar' E.V. Ramasamy Naicker (1879–1973) however turned the racial theory inside out.

They, and several indigenist first-of-the-soil 'Adi' movements of the marginalized communities (see Juergensmeyer 2009 on the Ad Dharm challenge to caste in Punjab), postulated a pre-Aryan golden age and regarded the Brahmins as Aryans, and hence foreigners, who imposed the caste system upon the non-Brahmins, who were seen as an indigenous race. For Phule's writings, especially *Gulamgiri* (*Slavery*, 1873), see G.P. Deshpande (2002, 23–101). While communities placed low in the caste hierarchy sought to rally around the memory of equality (even when it was not backed by the rigours of research and science), the Brahmanic belief in the Aryan story, such as by B.G. Tilak who authored *The Arctic Home in the Vedas* (1903), is staked primarily on claiming racial superiority. (Related to this memory of a time of equality see p.132–3 note 18 as well as the essay on Broken Men theory that concludes this book.) Having dismissed the racial theories, Ambedkar turns to the theory of occupational origins in Chapter VIII only to conclude: 'The filthy and unclean occupations which the Untouchables perform are common to all human societies. In every human Society there are people who perform these occupations. Why were such people not treated as Untouchables in other parts of the world?' (Ambedkar 1990a, 205). He also does not place much premium on the purity–impurity binary that has often predominated in treatises on caste and Untouchability (such as with works that have come to enjoy the status of classics like Louis Dumont's *Homo Hierarchicus* (1966) or Michael Moffat's *An Untouchable Community in South India: Structure and Consensus* (1979) that are dictated by a functionalist understanding of hierarchy where caste is seen as a 'cultural resource' of the people, works that make no mention of Ambedkar's Broken Men theory). It is then that Ambedkar asks us to consider his very own 'New Theories of the Origin of Untouchability', starting with Chapter XI entitled 'Contempt for Buddhists as the Root of Untouchability'. Our selection begins here.

A crucial reason to not annotate the entire book is that such an exercise would have made for a rather unwieldy edition of close to six hundred pages. Our task has been primarily threefold. One, to illuminate to ourselves what we, as readers in a fractious present, cannot easily decipher of the argument when Ambedkar writes thus, for instance:

> Nilakantha in his *Prayaschit Mayukha* quotes a verse from Manu which says: 'If a person touches a Buddhist or a flower of Pachupat, Lokayata, Nastika and Mahapataki, he shall purify himself by a bath.' The same doctrine is preached by Apararka in his *Smriti*. Vrddha Harita goes further and declares entry into the Buddhist temple as sin requiring a purificatory bath for removing the impurity.

Most readers would find it next to impossible to understand the range of references. All that Ambedkar offers here is a cryptic footnote to the *Prayaschit Mayukha* indicating his source as an unreferenced volume edited by 'Gharpure, p. 95'. In the process of explaining to ourselves who Nilakantha and Gharpure were, or what *Prayaschit Mayukha* and the *Smriti* attributed to Apararka are, and so on, we not only return to the sources Ambedkar cites but also consider all the available commentary on such texts and the contexts, both contemporaneous with Ambedkar's time and the latest scholarship.

Our second concern has been to determine and sometimes project and build on the intellectual and philosophical coordinates of some of his ideas, such as his views on what makes a 'civilization' when he says what has come to be called 'Hinduism' is not one. Such annotations are both serendipitous and intentional. The task has not been restricted to bringing Ambedkar up to speed with contemporary academic findings; we try and bring contemporary academic discourse up to speed with Ambedkar, while also setting up the possibility of having Ambedkarite thought encounter disparate and seemingly unassociated investigations. We have maintained a sense of plasticity in our search for connections; Catherine Malabou's translation of the French expression *voir venir* embodies the effort: "To see (what is) coming' is to anticipate, to foresee, to presage, to project; it is to expect what is coming; but it is also to let what is coming come or to let oneself be surprised by the unexpected, by the sudden appearance of what is un-awaited' (Malabou 2005, ix). The third is our efforts to come to terms with the several tables that Ambedkar indefatigably offers when he seeks to hunt down the ways in which terms like Antyavasin, Antya, Antyaja, Asprashya, Svapaca, Pukkusa, Mleccha, Chandala and so forth have been used—each indicating, according to Ambedkar, the Untouchable-to-come, not yet having become 'Untouchable' as we understand it today (the 429 communities, including his own Mahar caste, designated Untouchable in the 1931 Census). In corroborating Ambedkar's investigations, especially in Chapters XV and XVI, our notes overwhelm Ambedkar's precise and clear arguments. This merely owes to the fact that we have set out to establish the truth value of each claim, and this we felt was necessary because historians of ancient India have blithely disregarded his efforts for being dictated more by politics, contingency and convenience than by 'objectivity'.

For these reasons, our notes run longer than the core text of Ambedkar. To be exact, for the thirty thousand words from *The Untouchables* featured here, our annotations come to just over fifty thousand words—an excess that we hope will seem as necessary to most readers as it did to us. We the annotators and editors become critical yet partisan readers who hope to bring the whole width of Ambedkar's scholarly enterprise to you. Any reader could of course choose to walk past us and read only Ambedkar's work, available freely online and in previous editions. For ease of reading, and for those who wish to only follow the supple thread of Ambedkar's argumentation, we have proposed a design wherein Ambedkar's text shall appear first, chapter-wise, and the notes, in a more compact yet readable typeface, shall run at the end of each chapter. We hope the reader will pause to consider the dialogue we seek to establish between Ambedkar and the present. Ambedkar's own notes and references are given in square parenthesis to distinguish them from our annotative notes. While spellings and capitalization have been standardized, we have stuck by Ambedkar's style of using capitals for caste and identity markers. Some of the extended informative notes, which we hope add to the force of Ambedkar's arguments, have been split across various entries to make them manageable.

As with other comparable texts like *Who Were the Shudras*, *Riddles in Hinduism* and "Revolution and Counter-revolution in Ancient India", Ambedkar often presumes a minimal familiarity with textual debates and knowledge of Brahmanic theology and mythology among his readers. It is, as if, he is writing both for a posterity, which is us and those who will come after us, as well as for the Brahmanic readers of his time who he fears will ignore his often-laborious efforts. It is indeed true that Ambedkar depends primarily on translations of Sanskrit texts by Orientalists, Indologists and colonialists, and Brahmanic Sanskritists for his readings—just as we as annotators do. However, this is perforce the case with most scholars even today. Anyone who reads this annotated edition will realise how Ambedkar reads these sources against the grain. None of them asks the kind of questions Ambedkar feels existentially driven to ask. To give but one instance, the renowned historian of the late nineteenth century, Rajendralal Mitra, has a long essay on beef-eating in ancient India in his 1881 work *Indo-Aryans*. However, not once in this thirty-five-page essay does he pause to consider the connection between beef-eating, caste and Untouchability. In more recent times, we have the historian D.N. Jha's *The Myth of the Holy Cow*, which upon first publication in 2001 ran into rough weather with the right-wing BJP, causing its publisher in India to withdraw the book. Jha—like most historians, anthropologists, political scientists, sociologists and philosophers engaging with caste and Hinduism—never once cites Ambedkar nor does he explore the connection between beef-eating and caste. Yet, often they both use the same sources, raising questions of both method and perceptions. When Navayana re-issued Jha's work in 2009, we appended to it a small selection from Ambedkar's *The Untouchables*, both to underscore Jha's own negligence and for *politics*—the imagined protection such a gesture might offer us from potential right-wing attacks. (The desire to annotate *The Untouchables* was seeded then, and we have since kept the Jha title in print.)

What struck us in this annotative effort is the relation Ambedkar forges between truth and method. Our effort partakes of this logic even when we feel free to call out Ambedkar where he gets carried away and errs in his readings, such as with his flawed interpretation of Sudraka's fourth-century play *Mricchakatika*, where he sees an anti-Buddhist bias where none exists, or with his condescending and dismissive views on the subcontinent's 'aboriginal' and 'primitive' tribes, quite in line with the views of the colonial authorities (Duncan 2005).

The final section of the book is an addendum which discusses Ambedkar's 'Broken Men Theory'. Its inception lies in the fundamental tension that is at the heart of *The Untouchables*. The arguments of the majority of the book have a deductive character; this is true about most of Ambedkar's investigative writing. However, the foundation which undergirds the meticulously crafted edifice of proofs, premises and conclusions is a speculation. The speculation is admitted and its possibility is defended with examples which aren't strictly related to the argument at hand.

This can be—and has been—quickly construed as an error by some scholars. At the very least, the contradiction between this basal argument and the logic that follows had led some scholars, who deal with a similar subject matter, to reject the systematic 'pretensions' of *The Untouchables*. At a fundamental level, any academic investigation is grounded in a method (or a set of methods) which comes with allied axiomatic rules. Ambedkar's method of logical deduction is not merely weakened by his opening speculation, rather he actively negates it by breaking its rules. The question we are posed with is: is this a mistake? Does this then relegate his text to mere cultural and literary significance? Must we just take specific arguments as valid, and deny the validity of the overall thesis?

We reject all these recourses. The addendum 'Broken Men Theory: Beginnings of a Reading' is a defence of Ambedkar's method specific to *The Untouchables*. The examination occurs at a formal level: indeed, we argue that the most fundamental level of truth is the method itself. With his specific formal treatment of the problem of the origin of Untouchability, Ambedkar invents for us the conceptual tools to connect the past and the future with an insurrectionary logic of the present. History is preserved not merely by discourses but also as a relation—and caste, in Ambedkar's words, is a regime of 'wrong relations'. Specifically, caste, as a historical development, privileges not merely specific castes, but rather it works in service of preserving the unnatural idea of caste itself. We find ourselves within this notion today as much as the past is steeped in it. Any study of caste runs the risk of being influenced not merely by the present configuration of caste, but also the material continuity of the past and the present. The problem is that the caste-organisation of the past is materially *different* from that of the present, not better or worse (that is a separate question) but different. The present interpellation, the relation we hold with caste as its unwilling and willing subjects, necessarily interacts with and infects the study of caste at least at the level of university discourse in ways that are multiple, differential and new.

But the Ambedkarite task is to annihilate this relation— this wrong relation—with the casteist past and bring forth the new. And Ambedkar's founding speculation, stripped of all its particularities, is of *different* relations. One would assume that to investigate Untouchability one would have to trawl the particular spatio-temporal plane within which it evolved, that is logical. Resisting this interpellation, Ambedkar forms new historical relations with British civilizational past, with general theories of world ancient history. In doing this, Ambedkar, like many anti-caste radicals of his time and those who came after him, exits the Brahmanical-mythical past (see for instance how Iyothee Thass anticipates Ambedkar but whose work in Tamil the latter is not familiar with, in Ayyathurai 2011). This is not a mere happenstance but is a wager that produces profound philosophical insights.

The methodology becomes militant. Ambedkar's fundamental fidelity to the truth of equality comes at play in the formal structure of his study. The now infamous declaration in the collective Laboria Cuboniks' *The Xenofeminist Manifesto* (2018) comes to mind: 'If nature is unjust, change nature!' Speculation replaces deduction, because deduction would mean maintaining a relation with caste and being restricted to the world this ideology would allow him to conceive. At the moment of impasse, where the study would halt, Ambedkar turns the dead end itself into a site where he can perform an equalizing gesture and speculate the possibility of a world where no subject is interpellated by Untouchability. He constructs (im)possible relations. And yet, in manufacturing new historical relations, he insists on the speculative nature of his thesis. This insistence is crucial. If he was simply declaring his work as the truth, he would be creating new superstition. But by placing a fundamental doubt at the centre of his argument—'I am not so vain as to claim any finality for my thesis. I do not ask them to accept it as the last word'—Ambedkar performs a radical epistemological exercise in service of the present. The task of annihilating caste is accompanied also by the envisaging of a world with new relations, this new relation is unknown because it hasn't come yet. Just like the past is unknown, for Dalits, because it has been violently erased by Brahmanism. In the present, which is a political present no less, the past as a relational continuity is what we must end. Historical material and 'data' are resources that allow us to construe the possibilities of new relations. These possibilities are thought in the universal domain of human experience, a domain defined (in Ambedkar's case, as the principle of equality, and even through his particular mode of deductive reasoning) at particular sites against the grain of a restrictive present. Ambedkar's method enables the exit from merely studying culture in our superstitious corners and offers an ontology of objects, a material possibility of the new. When he uses historical material to construct new relations, Ambedkar sets a precedent. Of thinking the possibilities in the past and the future.

And yet what remains true for Ambedkar, as also for other anti-caste thinkers, is the materialism that is inherent in their speculations and their general political position. The materialism we see in Ambedkar is one that does not restrict itself to mere critical analysis of Brahmanism and instead posits a real, positive statement about Untouchable subjects and their existence in history. This position comes with an underlying principle which is a judgement on what the nature of reality itself is. Having reached this highly abstract and philosophical point in analyzing Ambedkar's theory, we have explored its ontological stakes in light of the contemporary developments in the 'speculative realist' school of thought. Ours is an attempt to study Ambedkar in tandem with the latest understanding of what the term 'materialism' itself means, where materialism has become increasingly twinned with the term 'speculation'; we believe that we have uncovered a strange proximity in this unlikely juxtaposition. In 1951, the communist leader and writer S.A. Dange while criticizing Ambedkar referred to him as 'unprincipled and opportunist'. This has continued to be the usual Hindu attitude, albeit in different registers. Against this, we assert the force of Ambedkar's logic and systematicity.

Even in the preface to his 1946 work *Who Were the Shudras*—such as in the epigraph that frames this preface—Ambedkar anticipates criticisms that could, and have been, raised against him for breaching the disciplinary and caste lines, and for studying Sanskrit texts in translation, in order to reach his partisan conclusions, where he explains why he needs to enter 'the prohibited field':

> [S]ome may question my competence to handle the theme [of such a study]. I have already been warned that while I may have a right to speak on Indian politics, religion and religious history are not my field and that I must not enter it … I am ready to admit that I am not competent to speak even on Indian politics. If the warning is for the reason that I cannot claim mastery over the Sanskrit language, I admit this deficiency. But I do not see why this should disqualify me altogether (1990b, 11).

However, Ambedkar's approach to the question of history of Untouchability is not to be celebrated merely because he transgresses and breaches bastions of privilege, but because the questions he asks and the answers he offers have a renewed relevance in our times—not just for Untouchability but for the end of caste as such.

Hence this annotative exercise—*Beef, Brahmins and Broken Men*—is a fool's errand since the wise angels are still to wake from their sleep.

REFERENCES

Ambedkar, B.R. [1948] 1990a. *The Untouchables: Who Were They and Why They Became Untouchables?* In BAWS 7. Edited by Vasant Moon. Bombay: Education Department, Government of Maharashtra.229–382.

———. [1946] 1990b. *Who Were the Shudras? How they came to be the Fourth Varna in the Indo-Aryan Society.* In BAWS 7. Edited by Vasant Moon. Bombay: Education Department, Government of Maharashtra.1–227.

———. [1936] 2014. *Annihilation of Caste: The Annotated Critical Edition.* Edited by S. Anand. New Delhi: Navayana.

Ayyathurai, Gajendran. 2011. "Foundations of Anti-caste Consciousness: Pandit Iyothee Thass, Tamil Buddhism, and the Marginalized in South India". PhD thesis. New York: Columbia University.

Deliège, Robert. 1999. *The Untouchables of India.* Trans. from the French by Nora Scott. Oxford: Berg.

Desai, Ashwin, and Goolam Vahed. 2015. *The South African Gandhi: Stretcher-Bearer of Empire.* New Delhi: Navayana.

Deshpande, G.P. (ed.) 2002. *Selected Writings of Jotirao Phule.* New Delhi: LeftWord Books.

Dumont, Louis. 1966/1980. *Homo Hierarchicus: The Caste System and its Implications.* Complete revised English edition. Chicago: University of Chicago Press.

Duncan, Ian. 2005. "Ambedkar, Ambedkarites and the Adivasi: The Dog that Didn't Bark in the Night". Paper presented at the International Conference on Reinterpreting Adivasi Movements in South Asia, University of Sussex. Accessed from Academia.edu 20 January 2019.

Figueira, Dorothy M. 2015. *Aryans, Jews, Brahmins: Theorizing Authority Through Myths of Identity.* New Delhi: Navayana.

Gandhi, M.K. 1987. *The Essence of Hinduism*. Compiled and edited by V.B. Kher. Ahmedabad: Navajivan Publication House.

Jha, D. N. 2001/2009. *The Myth of the Holy Cow*. New Delhi: Navayana.

Juergensmeyer, Mark. 2009. *Religious Rebels in the Punjab: The Ad Dharm Challenge to Caste*. New Delhi: Navayana.

Keer, Dhananjay. 1954/2001. *Dr. Ambedkar: Life and Mission*. Mumbai: Popular Prakashan.

Laboria Cuboniks. 2018. *The Xenofeminist Manifesto: A Politics for Alienation*. London: Verso.

Malabou, Catherine. 2005. *The Future of Hegel: Plasticity, Temporality and Dialectic*, trans. from the French by Lisabeth During. London: Routledge.

Mitra, Rajendralal. 1881. *Indo-Aryans: Contributions towards the Elucidation of their Ancient and Mediaeval History* (2 vols). Calcutta: W. Newman & Co.

Moffatt, Michael. 1979. *An Untouchable Community in South India: Structure and Consensus*. Princeton: Princeton University Press.

Rattu, Nanak Chand. 1997. *Last Few Years of Dr Ambedkar*. New Delhi: Amrit Publishing House.

Rao, Anupama. 2009. *Dalits and the Politics of Modern India*. Berkeley: University of California Press.

Tilak, Lokmanya Bal Gangadhar. 1903. *The Arctic Home in the Vedas: Being Also a New Key to the Interpretation of Many Vedic Texts and Legends*. Poona: Tilak Bros.

Selections from B.R. Ambedkar's

The Untouchables
Who Were They and Why They
Became Untouchables?

Preface

This book is a sequel to my treatise called *The Shudras—Who they were and How they came to be the Fourth Varna of the Indo-Aryan Society*[1] which was published in 1946. Besides the Shudras, the Hindu Civilization has produced three social classes whose existence has not received the attention it deserves. The three classes are:

i. The Criminal Tribes[2] who number about 20 million or so;
ii. The Aboriginal Tribes[3] who number about 15 million; and
iii. The Untouchables who number about 50 million.

The existence of these classes is an abomination. The Hindu Civilization, gauged in the light of these social products, could hardly be called civilization.[4] It is a diabolical contrivance to suppress and enslave humanity. Its proper name would be infamy. What else can be said of a civilization which has produced a mass of people who are taught to accept crime as an approved means of earning their livelihood, another mass of people who are left to live in full bloom of their primitive barbarism in the midst of civilization and a third mass of people who are treated as an entity beyond human intercourse and whose mere touch is enough to cause pollution?

In any other country the existence of these classes would have led to searching of the heart and to investigation of their origin. But neither of these has occurred to the mind of the Hindu. The reason is simple. The Hindu does not regard the existence of these classes as a matter of apology or shame and feels no responsibility either to atone for it or to inquire into its origin and growth. On the other hand, every Hindu is taught to believe that his civilization is not only the most ancient but that it is also in many respects altogether unique. No Hindu ever feels tired of repeating these claims. That the Hindu Civilization is the most ancient, one can understand and even allow. But it is not quite so easy to understand on what grounds they rely for claiming that the Hindu Civilization is a unique one. The Hindus may not like it, but so far as it strikes non-Hindus, such a claim can rest only on one ground. It is the existence of these classes for which the Hindu Civilization is responsible. That the existence of such classes is a unique phenomenon, no Hindu need repeat, for nobody can deny the fact. One only wishes that the Hindu realized that it was a matter for which there was more cause for shame than pride.

The inculcation of these false beliefs in the sanity, superiority and sanctity of Hindu Civilization is due entirely to the peculiar social psychology of Hindu scholars.

To-day all scholarship is confined to the Brahmins. But unfortunately no Brahmin scholar has so far come forward to play the part of a Voltaire[5] who had the intellectual honesty to rise against the doctrines of the Catholic Church in which he was brought up; nor is one likely to appear on the scene in the future. It is a grave reflection on the scholarship of the Brahmins that they should not have produced a Voltaire. This will not cause surprise if it is remembered that the Brahmin scholar is only a learned man. He is not an intellectual. There is a world of difference between one who is learned and one who is an intellectual. The former is class-conscious and is alive to the interests of his class. The latter is an emancipated being who is free to act without being swayed by class considerations. It is because the Brahmins have been only learned men that they have not produced a Voltaire.

Why have the Brahmins not produced a Voltaire? The question can be answered only by another question. Why did the Sultan of Turkey not abolish the religion of the Mohammedan World? Why has no Pope denounced Catholicism? Why has the British Parliament not made a law ordering the killing of all blue-eyed babies? The reason why the Sultan or the Pope or the British Parliament has not done these things is the same as why the Brahmins have not been able to produce a Voltaire. It must be recognized that the selfish interest of a person or of the class to which he belongs always acts as an internal limitation which regulates the direction of his intellect. The power and position which the Brahmins possess is entirely due to the Hindu Civilization which treats them as supermen and subjects the lower classes to all sorts of disabilities so that they may never rise and challenge or threaten the superiority of the Brahmins over them. As is natural, every Brahmin is interested in the maintenance of Brahmanic supremacy be he orthodox or unorthodox, be he a priest or a grahastha, be he a scholar or not. How can the Brahmins afford to be Voltaires? A Voltaire among the Brahmins would be a positive danger to the maintenance of a civilization which is contrived to maintain Brahmanic supremacy. The point is that the intellect of a Brahmin scholar is severely limited by anxiety to preserve his interest. He suffers from this internal limitation as a result of which he does not allow his intellect full play which honesty and integrity demands. For, he fears that it may affect the interests of his class and therefore his own.

But what annoys one is the intolerance of the Brahmin

scholar towards any attempt to expose the Brahmanic literature. He himself would not play the part of an iconoclast even where it is necessary. And he would not allow such non-Brahmins as have the capacity to do so to play it. If any non-Brahmin were to make such an attempt the Brahmin scholars would engage in a conspiracy of silence, take no notice of him, condemn him outright on some flimsy grounds or dub his work useless. As a writer engaged in the exposition of the Brahmanic literature I have been a victim of such mean tricks.[6]

Notwithstanding the attitude of the Brahmin scholars, I must pursue the task I have undertaken. For the origin of these classes is a subject which still awaits investigation. This book deals with one of these unfortunate classes namely, the Untouchables. The Untouchables are the most numerous of the three. Their existence is also the most unnatural. And yet there has so far been no investigation into their origin. That the Hindus should not have undertaken such an investigation is perfectly understandable. The old orthodox Hindu does not think that there is anything wrong in the observance of Untouchability. To him it is a normal and natural thing. As such it neither calls for expiation nor explanation. The new modern Hindu realizes the wrong. But he is ashamed to discuss it in public for fear of letting the foreigner know that Hindu Civilization can be guilty of such a vicious and infamous system or social code as evidenced by Untouchability. But what is strange is that Untouchability should have failed to attract the attention of the European student of social institutions. It is difficult to understand why. The fact, however, is there.

This book may, therefore, be taken as a pioneer attempt in the exploration of a field so completely neglected by everybody. The book, if I may say so, deals not only with every aspect of the main question set out for inquiry, namely, the origin of Untouchability, but it also deals with almost all questions connected with it. Some of the questions are such that very few people are even aware of them; and those who are aware of them are puzzled by them and do not know how to answer them. To mention only a few, the book deals with such questions as: Why do the Untouchables live outside the village? Why did beef-eating give rise to Untouchability? Did the Hindus never eat beef? Why did non-Brahmins give up beef-eating? What made the Brahmins become vegetarians, etc.? To each one of these, the book suggests an answer. It may be that the answers given in the book to these questions are not all-embracing. Nonetheless it will be found that the book points to a new way of looking at old things.

The thesis on the origin of Untouchability advanced in the book is an altogether novel thesis. It comprises the following propositions:

1. There is no racial difference between the Hindus and the Untouchables;
2. The distinction between the Hindus and Untouchables in its original form, before the advent of Untouchability, was the distinction between Tribesmen and Broken Men from alien Tribes. It is the Broken Men who subsequently came to be treated as Untouchables;
3. Just as Untouchability has no racial basis so also has it no occupational basis;
4. There are two roots from which Untouchability has sprung:
    a. Contempt and hatred of the Broken Men as of Buddhists by the Brahmins:
    b. Continuation of beef-eating by the Broken Men after it had been given up by others.

5. In searching for the origin of Untouchability care must be taken to distinguish the Untouchables from the Impure. All orthodox Hindu writers have identified the Impure with the Untouchables. This is an error. Untouchables are distinct from the Impure.

6. While the Impure as a class came into existence at the time of the *Dharma Sutras* the Untouchables came into being much later than 400 AD.

These conclusions are the result of such historical research as I have been able to make. The ideal which a historian should place before himself has been well defined by Goethe[7] who said:[8]

> [453] The historian's duty is to separate the true from the false, the certain from the uncertain, and the doubtful from that which cannot be accepted ... [543] Every investigator must before all things look upon himself as one who is summoned to serve on a jury. He has only to consider how far the statement of the case is complete and clearly set forth by the evidence. Then he draws his conclusion and gives his vote, whether it be that his opinion coincides with that of the foreman or not.

There can be no difficulty in giving effect to Goethe's direction when the relevant and necessary facts are forthcoming. All this advice is of course very valuable and very necessary. But Goethe does not tell what the historian is to do when he comes across a missing link, when no direct evidence of connected relations between important events is available. I mention this because in the course of my investigations into the origin of Untouchability and other interconnected problems I have been confronted with many missing links. It is true that I am not the only one who has been confronted with them. All students of ancient Indian history have had to face them. For as Mountstuart Elphinstone[9] has observed in Indian history 'no date of a public event can be fixed before the invasion of Alexander; and no *connected* relation of the natural transactions can be attempted until after the Mohametan conquest.'[10] This is a sad confession but that again does not help. The question is: 'What is a student of history to do? Is he to cry halt and stop his work until the link is discovered?' I think not. I believe that in such cases it is permissible for him to use his imagination and intuition to bridge the gaps left in the chain of facts by links not yet discovered and to propound a working hypothesis suggesting how facts which cannot be connected by known facts might have been interconnected. I must admit that rather than hold up the work, I have preferred to resort to this means to get over the difficulty created by the missing links which have come in my way.

Critics may use this weakness to condemn the thesis as violating the canons of historical research. If such be the attitude of the critics I must remind them that if there is a law which governs the evaluation of the results of historical results then refusal to accept a thesis on the ground that it is based on direct evidence is bad law. Instead of concentrating themselves on the issue of direct evidence versus inferential evidence and inferential evidence versus speculation, what the critics should concern themselves with is to examine (i) whether the thesis is based on pure conjecture, and (ii) whether the thesis is possible and if so does it fit in with facts better than mine does?

On the first issue I could say that the thesis would not be unsound merely because in some parts it is based on guess. My critics should remember that we are dealing with an institution the origin of which is lost in antiquity. The present attempt to explain the origin of Untouchability is not the same as writing history from texts which speak with certainty. It is a case of reconstructing history where there are no texts, and if there are, they have no direct bearing on the question. In such circumstances what one has to do is to strive to divine what the texts conceal or suggest without being even quite certain of having found the truth. The task is one of gathering survivals of the past, placing them together and making them tell the story of their birth. The task is analogous to that of the archaeologist who constructs a city from broken stones or of the palaeontologist who conceives an extinct animal from scattered bones and teeth or of a painter who reads the lines of the horizon and the smallest vestiges on the slopes of the hill to make up a scene. In this sense the book is a work of art even more than of history. The origin of Untouchability lies buried in a dead past which nobody knows. To make it alive is like an attempt to reclaim to history a city which has been dead since ages past and present it as it was in its original condition. It cannot but be that imagination and hypothesis should play a large part in such a work. But that in itself cannot be a ground for the condemnation of the thesis. For without trained imagination no scientific inquiry[11] can be fruitful and hypothesis is the very soul of science. As Maxim Gorky[12] has said:[13]

> Science and literature have much in common; in both, observation, comparison and study are of fundamental importance; the artist like the scientist, needs both imagination and intuition. Imagination and intuition bridge the gaps in the chain of facts by its as yet undiscovered links and permit the scientist to create hypothesis and theories which more or less correctly and successfully direct the searching of the mind in its study of the forms and phenomenon of nature. They are of literary creation; the

art of creating characters and types demands imagination, intuition, the ability to make things up in one's own mind.

It is therefore unnecessary for me to apologize for having resorted to constructing links where they were missing. Nor can my thesis be said to be vitiated on that account for nowhere is the construction of links based on pure conjecture. The thesis in great part is based on facts and inferences from facts. And where it is not based on facts or inferences from facts, it is based on circumstantial evidence of presumptive character resting on considerable degree of probability. There is nothing that I have urged in support of my thesis which I have asked my readers to accept on trust. I have at least shown that there exists a preponderance of probability in favour of what I have asserted. It would be nothing but pedantry to say that a preponderance of probability is not a sufficient basis for a valid decision.

On the second point with the examination of which, I said, my critics should concern themselves what I would like to say is that I am not so vain as to claim any finality for my thesis. I do not ask them to accept it as the last word. I do not wish to influence their judgement. They are of course free to come to their own conclusion. All I say to them is to consider whether this thesis is not a workable and therefore, for the time being, a valid hypothesis, if the test of a valid hypothesis is that it should fit in with all surrounding facts, explain them and give them a meaning which in its absence they do not appear to have.[14] I do not want anything more from my critics than a fair and unbiased appraisal.

B.R. AMBEDKAR
January 1, 1948
1, Hardinge Avenue,
New Delhi.

Annotations

1 Ambedkar's *Who were the Shudras?: How they came to be the Fourth Varna in the Indo-Aryan Society*, first published in 1946, two years before the publication of *The Untouchables: Who Were They and Why They Became Untouchables?*, charts a history of the emergence of the Shudra caste. Ambedkar hyposthesizes: to begin with there was no such varna as 'Shudra'; those that became Shudras were originally Kshatriyas; a section of these Kshatriya kings subjected Brahmins to tyrannies and persecution as a result of a feud; this led the Brahmins to refuse to perform Upanayana ceremonies on their enemies; not having access to the Upanayana meant that the antagonized Kshatriyas lost their status and position in the caste hierarchy and fell below other Kshatriyas and the Vaishyas (who had access to the Upanayana) leading to the the creation of a new jati: the Shudras. The justification for these hypotheses is given by providing minute readings of several Brahmanical texts. In the preface to this edition Ambedkar anticipates criticisms that could, and have been, raised against him for breaching the disciplinary and caste lines, and studying the original Sanskrit texts in order to reach his partisan conclusions. '[S]ome may question my competence to handle the theme [of such a study]. I have already been warned that while I may have a right to speak on Indian politics, religion and religious history are not my field and that I must not enter it [...] I am ready to admit that I am not competent to speak even on Indian politics. If the warning is for the reason that I cannot claim mastery over the Sanskrit language, I admit this deficiency. But I do not see why this should disqualify me altogether [...] There is very little literature in the Sanskrit language which is not available in English [...] I venture to say that a study of the relevant literature, albeit in English translations, ought to be enough to invest even

a person endowed with such moderate intelligence like myself with sufficient degree of competence for the task [...] It may well turn out that this attempt of mine is only an illustration of the proverbial fool rushing in where the angels dare not tread. But I take refuge in the belief that even the fool has a duty to perform, namely, to do his bit if the angel has gone to sleep or is unwilling to proclaim the truth. This is my justification for entering the prohibited field' (1990b, 11).

2   The classification of entire communities as 'Criminal Tribes' was in large part a colonial construction. This occurred in the wake of the 1857 mutiny when India came under the direct dominion of the British crown. Extensive Census activities were undertaken to take stock of the newly acquired subjects. The colonial encounter with bands of roaming dacoits resulted in their becoming an ethnic category with two hundred communities brought under the fold of 'Criminal Tribes' through the Criminal Tribes Act, 1871. These communities were declared as addicted to committing criminal offence, and authorities were asked to 'notify' those 'fitting such description' to register themselves with the government. This was a means of keeping these communities under surveillance. The government assumed that crime, like other Indian practices, could be explained by the hereditary caste principle. Other than the stigma of being named criminal, people belonging to the notified tribes were systematically persecuted, their nomadic lifestyle made unacceptable to state and society, and their activities curbed at every step by constant scrutiny, making them unable to perform their traditional occupations. Once stigmatized and disenfranchized, the colonial government came to use the now unemployed population as cheap labour and strikebreakers. After independence, the so-called criminal tribes were 'de-notified' and are now known as Denotified Tribes (DNTs); the stigma of 'thugee' in Indian popular imagination remains.

The discrimination faced in contemporary times by such communities often becomes difficult to counter because of the specific nature of institutional brutality meted out, stemming from the behaviour-based identity assigned to them. 'The category of the criminal tribe [...] is not well described by [the flexible ethnic] framework, since it involved the uneven superimposition of both modern (and early-modern) concepts of "criminality" on a broad array of highly differentiated pre-existing ethnicities. In many cases, these identities were already associated with law breaking. But [...] the cultures of illegality that such definitions implied hardly lent themselves to a straightforward strategy of community based rights claims. Unlike Scheduled Castes or Dalits and more recently Backward Castes, groups described as Criminal Tribes were structurally hindered in negotiating strategies of ethnic mobilisation. Any concept of disadvantage they might publicize in this milieu would always imply a heritage of law breaking, and therefore voluntary social marginality' (Bajrange et al 2018). The Criminal Tribes Act was christened Habitual Offenders' Act after Independence. In the fight against continued repression, the moniker of Vimukta jatis has been adopted by several members of the community as they struggle against the presumed moral superiority of the state machinery which continues to view their existence as opposed to the ethical sensibilities of Indian citizenry (Bajrange et al. 2018; Schwarz 2010).

3   While Ambedkar attests to the tribal origins of society as a whole, here we see a separation of a community which is referred to as 'aboriginal'. Several communities across the world have been termed as 'aborigine', a word in Latin used to denote 'original inhabitants'. First used in mythology to refer to the original inhabitants of Rome (Kimball et al. 1845, 275, 288), the word was later used by European colonizers as a catch-all term in order to establish superiority and to unify

the multiplicity of cultures across the world into a position of lowliness when compared to the Western world. In India, 'aboriginal tribes', now termed as 'Scheduled Tribes', is again used to denote a wide multiplicity of cultures: from the tribes in Nagaland to those in Kerala. This denotation only arises when one sees Hinduism as the superior order against which all the various tribal practices are juxtaposed as inferior. But Hinduism itself has tribal origins. The *Rig Veda* was essentially a tribal text (Jamison and Brereton 2014, 54–5). It is the rise of caste and Brahmanism with its need to expand and assimilate differences into a singular order that gave rise to a subjectivity such as 'Adivasi' and 'aboriginal', relegating them to outside the fold. Indeed, many Hindu deities including Shiva, Krishna, Murugan, the many versions of Durga/Bhavani/Kali were all tribal gods absorbed into the caste-fold of Brahmanism. In *Beyond Caste: Identity and Power in South Asia, Past and Present* (2017), historian Sumit Guha problematizes the notion that 'tribe' as a concept is some sort of an originary stage in the evolution of human society. Citing several examples he asserts that organization of society in the Iron Age cannot be determined due to lack of evidence, and that their continuity with later 'tribes', which are described as 'large, stratified, socio-political organizations characterized by diffused authority and collective leadership' (71), cannot be established. Guha claims that tribes existed in conversation with, and under varying degrees of reciprocity with, larger kingdoms and imperial powers. Their institutions weren't maintained out of ignorance, as is implied by most scholarship, but as a means of preservation in particular natural and social environments. Tribes often got transformed into dominant castes and their coexistence with monarchies has been noted across South Asia. Ambedkar's own understanding of tribal communities in his time was influenced largely by colonial interpretations and seems woefully incorrect as has been asserted by scholars who came after him. In his paper "Ambedkar, Ambedkarites and the Adivasi: The Dog that Didn't Bark in the Night" (2005), Ian Duncan charts Ambedkar's view of Adivasis and attempts to find in history the answers to the question which plagues contemporary Dalit-Bahujan activists: why did Ambedkar not attempt to form a political union with oppressed Adivasi communities, a solidary conjunction which seems natural and imperative now? For Duncan, the answer lies in how political movements engaged with the colonial government and how in the struggle for representation, those who didn't fit into the parliamentary paradigm were excluded as unimportant and 'undeveloped' for the exegencies of politics. Duncan says this attitude was a result of how colonial politics of representation was grounded in the search for the 'right man' who could effectively manoeuvre within existent legislative bodies: within this framework, Adivasis were deemed, as Ambedkar says, to 'have not as yet developed any political sense to make the best use of their political opportunities and they may easily become mere instruments in the hands either of a majority or a minority and thereby disturb the balance without doing any good to themselves' (Ambedkar 1989a, 375). Unsurprisingly, colonial officials held similar views about Untouchables who tried to enter politics. Duncan cites the example of Governor Wylie of the United Provinces who wrote to the Viceroy the following in a letter in 1947: 'The danger in their [the Untouchables'] case is that they lack both education and integrity; their presence in local bodies in appreciable numbers may only aggravate the intrigues and corruption which at present mar the working of almost all local bodies in the Province' (Duncan 2005).

4 In Ambedkar's time, one of the more influential thinkers of the term 'civilization' was the Australian Marxist archaeologist V. Gordon Childe (1892–1957). Childe formalized ten

characteristics that determined a civilization with urbanization as key to this determination: 1) densely populated urban settlements; 2) presence of full-time specialist craftsmen, merchants, transport-people, officials and priests; 3) some kind of taxation levied by a divine king from the surplus produced by his subjects; 4) distinguishing architecture and monuments; 5) presence of a ruling class, which included priests, and civil and military officials who absorbed a large share of the surplus wealth produced; 6) writing; 7) the emergence and expansion of exact, predictive sciences; 8) conceptualization of sophisticated artistic styles; 9) trade over long distances with foreign societies; 10) citizenship determined by place of residence rather than kinship (Childe 1950). Childe also used the term 'revolution' in a manner which is similar to Ambedkar's employment of the term with regard to Buddhism. In fact, Childe's main contribution to archaeology, and it is a contribution which has been heavily criticized since his rise in influence, was the understanding of development of societies on the basis of revolutions. He also formulated a Marxist and scientific understanding of the triad 'savage–barbarian–civilized' to explain the progress of history. It is unlikely that Ambedkar read Childe, however one can perhaps read similarities into their separate works owing to their involvement in the progressive movements of their time. Childe's specific claims and even understanding of history have been been debunked by several archaeologists with access to more accurate data; however, in recent years there has been a growing interest in some aspects of his work, such as his claim that archaeology was influenced by the subjective interpretation and biases of the researcher, the stress he lay on the importance of difference in various cultures which led to a differential progress in history and his disbelief in any progressive nature of our journey into the future from the present (Smith 2009; Trigger 1994).

5   Voltaire was the pen-name of François-Marie d'Arouet (1694–1778), a leading figure of the European Enlightenment in the eighteenth century. Though primarily a writer and activist, his philosophical tracts had a profound impact on Western thought. Born into an elite family of noblemen, he gained infamy for his critical stances and his defiant writing in a society which was heavily censored and controlled. Although his rebellious spirit is often exaggerated, as throughout his life he did try to fit into the ruling establishment, he was also a prolific attractor of scandals. Several of his books were publicly burnt, and he had to flee into exile many times. The last period of his life was characterized with radical opposition to the fanaticism and superstition of the ecclesiastical and the monarchical orders. The foundational elements of his philosophical programme were individual human liberty, hedonistic ethics of voluptuousness, scepticism and a belief in Newtonian empirical science (Shank 2015). Yet, Voltaire was also a virulent racist and an anti-semite. Strangely enough, his racism stemmed from his anti-religious views. He reckoned that racial difference indicated that god didn't create man as was claimed in the Book of Genesis. He cited the inherent racial superiority of the white man as the reason behind the enslavement of Africans and the conquest of the 'New World' in the Americas. The races that dwelled in the tropics were seen by him as savages who had never written a philosophical treatise and never would either (Harvey 2012). His attitude towards Jewish people was similarly appaling, referring to them as animals and an inferior species of man (Poliakov 2003, 88–9).

6   Critics of Ambedkar were scattered across all quarters of Hindu society. For instance, on 11 January 1950, the RSS mouthpiece *Organiser* published a long letter by K.D.P. Shastri that ridiculed Ambedkar for piloting the Hindu Code Bill: '[Calling Ambedkar the Modern Manu] is an instance of depicting

a Lilliput as a Brobdingnag. It borders on ridicule to put Dr Ambedkar on par with the learned and god-like Manu' (Guha 2016). A more dangerous opposition to Ambedkar could be sensed in the 'sensible' writings of Congressist leaders such as C. Rajagopalachari, a Tamil Brahmin, also known as Rajaji. In a book entitled *Ambedkar Refuted*, which came out in the year 1946, just two years prior to the publication of Ambedkar's *The Untouchables*, Rajaji took a more condescending route to belittle Ambedkar. The book was a response to Ambedkar's *What Congress and Gandhi Have Done to the Untouchables* (1945), a precise theoretical attack on the pretensions of Gandhism and centrist Congressism. Rajagopalachari, true to his ideological character, says: 'We have to look for a materialist explanation for [why] Dr Ambedkar and other educated leaders of the Scheduled Castes [ignore and understate the achievements of Congress under Gandhi]. These castes are scheduled for special favours intended for their uplift. Though these concessions are made for the benefit of the scheduled communities as a whole, the advantages accrue most to the educated leaders. Thriving on the scheduled status it is no wonder that many of them want that undesirable status to continue intact. They become detractors and enemies of any efforts that seek to remove the bar, for it may tend to the termination of the special favours based in the depressed condition of their community. It is a paradox but it is true that it is natural for educated and favoured leaders of Scheduleld Classes to do their utmost for the continuation of the isolation of their community and to oppose and belittle all efforts at the removal of untouchability. This is the material explanation for the violent dislike of Gandhiji exhibited by Dr Ambedkar who looks upon this great and inspired reformer as the worst enemy of the "untouchables", meaning thereby of the educated and ambitious among them who find that the depressed status furnishes a short cut to positions' (Rajagopalachari 1946, 33–4).

7 Johann Wolfgang von Goethe (1749–1832) was a poet, dramatist and novelist who came to symbolize the Germany of his times more than any other figure. Philosopher Robert Solomon writes about Goethe, '[His] rich and varied life, as a conservative and libertine, as a young lawyer and as author-autocrat of Weimar, as an artist, a scientist, and above all, a poet, has often been compared to the rich and varied experience of Germany from the first waves of chauvinism and sentiment with the poet Klopstock to the beginnings of militaristic nationalism' (Solomon 1983, 37n2). In the early years of his life, Germany was a confederation of 234 principalities without a concrete unified identity, still weighed down by medieval rulers and memories of the Thirty Years War. It was with the arrival of the 'world-soul', Napoleon, who evoked great regard in the minds of young Germans, that the hope for a new revolutionary and modernized era was kindled in Rhineland. Napoleon's annexation, though not a benevolent gesture, spurred German thought with a new vitality, with Goethe as its leading cultural figure (Solomon 1983, 35–9).

8 [Maxims and Reflections of Goethe, Nos. 453, 543.] *Maxims and Reflections of Goethe* is a collection of aphorisms that Goethe collected in the later period of his life on a varied field of subjects. Some reflections he developed himself, some he borrowed from other thinkers and still some he gathered from conversations with acquanintances. The subjects included: life and character, literature and art, science and nature. Ambedkar here is quoting from pages 164 and 190 in Bailey Saunders's 1906 translation of the book. The maxim numbered 452 also seems to have particular resonance with Ambedkar's enterprise: 'The historian's duty is twofold: first towards himself, then towards his readers. As regards himself, he must

carefully examine into the things that could have happened; and, for the reader's sake, he must determine what actually did happen. His action towards himself is a matter between himself and his colleagues; but the public must not see into the secret that there is little in history which can be said to be positively determined' (163–4). Ambedkar inverts Goethe; he first publicizes the indeterminacy of history and then proceeds to establish the truth despite this indeterminacy.

9   Mountstuart Elphinstone (1779–1859) was a Scottish diplomat and statesman who served the East India Company as envoy to Kabul and in the court of the Peshwas, before the Anglo–Maratha Wars. Once the Bombay province came under British dominion, Elphinstone was appointed as its Lieutenant-Governor. Here, he took on the white man's burden of educating the natives and set up several education programmes. Bombay's Elphinstone College, where Ambedkar himself did his undergraduate studies, was constructed in his honour (Cotton 1911).

10 The quote is taken from Elphinstone's magnum opus *The History of India* (1843, 19). The work was written in order to further the understanding of subcontinental history and the work of James Mill who had, before Elphinstone, written his own *The History of British India* (1817), unencumbered by the fact that he had never once visited India nor knew any Indian languages. Elphinstone proclaims that though Mill's 'ingenious, original and elaborate work [left little] room for doubt and discussion [...] the excellence of histories derived from European researches alone does not entirely set aside the utility of similar inquiries conducted under the guidance of impressions received in India' (xvii).

11 The nature of scientific inquiry and its claims of objectivity has been problematized by several thinkers in the humanities. Two figures who represent this critical approach are Michel Foucault

and Bruno Latour. Foucault subjected the apparent givenness of scientificity to his thesis that such historical concepts and cultural forms have to do with the exercise of power, thus showing us how they become tools developed by institutions that hold us in check. Latour held as suspect the objectiveness of scientific truths and their capability to describe the world independent of the actor who/which creates these truths and the networks of relationships she/it is embroiled in with other human and non-human actors. He inverted the lens to focus on non-human actors, and raised the possibility of thinking about non-human agency. Thus he was able to develop a method to subject scientific truths/things to an analysis that traces the way the networks are formed, how they operate, to arrive at the conclusion that scientific truths are 'matters of concern', things that gather, and are constituted in the human and non-human relationships that are formed around them—in a (reductive, admittedly) word, relational. Such critical approaches to objectivity, though of tremendous value, leave us with a problem. Can we, if we consider ourselves practitioners of the humanities, make objective claims about the universe and about being in general, or is our job restricted to the critique of what is given as truth? In the particular case of this study, Ambedkar makes truth claims of his own (the existence of Broken Men and the Buddhist origins of Untouchables, as we will see later), and doesn't stay restricted to critiquing the position of what he opposes. French speculative materialist Quentin Meillassoux addresses this very question: 'Doubtless, where science is concerned, philosophers have become modest—and even prudent. Thus, a philosopher will generally begin with an assurance to the effect that his theories in no way interfere with the work of the scientist, and that the manner in which the latter understands her own research is perfectly legitimate. But he will immediately add (or say to himself): legitimate, *as far as it goes*. What he means is that although it is normal, and even natural, for the scientist to adopt a spontaneously realist attitude, which she shares with the 'ordinary man', the philosopher possesses a specific type of knowledge which imposes a correction upon science's ancestral statements—a correction which seems to be minimal, but which suffices to introduce us to another dimension of thought in its relation to being' (2009, 13). It is in response to this woe that Meillassoux develops his theory that asks: What can be said to exist when we are not there to sense things? We delve into the possible relevance of Meillassoux in the Ambedkarite context in our note on the Broken Men theory at the end of this volume (p. 351). The stake of Ambedkar's argument in this book is this: Untouchability did not always exist; at some point in time some people were made Untouchable; all the historical evidence we have is suspect because they are all Brahmanical sources or influenced by Brahmanical ideology, but this doesn't take away from the *objective* fact that at some point in time some people were forcibly subjugated. It is in this problem that we find a parallel between Meillassoux's theory that allows us to think of the material world without its being mediated by human agency, and Amedkar's attempt to grasp the materially inaccessible past of Untouchability and its beginning. We assert the importance of the conjoined methods of speculation and science (see p. 356), and the necessity of claiming positive truths (as students of humanities) while also producing negative critiques. This is particularly important in the present where the critical energies of academia are still in the hands of Brahmanical forces, whose shape-shifting and even seemingly progressive stances keep enforcing caste ideology, rather than spurring on the annihilation of caste. Against such an institutional edifice, where the rules of engagement of appropriate academic language and ways of thinking, under the guise of professionalism and academic etiquette, serve the continuation of caste, the *truth* of anti-caste possibilities and realities must continue to be proclaimed and hypothesized in their full material force.

12 Maxim Gorky (1868–1936) was a leading figure of social-realist literature in pre-revolutionary Russia. He was praised for the simplicity of his writing and his concern for the indignity of the life of the working class. His work remained prototypical of the kind of literature expected from revolutionary writers. Needless to say, he was closely associated with the Bolsheviks and was an open critic of the Tsarist regime. After the revolution, he became critical of Lenin's authoritarian ways and spent several years in exile. However, he was first personally invited by Stalin to return to the Soviet Union in 1932 and later placed under house arrest once Stalin began to consolidate his power (Tikhonov 1946).

13 [*Literature and Life.* A selection from the writings of Maxim Gorky.] The volume Ambedkar is referring to is the 1946 edition of *Literature and Life*. As we are unable to track the edition down, we have referred to the 1982 collection of Maxim Gorky's non-fictional writings entitled *On Literature*. The quote can be found in an essay entitled "How I Learnt to Write". In it, Gorky responds to his readers' requests to teach them how to write stories. He first tells them to learn the history of literature, to study what drove men to be rebellious writers and how their writings pushed against class society in different periods of time. The rest of the essay maps out the importance of creativity in shaping the world and in helping us think the new. Speculation, something Ambedkar prizes, is revealed by Gorky as something that is imperative in all fields of thought in order to push possibilities and understanding forward. The quote Ambedkar refers to, which may have been translated differently in the edition we could access, is rendered thus: 'Science and letters have much in common: in both a leading

part is played by observation, comparison, and study; both the writer and the scientist must possess imagination and intuition. Imagination and intuition help fill in the gaps in a chain of facts, thus enabling the scientist to evolve hypotheses and theories, which more or less effectively guide the mind's inquiries into Nature's forces and phenomena. By gradually subordinating the latter, man's mind and will create human culture, which in effect is our "second nature"' (Gorky 1982, 31).

14 On the notion of 'hypothesis', Quentin Meillassoux offers this: '[T]he fundamental dimension presented by modern science from the moment of its inception was the fact that its assertions could become part of a *cognitive process*. They were no longer of the order of myths, theogonies, or fabulations, and instead became *hypotheses* susceptible to corroboration or refutation by actual experiments. The term 'hypothesis' here is not intended to suggest a kind of unverifiability that would be peculiar to such statements. We do not mean to imply the idea that no 'direct' verification of dia-chronic statements is possible by definition, since the occurrences to which they refer are posited as anterior or ulterior to the existence of human experience. For as a matter of fact, this absence of 'direct verification' holds for a great many scientific statements, if not for all of them, given that very few truths can be attained through immediate experience and that generally speaking, science is not based upon simple observations, but rather upon data that have already been processed and quantified by ever more elaborate measuring instruments. Thus, in qualifying the statements of empirical science as 'hypotheses', we do not seek to undermine their cognitive value but rather to confer upon them their full value as instances of knowledge. It is the discourse of empirical science which, for the first time, gives meaning to the idea of a rational *debate* about what did or did not exist prior to the emergence of humankind, as well as about what might eventually succeed

humanity. Theories can always be improved and amended, but the very fact that *there can be* such dia-chronic theories is the remarkable feature made possible by modern knowledge. It was science that made it meaningful to disagree about what there might have been when we did not exist, and what there might be when we no longer exist—just as it is science that provides us with the means to rationally favour one hypothesis over another concerning the nature of a world without us' (2009, 113–4).

Part IV
New theories of the origin of Untouchability

Chapter IX

Contempt for Buddhists as the root of untouchability

I

THE Census Reports for India published by the Census Commissioner at the interval of every ten years from 1870 onwards contain a wealth of information[1] nowhere else to be found regarding the social and religious life of the people of India. Before the Census of 1910 the Census Commissioner had a column called "Population by Religion". Under this heading the population was shown (1) Muslims, (2) Hindus, (3) Christians, etc. The Census Report for the year 1910 marked a new departure from the prevailing practice. For the first time it divided the Hindus under three separate categories, (i) Hindus, (ii) Animists and Tribal,[2] and (iii) the Depressed Classes or Untouchables. This new classification has been continued ever since.

II

This departure from the practice of the previous Census Commissioners raises three questions.[3] First is what led the Commissioner for the Census of 1910 to introduce this new classification.[4] The second is what were the criteria adopted as a basis for this classification. The third is what are the reasons for the growth of certain practices which justify the division of Hindus into three separate categories mentioned above.

The answer to the first question will be found in the address presented in 1909[5] by the Muslim Community under leadership of H.H. The Aga Khan[6] to the then Viceroy, Lord Minto, in which they asked for a separate and adequate representation for the Muslim community in the legislature, executive and the public services.

In the address[7] there occurs the following passage:

The Mohamedans of India number, according to the census taken in the year 1901, over sixty-two millions or between one-fifth and one-fourth of the total population of His Majesty's Indian dominions, *and if a reduction be made for the uncivilized portions of the community enumerated under the heads of animist and other minor religions, as well as for those classes who are ordinarily classified as Hindus but properly speaking are not Hindus at all, the proportion of Mohamedans to the Hindu Majority becomes much larger.*[8] We therefore desire to submit that under any system of representation extended or limited a community in itself more numerous than the entire population of any first class European power except Russia may justly lay claim to adequate recognition as an important factor in the State.

We venture, indeed, with Your Excellency's permission to go a step further, and urge that the position accorded to the Mohamedan community in any kind of representation direct or indirect, and in all other ways effecting their status and influence should be commensurate, not merely with their numerical strength but also with their political importance and the value of the contribution which they make to the defence of the empire, and we also hope that Your Excellency will in this connection be pleased to give due consideration to the position which they occupied in India a little more than hundred years ago and of which the traditions have naturally not faded from their minds.⁹

The portion in italics has a special significance. It was introduced in the address to suggest that in comprising the numerical strength of the Muslims with that of the Hindus the population of the Animists, tribals and the Untouchables should be excluded.[10] The reason for this new classification of 'Hindus' adopted by the Census Commissioner in 1910 lies in this demand of the Muslim community for separate representation on augmented scale. At any rate this is how the Hindus understood this demand.[11]

Interesting as it is, the first question as to why the Census Commissioner made this departure in the system of classification is of less importance than the second question. What is important is to know the basis adopted by the Census Commissioner for separating the different classes of Hindus into (1) those who were hundred per cent Hindus and (2) those who were not.

The basis adopted by the Census Commissioner for separation is to be found in the circular issued by him in which he laid down certain tests for the purpose[12] of distinguishing these two classes. Among those who were not hundred per cent Hindus were included castes and tribes which:

(1) Deny the supremacy of the Brahmins.

(2) Do not receive the mantra from a Brahmin or other recognized Hindu guru.

(3) Deny the authority of the Vedas.

(4) Do not worship the Hindu gods.

(5) Are not served by good Brahmins as family priests.

(6) Have no Brahmin priests at all.

(7) Are denied access to the interior of the Hindu temples.

(8) Cause pollution (a) by touch, or (b) within a certain distance.

(9) Bury their dead.

(10) Eat beef and do no reverence to the cow.

Out of these ten tests some divide the Hindus from the Animists and the Tribal.[13] The rest divide the Hindus from the Untouchables. Those that divide the Untouchables from the Hindus are (2), (5), (6), (7), and (10). It is with them that we are chiefly concerned.[14]

For the sake of clarity it is better to divide these tests into parts and consider them separately. This chapter will be devoted only to the consideration of (2), (5), and (6).

The replies received by the Census Commissioner to questions embodied in tests (2), (5) and (6) reveal, (a) that the Untouchables do not receive the mantra from a Brahmin; (b) that the Untouchables are not served by good Brahmin priests at all; and (c) that Untouchables have their own priests reared from themselves. On these facts the Census Commissioners of all provinces are unanimous.[15]

Of the three questions the third is the most important. Unfortunately the Census Commissioner did not realize this. For in making his inquiries he failed to go to the root of the matter to find out: Why were the Untouchables not receiving the mantra from the Brahmin? Why did Brahmins not serve the Untouchables as their family priests? Why do the Untouchables prefer to have their own priests? It is the 'why' of these facts which is more important than the existence of these facts. It is the 'why' of these facts which must be investigated. For the clue to the origin of Untouchability lies hidden behind it.

Before entering upon this investigation, it must be pointed out that the inquiries by the Census Commissioner were in a sense one-sided. They showed that the Brahmins shunned the Untouchables. They did not bring to light the fact that the Untouchables also shunned the Brahmins. Nonetheless, it is a fact. People are so much accustomed to thinking that the Brahmin is the superior of the Untouchable and that the Untouchable accepts himself as his inferior; that this statement that the Untouchables look upon the Brahmin as an impure person is sure to come to them as a matter of great surprise. The fact has however been noted by many writers who have observed and examined the social customs of the Untouchables. To remove any doubt on the point, attention is drawn to the following extracts from their writings.

The fact was noticed by Abbé Dubois who says:[16]

> Even to this day a Pariah is not allowed to pass a Brahmin Street in a village, though nobody can prevent, or prevents, his approaching or passing by a Brahmin's house in towns. The Pariahs, on their part will under no circumstances, allow a Brahmin to pass through their *paracherries* (collection of Pariah huts) as they firmly believe it will lead to their ruin.

Mr [F.R.] Hemingway, the Editor of the *Gazetteer* of the Tanjore District says:

> These castes (Parayan and Pallan or Chakkiliyan[17] castes of Tanjore District) strongly object to the entrance of a Brahmin into their quarters believing that harm will result to them there from.[18]

Speaking of the Holeyas[19] of the Hasan District of Mysore, Captain J.S.F. Mackenzie[20] says:

Every village has its Holegéri (as the quarters inhabited by the Holeyars is called), outside the village boundary hedge. This, I thought was because they were considered as impure race, whose touch carries defilement with it. Such is the reason generally given by the Brahman, who refuse to receive anything directly from the hands of a Holeyar. And yet the Brahmans consider great luck will wait upon them if they can manage to pass through the Holegéri without being molested. To this Holeyars have a strong objection, and, should a Brahmin attempt to enter their quarters, they turn out in a body and slipper him, in former times it is said to death. Members of the other castes may come as far as the door, but they must not (for that would bring the Holeyar bad luck) enter the house. If, by chance, a person happens to get in, the owner takes care to tear the intruder's cloth, tie up some salt in one corner of it, and turn him out. This is supposed to neutralise all the good luck which might have accrued to the tresspasser and avert any evil which ought to have befallen the owner of the house.[21]

What is the explanation of this strange phenomenon? The explanation must of course fit in with the situation as it stood at the start, i.e. when the Untouchables were not Untouchables but were only Broken Men.[22] We must ask why the Brahmins refused to officiate at the religious ceremonies of the Broken Men. Is it the case that the Brahmins refused to officiate? Or is it that the Broken Men refused to invite them? Why did the Brahmins regard Broken Men as impure? Why did the Broken Men regard the Brahmins as impure? What is the basis of this antipathy?

This antipathy can be explained on one hypothesis. It is that the Broken Men were Buddhists. As such they did not revere the Brahmins, did not employ them as their priests and regarded them as impure. The Brahmin on the other hand disliked the Broken Men because they were Buddhists and preached against them contempt and hatred with the result that the Broken Men came to be regarded as Untouchables.

We have no direct evidence that the Broken Men were Buddhists. No evidence is as a matter of fact necessary when the majority of Hindus were Buddhists.[23] We may take it that they were.

That there existed hatred and abhorrence against the Buddhists in the mind of the Hindus and that this feeling was created by the Brahmins is not without support.

Nilakantha[24] in his *Prayaschit Mayukha*[25] quotes a verse from Manu which says: 'If a person touches a Buddhist or a flower of Pachupat, Lokayala, Nastika and Mahapataki, he shall purify himself by a bath.'

The same doctrine is preached by Apararka[26] in his *Smriti*.[27] *Vrddha Harita*[28] goes further and declares entry into the Buddhist temple as sin requiring a purificatory bath for removing the impurity.

How widespread had become this spirit of hatred and contempt against the followers of Buddha can be observed from the scenes depicted in Sanskrit dramas.[29] The most striking illustration of this attitude towards the Buddhists is to be found in the *Mricchakatika*.[30] In Act VII of that drama the hero Charudatta and his friend Maitreya are shown waiting for Vasantasena in the park outside the city. She fails to turn up and Charudatta decides to leave the park. As they are leaving, they see the Buddhist monk by name Samvahaka. On seeing him, Charudatta says:

> Friend Maitreya, I am anxious to meet Vasantsena...
>   Come, let us go. (*After walking a little*) Ah! Here's an

inauspicious sight, a Buddhist monk coming towards us. (*After a little reflection*) Well, let him come this way, we shall follow this other path. (*Exit*.)

In Act VIII, the monk is in the park of Sakara, the king's brother-in-law, washing his clothes in a pool. Sakara, accompanied by Vita, turns up and threatens to kill the monk. The following conversation between them is revealing:

Sakara: Stay, you wicked monk.

Monk: Ah! Here's the king's brother-in-law! Because some monk has offended him, he now beats up any monk he happens to meet.

Sakara: Stay, I will now break your head as one breaks a radish in a tavern. *(Beats him)*.

Vita: Friend, it is not proper to beat a monk who has put on the saffron-robes, being disgusted with the world.[31]

Monk: (*Welcomes*) Be pleased, lay brother.

Sakara: Friend, see. He is abusing me.

Vita: What does he say?

Sakara: He calls me lay brother (*upasaka*). Am I a barber?

Vita: Oh! He is really praising you as a devotee of the Buddha.

Sakara: Why has he come here?

Monk: To wash these clothes.

Sakara: Ah! you wicked monk. Even I myself do not bathe in this pool; I shall kill you with one stroke.

After a lot of beating, the monk is allowed to go. Here is a Buddhist monk in the midst of the Hindu crowd. He is shunned and avoided. The feeling of disgust against him is so great that the people even shun the road the monk is travelling. The feeling of repulsion is so intense that the entry of the Buddhist was enough to cause the exit of the Hindus. The Buddhist monk is on a par with the Brahmin. A Brahmin is immune from death penalty.[32] He is even free from corporal punishment but the Buddhist monk is beaten and assaulted without remorse, without compunction as though there was nothing wrong in it.

If we accept that the Broken Men were the followers of Buddhism and did not care to return to Brahmanism when it became triumphant over Buddhism as easily as others did, we have an explanation for both the questions. It explains why the Untouchables regard the Brahmins as inauspicious, do not employ them as their priest and do not even allow them to enter into their quarters. It also explains why the Broken Men came to be regarded as Untouchables. The Broken Men hated the Brahmins because the Brahmins were the enemies of Buddhism and the Brahmins imposed Untouchability upon the Broken Men because they would not leave Buddhism. On this reasoning it is possible to conclude that one of the roots of Untouchability lies in the hatred and contempt which the Brahmins created against those who were Buddhist.[33]

Can the hatred between Buddhism and Brahmanism be taken to be the sole cause why Broken Men became Untouchables? Obviously, it cannot be. The hatred and contempt preached by the Brahmins was directed against Buddhists in general and not against the Broken Men in particular. Since Untouchability stuck to Broken Men only, it is obvious that there was some additional circumstance which has played its part in fastening Untouchability upon the Broken Men. What that circumstance could have been? We must next direct our effort in the direction of ascertaining it.

Annotations

1 The 'wealth of information' that Ambedkar speaks of, refers to the colonial ethnographic enterprise that through the mechanisms of census and survey attempted to collect, classify and codify identities in a heterogenous social space. In the aftermath of the 1857 revolt, the British colonial regime looked to create and mobilize a codified body of ethnographic knowledge to promulgate a totalizing governance of the subcontinent. According to Cohn, 'The census represents a model of the Victorian encyclopedic quest for total knowledge' (Cohn 1996, 8). Yet, the resulting 'wealth of information' did not just produce knowledge in the abstract but became the basis on which colonial rule over the subcontinent, in accordance with the customs of the land, was established. Scholars of the colonial archive have shown variously how particular forms this knowledge of native communities, when appropriated by the colonizers, transformed the workings of society, pitched the enumerated communities against each other, while also becoming a vehicle through which certain castes could achieve better status for themselves and the means for protesting British rule (Cohn 1987; Appadurai 1993). Eventually, as Ambedkar did, such information was also mobilized against Brahmanical dominance and was used in mounting a political challenge to Gandhi's claim of representing all Hindus. For the scholar Nicholas Dirks, following his mentor and advisor Bernard Cohn, they are proof that the Brahmin-centric model of the caste system was a colonial construction, a claim that has been heavily critiqued on the grounds of placing too much importance on the role of the British and ignoring the evidence of the precolonial workings of the caste system (Dirks 2001). Also, for Dirks, caste was socio-politically constituted rather than through religious interdiction. Alternatively, Christopher

Bayly posits a bi-directional dialectic of power. He argues for a pre-colonial system of knowledge within which the mechanisms of caste figured, only to be transmuted by the imposition of a colonial overlord (Bayly 1988). This conceptualization has now paved the way for studying alternative mechanisms of power that existed within the colonized people. Historian Sumit Guha (2017) traces, among other things, the Portugese racial lineage of the British understanding of caste. He also deduces the different geographic and socio-political factors that led to the creation of variant modalities of caste in different regions across South Asia. Guha complicates the history of caste through numerous examples that illustrate how maintenance of power and historical contingencies shaped caste consolidations, and how caste was a fluid and always changing identity marker. See also Susan Bayly (1999).

2 The conundrum of classifying various practices that fall within the superset 'Hindu' was also present in Census reports prior to 1910. In the 1901 Census report under the commissionership of ethnographer H.H. Risley, considerable attention was paid to distinguish animism from Hinduism. Risley regards animism as a lower order religion reducible to belief in magic, whereas Hinduism for him was important for its transcendental metaphysics. He also avers that animism would lead naturally to a pantheistic faith like Hinduism, which in turn was bound to transform into monotheism (Risley and Gait 1901, 357–9). This conception of development of religion echoes the theory set forth by Hegel in his *Phenomenology of Spirit*. Hegel divides religion into three stages: the first is 'Natural Religion' in which the divine is identified with natural phenomena such as light, wildlife and plants. The second stage is 'Religion in the Form of Art'. Here, the gods are represented sensuously in human forms, and tend to stand in for human failings and nobility. The third stage, unsurprisingly, is 'Revealed Religion', synonymous

with Christianity. In this stage the divine becomes human; god is alienated from himself and takes the human form. To what extent Risley was influenced by Hegel is hard to ascertain, but British philosophy during the late-nineteenth and early-twentieth century was in thrall of him (Mander 2011)—F.H. Bradley and J.M.E. McTaggart and even Bertrand Russell in his early years, for instance. In fact, Victorian England was quite fascinated by the post-unification romantic movements in Germany. The influence ran deep, with many English thinkers and artists looking to 'culturally superior' Germany to escape the rigid and mercantile life in England (Davis 2007). Risley here seems to be studying Hinduism through a Hegelian lens, though he cannot exactly define Hinduism, mired as it is in a multiplicity of beliefs and practices. His definition of Hinduism was not too wide off the mark: 'The most obvious characteristics of the ordinary Hindu are his acceptance of the Brahmanical supremacy and of the caste system, and when it is a question of whether a member of the Animistic tribes has or has not entered the fold of Hinduism, this seems the proper test to apply' (1901, 360). The Census Commissioner for 1911, when the separation of the Animists and Untouchables was made from Hindus, was E.A. Gait, co-author of the 1901 report with Risley. Also see the first riddle "The Difficulty of Knowing Why One is a Hindu" in the annotated edition of Ambedkar's *Riddles in Hinduism* (2016, 58–65). Risley also practised the racist pseudo-science of anthropometry and used it extensively in his field researches. More on this on p. 133–4 note 21.

3 The 1931 Census was the last to enumerate all castes; subsequently, following the Census Act of 1948, only the Scheduled Castes and Tribes were enumerated by caste. Ahead of the 2001 Census, it was under consideration if caste was a category appropriate for the census. The debate was renewed in 2011 (Deshpande and John 2010) and the Socio Economic

and Caste Census (SECC) was conducted as part of the 2011 Census, partial findings of which were revealed by the central government in July 2015. (See Ghosh 2015, for a critique of the methodology of the SECC where the caste data was collected but not released.)

4   Ambedkar rejects the Aryan invasion theory in an earlier chapter of the *The Untouchables*, "Racial Difference as the Origin of Untouchability". However, in the decade leading up to this annotated edition, some path-breaking DNA research combined with developments in archaelogy and linguistics have demonstrated that the self-styled Sanskrit-speaking Aryans did migrate to the northern subcontinent from West Eurasia around 2,000–1,500 BCE, and that they had little to do with the Harappans who on their part came from Zargos in Iran around 7000 BCE and went on to mix with the more ancient Out-of-Africa Indians to form the linguistic group called Dravidian. Genetic research based on an avalanche of new DNA evidence has been explained by the geneticist David Reich in *Who We Are and How We Got Here: Ancient DNA and the New Science of the Human Past* (2018). The political repercussions for a right-wing government in officially admitting that the Indo-Aryans (or the makers of the Vedic corpus) did come from elsewhere over three thousand years ago made 'nationalist' scientists look for acceptable ways of describing the facts. Even if the 'Aryans' had blended and mingled inextricably with the earlier populations that had settled here and with the subsequent waves of migrants over centuries, safer terminology was coined by the state-run Centre for Cellular and Molecular Biology in Hyderabad: "Ancestral North Indians" (ANI) and "Ancestral South Indians" (ASI). What the science and facts nevertheless tell us is that the Brahmins tend to have more ANI (or West Eurasian) ancestry than the groups they live among, even those speaking the same language (Reich 2018, 133–5). Reich offers us this bald fact: 'the

degree of genetic differentiation among Indian jati groups living side by side in the same village is typically two to three times higher than the genetic differentiation between northern and southern Europeans' (2018, 143). While Ambedkar did not put much blame or premium on the Aryan Invasion Theory, he did come close to seeing where the genetic evidence leads us now. He does this as early as in 1916 in an anthropology conference paper in Columbia University, "Castes in India": 'Caste in India means an artificial chopping off of the population into fixed and definite units, each one prevented from fusing into another through the custom of endogamy. Thus the conclusion is inevitable that *Endogamy is the only characteristic that is peculiar to caste*, and if we succeed in showing how endogamy is maintained, we shall practically have proved the genesis and also the mechanism of Caste.' (2013, 84–5). What this artificial chopping up leads to, in the language of genetics, is a 'population bottleneck'. 'These', says Reich, 'occur when relatively small numbers of individuals have many offspring and their descendants too have many offspring and remain genetically isolated from the people who surround them due to social or geographic barriers' (2018, 146). Reich concludes that population bottlenecks in India are often exceedingly old, dating back to over between 3,000 and 2,000 years ago. He tells us how the trading caste of Vysya in the Andhra region, constituting about five million people, would live cheek by jowl with other social groups over millennia and yet maintain severe endogamous integrity. 'Even an average rate of influx into the Vysya of as little as 1 percent per generation would have erased the genetic signal of a population bottleneck.' Yet, this does not happen. With such in-breeding, like with the Ashkenazi Jews community to which Reich belongs, what does happen is this: among Vysyas 'there's prolonged muscle paralysis in response to muscle relaxants given prior to surgery'. Ambedkar ends his preface to *Annihilation of Caste* by calling the upholders of caste 'sick' and that this 'sickness is causing danger to the health and happiness of other Indians'. What he meant figuratively has come to be the reality. See also the prefatory essay "A Fool's Errand" (p. 65).

5 Either Ambedkar errs in recording the year of the address or a proof error has been introduced by the editors of the BAWS (*Babasaheb Ambedkar Writings and Speeches*) volumes. The same quote appears in B.R. Nanda's biography of G.K. Gokhale, *Gokhale: The Indian Moderates and The British Raj* (1977, 328–9). Here, the year of the address is given as 1906, when, for the first time, a delegation of Muslim leaders headed by the Aga Khan III made concrete political demands for Mohamedan representation. Thirty-five prominent Muslims met Lord Minto in Simla (the deputation came to be known as the Simla Deputation) on 1 October 1906 and demanded separate representation to counter the Hindu–Congress hegemony.

6 Sir Sultan Muhammed Shah, Aga Khan III (1877–1957), was one of the founders and the first president of the All-India Muslim League. His petition to the then viceroy resulted in the Minto–Morley reforms, or the Indian Councils Act of 1909.

7 [For the text of the address see my *Pakistan*, p. 431]. In this work (1945), Ambedkar writes: 'These demands were granted and given effect to in the Act of 1909. Under this Act the Mohammedans were given (1) the right to elect their representatives, (2) the right to elect their representatives by separate electorates, (3) the right to vote in the general electorates as well, and (4) the right to weightage in representation' (Ambedkar 1990c, 251).

8 [Italics not in the original.]

9 The struggle for separate representation for Muslims in pre-independence India has a complex history. There is a general

consensus which tends to explain away the phenomenon of 'Pakistan' as the product of the machinations of Muhammad Ali Jinnah, lacking in both a cogent plan for nation-building and popular support, or as bargaining tool for more representation. See Jaffrelot 2002 for a critique of this position. Ayesha Jalal's influential 1985 study, *The Sole Spokesman: Jinnah, the Muslim League and the Demand for Pakistan*, presents the thesis that it was the concern of majority–minority relations in India, and the exegencies of dealing with this problem in the context of imminent independence, which was a driving factor in the Partition. Others highlight how support for Pakistan was generated in the United Provinces of Agra and Oudh (now Uttar Pradesh). The new state was envisaged not just as a refuge for Indian Muslims but also an Islamic utopia which would revitalize the Islamic world and be a successor to the Turkish Caliphate. The contribution of a section of the Deobandi Ulema and their collaboration with the Muslim League in creating a hybrid of the modern state and an Islamic nation is seen as the central driver of the two-nation theory (See Dhulipala 2015). Faisal Devji's *Muslim Zion: Pakistan as a Political Idea* (2013) rejects such a ground-up instrumental understanding of Pakistan as well as Jalal's theory of minoritarian concern (which he accuses of reducing 'Pakistan's history into nothing more than a failed conspiracy' [2013, 7]). Devji cuts through the 'police report' style investigation of history which tries to glean intentions and motives, all of which he claims can only be assigned retrospectively, and examines how religion as ideology unified a people into the 'imagined community' of Pakistan, in place of blood or geographic ties to hold together the people who came to populate the new land. Ambedkar's critical support for Pakistan was not insignificant. His book *Thoughts on Pakistan* (later retitled *Pakistan or the Partition of India*) was first published in 1940 and was used by both Gandhi and Jinnah against each other (Dhulipala 2015). Shabnum Tejani examined how Ambedkar maps out what it is that constitutes nationhood: 'Nationality is a social feeling. It is a feeling of corporate sentiment of oneness which makes those who are charged with it feel that they are kith and kin' (Ambedkar 1946, 31). It is a feeling simultaneously of inclusion, 'a feeling of fellowship', and exclusion, 'anti-fellowship' (Tejani 2013b). Tejani also notes Ambedkar's keen support for separate electorates for all minority communities for he 'believed that although electorates should be structured to reflect the communal divisions in India, their effect would not perpetuate these divisions, but, in bringing people who would not normally meet into public service, it would foster a new like-mindedness' (112).

10 In his paper, "Census enumeration, religious identity and communal polarisation in India" (2013), R.D. Bhagat points out that religion as a question in the Census of the United Kingdom was not included until 2001. The United States does not include it even today. Why then did the colonial regime impose this classification on India? As Edward W. Said critically argued, for the colonizers, the colonies were more real in their imagination of the 'Orient', than in the concrete multiplicity and difference of their realities. Within this framework, the heterogeneous, polytheistic—in a word, alien—cultures of the subcontinent that the colonizer encountered required a certain form of codification in order for it to make sense to the colonial regime. Caste was the most inconceivable and particular form encountered in the Subcontinent which had to be codified and archived through the ethnographic studies that compiled the 'history of the peoples of India' by assimilating various forms of knowledge—privileging Brahmin scholars—into a colonial project that would govern. (See also p. 121-2 note 1.) Bhagat emphasizes the definitional obsession of the British

ethnographers whose myopic perception of the subcontinent required them to segregate socio-cultural forms of living into religion(s), and further subject them to the monotheistic standards of Abrahamic religion consequently ignoring all evidence of heterogeneity. This led to the creation of concrete distinctions between Hindus, Animists, and tribals. Such fixing of religious identity and mathematizing their strength was crucial as far as the politics that followed was concerned. The struggle for representation in local bodies had a distinct communal character and the demand for rights were often articulated from the position of a particular community (Bhagat 2013, 438). At the same time, the methodology of the Census revealed the extent and magnitude of Untouchability, and the boundlessness of the caste system across the subcontinent.

11 [This operation came soon after the address given by Muslim community to Lord Minto in 1909 in which they asked for a separate and adequate representation for the Muslim community. The Hindu smelt a rat in it. As the Census Commissioner observed: 'Incidentally, the enquiry generated a certain amount of heat, because unfortunately it happened to be made at a time when the rival claims of Hindus and Mohammedans to representation on the Legislative Councils were being debated and some of the former feared that it would lead to the exclusion of certain classes from the category of Hindus and would thus react unfavourably on their political importance'. Part I. p. 116.]

12 [See Census of India (1911). Part 1. p. 117] This decision to take the 'Hindu' as the definitive centrality and classify others who are not-so-Hindu originates in the first ever partial Census of 1872, *Report of the Census of Bengal 1872* by H. Beverley.

13 A different kind of hegemonization is underway in contemporary times with the Rashtriya Swayamsevak Sangh labelling the Adivasis as 'vanvasi' (literally forest-dwellers). To this effect,

the RSS set up the Vanvasi Kalyan Ashram to counter the Christian missionary influence in tribal areas, especially in the field of education. Yet, the VKA makes no attempt to adopt tribal languages in its instruction, contributing to their increased disappearance. The propagation of Sanskritized Victorian values has also disturbed the more progressive tendencies found in tribal cultures, especially affecting gender roles (Sundar 2002). Several state school textbooks actively denigrate Adivasi communities: 'A second-grade textbook that Bonda children are made to learn has this to say: "Bonda life is very strange indeed. They live in tiny huts built of mud. The entrance to these huts is rather narrow. They enter the huts by bending forward..."' (Sundar 2002, 380).

14 Ambedkar, surprisingly, leaves out the criterion of burying the dead. Daya Pawar in his autobiography *Baluta* (2015) writes, 'In those days, we Mahars buried our dead; we did not cremate them as we do now. When we watched Babasaheb being cremated at Chaityabhoomi, we were watching the end of a tradition' (205). However, in his paper titled "The Mahars: Who Were They and How They Became Untouchable?", Ambedkar directly addresses this aspect of Mahar tradition: '[T]he Mahars [buried] the dead body when as a matter of theory and practice the Marathas and the Kshatriyas have the custom of burning the dead. The existence of this custom of burying the dead must be admitted...' (Ambedkar 2003, 141)

15 [See Census of 1911 for Assam p. 40; for Bengal, Bihar and Orisa p. 282; for CP. p. 73; for Madras p. 51; for Punjab p. 109; for U.P. p. 121; for Baroda p. 55; for Mysore p. 53; for Rajputana p. 94—105; for Travancore p. 198]

16 [*Hindu Manners and Customs* (3rd Edition) p. 61 f.n.] Jean-Antoine Dubois or Abbé Dubois (1765–1848) was a French missionary who arrived in Pondicherry in the wake of the French Revolu-

tion on a proselytizing mission. Travelling across South India and living according to the traditions of the natives, he prepared the book *Character, Manners and Customs of the People of India and of their Institutions Religious and Civil* which became an influential ethnographic text for both the British and the French colonizers. Based on first-hand experiences rather than textual analyses, Dubois's work reveals the French obsession with the glory of Brahmanical society. For him it was imperative to bring the 'cultured' Brahmins towards Christianity and he was contemptuous of the 'Pariah' converts, a common attitude among most missionaries of his time (Mohan 2004). 'While Dubois did mention other castes, it was merely in one single chapter describing the hundreds of groups of low castes, and he dismissed the lower castes—untouchables and pariahs—in passing, as entirely beyond the pale of civilization. […] What is interesting is that the abbé chose to focus on the Brahmans, considering that his primary reason for undertaking an observation of Indian society was to better effect conversions among Indians. By his own admission, the bulk of converts to Christianity continued to be the lowest castes—untouchables and pariahs. Lower castes were willing to convert to Christianity in exchange for a higher social status, material benefit, and the possibility of gaining employment with the colonizers. For Dubois this was of little spiritual interest compared with the conversion of a Brahman' (Mohan 2004, 233). In her study of Dubois's influence on colonial ethnography, Jyoti Mohan notes his baffling silence on the very existence of Muslims, even while he lived in Mysore under Muslim rulers. She also notes the difference between the French and British attitude towards Indians: whereas the former were deeply enamoured by native customs and believed in a colonization which accommodated them, the latter were more contemptuous. Though the British relied heavily on Dubois' extensive studies, they were pointedly dismissive of those aspects of his work which displayed an admiration of local culture.

17 The Paraiyars and Pallars are the most numerous Dalit castes in the Tamil-speaking region of the erstwhile Madras presidency. Rupa Viswanath (2014) says the Paraiyars were agrestic slaves till the colonial period, forced into a range of menial occupations in the northern districts of the state. The Pallars, predominant in the southern regions, were farm workers though today some of their spokespersons, abetted by the right-wing, claim they were originally wetland farmers and even rulers and never untouchable and wish to be excluded from the Scheduled Caste list (Krishnasamy 2018). The Chakkiliyars, who have now embraced the more 'respectable' though Hinduized label of 'Arundhatiyar', are traditionally leather workers predominant in the western districts of the state. Often native speakers of Telugu, they are also known as Madiga across Tamil, Telugu and Kannada-speaking regions.

18 [*Gazetteer of Tanjore District* (1906), p. 80] M.C. Rajah writes in *The Oppressed Hindus* (1925), which is considered the first ever nonfiction book in English by an Untouchable in India: 'It is not so well known that the Brahmin who considers himself polluted by the touch, the presence or the shadow of an Adi Dravida, will not be allowed to enter the *Cheri-natham*. Should a Brahmin venture into a *cheri*, water with which cow dung has been mixed, is thrown on his head and he is driven out. Some Brahmins consider a forsaken *cheri*, an auspicious site for an *agraharam*' (Rajah 1925/2005). Rajah, like Ambedkar, cites the case of Holeyas vide Mackenzie from the *Indian Antiquary*. This observation portends the central objective of Ambedkar's thesis. Through this text Ambedkar sets up a scene of a historical battle, where the opponents were equals-in-war. The memory of this adversarial relation and of the existence of a time of equality sets up an 'open history' which is ripe with lessons for contemporary

politics: the possibility of recapturing this originary egalitarianism in the contemporary body which kindles its memory.

19   Holeyas, belonging to the present-day state of Karnataka and its adjoining regions, are primarily agricultural labourers.

20   Little is known of James Stuart Francis Fraser Mackenzie except that as a colonial official he worked largely in Mysore and Southern India. His interests ranged far and wide and he authored scores of scholarly essays (including the much-cited "The Village Feast," in the *Indian Antiquary* in 1874 which describes a fire-walking ritual in Akka Timanhully in Bangalore as largely benign and harmless) and nine books from the 1870s to 1910s including *Description of the Halebid Temple* (1873) and the much-reprinted *Wild Flowers and How to Name them at a Glance Without Botany* (1917).

21   [*Indian Antiquary* 1873 11.65.] Some errors in spelling and punctuation in the BAWS edition have been edited after comparing with Mackenzie's essay in the *Indian Antiquary*. The quote also appears in the second volume of Edgar Thurston and K. Rangachari's *Castes and Tribes of Southern India* (1909). Whether Ambedkar obtained the particular extract from this volume is hard to ascertain. He does refer, in an earlier chapter of *The Untouchables*, to Thurston and Risley's list of social precedence of castes in different regions in India. Thurston had worked alongside Risley during his survey work for the 1901 Census. In *Castes and Tribes of Southern India*, he presents contradictory accounts of the origin of the Holeyas, all of which reveal an undercurrent of conflict with the Tulu Brahmins. Holeyas are said to have been the inhabitants of the land which stretched from the Western Ghats all the way to the Eastern Coast, until the arrival of the Tulu Brahmins. One particularly self-serving narrative is as follows: '...the Brahmins [...] from Ahi-Kshetra were again driven out by Nanda, a Holeya chief,

whose son Chandra Sayana had, however, learned respect for Brahmins from his mother, who had been a dancing-girl in a temple. His admiration for them became so great that he not only brought back the Brahmins, but actually made over all his authority to them, and reduced his people to the position of slaves' (Thurston and Rangachari 1909, 374–5). The first volume of *Castes and Tribes in Southern India* also offers mythical justification for the subdued reverence Brahmins had for the Holeyas as evidenced in the above quote. It goes back to the time of the twelfth century Vaishnavaite reformer Ramanuja and how he came to allow the Holeyas and Madigas temple entry. On learning that the Turk king of Delhi had stolen an image of Lord Krishna, Ramanuja tried to enlist the Brahmins to help retrieve it. When they refused, it was the Holeyas who offered assistance. In return they were allowed to enter the sanctum sanctorum of any temple and were also granted the title of 'Tiru-kulam' (sacred race). Importantly, Risley and Thurston were proponents of the racist pseudoscience of colonial anthropometry. They were together responsible for much of the systematization of colonial ethnography and contributed to the essentialization of caste characteristics (Dirks 1996). Thurston was particularly thoroughgoing in his categorizing fervour, personally measuring the skulls and noses of subjects across South India. His study of racial types seemed to extend from his hobby of labelling and pinning butterflies and collecting plants (Bates 1995). His methodology was heavily shaped by his 'personal touch', where subjective knowledge as anecdotal evidence was used to determine essential features of several castes (Philip 2004). For a detailed study of Thurston's work in India and his role in accentuating caste, see Dirks (1996; 2015).

22 The Broken Men theory is Ambedkar's novel explanation of the origin of Untouchability in India. It can be summarized in three points:

1. Primitive tribal society could be divided into two categories: Settled (which practised agriculture) and Nomadic.
2. The Nomadic Tribes found it favourable to attack Settled Tribes for food, who, because of their agrarian turn, had no defensive recourse. This system of warfare resulted in 'Broken Men': people who had their villages destroyed and were left tribe-less.
3. Tribal communities were built on blood relations, which meant that the Broken Men couldn't assimilate into a different tribe. However, Settled Communities would allow them to establish themselves outside their village, and would provide them with food in lieu of defensive services.

Ambedkar postulates that it is these groups of Broken Men who end up becoming Untouchables The present volume is a compendium of the justifications Ambedkar provides, including the rise of Buddhism and the Brahmins' decision to make beef consumption sacrilegious in its wake. See the extended note on the Broken Men theory addended to this annotated edition which explains the significance and strength of Ambedkar's speculative thesis.

23 Robert DeCaroli, in *Haunting the Buddha: Indian Popular Religions and the Formation of Buddhism* (2004), demonstrates how Buddhism became a mass religion through interpretations of textual and archaeological sources. DeCaroli argues that contrary to the usual understanding that extant local religious practices were at odds with the tenets of Buddhism, it was Buddhism's commensuration with the worship of spirit-deities that made it into a popular religion. Patanjali's differentiation of two types of gods is a useful tool in this regard: there were the vaidika (Vedic or prescribed) gods and the laukika (worldly, customary, or generally prevalent) ones (DeCaroli 2004, 13). The laukika deities would include yaksas, raksasas, pisacas, bhutas, kinnaras, kim-

purusas, mahoragas, gandharvas, asuras, nagas, vidyuts, suvarnas and tree-spirits (bhutanis). Despite a drop in state patronage for Buddhism during the Sunga period (second century BCE) it grew into a popular religion by directly engaging with the laukika beliefs of a majority of the population. Through this, the monks solidified the position of Buddhism as the supreme moral doctrine. Several fantastic texts reveal how the monks dealt with the menace of haunting spirits and brutish deities by non-violently (usually) winning them over into the Buddhist ethic. This indicates the willingness of monks to adopt local religious beliefs to push their own values. DeCaroli also says that tales of Buddha's life were modified after the fact (gleaned by dating particular texts) to show him engaging with local spirit-deities. Architectural study reveals that Buddhist monasteries were often built near or directly on top of megalithic burial sites. '[I]t would seem that the Buddhist monks and nuns quickly established themselves as experts in dealing with the dead. [...] All of this evidence, taken collectively, reveals a monastic world that frequently interacted with both spirit-deities and the dead' (2004, 102). DeCaroli concludes that, rather than sticking to dogma, Buddhism was able to flourish and gain ascendance as a popular religion because the monks had to incorporate it within already existing laukika traditions.

24 Nilakantha Bhatta was a seventeenth-century philosopher who wrote several texts which continue to have ritualistic influence in caste Hindu lives. He was the grandson of the influential Brahmin priest Narayana Bhatta who was close to Akbar's minister, Todar Mal, and with whose help he was able to reconstruct the Visvesvara temple in Kashi (O'Hanlon 2007). Nilakantha, best known for his encyclopaedic interpretation of Brahmanic laws collected together in the *Mayukhas* ('rays of light'), drew from various canonical sources, including the *Manusmriti*, to give a consistent rulebook for the dwijas.

25 [Edited by Gharpure, p. 95] J.R. Gharpure was a pleader in the Bombay High Court and a Sanskritist who offered scholarly Sanskrit editions of *Yajnavalkya Smriti* and *Manusmriti* among other texts. Ambedkar is citing from his *Santi Mayukha: A Treatise on Propitiatory Rituals* by Bhatta Nilakantha, self-published by Gharpure in Sanskrit in 1924 from Girgaon, Bombay, as part of his series, 'Collections of Hindu Law Texts'. Of Nilakantha's twelve *Mayukhas*, *Prayaschit Mayukha* is the tenth. It details the various ways in which sin (see p. 239 note 49 and p. 245–6 note 57) or crime and pollution can occur, the punishments that await sinners in hell and the means of repentance. Sin, for a dwija, can be induced by such actions as 'murder, drinking, theft, adultery, eating of forbidden things [flesh, onion, garlic, among other things], giving up vedic study, contact with *certain persons* ... [and] taking food from men of other castes or Sudras' [emphasis added] (Kane 1926, xxxii–xxxiii). Killing of the cow or the Brahmin were also considered grave sins. Nilakantha also lists the different births a person may be condemned to for living in sin. He gives extensive lists of means of repentance, which include shaving and applying cow-dung and mud to the body. Acts of penitence differ depending on the caste of the sinner. On Untouchability and avoidance of contact with lower castes, Nilakantha was, well, more liberal than his forebears: 'contact at *tirthas*, in marriage processions, fairs, battles, national calamities, burning of village' were all permissible (Kane 1926, xxxii–xxxiii). The *Mayukhas* were popular books of Hindu ethics in the regions of Gujarat, Konkan and Maharashtra, and are said to have been brought into prominence by the Marathas in the seventeenth and eighteenth centuries (Macnaghten 1860; Mitra 1881).

26 Apararka, or Aparaditya, was a monarch of the Shilahara dynasty who ruled over the Konkan region in the late twelfth century. He is best known for *Apararka-Yajnavalkya-Dharma-*

sastra nibandha, his commentary on the Yajnavalkya Smriti. Estimated to have been written anywhere between 100 BCE to 600 CE, the Yajnavalkya Smriti is regarded as second in importance only to the Manusmriti (Ghose 1917). The Smriti was likely written during the Gupta reign and can be seen as commissioned to grant legitimacy to the Brahmanical empire (Olivelle and Davis 2018, 26). Set in the anustup metre (see p. 232 note 27), the work sets out the ethical, social, political and religious imperatives of the lives of dwija men. Apararka, in his commentary, pulls from 108 other primary sources including the srutis, Grihya and Dharma Sutras, metrical Smritis and from twenty-one puranas. He tries to reconcile the various contradictions found in these texts and situates and discards codicils as he sees fit for contemporary society. Apararka's text still remains authoritative in Brahmanical society and is the principal book of the Kashmiri pandits (Ramdas 1986). The original text of the Yajnavalkya Smriti (Vidyarnava 1918) also contains references to Buddhism: in a list which describes in odious detail the qualities of a good wife, one of them is 'She never makes friendship with Buddhistic nuns (Sramana)' (149). In one section, among the obstacles mentioned in the non-fulfilment of wishes made during a sacrifice is if the sacrificer dreams of a head-shaven person, which the translator, Srisa Chandra Vidyarnava, notes could be a reference to Buddhist monks (367–8). Vidyarnava, in his introduction to the text, also notes the influence of the Buddhist period in the writing of several Smritis. He identifies the usage of the word 'vinaya' meant as 'discipline' among the Buddhist and not as 'modest' (an alternative translation of the term) to make this claim (xvi). He also notes that though there is no mention of Buddhists by name, they are references to them as 'munda', 'shaven-heads', and 'kashaya-vasas', 'yellow garments' (xvii).

27 [Smriti Sammuchaya I. p. 118]

28 Harita was an ancient composer of *Dharma Sutras* who is said to have lived anywhere between 600 and 300 BCE. The two main texts attributed to him are *Vrddha Harita* and *Laghu Harita*. That he is widely quoted in several ancient *Dharma Sutras* establishes him as a prolific composer with encyclopaedic ambitions (Kane 1930). The *Vrddha Harita*, which comprises eight chapters and about 2,600 verses, is said to have been recited by him to the mythological king, Ambarisa. It details the various obligatory duties that ought to be performed by individuals depending on their varna. It is also a theoretical study of the nature of the self, both individual and supreme, and it lists the various means by which one can attain moksha. Purification from different kinds of pollution, penances to be performed, rules of impurity in birth and death and of inheritance are also listed (Kane 1930).

29 There are not many Buddhist plays in Sanskrit, but Buddhist characters appear in Sanskrit plays from the time of Bhasa (third–fourth centuries CE). The treatment of Buddhist characters in Sanskrit dramas is not uniform. Bharata in his *Natyashastra* states that Buddhist monks should be addressed as 'bhadanta' or Blessed Sir, contravening the conclusion that Ambedkar chooses to draw from *Mricchakatika*. In the bhana play (a one-act monologue) *Padmaprabhrutakam* by Shudraka, the protagonist Sharvilaka makes love to a shakyabhikshaki, a Buddhist nun. In Bhavabhuti's romantic play *Malati-Madhava*, a Buddhist nun, Kamandaki, helps to unite the hero and the heroine. M.L. Varadpande in *History of Indian Theatre* (2005) says, 'Since seventh century A.D. onwards dramatic literature, particularly farces made fun of Shakya Shramanakas. Buddhism had started declining and it branched off into various tantric cults like Vajrayana and Sahajayana whose ritualistic practices included the five Ms or panchamakaras. But one must also note that the ascetics and monks of other cults too were not spared by the playwrights.

Collapse of morality was not confined to any one cult' (152).

30 Ambedkar appears to misread the play to make it work for his thesis. *Mricchakatika* (The Little Clay Cart), composed in the second century BCE by Sudraka, is classified as a prakarna (realistic) play reflecting society and its ordinary characters (as opposed to the nataka type where the temporal order subserves a celestial order, such as Kalidasa's *Sakuntala*). In the play, the hero Charudatta, a Brahmin merchant fallen upon hard times, loves a wealthy, beautiful courtesan, Vasantsena, who in turn is pursued by the king's ill-bred brother-in-law, Sakara, also the local governor. The historian D.D. Kosambi (2008) says the play 'flouts convention by ignoring court life and epic incidents in its choice of theme [...] The boorish villain, foiled several times, finally strangles the heroine and leaves her for dead, but accuses the hero of her murder [...] The heroine is revived and the hero rescued from the execution block. The Prakrit spoken by various characters has provincial variations that seem to be modelled upon life' (180). Such usage of language in *Mrichhakatika* was unique to the text. Kosambi points out the caste nature of this aspect of *Mrichhakatika*: 'The Prakrit spoken by different characters in the *Mrcchakatika* has been separated into varieties labelled with local names. But even the *Mrcchakatika* Candalas use a Prakit easily understood by the rest, while the Candalas of the Jatakas spoke a language among themselves incomprehensible to "Aryans"' (Kosambi 1985, 14). In the scene that Ambedkar chooses to discuss, subtle satire and the role of social distinctions are reflected in the depiction of the Buddhist monk. There is evidence in the play that the attitude towards Buddhists was not universally hostile. The scene that riles Ambedkar serves to further the comic element and Sakara's villainous character rather than establish the inferiority of Buddhists, for Samvahaka is not enclosed within a Hindu/Buddhist dichotomy but is a rounded character who

evolves through the play. A shampooer at the beginning, who works at the Brahmin merchant Charudutta's home, he's given to gambling. With financial help from Vasantasena, he gives up gambling and turns to Buddhism and becomes a monk. In a line of the play he says, 'Treasure these words in your memory: "He was a shampooer, a gambler, a Buddhist monk"' (Ryder 1905, 40). In Act VIII, when the villainous Sakara assaults Vasantasena and leaves her for dead, it is Samvahaka who rescues and nurses her. In Act X, he averts the execution of Charudutta and reunites Vasantasena and Charudatta. Contrary to the conclusion Ambedkar draws, being a Brahmin does not exempt Charudatta from being awarded capital punishment at the hands of Chandala executioners. Nevertheless, the question of why, within the text, Sakara as governor maintains such a hostility towards Samvahaka remains. Ambedkar is right in making much of this thread he extracts from within the play. Though the play may not be itself contemptuous towards Buddhism, that the element of contempt does exist, in the mind of a character, is of use for Ambedkar's purpose.

31 In the 1905 translation of the play by Arthur William Ryder (for Harvard University), and in all other translations, we see that the courtier Vita brazenly mocking Sakara, referred to as Sansthanaka (the governor). Three times in the course of the scene by the pool and garden, Vita addresses the loutish governor not as 'Friend' but as 'You jackass' (as he does in almost every other scene he shares with him). Vita admonishes Sakara for going after a harmless monk. In fact, in almost all the scenes involving the courtier and the governor, the latter is shown to be a comic villain who exercises brute authority. It has not been possible to establish which translation Ambedkar is referring to, but crucial elements in the dialogue between Vita and Sakara that figure in Ryder's and A.L. Basham's translations—both dateable to Ambedkar's time—are missing here.

32 While the Brahmin is exempted from capital punishment irrespective of his crime in texts such as the *Manusmriti*, it is not a rule that was necessarily followed. At variance with the conclusion Ambedkar draws from within the play, the Brahmin Charudatta is indeed sentenced to capital punishment. He is of course saved in the last act thanks to the Buddhist monk Samvahaka's crucial role.

33 Gail Omvedt (2003) points out the considerable lack of evidence to substantiate the decline of Buddhism. She rejects the accepted theories, one of the main claims being that persecution of Buddhists only played a minor role in the process. Rather, it is generally held that the system of monasteries that increasingly became involved in commercial activities and banking, drained surplus labour into itself leading to increased irrelevance to people's everyday lives. The monasteries have also been termed as decadent and as having moved away from the central tenets of austerity. They are described as exploitative centers which flourished on tax incentives and offered nothing in return. On the other hand, the adoption (at least nominally) of the Buddhist tenet Ahimsa by the Brahmins is said to have transformed Hinduism into devotional worship of Shiva and Vishnu (whose various avatars could easily subsume local deities). This came to fill the religious gap left by Buddhist (anti-) theism in popular consciousness. Moreover, the Brahmanical expertise in sacrificial rites and knowledge of seasons is said to have been crucial in rallying the agricultural populace into the Hindu fold. The eighth century Adi Sankara is said to have been crucial in this transformative process with his revivalist institution-building project. The deathblow to Buddhism is said to have been dealt by the Turkish invaders who put the final nail in the coffin of a religion already in decline. Drawing upon colonialist readings of Islam, Ambedkar, too, believes this. In the unfinished unpublished manuscript, "The Decline and Fall of

Buddhism", (1987a, 229–38), he writes: 'There can be no doubt that the fall of Buddhism in India was due to the invasions of the Musalmans. Islam came out as the enemy of the *'But'*. The word *'But'* as everybody knows is an Arabic word and means an idol. Not many people however know what the derivation of the word *'But'* is *'But'* is the Arabic corruption of Buddha. Thus the origin of the word indicates that in the Moslem mind idol worship had come to be identified with the Religion of the Buddha' (229–30). Regretting that the 'sword of Islam' thesis was accepted even by Ambedkar, Omvedt labels all the above theories as 'facile generalisations' and laments the absence of any evidentiary Buddhist texts from this period, which is part of the larger problem of lack of historiographical evidence from ancient times in Indian history in general. She says there is a glaring lack of sociological texts which serve as direct chronicles of the lived experiences of subcontinental peoples. The lack of descriptive texts is matched by an abundance of Brahmanic prescriptive ones. Relying on Hsuan Tsang's descriptions of violence against Buddhists and noting that it was much more beneficial for the ruling classes to maintain Brahmanism rather than a more egalitarian Buddhism, Omvedt concludes that large-scale violent reprisal remains the most probable explanation for the disappearance of the religion. Omvedt: 'To view "Muslims" uniquely as destroyers and looters of monasteries and temples in contrast to people of other religions (e.g. 'Hindus') is an erroneous concept, a product of the Hindutva ideology that began to take shape in 19th century India' (2004, 174). Omvedt points out several contradictions that plague the above-mentioned theories. For instance, how could the mere agricultural orientation of Brahmins supplant the commercial strength of the Buddhist, especially in an age where foreign trade was becoming widespread? Moreover, if indeed the Buddhists were closely tied to the commercial realm of things, how then would their existence be seen as parasitic and unproductive? If they were instrumental in moving the people away from the 'productive' lives of ritualistic-agrarianism, could this not be construed as more of a threat to the ruling classes by creating a new configuration of power? It is also known that Buddhism very easily accommodated itself with local ritual cultures and that its questioning of the previous Vedic hegemony didn't merely result in a belief-void, but instead offered simple tenets of a moral life. The main problem, Omvedt reckons, is that historians have relied on Brahmanic texts to map out the situation of the past. Buddhist texts on the other hand have mostly been destroyed and the only ones available are from outside the subcontinent. Also, Brahmanic texts quite openly sanction the use of violence to get rid of 'heretics' (Pashandas). Although, DeCaroli (2004) notes that Buddhism was extremely flexible in incorporating itself into existing local traditions (see p. 135–6 note 23), Kosambi (2008, 166–76) identifies the decline in importance of yajna rituals after the proliferation of Sramanic traditions, like Buddhism and Jainism, as central to the branching out of Brahmin priests into more accommodative of laukika traditions that included tribes who previously weren't a part of caste society. The adoption of tribal gods like Shiva, Nandi, the various avatars of Vishnu are good examples. Further Kosambi points out that even during the reign of Buddhist kings, Brahmins held important positions and were important in securing 'illustrious' lineages in order to legitimize and grant prestige to the kings.

Part V

The new theories and some hard questions

Chapter X

Beef-eating as the root of untouchability

We now take up test No. 10 referred to in the circular issued by the Census Commissioner and to which reference has already been made in the previous chapter. The test refers to beef-eating.

The Census Returns show that the meat of the dead cow forms the chief item of food consumed by communities which are generally classified as untouchable communities. No Hindu community, however low, will touch cow's flesh. On the other hand, there is no community which is really an Untouchable community which has not something to do with the dead cow. Some eat her flesh, some remove the skin, some manufacture articles out of her skin and bones.

From the survey of the Census Commissioner, it is well established that Untouchables eat beef. The question however is: Has beef-eating any relation to the origin of Untouchability? Or is it merely an incident in the economic life of the Untouchables? Can we say that the Broken Men came to be treated as Untouchables because they ate beef? There need be no hesitation in returning an affirmative answer to this question. No other answer is consistent with facts as we know them.

In the first place, we have the fact that the Untouchables, or the main communities which compose them, eat the dead cow and those who eat the dead cow are tainted with Untouchability and no others. The co-relation between Untouchability and the use of the dead cow is so great and so close that the thesis that it is the root of Untouchability seems to be incontrovertible.[1] In the second place if there is anything that separates the Untouchables from the Hindus, it is beef-eating. Even a superficial view of the food taboos of the Hindus will show that there are two taboos regarding food which serve as dividing lines. There is one taboo against meat-eating. It divides Hindus into vegetarians and flesh eaters. There is another taboo which is against beef-eating. It divides Hindus into those who eat cow's flesh and those who do not. From the point of view of Untouchability the first dividing line is of no importance. But the second is. For it completely marks off the Touchables from the Untouchables. The Touchables whether they are vegetarians or flesh-eaters are united in their objection to eat cow's flesh. As against them stand the Untouchables who eat cow's flesh without compunction and as a matter of course and habit.[2]

In this context it is not far-fetched to suggest that those who have a nausea against beef-eating should treat those who eat beef as Untouchables. There is really no necessity to enter upon any speculation as to whether beef-eating was or was not the principal reason for the rise of Untouchability. This new theory receives support from the Hindu Shastras. The *Veda Vyas Smriti*[3] contains the following verse which specifies the communities which are included in the category of Antyajas and the reasons why they were so included.[4]

> I. 12–13: The *Charmakars* (cobbler), the *Bhatta* (soldier), the *Bhilla*, the *Rajaka* (washerman), the *Puskara*, the *Nata* (actor), the *Vrata*, the *Meda*, the *Chandala*, the *Dasa*, the *Svapaka*, and

the *Kolika*—these are known as Antyajas as well as others who eat cow's flesh.

Generally speaking the smritikars never care to explain the why and the how of their dogmas. But this case is [an] exception. For in this case, Veda Vyas does explain the cause of Untouchability. The clause 'as well as others who eat cow's flesh' is very important. It shows that the smritikars knew that the origin of Untouchability is to be found in the eating of beef. The dictum of Veda Vyas must close the argument. It comes, so to say, straight from the horse's mouth and what is important is that it is also rational for it accords with facts as we know them.

The new approach in the search for the origin of Untouchability has brought to the surface two sources of the origin of Untouchability. One is the general atmosphere of scorn and contempt spread by the Brahmins against those who were Buddhists and the second is the habit of beef-eating kept on by the Broken Men. As has been said, the first circumstance could not be sufficient to account for stigma of Untouchability attaching itself to the Broken Men. For the scorn and contempt for Buddhists spread by the Brahmins was too general and affected all Buddhists and not merely the Broken Men. The reason why Broken Men only became Untouchables was because in addition to being Buddhists they retained their habit of beef-eating which gave additional ground for offence to the Brahmins to carry their newfound love and reverence to the cow to its logical conclusion. We may therefore conclude that [while] the Broken Men were exposed to scorn and contempt on the ground that they were Buddhists, the main cause of their Untouchability was beef-eating.

The theory of beef-eating as the cause of untouchability also gives rise to many questions. Critics are sure to ask: What is the cause of the nausea which the Hindus have against beef-eating? Were the Hindus always opposed to beef-eating? If not, why did they develop such a nausea against it? Were the Untouchables given to beef-eating from the very start? Why did they not give up beef-eating when it was abandoned by the Hindus? Were the Untouchables always Untouchables? If there was a time when the Untouchables were not Untouchables even though they ate beef why should beef-eating give rise to Untouchability at a later-stage? If the Hindus were eating beef, when did they give it up? If Untouchability is a reflex of the nausea of the Hindus against beef-eating, how long after the Hindus had given up beef-eating did Untouchability come into being? These questions must be answered. Without an answer to these questions, the theory will remain under cloud. It will be considered as plausible but may not be accepted as conclusive. Having put forth the theory, I am bound to answer these questions. I propose to take up the following heads:

(1) Did the Hindus never eat beef?

(2) What led the Hindus to give up beef-eating?

(3) What led the Brahmins to become vegetarians?

(4) Why did beef-eating give rise to Untouchability? and

(5) When was Untouchability born?

Annotations

1 The entrenched association of 'impurity' and the 'dead cow' was institutionalized through a mechanism of taxation between the Savarnas and the Antyajas. Shalini Randeria provides an account of such a system of discrimination in Gujarat. 'The right (*hak*) to drag and flay [the carrion] had to be secured against payment of a tax to the local ruler at a periodic auction. In Sabarkantha district [of Gujarat] this tax was known as *bhambh*, which means dead animal' (Randeria 1989, 175). Hiroyuki Kotani, in his study of Mahar vatan in the colonial period in the Bombay presidency says, apropos of a Bombay High Court verdict of 1870, that 'in the course of the nineteenth century conflicts often arose between Vatandar Mahars and peasants over the problem of who should be awarded possession of the skins of dead cattle. In these cases, the parties to the conflicts frequently resorted to taking legal action. Through these actions a new precedent came to be consolidated in that the owner of the animal while alive was also the owner of the skin of the animal when dead' (1997a, 112). In another essay, Kotani also points to occasional conflicts between Mahars and Mangs over the right to the hides of dead cattle in a Mang house over which Mahars tended to stake a 'vatan' claim (1997b, 60).

2 [The Untouchables have felt the force of the accusation levelled against them by the Hindus for eating beef. Instead of giving up the habit, the Untouchables have invented a philosophy which justifies eating the beef of the dead cow. The gist of the philosophy is that eating the flesh of the dead cow is a better way of showing respect to the cow than throwing her carcass to the wind.] In the various origin myths of many untouchable jatis that are forced to dispose of and eat the dead cow, across the north and south of the subcontinent, often the narrative revolves around a fall from a higher caste, often from being

a Brahmin. G.W. Briggs in his classic study *The Chamars* (1920) documents several such legends. In one, 'five brothers, Brahmans, while out walking one day, saw the carcass of a cow by the roadside. Four of the brothers passed it by, but the fifth removed the body. Thereupon he was excommunicated by his brothers. His descendants continue to remove the carcasses of cattle' (17). More recently, the social anthropologist Simon Charsley (2004) has documented what he calls a living purana, the Jamba Purana that is performed by the Chindus among the Madigas of present-day Andhra Pradesh and Tamil Nadu. The Madigas are the equivalent of the Chamars of North India. In this telling of history as fable, performed as a *yakshagana*, the Madiga claims an origin more original than the primal birth of the Brahman. This story, claiming a Puranic status of circa fifth century CE, features the gods Parvati and Siva, among others, the Dalit forebears Chennaiah and Jamabvan and Kamadhenu, the holiest of cows. G. Kalyana Rao, Telugu Marxist writer with a Maoist orientation, retells this tale in his acclaimed novel *Antarani Vasantam* (2000, translated as *Untouchable Spring* into English and several Indian languages). The Jamba Purana as narrated in *Antarani Vasantam* in a nutshell: Chennaiah, miraculously born to Parvati, has the job of grazing Kamadhenu the cow. One day, he has the urge to drink its milk. He asks Parvati, and she tells him to tell the cow of his urge. On hearing his request, Kamadhenu drops dead. If its milk is so sweet, how must its flesh taste, Siva and Parvati wonder. All the devas and devatas, gods and godlings, come to see, and stand salivating around the dead Kamadhenu. But all of them together cannot lift its body. Chennaiah, at Siva's behest, then summons his ancestor, Jambavan. He is stronger than all the gods and lifts the dead cow with his left hand. The gods then butcher the cow and tell Jamabavan how to cook it, asking him to make two halves of the meat. He does not heed them and cooks the entire meat in one pot. While being stirred, a piece of meat falls to the ground and is muddied. It becomes impure. The lad Chennaiah cleans it and puts it back into the pot. This angers the gods, and Siva curses Jambavan and Chennaiah: You will live in Kaliyuga, eating the meat of dead cows and sweeping the streets forever and ever. Heedless, Jambavan and Chennaiah eat the beef. And so it happens that in Kaliyuga, Jambavan's progeny become Madigas and Chennaiah's children become Malas.

3   Vyasa was a mythic sage who is credited with the authorship of the *Mahabharata* and for rendering the *Vedas* in their present four-part structure. His given name was Krishna Dvaipayana; the name 'Vyasa', which means 'editor' or 'divider', was attributed to him because he divided the unified Vedic knowledge system to make it more understandable in the coming Kaliyuga (White 2014, 227–8). In addition, he is said to have composed the *Puranas* and the *Upapuranas*. He was also the originator of the Brahmin tradition of 'smrti': the practice of writing down that which has been remembered (Sullivan 1989). After he formalized the *Vedas*, which had previously only been transmitted aurally (or so it is claimed), he went on to influence various disciples, who themselves produced written interpretive tracts (Mani 1975, 885–8).

4   [Quoted in Kane's *History of Dharmasastras*, Vol. II, Part 1, p. 71.] The following quote appears in its original Sanskrit form in Kane's text (1941a). Kane here discusses the term Antyaja and all its various occurrences and cadences across the Shastras. It is possible that Ambedkar has translated the extract himself based on the explanation Kane provides in pages 70–1 of the aforementioned book.

Chapter XI

Did the Hindus never eat beef?

To the question whether the Hindus ever ate beef, every Touchable[1] Hindu, whether he is a Brahmin or a non-Brahmin, will say 'no, never'. In a certain sense, he is right. From times [sic], no Hindu has eaten beef. If this is all that the Touchable Hindu wants to convey by his answer there need be no quarrel over it. But when the learned Brahmins argue that the Hindus not only never ate beef but they always held the cow to be sacred and were always opposed to the killing of the cow, it is impossible to accept their view.

What is the evidence in support of the construction that the Hindus never ate beef and were opposed to the killing of the cow?

There are two series of references in the *Rig Veda*[2] on which reliance is placed. In one of these, the cow is spoken of as *Aghnya*. They are *Rig Veda* I.164.27;[3] IV.1.6;[4] V.82.8;[5] VII.69.71;[6] X.87.[7] Aghnya means 'one who does not deserve to be killed'. From this, it is argued that this was a prohibition against the killing of the cow and that since the *Vedas* are the final authority in the matter of religion, it is concluded that the Aryans could not have killed the cows, much less could they have eaten beef. In another series of references the cow is spoken of as sacred. They are *Rig Veda* VI.28.1.8[8] and VIII.101.15.[9] In these verses the cow is addressed as Mother of Rudras, the Daughter of Vasus, the Sister of the Adityas and the Centre of Nectar. Another reference on the subject is in *Rig Veda* VIII.101.16 where the cow is called Devi (Goddess).

Reliance is also placed on certain passages in the *Brahmanas* and *Sutras*.

There are two passages in the *Satapatha Brahmana*[10] which relate to animal sacrifice and beef-eating. One is at III.1.2.21 and reads as follows:

> He (the Adhvaryu) then makes him enter the hall. Let him not eat (the flesh) of either the cow or the ox, for the cow and the ox doubtless support everything here on earth. The gods spake, 'Verily, the cow and the ox support everything here: come, let us bestow on the cow and the ox whatever vigour belongs to other species (of animals)' [...] and therefore the cow and the ox eat most. Hence were one to eat (the flesh) of an ox or a cow, there would be, as it were, an eating of everything, or, as it were, a going to the end (or, to destruction) ... Let him therefore not eat (the flesh) of the cow and the ox.[11]

The other passage is at I.2.3.6.[12] It speaks against animal sacrifice and on ethical grounds. A similar statement is contained in the *Apastamba Dharma Sutra*[13] at I.5.17.29.[14] Apastamba lays a general embargo on the eating of cow's flesh.[15] Such is the evidence in support of the contention that the Hindus never ate beef. What conclusion can be drawn from this evidence? So far as the evidence from the *Rig Veda* is concerned the conclusion is based on a misreading and misunderstanding of the texts. The adjective Aghnya applied to the cow in the *Rig Veda* means a cow that was yielding milk and therefore not fit for being killed.[16]

That the cow is venerated in the *Rig Veda* is of course true. But this regard and venerations of the cow are only to be expected from an agricultural community like the Indo-Aryans. This application of the utility of the cow did not prevent the Aryan from killing the cow for purposes of food. Indeed the cow was killed because the cow was regarded as sacred. As observed by Mr Kane:[17] 'It was not that the cow was not sacred in Vedic times, it was because of her sacredness that it is ordained in the Vajasaneyi Samhita[18] that beef should be eaten.'[19]

That the Aryans of the *Rig Veda* did kill cows for purposes of food and ate beef is abundantly clear from the *Rig Veda* itself. In the *Rig Veda* (X.86.14),[20] Indra says: "They cook for one fifteen plus twenty oxen". The *Rig Veda* (X.91.14)[21] says that for Agni were sacrificed horses, bulls, oxen, barren cows and rams. From the *Rig Veda* (X.72.6)[22] it appears that the cow was killed with a sword or axe. As to the testimony of the *Satapatha Brahmana*, can it be said to be conclusive? Obviously, it cannot be. For there are passages in the other *Brahmanas* which give a different opinion.

To give only one instance. Among the *Kamyashtis*[23] set forth in the *Taittiriya Brahmana*,[24] not only the sacrifice of oxen and cows are laid down, but we are even told what kind and description of oxen and cows are to be offered to what deities. Thus, a dwarf ox is to be chosen for sacrifice to Vishnu; a drooping horned bull with a blaze on the forehead to Indra as the destroyer of Vritra; a black cow to Pushan; a red cow to Rudra;[25] and so on. The *Taittiriya Brahmana* notes another sacrifice called *Panchasaradiya-seva*,[26] the most important element of which was the immolation of seventeen five-year old humpless, dwarf-bulls, and as many dwarf heifers under three years old.

As against the statement of the *Apastamba Dharma Sutra*, the following points may be noted. First is the contrary statement contained in that very Sutra. At 14.15.29, the Sutra says: 'The cow and the bull are sacred and therefore should be eaten.'[27]

The second is the prescription of Madhuparka[28] contained in the *Grihya Sutras*[29]. Among the Aryans the etiquette for receiving important guests had become settled into custom and had become a ceremony. The most important offering was Madhuparka. [D]etailed descriptions regarding Madhuparka are to be found in the various *Grihya Sutras*. According to most of the *Grihya Sutras* there are six persons who have a right to be served with Madhuparka namely; (1) Ritvija or the Brahmin called to perform a sacrifice, (2) Acharya, the teacher, (3) The bridegroom (4) The king (5) The Snataka, the student who has just finished his studies at the Gurukul and (6) Any person who is dear to the host. Some add Atithi[30] to this list. Except in the case of Ritvija, king and Acharya, Madhuparka is to be offered to the rest once in a year. To the Ritvija, king and Acharya it is to be offered each time they come.

What was this Madhuparka made of?

> There is divergence about the substances mixed in offering Madhuparka. Asv.gr[31] and Ap.gr. (13.10)[32] prescribe a mixture of honey and curds or clarified butter and curds. Others like Par.gr. 13[33] prescribe a mixture of three (curds, honey and butter). Ap.gr. (13.11–12) states the view of some that those three may be mixed or five (those three with fried yava grain and barley). Hir.gr. I, 12, 10–12 give the option of mixing three of five (curds, honey, ghee, water and ground grain). The *Kausika Sutra*[34] (92) speaks of nine kinds of mixtures, viz., Brahma (honey and curds). Aindra (of payasa), Saumya (curds and ghee), Pausna (ghee and mantha), Sarasvata (milk and ghee), Mausala (wine and ghee, this being used only in

Sautramanai and Rajasuya sacrifices), Parivrajaka (sesame oil and oil cake). The Madhava[35] gr I.9.22 says that the Veda declares that the Madhuparka must not be without flesh and so it recommends that if the cow is let loose, goat's meat or payasa (rice cooked in milk) may be offered; the Hir.gr. I.13, 14 says that other meat should be offered; Baud.gr. (I.2,51-54) says that when the cow is let off, the flesh of a goat or ram may be offered or some forest flesh (of a deer, etc.) may be offered, as there can be no Madhuparka without flesh or if one is unable to offer flesh one may cook ground grains.[36]

Thus the essential element in Madhuparka is flesh and particularly cow's flesh.

The killing of cow for the guest had grown to such an extent that the guest came to be called 'Go-ghna'[37] which means the killer of the cow. To avoid this slaughter of the cows the Asvalayana[38] Grahya Sutra (1.24.25) suggests that the cow should be let loose when the guest comes so as to escape the rule of etiquette.

Thirdly, reference may be made to the ritual relating to disposal of the dead to counter the testimony of the *Apastamba Dharma Sutra*.[39] The Sutra says:

1. He should then put the following (sacrificial) implements (on the dead body)
2. Into the right hand the (spoon called) Guhu.
3. Into the left the (other spoon called) Upabhrit.
4. On his right side the (wooden sacrificial sword called) Sphya, on his left (side) the Agnihotrahavani (i.e., the laddle with which the Agnihotra oblations are sacrifi[c]ed).
5. On his chest the (big sacrificial ladle called) Dhruva. On his head the dishes. On his teeth the pressing-stones.

6. On the two sides of his nose, the two (smaller sacrificial ladles called) Sruvas.
7. Or, if there is only one (Sruva), breaking it (in two pieces).
8. On his two ears the two Prasitraharanas (i.e. the vessels into which the portion of the sacrificial food belonging to the Brahmin) is put.
9. Or, if there is only one (Prasitraharana), breaking it (in two pieces).
10. On his belly the (vessel called) Patri.
11. And the cup into which the cut-off portion (of the sacrificial food) are put.
12. On his secret parts the (staff called) Samy[a].
13. On his thighs two kindling woods.
14. On his legs the mortar and the pestle.
15. On his feet the two baskets.
16. Or, if there is only one (basket), breaking it in two pieces.
17. Those (of the implements) which have a hollow (into which liquids can be poured) are filled with sprinkled butter.
18. The son (of the deceased person) should take the under and the upper mill-stone for himself.
19. And the implements made of copper, iron and earthenware.
20. Taking out the omentum of the she-animal he should cover therewith the head and the mouth (of the dead person) with the verse, '[P]ut on the armour (which will protect thee) against Agni, by (that which comes from) the cows' (Rig Veda X.16.7).
21. Taking out the kidneys (of the animal) he should lay them into the hands (of the dead body) with the verse, '[E]scape the two hounds, the sons of Sar[a]ma (Rig Veda X.14.10) the

right (kidney) into the right (hand) and the left into the left hand.

22. The heart (of the animal he puts) on the heart (of the deceased).

23. And two lumps (of flour or rice), according to some (teachers).

24. (Only) if there are no kidneys, according to some (teachers).

25. Having distributed the whole (animal), limb by limb (placing its different limbs on the corresponding limbs of the deceased) and having covered it with its hide, he recites, when the Pranita water is carried forward, (the verse), 'Agni, do not overturn this cup' (Rig Veda X.16.8).

26. Bending his left knee he should sacrifice Agya oblation[s] into the Dakshina fire with (the formulas), 'To Agni svaha! [T]o Kama svaha! [T]o the world svaha! [T]o Anumati Svaha.'

27. A fifth (oblation) on the chest of the deceased with (the formula), '[F]rom this one verily thou hast been born. May he now be born out of thee, N.N! To the heaven worlds Svaha.'

From the above passage quoted from the *Asvalayana Grihya Sutra* it is clear that among the ancient Indo-Aryans when a person died, an animal had to be killed and the parts of the animal were placed on the appropriate parts of the dead body before the dead body was burned.

Such is the state of the evidence on the subject of cow-killing and beef-eating. Which part of it is to be accepted as true? The correct view is that the testimony of the *Satapatha Brahmana* and the *Apastamba Dharma Sutra* in so far as it supports the view that Hindus were against cow-killing and beef-eating, are merely exhortations against the excesses of cow-killing and not prohibitions against cow-killing. Indeed the exhortations prove that cow-killing and eating of beef had become a common practice.⁴⁰ That notwithstanding these exhortations cow-killing and beef-eating continued. That most often they fell on deaf ears is proved by the conduct of Yajnavalkya,⁴¹ the great Rishi of the Aryans. The first passage quoted above from the *Satapatha Brahmana* was really addressed to Yajnavalkya as an exhortation. How did Yajnavalkya respond? After listening to the exhortation this is what Yajnavalkya said: 'I, for one, eat it, provided that it is tender.'⁴²

That the Hindus at one time did kill cows and did eat beef is proved abundantly by the description of the Yajnas given in the Buddhist Sutras which relate to periods much later than the *Vedas* and the *Brahmanas*. The scale on which the slaughter of cows and animals took place was colossal. It is not possible to give a total of such slaughter on all accounts committed by the Brahmins in the name of religion. Some idea of the extent of this slaughter can however be had from references to it in the Buddhist literature. As an illustration reference may be made to the *Kutadanta Sutta*⁴³ in which Buddha preached against the performance of animal sacrifices to Brahmin Kutadanta.⁴⁴ Buddha, though speaking in a tone of sarcastic travesty, gives a good idea of the practices and rituals of the Vedic sacrifices when he said:

> And further, O Brahman, at that sacrifice neither were any oxen slain, neither goats, nor fowls, nor fatted pigs, nor were any kind of living creatures put to death. No trees were cut down to be used as posts, no Dabbha grasses mown to strew around the sacrificial spot. And the slaves and messengers and workmen there employed were driven neither by rods nor fear, nor carried on their work weeping with tears upon their faces.⁴⁵

Kutadanta on the other hand in thanking Buddha for his conversion gives an idea of the magnitude of the slaughter of animals which took place at such sacrifices when he says:

> I, even I betake myself to the venerable Gotama as my guide, to the Doctrine and the Order. May the venerable One accept me as a disciple, as one who, from this day forth, as long as life endures, has taken him as his guide. And I myself, O, Gotama, will have the seven hundred bulls, and the seven hundred steers, and the seven hundred heifers, and the seven hundred goats, and the seven hundred rams set free. To them I grant their life. Let them eat grass and drink fresh water and may cool breezes waft around them.[46]

In the *Samyuta Nikaya* (III,1–9)[47] we have another description of a Yajna performed by Pasenadi, king of Kosala. It is said that five hundred bulls, five hundred calves and many heifers, goats and rams were led to the pillar to be sacrificed.

With this evidence no one can doubt that there was a time when Hindus—both Brahmins and non-Brahmins—ate not only flesh but also beef.

Annotations

1 In Brahmanical ideology there is no prescription of who is 'touchable', rather it exclusively makes prescriptions of excommunication. 'Touchable' as a category could only have been asserted through the emergence of anti-caste figures like Ambedkar and the burgeoning Dalit subjectivity, which rebelled against the label 'untouchable' and against the totalizing force of Brahmanism. Using the word 'touchable', almost aseptically, was an assertion of the annihilation project, of the separate subjectivities engendered by the caste system. Linguist Laurie Bauer, in her book *English Word-Formation* (1983, 20–1), coincidentally uses the word 'untouchable' as an example to explain the linguistic terms 'root', 'stem' and 'base'. To simplify her definitions, the 'root' is the indivisible unit within the word from which the whole word derives: e.g. in 'untouchable' the root is 'touch'. The 'stem' of a word is that part to which suffixes which change the inflections of the word are added, but the meaning of the word remains the same: e.g. the word 'untouchable' acts as the stem of the word 'untouchables'. A suffix is added to change the usage of the word depending on the context, but the essential meaning is unchanged. The 'base' of a word is any smaller unit within a word to which suffixes or prefixes are added; the base isn't the root of the larger word, rather a smaller word which may or may not have a connection with the larger word. Thus, one can see that 'touchable' is the base of the word 'untouchable'. They share the root 'touch', but linguistically, they only have a relation of the added prefix 'un-'. Of course, in a meaningful sense the two words are antonymous. However, politically, touchability and untouchability don't derive from each other but rather from the notion of 'touch' itself. Ambedkar's politicization of the word 'Touchable' here is crucial: it indicates an oppositional relation of the two classes

of people within the larger category of 'touch'. It is this notion of 'touch' as an associational category itself which he calls into question. For a discussion on the various modalities of touch and how it associates with caste, the material and philosophical underpinnings of touch as a driver of caste, see Aniket Jaaware's *Practicing Caste: On Touching and Not Touching* (2019).

2 The *Rig Veda* is considered the most important of the four *Vedas* and is one of the oldest surviving texts in human history. It is divided into ten mandalas (chapters) and contains 1,017 suktas with eleven additional 'khilas'. Most of the hymns take the form of praises and were chanted at sacrifices, which involved slaughter of animals and their burning on a sacrificial fire, to invoke deities like Indra, Agni, Soma and Varuna. The Purusha Sukta hymn, found in the tenth book, contains the first known articulation of the four major social groups (varna) along with their symbolic functions (Mani 1975). In most of his works, Ambedkar refers to *Rig-Veda Sanhita* compiled and translated by Horace Hayman Wilson from 1850–88 (6 vols), London, Trübner & Co., though he does not always provide citations. All further references here are from the exhaustively annotated 1,725-page Jamison and Brereton edition of 2014.

3 The verse goes: 'Making the sound *hin*, the goods-mistress of goods, seeking her calf, has come near through (my) thinking/ Let this inviolable cow give milk to the Aśvins. Let her increase for our great good fortune' (Jamison and Brereton 2014, 357).

4 'Of this well-portioned god here his manifestation is the fairest, the most brilliant one among mortals/ Gleaming like the heated ghee of the inviolable (cow), (the manifestation) of the god is eagerly sought like the largesse of a milk-cow' (Jamison and Brereton 2014, 557).

5 V.82.8 makes no reference to the cow, and 82 is about 'Savitar'. The numbering here seems to be a proof error (either

by Ambedkar or the BAWS editors). V.84.8 offers the closest match: 'The great bucket—turn it up, pour it down. Let the brooks, unleashed, flow forward/ Inundate Heaven and Earth with ghee. Let there be a good watering hole for the prized cows' (Jamison and Brereton 2014, 766).

6 There's no verse at VII.69.71, but there's VII.69, focused on Asvins, featuring eight verses with none referring to a cow. A proximal one is VII.68.9: 'This praise-poet here awakens with good hymns, rousing himself at the beginning of the dawns, bringing good thoughts./ The fertile cow makes him grow strong with her refreshing drink, with her milk. – Do you protect us always with your blessings' (Jamison and Brereton 2014, 968). Jamison and Brereton warn us about how the poets of the *Rig Veda* were often having fun with language, deploying wit and irony. They say we cannot ever be alert enough to the panoply of meanings that arise from implied puns that often come aurally alive, in the recitation of the verse. In their general introduction, Jamison and Brereton go to great lengths to explain how and why 'obscurity [is] so highly prized' by the Rig Vedic poets. 'The most significant and salient feature of the poets' relationship to language is their deliberate pursuit of obscurity and complexity. The strong privileging of obscurity is found in all aspects of Rigvedic poetry' (61). For instance, they say, 'In verse [VII.15] 9, as also in VII.1.14, the *ákṣarā* refers to both a syllable—its primary meaning—and a cow that always gives milk. Thus, the "syllable" of the poets comes with thousands of syllables, and because their speech is an inexhaustible cow, it brings thousands of cattle' (899). Elsewhere, considering VII.87, they say, of 4b, '"The inviolable cow bears three times seven names." As often, the "cow" in this verse is speech (e.g., Thompson 1995: 20), and it is speech, or more specifically this hymn, that carries within it twenty-one "names"' (Jamison and Brereton 2014, 992–3). Consider, also, the expert commentary

on X.85 which is an account of the wedding of Surya to the groom Soma (here the moon and not the drink): '...menace returns in verse 34, where an unidentified object is ascribed all sorts of harmful qualities. Only a Brahmin can neutralize them. Similarly, in verse 35, various violent actions are depicted, which a Brahmin can absolve' (1519). The Brahmin calls all the shots. In verse 34, where a cow is killed for a wedding feast, it is said: 'But Brahmins who understand "Sūryā," that is, the nature of marriage, including its negative qualities, can safely eat the offered cow' (1521). All these layers of obscurity, poetic flights of fancy and penchant for quibbling do not take away from Ambedkar's two key points: one, the cow was both revered and loved, sacrificed and eaten; and two, the supremacy of the Brahmin and the need for hierarchy are established over and over.

7 X.87 is dedicated to Agni Rakshohan ("Demon-Smiter"), and the reference to a cow that ought not be killed comes at verse 17: 'A year's worth of the milk of the ruddy cow: let the sorcerer not eat of that, o you with your eye on men. Whoever seeks to gorge himself on [/steal] the beestings, with your flame pierce him face-to-face in his vulnerable spot, o Agni' (1531).

8 VI.28 is a hymn focused on the well-being of the cows and its eight verses, seen in isolation, could well be the charter of contemporary far-right go-rakshaks (cow-protectors). Jamison and Brereton: 'The safety of the cows of the pious man as they graze is the subject of much of the hymn, and the various dangers that could befall them are detailed: being stolen by a thief or in a cattle raid, getting lost, going to the slaughterhouse' (2014, 812). The hymn begins with: 'The cows have come here and have made (the house) blessed. Let them find a place in the cow-stall; let them find enjoyment among us' (812); but verse three makes it clear that only the sacrificer (the Hotar Brahmin) has absolute rights over his cows: 'Those (cows) with which he

sacrifices and gives to the gods, he keeps company with them as their cowherd for a very long time'. The Brahmin is both the protector and slayer of cows. Note, too, the difference between simple slaughter for food (proscribed) and the taller claims of sacrifice (extolled).

9 The verse reads: 'Mother of the Rudras, daughter of the Vasus, sister of the Ādityas, navel of immortality—/ I now proclaim to observant people: do not smite the blameless cow—Aditi' (Jamison and Brereton 2014, 1213).

10 *Brahmanas*, instruction manuals for performing Vedic rituals, form the second literary stratum of the *Vedas*. Although the composition of these texts is not linear, the *Brahmanas* generally come after the hymns of praise to gods, known as *Samhitas*, and precede the speculative texts known as the *Aranyakas* and the *Upanishads*. The *Aitareya Brahmana* and *Satapatha Brahmana* (*Brahmanas* of one hundred parts) are the most important ones, the latter being the most recent. They indicate a shift from an emphasis on the importance of ritual to invoke gods to stressing the power of rituals in and of themselves (Lochtefeld 19, 122). The *Satapatha Brahmana* is linked to the school of Brahmin priests known as Vajasaneyins, who looked to excise the various exegetical contents of the *Yajur Veda*, and solely focus on the formulas necessary for ritualistic purposes. The Vajasaneyins were primarily Adhvaryu priests who were secondary in importance to the Hotars (see p. 228 note 9). The *Satapatha Brahmana* has two recensions: the *Madhyandina* and the *Kanva*, of which only the former has survived in its entirety (Eggeling 1882, xxv–xxix).

11 The above passage is immediately followed by: 'Such a one indeed would be likely to be born (again) as a strange being, (as one of whom there is) evil report, such as "he has expelled an embryo from a woman," "he has committed a sin;" let him

therefore not eat (the flesh) of the cow and the ox. Nevertheless Yâgñavalkya said, "I, for one, eat it, provided that it is tender"' (Eggeling 1885, 11). Here the prohibition of beef is immediately overturned by the sage Yajnavalkya. Ambedkar refers to this overturning later in the text (see p. 160 and p. 176 note 42).

12   The verse is as follows: 'At first, namely, the gods offered up a man as the victim. When he was offered up, the sacrificial essence went out of him. It entered into the horse. They offered up the horse. When it was offered up, the sacrificial essence went out of it. It entered into the ox. They offered up the ox. When it was offered up, the sacrificial essence went out of it. It entered into the sheep. They offered up the sheep. When it was offered up, the sacrificial essence went out of it. It entered into the goat. They offered up the goat. When it was offered up, the sacrificial essence went out of it' (Eggeling 1882, 50). A near-identical verse can also be found in the *Aitareya Brahmana*; see p. 232 note 29 for our exegesis on the verse.

13   Apastamba was a sage, writer and commentator. The *Dharma Sutra* that bears his name (roughly 400 BCE) is considered a major source for the law code attributed to Manu which was considered a traditional source of Hindu law by the British rulers. *Dharma Sutras*, the earliest literature of dharma, are in prose, unlike the verse *Dharmashastras* which succeeded them. They deal with sources of dharma, upanayana, *Veda* study, the ashramas (but not as a succession of four stages) (Olivelle 1999, 73–93), food, purity, means of livelihood, marriage, succession, property, the dharma of women, penances, punishments and duties of a king.

14   The reference to the verse is wrong here. Ambedkar is referring I.17.29 in the *Apastamba Dharma Sutra*. It goes: 'The meat of one-hoofed animals, camels, Gayal oxen, village pigs, and Sarabha cattle are forbidden' (Olivelle 1999, 28). However,

Ambedkar fails to mention the next verses which go: 'It is permitted to eat the meat of milch cows and oxen./ A text of the Vajasaneyins states: "The meat of oxen is fit for sacrifice"' (I.17.30–1).

15 The previous endnote contradicts Ambedkar's claim. *Apastamba Dharma Sutra* appears to be quite permissive of beef consumption: cow was both sacrifice and food.

16 Ludwig Alsdorf (2010) points out the Iranian origin of the word 'Aghnya'; the Persian word for cow was 'agznya'. He tentatively puts forth an interpretation of the word to indicate 'that which cannot be killed', rather than 'that which must not be killed'. Even though one may concede that the cow was indeed sacred in ancient India, it didn't mean that it was not sacrificed or consumed: it was its 'unkillable' nature that made it more sacred as a sacrifice. Sebastian Carri (2000) points out the even bolder interpretation of 'Aghnya' made by Hanns-Peter Schmidt, a German Indo-Iranist and scholar of Sanskrit. The word can be read in two ways according to Schmidt: as the tame animal par excellence (domestic rather than wild) and as that which is characterized by its non-killing, i.e. life-giving, nurturing nature.

17 Pandurang Vaman Kane (1880–1972) was an Indologist and Sanskritist. He was given the honorific of Mahamahopadhyaya in 1941, won the Sahitya Akademi award under the Sanskrit translation category for *History of Dharmasastra*, Volume IV, in 1956 and was bestowed with the Bharat Ratna in 1963. Kane was a practising lawyer and also a teacher of Sanskrit at various schools and colleges. *History of Dharmasastras*, an encyclopaedic study of all the major scriptural and prescriptive Hindu texts spanning five volumes, is considered his most important and influential work. Although an orthodox Hindu himself, it was his reading which helped several scholars, including Ambed-

kar and D.N. Jha, assert that beef was indeed a commonly consumed food item in Vedic times. In his autobiographical note in the Epilogue to the fifth volume of the *History of Dharmasastras*, he writes about an incident in 1927 when during Ganesh Chaturthi festival in Bombay, a group of Mahar devotees requested a Brahman Sabha, of which he was chairman, to grant permission for temple entry. Kane called the managing committee to a vote and noted that half of them were opposed to the entry of the Mahars. It was his deciding vote that led to the resolution of allowing the Mahars into the shrine. Several aggravated members filed a suit in the High Court against the committee, calling for a temporary injunction. Since temple entry for Untouchables had become a legal right by then, the suit fell through. Nominated by the then President Rajendra Prasad, Kane served as a member of parliament in the Rajya Sabha from 1953 to 1959.

18 The literal translation of the word samhita is 'collection'. In the *Vedas*, the *Samhitas* form the central and most ancient layer of the text. The mantras collected within the various *Samhitas* include hymns, benedictions, prayers, spells and litanies usually directed to a Vedic diety. These texts have a special significance as rites of sacrifice, which were considered the most important aspect of early Hinduism (Lochtefeld 2001).

19 [*Dharm Shastra Vichar* (Marathi) p. 180]

20 Jamison and Brereton (2014, 1528): '[Indra:] "For they cook fifteen, twenty oxen at a time for me. And I eat only the fat meat. They fill both my cheeks." – Above all Indra!'

21 Jamison and Brereton (2014, 1542): '(For him) into whom horses, bulls, oxen, mated cows, rams, once released, are poured out [=offered] ...'

22 The reference Ambedkar makes here does not have any mention of cow slaughter. Ralph Griffith's translation of X.72.6 is: 'When

ye, O Gods, in yonder deep closeclasping one another stood,/ Thence, as of dancers, from your feet a thickening cloud of dust arose.' In the Jamison and Brereton translation of the *Rig Veda*, the following is found at X.44.9 (2014, 1448): 'Let the axe [=fire] arise, together with its light. The (cow) of truth,/ yielding good milk, should come into being as of old./ Let the ruddy, blazing (fire) shine out with its radiance. The master of/ settlements should blaze like the blazing sun.' The next verse is as follows: 'With cows we would overcome neglect that goes ill, and with barley we/ would overcome all hunger, o you who are much invoked.' The hymn from which these verses are taken extolls the marauding prowess of the Aryas, mythically embodied in the figures of Indra and Manu. One can argue that the verses given here seem to indicate a sort of cow-sacrifice; however, the layers of metaphor imbued in the text dissuade any definitive claim.

23 The *Kamyashtis* or *Kamya Ishtis* are the minor sacrifices prescribed in the *Taittiriya Brahmana* (Chakravarti 1979). Kamya sacrifices are made primarily for the fulfilment of special wishes, like the success of a particular undertaking (Kittel 1872).

24 Each of the *Vedas* is broadly divided into four sections: the *Samhitas*, the *Brahmanas*, the *Aranyakas* and the *Upanishads*. The *Vedas* were studied by several rishis who went on to form their own schools and editions of the original text. These schools were known as shakhas (Mani 1975). One such shakha was the Taittirya, which was a recension of the *Krishna (Black) Yajur Veda* (Dalal 2014). According to legend, the Taittiriya shakha originates from Vyasa's disciple Yajnavalkya. His guru, on being annoyed with Yajnavalkya, orders him to return all that he had taught him about the *Vedas*. Yajnavalkya is then said to have 'vomited' all that he had learnt. But such was the extent of his knowledge that the guru tells the lesser disciples to consume this 'vomit' like *tittiris* (sparrows) (Chinmayananda 2013). From

this body of knowledge arose the Taittiriya shakha. This recension of the *Yajur Veda* is most popular in Southern India and the Konkan region.

25 Ralph T.B. Griffith quotes this same text from the *Taittiriya Brahmana* in *The Vedas: With Illustrative Extracts*. It is as follows: 'A thick-legged cow to Indra; a barren cow to Vishnu and Varuna; a black cow to Pushan; a cow that has brought forth only once to Vayu; a cow having two colours to Mitra and Varuna; a red cow to Rudra; a white barren cow to Surya, &c' ([1892] 2003, 56).

26 Griffith, whom Ambedkar often consults, also refers to the *Panchasaradiya-seva* in his work ([1892] 2003). Rather than the immolation of five-year-old humpless, dwarf bulls, he claims that it is young cows that are sacrificed. The *Brahmana* says about the ritual: 'Whoever wishes to be great, let him worship through the Panchasaradiya. Thereby, verily, he will be great.' Pratapacandra Ghosa (1871) notes that the Panchasaradiya is an autumnal rite, as one can glean from the '-sarad-' that occurs in the term.

27 Such a verse reference number is not found in Patrick Olivelle's translation of the *Apastamba Dharma Sutra*. However, the following quote can be found: (1.17.24) 'It is permitted to eat the meat of milch cows and oxen. A text of the Vajasaneyins states: "The meat of oxen is fit for sacrifice"' (Olivelle 1999, 28). Elsewhere in the text, the following is said with regard to sacrificial offerings: (2.16.24–28) 'When the food is made greasy, however, the gratification it gives the ancestors is more ample and lasts longer, as also when one gives righteously (dharma) acquired wealth to a worthy person. With cow's meat their gratification lasts for a year, and even longer than that with buffalo meat. This rule makes clear that the meat of domestic and wild animals is fit to be offered' (60). See also p. 175 note 40.

28 The oldest usage of the word 'Madhuparka' is found in the *Jaiminiya Upanisad-Brahmana* (Jha 2009), and references to it are also found in the *Satapatha* and *Aitareya Brahmana* (Chakravarti 1979). The popular ceremony, employed for welcoming guests, is both a Srauta ritual (performed by someone versed in the srutis) and a Grihya (domestic) ritual. It is also part of Soma sacrifices (Valhe 2015).

29 The *Grihya Sutras* are manuals that prescribe domestic behaviour, religious ceremonies and rituals. Among other things, these texts outline daily sacred-fire rites and the life-cycles rites (Samskaras). The samskaras encompass all stages of a person's life: from offerings to be made at the time of birth, to the memorials to be made after death. These domestic rituals, though they have evolved with time, continue to be performed by a majority of caste Hindus.

30 According to D.N. Jha (2009, 33–4): 'The killing of the kine to honour guests seems to have been prevalent from earlier times. The *Rig Veda* (X.68.3) mentions the word atithinir, which has been interpreted as 'cows fit for guests' and refers to at least one Vedic hero, Atithigva, meaning literally 'slaying cows for guests'. The cow was also killed on festive occasions like marriage. A Rig Vedic passage, for instance X.85 discussed earlier on p. 164–5 note 6, refers to the slaughter of a cow on the occasion of marriage and, later, in the *Aitareya Brahmana*, we are told, that 'Just as in the world when a human king has come, or another deserving person, they slay an ox or a cow that miscarries; so for him [Soma] they slay in that they kindle the fire, for Agni is the victim of the gods' (Keith 1920, 118).'

31 The Asv.gr. is the *Asvalayana Grihya Sutra*. There is debate whether the sutra should be attributed to the writer Asvalayana or his teacher Saunaka. The ingredients of the Madhuparka are mentioned in 24.5–6: 'He pours honey into curds,/ Or butter, if he can get no honey' (Oldenberg 1886, 82).

32 The reference to the Madhuparka in the *Apastamba Grihya Sutra* is spread across 13.10–12: '(The host) pours together curds and honey in a brass vessel, covers it with a larger (brass cover), takes hold of it with two bunches of grass, and announces (to the guest), "The honey-mixture!"/ Some take three substances, (those stated before) and ghee./ Some take five, (the three stated before), and grains, and flour' (Oldenberg 1886, 270).

33 The *Paraskara Grihya Sutra* is an appendix of Katyayana's *Srauta-sutra* and forms a part of the *White Yajur Veda*. The Kandika thirteen Ambedkar mentions above does not speak about the Madhuparka; however, at 10.5, the following is given: 'Let them announce three times (to the guest) separately (each of the following things which are brought to him): a bed (of grass to sit down on), water for washing the feet, the Argha water, water for sipping, and the Madhuparka (i.e. a mixture of ghee, curds, and honey)' (Oldenberg 1886, 214).

34 The *Kausika Sutra* is an accessory text to the *Atharva Veda*. Similar in vein to the *Grihya Sutras*, it contains additional exegesis on medicinal and abhicara practices (incantations by a priest to defeat any enemy). The Sutra is part of the Sunikya shakha of the *Atharva Veda* and is one of the earliest works belonging to the school. Some scholars date the text back to the Sutra period (first and second centuries CE), but references to the work have been made as far back as the time of Panini (sixth to fifth centuries BCE). It can be held that the *Kausika Sutra* is a fusion of the earlier *Atharva Sutras* and the *Grihya Sutras* that were brought together in the Sutra period (see Gopalan 1992).

35 Ambedkar is probably referring to the *Manava Grihya Sutra* here. This *Grihya Sutra* belongs to the Manava school of the *Krishna (Black) Yajur Veda*. Unlike other *Grihya Sutras*, which begin by detailing either the marriage or the Upanayana ceremonies, this one begins by listing all the rules that ought to

be followed by a good Brahmacharin. The *Manava Grihya Sutra* has three other names: *Maitrayaniya Grihya, Maitrayaniya Manava Grihya* and *Manava Grihya*. The text of *Manava Grihya Sutra* attributes Manavacaryya as its author, but the name can also signify 'teacher of the manavas (people)' (Sastri 1926). In his preface to the 1926 edition of the Sutra, B.C. Lele writes: 'The *Manava Grhya Sutra* points to a very ancient state of Indian society. In the opening section the Brahmacarin is enjoined not to eat meat and partake of wine. This shows that meat-eating was not forbidden wholesale but only in certain cases. In the Madhuparka rite the killing of a cow is a necessity and the author quotes at 1.9.22 the Sruti: 'namaanso madhuparkah iti shrutih' [which, according to Bibek Debroy means: 'Without flesh, it is not madhuparka. The sacred texts have said this']. However, an option is given later and the cow instead of being killed might be let loose... The elaborate rules about the Upanayana of the four different castes are not given in this Sutra. The killing of a cow was also compulsory at the time of another rite namely the final *Astaka*' (Lele in Sastri 1926, 7–8). The *Manava Grihya Sutra* is also said to have influenced the development of the *Manusmriti* (Weber 1882). Debroy says: while the primary meaning of mamsa is flesh, it also means fish and the fleshy part of a fruit.

36 [Kane's vol. II. Part I p. 545.] In the BAWS edition of *The Untouchables*, the above quote is given as part of Ambedkar's own text and the footnote is placed wrongly. The correction has been made here.

37 The term 'goghna' is used by Panini, the Sanskrit grammarian, to connote 'guests' (Jha 2009, 33). Although, the word is used in pejorative sense by Manu's time, its original meaning was 'one for whom the cow is killed'. Sanskrit scholars like S.D. Joshi and J.A.F. Roodbergen also emphasize the point that the word may

have had a mocking application, where guests may have been called 'cow-killers' in jest (Cardona 1999, 280–1n16).

38   Asvalayana was the most noted disciple of Saunaka, a celebrated teacher of the *Atharva Veda*, and the author of works on Vedic ritual, most notably the *Srautasutras* and the *Grihya Sutras*. Asvalayana was also the founder of a Sakha of the *Rig Veda*, one of the many variations of the texts traditionally handed down orally by teachers and leading to the formation of various schools. Most of his Rigvedic recensions however have been lost.

39   The following twenty-seven instructions occur in the third kandika of the fourth adhyaya of the *Asvalayana Grihya Sutra* and not the *Apastamba Grihya Sutra*. (See IV.3.1–27, Oldenberg 1886.) Ambedkar here is citing the Oldenberg translation of the *Grihya Sutras*, which appeared as a single volume edition in 1886. The errors in Ambedkar's version of the quote have been corrected here.

40   In the *Apastamba Dharma Sutra*, direction is taken from Manu concerning the rituals of ancestral offering. 'In this rite, the ancestors are the deity to whom the offering is made, while the Brahmins stand in the place of the offertorial fire' (Olivelle 1999, 60). In the elucidation of rites, a variety of vegetarian food items—rice, barley, water, roots, fruits, sesame and beans—are specified as materials to be used in the 'sacrifice'. 'When the food is *greasy*, however, the gratification it gives the ancestors is more ample and lasts longer ... With cow's meat their gratification lasts for a year, and even longer than that with buffalo meat' (Olivelle 1999, 60, emphasis added). Simply put, the Brahmin is the recipient of the beef which is sacrificed in the ritual.

41   Yajnavalkya, the purported author of the *Yajnavalkya Smriti*, was a sage in the court of mythical king Janaka and a disciple

of Sanatkumara. He is also said to have been a part of Yudhistira's court as also Indra's assembly. His dialogues pertaining to the relationship between atman, Brahman and the world and perceived support for a non-dualistic philosophy with respect to reality and being has influenced the followers of Advaita Vedanta (Mani 1975, 891–2). See p. 138 note 26 on the *Yajnavalkya Smriti*.

42 As far as the prohibition of food is concerned, Yajnavalkya does not much differ from Manu, which points to the profound influence of the *Manusmriti* on most of the dharmshastra writers (Olivelle and Davis 2018, 26). Much like Manu, he gives lists of specific animals not to be eaten (deer, sheep, goat, boar, rhinoceros, partridges, etc.). References to the arghya, Madhuparka and rituals of welcoming learned Brahmins, indicate that consumption of consecrated meat was not merely enjoined but necessitated. However, the bottomless pit of rules and sub-rules (typical to Brahmanism) meant that meat consumption was not so much about meat consumption itself but about following the correct rules and rituals, and about who was the one consuming the meat, under what circumstances, for what purpose, at what time, and so on; these were all only so many ways of creating an abstract web of control which maintained power and supremacy through an infinite set of forever amendable rules at the centre of which sat the illusory (but ever-present) notion of purity (Jha 2009, 93).

43 The Canon of Buddhist religious texts was set in its written form around the first century BCE in Pali. Until then the doctrines were preserved through oral transmission. It is Vattagamini (who was king of Ceylon between the first and second centuries BCE) who is credited for having commissioned the preservation of the canon in written form. The Pali Canon is divided into three sections (and therefore is known as *Tipitaka*, or The Three Baskets): *Vinaya Pitaka*, The Book of Discipline, which is

meant for monks and nuns and pertains to the discipline they must adhere to; *Sutta Pitaka*, the Discourses, which contain the dialogues of the Buddha; and *Abhidhamma Pitaka*, the further doctrines, which is a collection of seven books that contain further setting down of Buddhist philosophical doctrines. The *Sutta Pitaka* itself is divided into five further sections or *Nikayas*: *Digha Nikaya, Majjhima Nikaya, Samyutta Nikaya; Anguttara Nikaya* and *Khuddaka Nikaya*. Of these, the *Digha Nikaya* is the longest collection and it contains thirty-four Suttas, one of which is the *Kutadanta Sutta* (Walshe 1987, 46–53).

44 The *Kutadanta Sutta* recounts the tale of the Buddha's encounter with an influential Brahmin named Kutadanta. On learning that the Buddha was set up in a park in his village, the Brahmin makes his way to meet the illustrious teacher, in order to clarify how best to perform a sacrifice. Kutadanta had already prepared 'seven hundred bulls, seven hundred bullocks, seven hundred heifers, seven hundred he-goats and seven hundred rams' (Walshe 1987, 133) for this purpose. On being posed the question, the Buddha recounts a story. Once there was a great and powerful king named Mahavijita who had amassed much wealth and glory in his lifetime. Having done so, he summons his Brahmin chaplain and consults him about how best he should make a sacrifice so that his good fortune wouldn't wane. The chaplain tells him to distribute more crops and cattle to those in his kingdom who are engaged in agricultural work, to distribute more capital to the traders, and to increase the wages of those engaged in other services. The king agrees to this and lo and behold his kingdom grows happier and him wealthier. Joyous, Mahavijita once again summons the chaplain and makes known his wish to perform yet another sacrifice. The chaplain tells him that he should send for all the Kshatriyas, advisers, counsellors, influential Brahmins and wealthy householders in his kingdom and ask them to present their sacrifices

to him. The Buddha says that in these sacrifices no animals were slain, no trees were cut, and no harm was done to any creature. Having done so, the Kshatriyas, advisers, counsellors, influential Brahmins and wealthy householders then return with the wealth they have amassed thanks to the earlier sacrifice and present it to the king. But the king refuses to accept it saying that he has no need for further wealth and asks them to keep it for themselves. The subjects, affected by the king's generosity, in turn decide to distribute what they had amassed among the people. Having heard the story, Kutadanta wonders how the Buddha is able to tell it with such authority: 'But it strikes me that the ascetic Gotama does not say: "I have heard this", or "It must have been like this", but he says: "It was like this or like that at the time"' (Walshe 1987, 139). He concludes that the Buddha must have been the lord of sacrifice in king Mahavijita's court in his previous incarnation. The Buddha confirms this hypothesis and reveals himself to be Mahavijita's chaplain in a previous life. The Brahmin then enquires about the best sacrifice he can make, and he is told that it is the acceptance of the dhamma. Kutadanta accedes and becomes a disciple of the Buddha (Walshe 1987, 131–41).

45 The above quote is taken from *Dialogues of the Buddha* (1899, 180), which is a translation of the *Digha Nikaya* by T.W. Rhys Davids. T.W. Rhys Davids and wife Caroline Foley Rhys Davids often worken together on Buddhist translations. Although, Caroline Foley started out as an economist, she soon set her sights on philosophy, particularly Buddhist philosophy, under the influence of her professor and to-be husband T.W. Rhys Davids. She was the foremost interpreter and translator of several works from Pali to English and was an early scholar of Theravada Buddhism. Her translation of the *Therigatha* was the first ever in English. She was also a proponent of women's suffrage and closely studied the role of women

in early Buddhist society (Neal 2014). Ambedkar quotes C.A.F. Rhys Davids several times in his career, the oldest of which can be found in an abandoned draft of his Master's dissertation at Columbia in which he quotes Rhys Davids' 1901 paper entitled "Notes on Early Economic Conditions in Northern India" (860). In it, Rhys Davids draws from Buddhist texts and cites instances where caste seemed to have weakened under Buddhist rule. The *Jataka* depicts Kshatriyas, Brahmins and Vaishyas (Savarnas) having meals and learning together, and intermarrying. She also cites instances where a deer-trapper forms an inseparable friendship with a Sethi, and a prince adopts the garb of a potter, basket-maker, florist and chef without losing his caste. However, it is made clear that the Chandalas were despised and faced the wrath of the Brahmins (867–8). Y. Krishan further documents the following events in the *Jatakas* (1986, 74): 'In the Setaketu Jataka (no. 377), brahmana Setaketu, on seeing a candala fears that "the wind, after striking the candala's body, might touch his own body" and thereby pollute him. He calls the candala ill-omened. In the Matanga Jataka (no. 497), Dittha-mangalika, on seeing a candala, says "Bah, I have seen something that brings bad luck" and washes her eyes with scented water. This is repeated in the Citta Sambhutta Jataka (no. 498). In the same Jataka a man describes a candala as "the blot in the blood" (jatiya doso). The dwellings of the candalas were outside the towns.' The Orientalist French scholar Eugène Burnouf (1801–1852), in his pioneering work *Introduction à l'histoire du Buddhisme Indien* recently translated (2010) in a critical edition, is highly critical of Brahmanism as a persecutor of Buddhism that eventually drove it away from the subcontinent, but also speaks of how institutionalized Buddhism did not quite shake up caste the way earlier European scholars had rushed to say it did. While the Buddha's teaching is offered to all castes, the right to be a Bodhisatta is limited to

Brahmins and Kshatriyas. In Buddhist sutras, 'the brahmans are those whose name occurs most often; they figure in almost all the sūtras, and their superiority over the other castes is always uncontested' (168–9). In *Lalitavistara Sutra* of Mahayana Buddhism dated to the third century CE, it is explicitly said that 'bodhisattvas are not born into the womb of abject families, like those of the candalas, of flute players, of cart makers, and of the puskasas. There are only two races into which they are born, the race of the brahmans and that of the ksatriyas. When it is principally to the brahmans that the world shows respect, it is in a family of brahmans that bodhisattvas descend to earth. When, on the contrary, it is principally to the ksatriyas that the world shows respect, then they are born into a family of ksatriyas. Today, O monks, the ksatriyas obtain all the respect of the people: it is for this that bodhisattvas are born among the ksatriyas' (173). Ambedkar of course rejects all this and formulates a new Buddhism by writing a new book toward the end of his life (*The Buddha and His Dhamma*, 1956) where he rejects all the stories that 'do not appeal to reason', stopping often to ask, 'Do they form part of the original teachings of the Buddha?' (13–4). Rejecting texts and stories often written three to five hundred years after Siddhartha Gautama's passing, he contends that the Buddha 'was the strongest opponent of caste and the earliest and staunchest upholder of equality' and 'there is no argument in favour of caste and inequality which he [Buddha] did not refute' (301–2). The *Jatakas* were of course later constructions of the Buddha's life. The precise dating of Buddhist texts is crucial here to understand attitudes towards caste; those written during or after the Brahmanic revival have much stronger affirmation of hierarchy than those that were written closer to the time of the Buddha. The *Nikayas* for instance form the earliest expression of Buddhist thought and may have been set down when the sangha was still a united body and hadn't broken into differing factions. They can be dated back to the first half of the fourth century BCE (Pande 1974). Uma Chakravarti notes that the Buddhists had a three-fold 'kula' system with the Khattiyas, Brahmanas and the Gahapatis, as opposed to the four-fold varna of the Brahmins. She further cites the *Majjhima Nikaya* where 'the Buddha pertinently refuted the *brahmana* claim to superiority based on the criteria of the lower vanna serving the higher. He pointed out that anyone including *suddas* who had wealth, corn, gold, and silver could have in their employment others who would rise earlier than the employer, rest later, carry out his pleasure, and speak affably to him' (1987, 99–100). The core of Chakravarti's argument is that though there was acknowledged caste stratification in Buddhism, and sometimes the Buddha even spoke in the idiom of caste, the attitude was markedly different from the rigid Brahmanical order. Further, the organizational structure of the Buddha's sangha, which placed a premium on egalitarianism over caste, is further indication of an anti-Brahmanic attitude.

46 Also taken from *Dialogues of the Buddha* (Rhys Davids 1899, 184).

47 The *Samyutta* is the third *Nikaya* in the *Sutta Pitaka*. It is a collection of various suttas grouped into specific categories: for instance the reference Ambedkar makes here is from the *Kosalasamyutta* which is a collection of dialogues the Buddha has with the Kosalan king Pasenadi. The ninth section of the Kosalasamyutta is an exegesis on the morality of sacrifices. In preparation for a sacrifice made in the name of king Pasenadi '[f]ive hundred bulls, five hundred bullocks and as many heifers, goats, and rams, were led to the pillar to be sacrificed' (Rhys Davids 1917, 102). The Buddha exhorts: 'These are not rites that bring a rich result./ Where divers goats and sheep and kine are slain [...] The noble seers who walk the perfect way./ These are the rites entailing great results./ These to the

celebrant are blest, not cursed./ Th' oblation runneth o'er; the gods are pleased' (Rhys Davids 1917, 103). Pasenadi was the king of Kosala and was the sovereign to whom the Sakhyas, the clan of the Buddha, swore fealty. Like the Magadhan kings of his time, he was of 'low-birth' and did not have tribal affiliations, leading to his ability to create a large army not based on tribal origin. He also didn't have much regard for Vedic rituals and was quite willing to patronize cults like Buddhism and Jainism. However, this wasn't a result of strong convictions or a principled stand: he was as much a patron of Brahmin pandits and open to performing yajnas when desirable (Kosambi 2008, 108–9,127–30).

Chapter XII

Why did non-Brahmins give up beef-eating?

The food habits of the different classes of Hindus have been as fixed and stratified as their cults. Just as Hindus can be classified on their basis of their cults so also they can be classified on the basis of their habits of food. On the basis of their cults, Hindus are either Saivites (followers of Siva) or Vaishnavites (followers of Vishnu).[1] Similarly, Hindus are either Mansahari (those who eat flesh) or Shakahari (those who are vegetarians).

For ordinary purposes the division of Hindus into two classes Mansahari and Shakahari may be enough. But it must be admitted that it is not exhaustive and does not take account of all the classes which exist in Hindu society. For an exhaustive classification, the class of Hindus called Mansahari shall have to be further divided into two sub-classes: (i) Those who eat flesh but do not eat cow's flesh; and (ii) Those who eat flesh including cow's flesh; In other words, on the basis of food taboos, Hindu society falls into three classes : (i) Those who are vegetarians; (ii) Those who eat flesh but do not eat cow's flesh; and (iii) Those who eat flesh including cow's flesh. Corresponding to this classification, we have in Hindu society three classes: (1) Brahmins; (2) non-Brahmins; and (3) The Untouchables. This division though not in accord with the fourfold division of society called Chaturvarnya, yet it is in accord with facts as they exist. For, in the Brahmins[2] we have a class which is vegetarian, in the non-Brahmins the class which eats flesh but does not eat cow's flesh and in the Untouchables a class which eats flesh including cow's flesh.

This threefold division is therefore substantial and is in accord with facts. Anyone who stops to turn over this classification in his mind is bound to be struck by the position of the non-Brahmins. One can quite understand vegetarianism. One can quite understand meat-eating. But it is difficult to understand why a person who is a flesh-eater should object to one kind of flesh namely cow's flesh. This is an anomaly which calls for explanation. Why did the non-Brahmin give up beef-eating? For this purpose it is necessary to examine laws on the subject. The relevant legislation must be found either in the Law of Asoka or the Law of Manu.

II

To begin with Asoka.[3] The edicts of Asoka which have reference to this matter are Rock Edict No. I[4] and Pillar Edict Nos. II and V[5]. Rock Edict No. I[6] reads as follows:

> This pious Edict has been written by command of His Sacred and Gracious Majesty the King.
>
> Here [in the capital] no animal may be slaughtered for sacrifice, nor may the holiday-feast be held, because His Sacred and Gracious Majesty, the King sees much offence in the holiday feast, although in certain places holiday-feasts are excellent in the sight of His Sacred and Gracious Majesty the King.
>
> Formerly, in the kitchen of His Sacred and Gracious Majesty the King each day many hundred thousands of living

creatures were slaughtered to make curries. But now, when this pious edict is being written, only three living creatures are slaughtered [daily] for curry, to wit, two peacocks and one antelope—the antelope, however, not invariably. Even those three living creatures henceforth shall not be slaughtered.

Pillar Edict No. II is in the following terms:[7]

Thus saith His Sacred and Gracious Majesty, the King:
"The Law of Piety is excellent." But wherein consists the Law of Piety? In these things, to wit, little impiety, many good deeds, compassion, liberality, truthfulness and purity.

The gift of spiritual insight I have given in manifold ways; whilst on two-footed and four-footed beings, on birds and the denizens of the waters, I have conferred various favours—even unto the boon of life; and many other good deeds have I done.

For this my purpose have I caused this pious edict to be written, that men may walk after its teaching, and that it may long endure; and he who will follow its teaching will do well.

Pillar Edict V says:[8]

Thus saith His Sacred and Gracious Majesty the King:
When I had been consecrated twenty-six years the following species were declared *exempt from slaughter,*[9] namely:
Parrots, starlings (?) adjutants, "Brahmany ducks", geese, *nandimukhas, gelatas,* bats, queen-ants, female tortoises, "boneless fish", *vedaveyakas, gangapuputakas,* (?) skate, (river) tortoises, porcupines, tree-squirrels, (?) *barasingha* stag, "Brahmany bulls", (?) monkeys, rhinoceros, grey doves, village pigeons, and *all four-footed animals which are not utilised or eaten.*[10]
She-goats, ewes, and sows, that is to say, those either with young or in milk, are exempt from slaughter as well as their off-spring up to six months of age.

The caponing of cocks must not be done.

Chaff must not be burned along with the living things in it.

Forests must not be burned either for mischief or so as to destroy living creatures.

The living must not be fed with the living. At each of the three seasonal full moons, and at the full moon of the month Tishya (December–January), for three days in each case, namely the fourteenth and fifteenth days of the first fortnight, and the first day of the second fortnight, as well as on the fast days throughout the year, fish is exempt from killing and may not be sold.

On the same days, in elephant-preserves or fish-ponds no other classes of animals may be destroyed.

On the eighth, fourteenth, and fifteenth days of each fortnight, as well as on the Tishya and Punarvasa[11] days and festival days, the castration of bulls must not be performed, nor may he-goats, rams, boars and other animals liable to castration be castrated.

On the Tishya and Punarvasa days, on the seasonal full moon days, and during the fortnights of the seasonal full moons the branding of horses and oxen must not be done.

During the time up to the twenty-sixth anniversary of my consecration twenty-five jail deliveries have been effected.

So much for the legislation of Asoka.

III

Let us turn to Manu.[12] His Laws contain the the following provisions regarding meat-eating:[13]

> V.11. Let him avoid all carnivorous birds and those living in villages, and one-hoofed animals which are not specially permitted (to be eaten), and the Tittibha (Parra Jacana).

V.12. The sparrow, the Plava, the Hamsa, the Brahmani duck, the village-cock, the Sarasa crane, the Raggudala, the woodpecker, the parrot, and the starling.

V.13. Those which feed striking with their beaks, web-footed birds, the Koyashti, those which scratch with their toes, those which dive and live on fish, meat from a slaughter-house and dried meat.

V.14. The Baka and the Balaka crane, the raven, the Khangarilaka (animals) that eat fish, village-pigs, and all kinds of fishes.

V.15. He who eats the flesh of any (animal) is called the eater of the flesh of that (particular creature), he who eats fish is an eater of every (kind of) flesh; let him therefore avoid fish.

V.16. (But the fish called) Pathina and (that called) Rohita may be eaten, if used for offering to the gods or to the manes; (one may eat) likewise Ragivas, Simhatundas, and Sasalkas on all (occasions).

V.17. Let him not eat solitary or unknown beasts and birds, though they may fall under (the categories of) eatable (creatures), nor any five-toed (animals).

V.18. The porcupine, the hedgehog, the iguana, the rhinoceros, the tortoise, and the hare they declare to be eatable; likewise those (domestic animals) that have teeth in one jaw excepting camels.

IV

Here is survey of the legislation both by Asoka and by Manu on the slaughter of animals. We are of course principally concerned with the cow. Examining the legislation of Asoka the question is: Did he prohibit the killing of the cow? On this issue there seems to be a difference of opinion. Prof Vincent Smith is of opinion that Asoka did not prohibit the killing of the cow. Commenting on the legislation of Asoka on the subject, Prof Smith says: 'It is noteworthy that Asoka's rules do not forbid the slaughter of cow, which, apparently, continued to be lawful.'[14]

Prof Radhakumud Mookerji joins issue with Prof Smith and says[15] that Asoka did prohibit the slaughter of the cow. Prof Mookerji relies upon the reference in Pillar Edict V to the rule of exemption which was made applicable to all four-footed animals and argues that under this rule cow was exempted from killing. This is not a correct reading of the statement in the Edict. The statement in the Edict is a qualified statement. It does not refer to all four-footed animals but only to four-footed animals, *which are not utilised or eaten*. A cow cannot be said to be a four-footed animal which was not utilized or eaten. Prof Vincent Smith seems to be correct in saying that Asoka did not prohibit the slaughter of the cow. Prof Mookerji tries to get out of the difficulty by saying that at the time of Asoka the cow was not eaten and therefore came within the prohibition. His statement is simply absurd for the cow was an animal which was very much eaten by all classes.

It is quite unnecessary to resort as does Prof Mookerji to a forced construction of the Edict and to make Asoka prohibit the slaughter of the cow as though it was his duty to do so. Asoka had no particular interest in the cow and owed no special duty to protect her against killing. Asoka was interested in the sanctity of all life human as well as animal. He felt [it] his duty to prohibit the taking of life where taking of life was not necessary. That is why he prohibited slaughtering animal for sacrifice which he regarded as unnecessary and of animals which are not utilized nor eaten which again would be wanton and unnecessary. That he did not prohibit the slaughter of the cow in specie may well be taken as a fact which for having regard to the Buddhist attitude in the matter cannot be used against Asoka as a ground for casting blame.

Coming to Manu there is no doubt that he too did not prohibit the slaughter of the cow. On the other hand he made the eating of cow's flesh on certain occasions obligatory.

Why then did the non-Brahmins give up eating beef? There appears to be no apparent reason for this departure on their part. But there must be some reason behind it. The reason I like to suggest is that it was due to their desire to imitate the Brahmins that the non-Brahmins gave up beef-eating. This may be a novel theory but it is not an impossible theory. As the French author, Gabriel Tarde[16] has explained that culture within a society spreads by imitation of the ways and manners of the superior classes by the inferior classes. This imitation is so regular in its flow that its working is as mechanical as the working of a natural law. Gabriel Tarde speaks of the laws of imitation. One of these laws is that the lower classes always imitate the higher classes. This is a matter of such common knowledge that hardly any individual can be found to question its validity.

That the spread of the cow-worship among and cessation of beef-eating by the non-Brahmins has taken place by reason of the habit of the non-Brahmins to imitate the Brahmins who were undoubtedly their superiors is beyond dispute. Of course there was an extensive propaganda in favour of cow-worship by the Brahmins. The *Gayatri Purana*[17] is a piece of this propaganda. But initially it is the result of the natural law of imitation. This, of course, raises another question: Why did the Brahmins give up beef-eating?

Annotations

1 Although it is untenable to claim that all Hindus are either Vaisnavites or Saivites (such a claim would require a strict definition of Hinduism), yet the reverence and worship of Vishnu and Shiva is undoubtedly extremely widespread throughout the subcontinent. This spread of worship can be attributed to the Puranas which began to be written towards the beginning of the fourth century CE. They were compendiums of myth and rituals which, interestingly, were written during a time when Brahmanism was on the retreat. The writers of the Puranas are said to have appropriated several folktales and popular beliefs and plagiarized local storytellers in order to construct myths with a uniform cast of protagonists: Brahma, Vishnu, Shiva and Devi. Needless to say, of these Vishnu and Shiva were most popular (Doniger 2015, 231–78). Another aspect that needs to be considered is the rise of bhakti as a philosophy, under the aegis of Sankara and Ramanuja. Here, the focus moved from ritualistic and repetitional aspects of religious rites towards a faith in a personal god, and towards devotion to the figure (usually) Vishnu and Shiva, in one form or another (Doniger 2015, 295–304).

2 [The Brahmins of India fall into two divisions (1) Pancha Dravid and (2) Pancha Gauda. The former are vegetarians, the latter are not.] In *Castes and Tribes of Southern India*, Edgar Thurston notes that 'it is *customary* to group them [the Brahmins] in two main divisions, the Pancha Dravidas and Pancha Gaudas' (Thurston & Rangachari 1909, 268; emphasis added). Thurston sheds some light on the basis of this division, writing that 'the Pancha Dravidas are pure vegetarians, whereas the Pancha Gaudas need not abstain from meat and fish, though some, who live amidst the Pancha Dravidas, do so' (1909, 268). It is in the context of these flesh-eating habits that Ambedkar cites this

distinction. On the other hand, Walter Elliot in his ethnographic survey, "On the Characteristics of the Population of Central and Southern India" (1869) notes that 'the people themselves arrange their countrymen under two heads; five termed *Panch-gaura*, belonging to the Hindi, or as is now generally called the Aryan group, and the remaining five or *Panch-Dravida* to the Tamil type. The latter is restricted in native parlance to the more civilized societies speaking languages closely affiliated to Tamil' (Elliot 1869, 94). Swati Datta (1989) drives home a similar, geographic basis for this division: Gauda was, at least in the tenth century CE, a large section of Northern India, and the Pancha Gaudas (Saraswats, Kanyakubjas, Gaudas, Maithilas, Utkalas) were those who had the freedom to travel anywhere within the Gauda region. Rosalind O'Hanlon (2013) claims that the concretization of the Pancha Dravida and Pancha Gauda categories is relatively new. The new classification became necessary in the sixteenth and seventeenth centuries, when there was a marked inequality between Brahmins, some of whom were quite poor while others prospered. This necessitated a renewed need to look at what exactly made a Brahmin (to weed out the unworthies). So while up until the early centuries of the second millennium Brahmins identified themselves through the Vedic shakhas they studied and their gotras, now Benarasi Brahmins sought to classify all Brahmins within ten large groupings, five each for Northern and Southern India: Pancha Gaudas and Pancha Dravidas.

3   Asoka was the emperor of the Maurya dynasty from 268 to 232 BCE. He was the grandson of Chandragupta Maurya and ruled over the largest empire known to the subcontinent. He famously adopted the Buddhist dhamma and propagated it within and beyond the borders of South Asia. Just like Buddhism was stamped out of Indian soil by a resurgent Brahmanism, so was the life and work of Asoka, who stepped out of the mists of

academic history owing to the work of European archaeologists and philologists as outlined by Charles Allen in *Ashoka: The Search for India's Lost Emperor* (2012). Among the primary sources on Asoka are the Pillar and Rock Edicts erected by him. Asoka's religious paradigm was defined by his conception of dhamma. 'For Asoka, dhamma was essentially a code of ethical behaviour and the benefits thereof.' As sovereign of his empire, his dhamma strived to strike a middle ground between the 'welfare of his praja (subjects)' and his obligations as Emperor. He did not subscribe to a specific religious code because 'he was attempting to universalize a code focused on social ethics and on the accommodation of diverse views' (Thapar 2009, 31). In his ethical system, taking life was immoral and therefore prohibited. Romila Thapar argues that 'his formulations of dhamma were intended to influence the conduct of categories of people in relation to each other, especially where they involved unequal relationships'. This new formalized code of ethics was 'virtually the reversal of the other system, varnashrama dharma' (Thapar 2009, 32).

4   The Rock Edict No. I was found inscribed onto a boulder in Girnar near Junagad, Gujarat. It covers about a hundred square-feet area, rising to twelve feet in height and having a circumference of seventy-five feet. There is a total of fourteen inscriptions on the Girnar rock. Besides Asoka's directives it also contains an inscription which records the restoration of lake Sudarsana, which dates back to the reign of Chandragupta Maurya, by king Rudradaman of the Satavahana dynasty, and a third inscription which records the Gupta king, Skandagupta's, work in carrying out repairs of the same lake (Hultzsch 1925, ix–x).

5   The second and fifth pillar edicts Ambedkar refers to here are found on the Delhi-Topra pillar, which is one among the six pillars discovered which possess Asokan edicts. Made out of

pink sandstone and forty-two feet and seven inches in length, the Delhi-Topra pillar contains seven edicts. It originally stood in the village of Topra (in present-day Haryana) and was moved to Delhi by Sultan Firoz Shah (1351–88 CE) of the Tughlaq dynasty. Besides Asoka's edicts the pillar also contains minor records of several pilgrims and travellers and three inscriptions by Visaladeva, the Chahamana ruler of Sakambari (in present-day Rajasthan), which has been dated 1164 CE. The first translation of the pillar texts was done by James Prinsep in 1837 (Hultzsch 1925, xv–xvi).

6 The following reference is taken from Vincent Smith's *Asoka— The Buddhist Emperor of India* (1909), pages 155–6. Smith (1848–1920) was a British Indologist and art historian who taught at St John's College, Oxford, and worked as a Curator of the Indian Institute (Oxford) after a stint as an administrator in the then United Provinces, India.

7 Taken from Smith 1909, 183–4, under the title 'The Royal Example'. Inconsistencies in Ambedkar's reference have been fixed here.

8 Smith 1909, 186–9. The title under which Pillar Edict No. V occurs in Smith's rendition is: 'Regulations restricting slaughter and mutilation of animals'.

9 Emphasis added by Ambedkar.

10 Emphasis added by Ambedkar. In E. Hultzsch's 1925 work, *Inscriptions of Asoka*, the above paragraph is translated so: '...the following animals were declared by me inviolable, viz. parrots, mainas, the *aruna*, ruddy geese, wild geese, the *nandimukha*, the *gelata*, bats, queen-ants, terrapins, boneless fish, the *vedaveyaka*, the *Ganga-puputaka*, skate-fish, tortoises and porcupines, squirrels, the *srimara*, bulls set at liberty, iguanas, the rhinoceros, white doves, domestic doves, (and) all the quadrupeds which are neither useful nor edible' (Hultzsch 1925, 127).

11 Tishya and Punarvasu are lunar constellations, and the day of the full moon for the particular constellation is considered an auspicious day, seeing as they had a special significance for Asoka. The scholar Nayanjot Lahiri writes, 'Possibly, Tishya signified Asoka's birth-star and Punarvasu his anointment' (Lahiri 2015, 274)

12 In the *Manusmriti* it is established that 'those that do not move are food for those that move, and those that have no fangs are food for those with fangs; those that have no hands are food for those with hands; and cowards are the food of the brave' (5.29, Doniger and Smith 1991, 110). While the cow is the most revered animal in the text, there is no injunction against its slaughter. Only the caveat that the consumption of meat must be treated as, and preceded by, a 'sacrifice'. In their introduction to the *Laws of Manu* (1991), Wendy Doniger and Brian K. Smith observe that 'the vedic description of the natural and social orders as determined by power and violence (*himsa*, literally 'the desire to inflict injury') was preserved in later Indian thought' (1991, xxx). In the preservation of this order, 'eating and killing were regarded as two sides of the same coin. But eating was also frankly envisioned as the perpetual re-enactment of the defeat and subjugation of one's rival' (xxv). It is within this paradigm that, in 'sacrifice' to the gods, meat was consumed. The proliferation of vegetarianism and Ahmisa was a radical intervention into this space, and the Brahmins upholding it points to a shift in the status quo between the social groups. 'It was no longer a matter of courage and fear, domination and servitude; it was instead an opposition between the pure and the impure and a hierarchy of castes. Abstention from eating meat became a criterion of purity' (xxxiii).

13 The following extract is taken from Georg Bühler's translation of the *Manusmriti* (1886, 171–2). Professor Johann Georg Bühler was a scholar of ancient India who was born in Han-

nover, Germany, in 1837. He completed his education at Göttingen University, and besides being fluent in the classical languages he also undertook study in classical philology, Sanskrit, Zend, Arabic, Persian, Armenian, Archaeology and Philosophy. After fruitful stints in Paris and Oxford where he developed his research in Oriental Studies, with the help of Max Müller, he was appointed as Professor of Oriental Languages at Elphinstone College, Bombay, in December 1862. In the following years his health deteriorated and he accepeted the position of Professor of Sanskrit at Deccan College which was previously held by Martin Haug. During this period, Bühler was a frequent contributor in the Bombay Sanskrit Series, which produced cheap textbooks for students. In 1868, he also published the first volume of his translation of the *Apastamba Dharma Sutra* through the Bombay government. Apart from his books on grammar, like the Prakrit dictionary and *On the Origin of the Indian Brahma Alphabet*, he also produced translations of Indian classics like the *Panchatantra* and the *Laws of Manu*. Bühler's translation of the *Laws of Manu* was part of Max Müller's prestigious *Sacred Books of the East* series, for which he produced two other volumes, both of which were translations of ancient Indian law books (Jolly 2010). For criticisms of various aspects of Bühler's translation of *Laws of Manu*, see Doniger and Smith (1991, lxi–lxxi).

14 [Smith – Asoka, p. 58] The quote is from Vincent Smith's *Asoka: The Buddhist Emperor of India* (1909). Although Smith accedes to the point that Jains and Brahmanical Hindus do conform to the same notion of sanctity of (animal) life, he does concede that early Hinduism did not have similar values and that sacrificial killing of animals was an important part of their sacred rituals. He states that the origin of present-day reverence Hindus hold for cows was 'very curious [and] imperfectly solved' (Smith 1909, 58). He further notes that during Asoka's

time, though a great amount of sympathy was garnered for animal life, the same was not the case for the human one. For Asoka to enact the new rules of conduct as far as treatment of animals was concerned must have been a vexatious task, one that flew in the face of the common morality of the time, when sacrifices were deemed necessary to a large extent. Yet, the 'revolutionary' task of undertaking such a massive change in practice seems to have been taken in earnest. When this is juxtaposed against the treatment of human life, particularly in the case of the death penalty, it is strange to see that the same rules of sanctity of life didn't apply, even though, as Smith notes, his position was much more liberal when compared to other rulers of his time: 'The monkish legend that Asoka abolished the death penalty is not true. His legislation proves that the idea of such abolition never entered his thoughts, and that like other Buddhist monarchs, he regarded the extreme penalty of the law as an unavoidable necessity, which might be made less horrible than it had been, but could not be dispensed with. Late in his reign, in B.C. 243, he published an ordinance that every prisoner condemned to death should invariably be granted before execution a respite of three days in which to prepare himself for the next world' (Smith 1909, 59).

15 [Mookerji, Asoka, p. 21, 182, 184] Radhakumud Mookerji (1884–1964) belonged to the school of nationalist historiography, a characteristic evident in his works such as *The Fundamental Unity of India* and *Asoka*, where he argues against the perception that a cohesive feeling of nationhood was the effect of the colonial rule and refutes the prevalence of beef-eating in ancient India. On page 21 he says: '[Asoka's proclamation prohibited] the slaughter of numerous birds and beasts specified besides "all four-footed animals which are neither utilised nor eaten," such as the cow, for example, which was never used as a pack-animal nor for food in India' (Mookeri 1928, 21). He also

states: 'But a similar inference from the omission of the cow in the list, as made by V. A. Smith, is untenable, because the cow had been protected by popular religious opinion long before Asoka, and would also come under the class of quadrupeds which are 'not eaten' (khadiyati)' (1928, 182). Mookerji goes on to substantiate this by citing Kautilya's *Arthashastra* where it is forbidden to kill animals which do not prey on others as well as those which are considered auspicious (1928, 182). This, yet, seems to not point at the cow definitively.

16 Gabriel Tarde (1843–1894) was a French sociologist, criminologist and social psychologist who significantly contributed to 'social interaction theory and to diffusion research' (Kinnunen 1996, 431). Diffusion here refers to the 'spreading of social or cultural properties from one society to another'. Tarde's theories of social behaviour were based on psychology and were designed such that they could explain a whole nexus of social activity, 'from [the] development of cultures to [the] acts of an individual' (Kinnunen 1996, 431). This diffusion, according to Tarde, were carried out through the process of *imitation*. 'People imitate beliefs and desires or *motives* transmitted from one individual to another' (Kinnunen 1996, 433). His interest in criminology, and time spent at courts, lent to his conception of the 'motive' in human agency. In his lifetime, Tarde found himself eclipsed by the rising star of the other great sociologist, Emile Durkheim. His theories fell out of fashion and were soon forgotten. But in recent years, his monadism-influenced views of social organization which rejected the a priori assumptions of society, had come back into vogue among proponents of 'Actor–Network Theory', like Bruno Latour (see Candea 2010). This, rather than a theory, is a methodological approach towards viewing constellations and networks of relations and their effects, primarily in the sciences, rather than a predefined society or social group identified and governed by a set of

pregiven parameters. To see how Ambedkar utilized Tarde's theory of imitation to explain caste, see p. 275–6 note 17.

17 It has not been possible to establish the existence or provenance of such a purana; no scholar mentions it.

Chapter XIII

What made the Brahmins become vegetarian?

The non-Brahmins have evidently undergone a revolution. From being beef-eaters to have become non-beef-eaters was indeed a revolution. But if the non-Brahmins underwent one revolution, the Brahmins had undergone two. They gave up beef-eating which was one revolution. To have given up meat-eating altogether and become vegetarians was another revolution.[1]

That this was a revolution is beyond question. For as has been shown in the previous chapters there was a time when the Brahmins were the greatest beef-eaters. Although the non-Brahmins did eat beef they could not have had it every day. The cow was a costly animal and the non-Brahmins could ill afford to slaughter it just for food. He only did it on special occasion when his religious duty or personal interest to propitiate a deity compelled him to do. But the case with the Brahmin was different. He was a priest. In a period overridden by ritualism there was hardly a day on which there was no cow sacrifice to which the Brahmin was not invited by some non-Brahmin. For the Brahmin every day was a beef-steak day. The Brahmins were therefore the greatest beef-eaters. The yajna of the Brahmins was nothing but the killing of innocent animals carried on in the name of religion with pomp and ceremony with an attempt to enshroud it in mystery with a view to conceal their appetite for beef. Some idea of this mystery pomp and ceremony can be had from the directions contained in the *Aitareya Brahmana*[2] touching the killing of animals in a yajna.[3]

The actual killing of the animal is preceded by certain initiatory rites accompanied by incantations too long and too many to be detailed here. It is enough to give an idea of the main features of the sacrifice. The sacrifice commences with the erection of the sacrificial post called the Yupa[4] to which the animal is tied before it is slaughtered. After setting out why the Yupa is necessary the *Aitareya Brahmana* proceeds to state what it stands for. It says:[5]

> This Yupa is a weapon. Its point must have eight edges. For a weapon (or iron club) has eight edges. Whenever he strikes with it an enemy or adversary, he kills him. (This weapon serves) to put down him (every one) who is to be put down by him (the sacrificer). The Yupa is a weapon which stands erected (being ready) to slay an enemy. Thence an enemy (of the sacrificer) who might be present (at the sacrifice) comes of all ill after having seen the Yupa of such or such one.

The selection of the wood to be used for the Yupa is made to vary with the purposes which the sacrificer wishes to achieve by the sacrifice. The *Aitareya Brahmana* says:

> He who desires heaven, ought to make his Yupa of Khadira wood. For the gods conquered the celestial world by means of a Yupa, made of Khadira wood. In the same way the sacrificer conquers the celestial world by means of a Yupa, made of Khadira wood.
>
> He who desires food and wishes to grow fat ought to make his Yupa of Bilva[6] wood. For the Bilva tree bears fruits every year; it is the symbol of fertility; for it increases (every

year) in size from the roots up to the branches, therefore it is a symbol of fatness. He who having such [a] knowledge makes his Yupa of Bilva wood, makes fat his children and cattle.

As regards the Yupa made of Bilva wood (it is further to be remarked), that they call 'light' *bilva*. He who has such a knowledge becomes a light among his own people, the most distinguished among his own people.

He who desires beauty and sacred knowledge ought to make his Yupa of Palasa[7] wood. For the Palasa is among the trees [of] beauty and sacred knowledge. He who having such a knowledge makes his Yupa of Palasa wood, becomes beautiful and acquires sacred knowledge.

As regards the Yupa made of Palasa wood (there is further to be remarked), that the Palasa is the womb of all trees. Thence they speak on account of the *palasam* (foliage) [of the Palasa tree, of the *palasam*] of this or that tree (i.e. they call the foliage of every tree *palasam*). He who has such knowledge obtains (the gratification of) any desire, he might have regarding all trees (i.e. he obtains from all trees anything he might wish for).

This is followed by the ceremony of anointing the sacrificial post.[8]

The Adhvaryu says (to the Hotar[9]): "We anoint the sacrificial post (Yupa); repeat the mantra (required)". The Hotar then repeats the verse: "Amjanti tvam adhvare" (3, 8, 1), i.e. "The priests anoint thee, O tree! with celestial honey (butter); provide (us) with wealth if thou standest here erected, or if thou art lying on thy mother (earth)." The "celestial honey" is the melted butter (with which the priests anoint the Yupa). (The second half verse from) "provide us" &c. means: "thou mayest stand or lie, provide us with wealth.

[...]

(The Hotar then repeats :) "jato jayate sudinatve" & c. (3, 8, 5) i.e. "After having been born, he (the Yupa) is growing (to serve) in the prime of his life the sacrifice of mortal men. The wise are busy in decorating (him, the Yupa) with skill. He, as an eloquent messenger of the gods, lifts his voice (that it might be heard by the gods)." He (the Yupa) is called jata, i.e., born, because he is born by this (by the recital of the first quarter of this verse). (By the word) vardhamana, i.e. growing, they make him (the Yupa) grow in this manner. (By the words:) punanti (i.e. to clean, decorate), they clean him in this manner. (By the words:) "he as an eloquent messenger, &c." he announces the Yupa (the fact of his existence), to the gods.

The Hotar then concludes (the ceremony of anointing the sacrificial post) with the verse "yuva suvasah parivitah" (3, 8, 4), i.e. "the youth decorated with ribands, has arrived; he is finer (than all trees) which ever grew; the wise priests raise him up under recital of well-framed thoughts of their mind." The youth decorated with ribands, is the vital air (the soul), which is covered by the limbs of the body. (By the words:) "he is finer," &c. he means that he (the Yupa) is becoming finer (more excellent, beautiful) by this (mantra)."

The next ceremony is the carrying of fire round the sacrificial animal.[10] The *Aitareya Brahmana* gives the following directions on this point. It says:[11]

> When the fire is carried round (the animal) the Adhvaryu[12] says to the Hotar: repeat (thy mantras). The Hotar then repeats this triplet of verses, addressed to Agni, and composed in the Gayatri metre: agnir hota no adhvare (4,15,1–3) i.e., (1) Agni, our priest, is carried round about like a horse, he who is among gods, the god of sacrifices, (2) Like a charioteer

Agni passes thrice by the sacrifice; to the gods he carries the offering, (3) The master of food, the seer of Agni, went round the offering; he bestows riches on the sacrificer.

When the fire is carried round (the animal) then he makes him (Agni) prosper by means of his own deity and his own metre. 'As a horse he is carried' means: they carry him as if he were a horse, round about. Like a charioteer Agni passes thrice by the sacrifice means: he goes round the sacrifice like a charioteer (swiftly). He is called *vajapati* (master of food) because he is the master of (different kinds of) food.

The Advaryu says: give Hotar! the additional order for dispatching offerings to the gods.

[...]

The Hotar then says (to the slaughterers): *Ye divine slaughterers, commence* (your work), *as well as ye who are human!* that is to say, he orders all the slaughterers among gods as well as among men (to commence).

Bring hither the instruments for killing, ye who are ordering the sacrifice, in behalf of the two masters of the sacrifice.

The animal is the offering, the sacrificer the master of the offering. Thus he (the Hotar) makes prosper the sacrificer by means of his (the sacrifcer's) own offering. Thence they truly say: for whatever deity the animal is killed, that one is the master of the offering. If the animal is to be offered to one deity only, the priest should say: *medhapataye* 'to the master of the sacrifice (singular)'; if to two deities, then he should use the dual 'to both masters of the offering', and if to several deities, then he should use the plural, 'to the masters of the offering'. This is the established custom.

Bring ye for him fire! For the animal when carried (to the slaughter) saw death before it Not wishing to go to the gods, the gods said to it: Come we will bring thee to heaven! The animal consented and said: One of you should walk before me.

They consented. Agni then walked before it, and it followed after Agni. Thence they say, every animal belongs to Agni, for it followed after him. Thence they carry before the animal fire (Agni).

Spread the (sacred) grass! The animal lives on herbs. He (the Hotar) thus provides the animal with its entire soul (the herbs being supposed to form part of it).

After the ceremony of carrying fire round the animal comes the delivery of the animal to the priests for sacrifice. Who should offer the animal for sacrifice? On this point the direction of the *Aitareya Brahmana* is[13]—

The mother, the father, the brother, sister, friend, and *companion should give this (animal) up* (for being slaughtered)! When these words are pronounced, they seize the animal which is (regarded as) entirely given up by its relations (parents, &c.)

On reading this direction one wonders why almost everybody is required to join in offering the animal for sacrifice. The reason is simple. There were altogether seventeen Brahmin priests who were entitled to take part in performing the sacrifice.[14] Naturally enough they wanted the whole carcass to themselves.[15] Indeed they could not give enough to each of the seventeen priests[16] unless they had the whole carcass to distribute. Legally the Brahmins could not claim the whole carcass unless everybody who could not claim any right over the animal had been divested of it. Hence the direction requiring even the companion of the sacrificer to take part in offering the animal. Then comes the ceremony of actually killing the animal. The *Aitareya Brahmana* gives the details of the mode and manner of killing the animal. Its directions are:[17]

Turn its feet northwards! Make its eye to go to the sun, dismiss its breath to the wind, its life to the air, its hearing to the directions, its body to the earth.

In this way he (the Hotar) places it (connects it) with these worlds.

Take off the skin entire (without cutting it). Before operating the naval, tear out omentum! Stop its breathing within (by stopping its mouth)! Thus he (the Hotar) puts its breath in the animals.

Make of its breast a piece like an eagle, of its arms (two pieces like) *two hatchets, of its forearms* (two pieces like) *two spikes, of its shoulders* (two pieces like) *two kashyapas, its loins should be unbroken* (entire); (make of) *its thighs* (two pieces like) *two shields, of the two kneepans* (two pieces like) *two oleander leaves; take out its twenty six ribs according to their order; preserve every limb of it in its integrity.* Thus he benefits all its limbs.

There remain two ceremonies to complete the sacrificial killing of the animal. One is to absolve the Brahmin priests who played the butcher's part. Theoretically they are guilty of murder for the animal is only a substitute for the sacrificer. To absolve them from the consequences of murder, the Hotar is directed by the *Aitareya Brahmana* to observe the following injunction:[18]

Do not cut the entrails which resemble on owl (when taking out the omentum), *nor should among your children, O slaughterers! or among their offspring any one be found who might cut them.* By speaking these words, he presents these entrails to the slaughterers among the gods as well as to those among men.

The Hotar shall then say thrice: O *Adhrigu* (and ye others), *kill* (the animal), *do it well;* kill it, O *Adhrigu*.

[...]

After the animal has been killed, (he should say thrice:) *Far may it* (the consequences of murder) be (from us). For *Adhrigu*[19] among the gods is he who silences (the animal) and the *Apapa*[20] (away, away!) is he who puts it down. By speaking those words he surrenders the animal to those who silence it (by stopping its mouth) and to those who butcher it.

The Hotar then mutters (he makes, *japa*[21]); 'O slaughterers! may all good you might do abide by us! and all mischief you might do go elsewhere!' The Hotar gives by (this) speech the order (for killing the animal), for Agni had given the order for killing (the animal) with the same words when he was the Hotar of the gods.

By those words (the *japa* mentioned) the Hotar removes (all evil consequences) from those who suffocate the animal and those who butcher it, in all that they might transgress the rule by cutting one piece too soon, the other too late, or by cutting a too large, or a too small piece. The Hotar enjoying this happiness clears himself (from all guilt), and attains the full length of his life (and it serves the sacrificer) for obtaining his full life. He who has such a knowledge, attains the full length of his life.

The *Aitareya Bramhana* next deals with the question of disposing of the parts of the dead animal. In this connection its direction is[22]—

Dig a ditch in the earth to hide its excrements. The excrements consist of vegetable food; for the earth is the place for the herbs. Thus the Hotar puts them (the excrements) finally in their proper places.

Present the evil spirits with the blood! For the gods having deprived (once) the evil spirits of their share in the Haviryajnas[23] (such as the Full and New Moon offerings) apportioned to them the husks and smallest grains, and after having them turned out of the great sacrifice (such as the Soma and animal sacrifices), presented to them the blood. Thence the Hotar pronounces the words: *present the evil spirits with the blood!* By giving them this share he deprives the evil spirits of any other share in the sacrifice. They say: one should not address the evil spirits in the sacrifice, any evil spirits whichever they might be (Rakshasa, Asuras, &c.); for the sacrifice is to be without the evil spirits (not to be disturbed by them). But others say: one should address them; for who deprives any one, entitled to a share, of this share, will be punished (by him whom he deprives); and if he himself does not suffer the penalty, then his son, and if his son be spared, then his grandson will suffer it, and thus he resents on him (the son or grandson) what he wanted to resent on you.

However, if the Hotar addresses them, he should do so with a low voice. For both, the low voice and the evil spirits, are, as it were, hidden. If he addresses them with a loud voice, then such one speaks in the voice of the evil spirits, and is capable of producing Rakshasa-sounds (a horrible, terrific voice). The voice in which the haughty man and the drunkard speak is that of the evil spirits (Rakshasas). He who has such knowledge will neither himself become haughty nor will such a man be among his offspring.

Then follows the last and the concluding ceremony that of offering parts of the body of the animal to the gods. It is called the Manota. According to the *Aitareya Brahmana*[24]—

The Adhvaryu [now] says (to the Hotar): recite the verses appropriate to the offering of the parts of the sacrificial animal which are cut off for the Manota. He then repeats the hymn: Thou, O Agni, art the first Manota[25] (6, 1).

There remains the question of sharing the flesh of the animal. On this issue the division was settled by the *Aitareya Brahmana* in the following terms:[26]

Now follows the division of the different parts of the sacrificial animal (among the priests). We shall describe it. The two jawbones with the tongue are to be given to the Prastotar; the breast in the form of an eagle to the Udgatar; the throat with the palate to the Pratihartar; the lower part of the right loins to the Hotar: the left to the Brahma; the right thigh to the Maitravaruna; the left to the Brahmanachhamsi; the right side with the shoulder to the Adhvaryu; the left side to those who accompany the chants; the left shoulder to the Pratipashatar; the lower part of the right arm to the Neshtar; the lower part of the left arm to the Potar; the upper of the right thigh to the Achhavaka; the left to the Agnidhara; the upper part of the right arm to the Atreya; the left to the Sadasya; the back bone and the urinal bladder to the Grihapati (sacrificer); the right feet to the Grihapati who gives a feasting; the left feet to the wife of that Grihapati who gives a feasting; the upper lip is common to both (the Grihapati and his wife), which is to be divided by the Grihapati. They offer the tail of the animal to wives, but they should give it to a Brahmana; the fleshy processes *(manikah)* on the neck and three gristles *(kikasah)* to the Gravastut; three other gristles and one-half of the fleshy part on the back *(vaikartta)* to the Unnetar; the other half of the fleshy part on the neck and the left lobe *(kloma)* to the slaughterer, who should present it to a Brahmana, if he himself would not happen to be a Brahmana. The head is to be given to the Subrahmanya, the skin belongs to him (the Subrahmanya), who spoke, *svah sutyam* (tomorrow at the Soma sacrifice); that part of the sacrificial animal at a Soma sacrifice which belongs to Ila (sacrificial food) is common to all the priests; only for the Hotar it is optional.

All these portions of the sacrificial animal amount to thirty-six single pieces, each of which represents the pada (foot) of a verse by which the sacrifice is carried up. The Brihati metre[27] consists of thirty-six syllables; and the heavenly worlds are of the Brihati nature. In this way (by dividing the animal into thirty-six parts) they gain life (in this world) and the heavens, and having become established in both (this and that world) they walk there.

To those who divide the sacrificial animal in the way mentioned, it becomes the guide to heaven. But those who make the division otherwise are like scoundrels and miscreants who kill an animal merely (for gratifying their lust after flesh).

This division of the sacrificial animal was invented by the Rishi (*Devabhaga*,[28] a son of *Sruta*). When he was departing from this life, he did not entrust (the secret to anyone). But a supernatural being communicated it to *Girija*, the son of *Babhru*. Since his time men study it.

What is said by the *Aitareya Brahmana* places two things beyond dispute. One is that the Brahmins monopolized the whole of the flesh of the sacrificial animal. Except for a paltry bit they did not even allow the sacrificer to share in it. The second is that the Brahmins themselves played the part of butchers in the slaughter of the animal. As a matter of principle the Brahmins should not eat the flesh of the animal killed at a sacrifice. The principle underlying yajna is that man should offer himself as sacrifice to the gods. He offers an animal only to release himself from this obligation. From this it followed that the animal, being only a substitute for the man, eating the flesh of animal meant eating human flesh.[29] This theory was very detrimental to the interest of the Brahmins who had a complete monopoly of the flesh of the animal offered for sacrifice. The *Aitareya Brahmana* which had seen in this theory the danger of the Brahmins being deprived of the flesh of the sacrificial animal takes pains to explain away the theory by a simple negation. It says:[30]

> The man who is initiated (into the sacrificial mysteries) offers himself to all deities. Agni represents all deities, and Soma represents all deities. When he (the sacrificer) offers the animal to *Agni-Soma* he releases himself (by being represented by the animal) from being offered to all deities.
>
> [...]
>
> They say: 'do not eat from the animal offered to Agni-Soma.' 'Who eats from this animal, eats from human flesh; because the sacrificer releases himself (from being sacrificed) by means of the animal'. But this (precept) is not to be attended to.

Given these facts, no further evidence seems to be necessary to support the statement that the Brahmins were not merely beef-eaters but they were also butchers.³¹

Why then did the Brahmins change front? Let us deal with their change of front in two stages. First, why did they give up beef-eating?

II

As has already been shown cow-killing was not legally prohibited by Asoka. Even if it had been prohibited, a law made by the Buddhist Emperor could never have been accepted by the Brahmins as binding upon them.

Did Manu prohibit beef-eating? If he did, then that would be binding on the Brahmins and would afford an adequate explanation of their change of front. Looking into the *Manusmriti* one does find the following verses:³²

> V.46. He who does not seek to cause the sufferings of bonds and death to living creatures, (but) desires the good of all (beings), obtains endless bliss.
>
> V.47. He who does not injure any (creature), attains without an effort what he thinks of, what he undertakes, and

what he fixes his mind on.

V.48. Meat can never be obtained without injury to living creatures, and injury to sentient beings is detrimental to (the attainment of) heavenly bliss; let him therefore shun (the use of) meat.

V.49. Having well considered the (disgusting) origin of flesh and the (cruelty of) fettering and slaying corporeal beings, let him entirely abstain from eating flesh.

If these verses can be treated as containing positive injunctions they would be sufficient to explain why the Brahmins gave up meat-eating and became vegetarians. But it is impossible to treat these verses as positive injunctions, carrying the force of law. They are either exhortations or interpolations introduced after the Brahmins had become vegetarians in praise of the change. That the latter is the correct view is proved by the following verses which occur in the same chapter of the *Manusmriti*:

V.28. The Lord of creatures (Prajapati)[33] created this whole (world to be) the sustenance of the vital spirit; both the immovable and the movable (creation is) the food of the vital spirit.

V.29. What is destitute of motion is the food of those endowed with locomotion; (animals) without fangs (are the food) of those with fangs, those without hands of those who possess hands, and the timid of the bold.

V.30. The eater who daily even devours those destined to be his food, commits no sin; for the creator himself created both the eaters and those who are to be eaten (for those special purposes).

"V. 56. There is no sin in eating meat, in (drinking) spirituous liquor, and in carnal intercourse for that is the natural way of created beings, but abstention brings great rewards.

"V. 27. One may eat meat when it has been sprinkled with water, while Mantras were recited, when Brahmanas desire (one's doing it) when one is engaged (in the performance of a rite) according to the law, and when one's life is in danger.

"V. 31. 'The consumption of meat (is befitting) for sacrifices,' that is declared to be a rule made by the gods, but to persist (in using it) on other (occasions) is said to be a proceeding worthy of Rakshasas.

"V. 32. He who eats meat, when he honours the gods and manes commits no sin, whether he has bought it, or himself has killed (the animal) or has received it as a present from others.

"V. 42. A twice-born man who, knowing the true meaning of the Veda, slays an animal for these purposes, causes both himself and the animal to enter a most blessed state.

"V. 39. Svayambhu (the Self-existent) himself created animals for the sake of sacrifices; sacrifices (have been instituted) for the good of this whole (world); hence the slaughtering (of beasts) for sacrifice is not slaughtering (in the ordinary sense of the word).

"V. 40. Herbs, trees, cattle, birds, and (other) animals that have been destroyed for sacrifices, receive (being reborn) higher existences."

Manu goes further and makes eating of flesh compulsory. Note the following verse:

"V. 35. But a man who, being duly engaged (to officiate or to dine at a sacred rite), refuses to eat meat, becomes after death an animal during twenty-one existences."

That Manu did not prohibit meat-eating is evident enough.[34] That *Manusmriti* did not prohibit cow-killing can also be proved from the *Smriti* itself. In the first place, the only references to cow in the *Manusmriti* are to be found in the catalogue of rules which are made applicable by Manu to the Snataka.[35] They are set out below:

1. A Snataka should not eat food which a cow has smelt.[36]
2. A Snataka should not step over a rope to which a calf is tied.[37]
3. A Snataka should not urinate in a cow-pen.[38]
4. A Snataka should not answer call of nature facing a cow.[39]
5. A Snataka should not keep his right arm uncovered when he enters a cow-pen.[40]
6. A Snataka should not interrupt a cow which is sucking her calf, nor tell anybody of it.[41]
7. A Snataka should not ride on the back of the cow.[42]
8. A Snataka should not offend the cow.[43]
9. A Snataka who is impure must not touch a cow with his hand.[44]

From these references it will be seen that Manu did not regard the cow as a sacred animal. On the other hand, he regarded it as an impure animal whose touch caused ceremonial pollution.[45]

There are verses in Manu which show that he did not prohibit the eating of beef. In this connection, reference may be made to Chapter III.3. It says:

> He (Snataka) who is famous (for the strict performance of) his duties and has received his heritage, the Veda from his father, shall be honoured, sitting on couch and adorned with a garland with (the present of) a cow (the honey-mixture).[46]

The question is why should Manu recommend the gift of a cow to a Snataka? Obviously, to enable him to perform

Madhuparka. If that is so, it follows that Manu knew that Brahmins did eat beef and he had no objection to it.

Another reference would be to Manu's discussion of the animals whose meat is eatable and those whose meat is not. In Chapter V.18. he says:

> The porcupine, the hedgehog, the iguana, the rhinoceros, the tortoise, and the hare they declare to be eatable: likewise those (domestic animals) that have teeth in one jaw only, excepting camels.[47]

In this verse Manu gives general permission to eat the flesh of all domestic animals that have teeth in one jaw only. To this rule Manu makes one exception, namely, the camel. In this class of domestic animals—those that have teeth in one jaw only—falls not only the camel but also the cow. It is noteworthy that Manu does not make an exception in the case of the cow. This means that Manu had no objection to the eating of the cow's flesh.[48]

Manu did not make the killing of the cow an offence. Manu divides sins into two classes (i) mortal sins and (ii) minor sins.[49] Among the mortal sins Manu includes:

> XI.55. Killing a Brahmana, drinking (the spirituous liquor called) Sura, stealing (the gold of Brahmana), adultery with a Guru's wife, and associating with such offenders they declare (to be) mortal sins (mahapataka).[50]

Among minor sins Manu includes:

> XI.60. Killing the cow, sacrificing for those unworthy to sacrifice, adultery, selling oneself, casting off one's teacher, mother, father or son, giving up the (daily) study of the Veda and neglecting the (sacred domestic) fire.[51]

From this it will be clear that according to Manu cow-killing was only a minor sin.[52] It was reprehensible only if the cow was killed without good and sufficient reason. Even if it was otherwise, it was not heinous or inexplicable. The same was the attitude of Yajnavalkya.[53]

All this proves that for generations the Brahmins had been eating beef. Why did they give up beef-eating? Why did they, as an extreme step, give up meat eating altogether and become vegetarians? It is two revolutions rolled into one. As has been shown it has not been done as a result of the preachings of Manu, their Divine Law-maker. The revolution has taken place in spite of Manu and contrary to his directions. What made the Brahmins take this step? Was philosophy responsible for it? Or was it dictated by strategy? Two explanations are offered. One explanation is that this deification of the cow was a manifestation of the Advaita philosophy that one supreme entity pervaded the whole universe, that on that account all life human as well as animal was sacred. This explanation is obviously unsatisfactory. In the first place, it does not fit in with facts. The *Vedanta Sutra*[54] which proclaims the doctrine of oneness of life does not prohibit the killing of animals for sacrificial purposes as is evident from II.1.28.[55] In the second place, if the transformation was due to the desire to realize the ideal of Advaita then there is no reason why it should have stopped with the cow. It should have extended to all other animals.

Another explanation[56] more ingenious than the first, is that this transformation in the life of the Brahmin was due to the rise of the doctrine of the Transmigration of the Soul.[57] Even this explanation does not fit in with facts. The *Brahadaranyaka Upanishad*[58] upholds the doctrine of transmigration (VI.2)[59] and yet recommends that if a man desires to have a learned son born to him he should prepare a mass of the flesh of the bull or ox or of other flesh with rice and ghee.[60] Again, how is it that this doctrine which is propounded in the *Upanishads* did not have any effect on the Brahmins upto the time of the *Manusmriti*, a period of at least 400 years. Obviously, this explanation is no explanation. Thirdly, if Brahmins became vegetarians by reason of the doctrine of transmigration of the soul how is it that it did not make the non-Brahmins take to vegetarianism?

To my mind, it was strategy which made the Brahmins give up beef-eating and start worshipping the cow. The clue to the worship of the cow is to be found in the struggle between Buddhism and Brahmanism and the means adopted by Brahmanism to establish its supremacy over Buddhism.[61] The strife between Buddhism and Brahmanism is a crucial fact in Indian history. Without the realization of this fact, it is impossible to explain some of the features of Hinduism. Unfortunately students of Indian history have entirely missed the importance of this strife. They knew there was Brahmanism. But they seem to be entirely unaware of the struggle for supremacy in which these creeds were engaged and that their struggle which extended for 400 years has left some indelible marks on religion, society and politics of India.

This is not the place for describing the full story of the struggle. All one can do is to mention a few salient points. Buddhism was at one time the religion of the majority of the people of India. It continued to be the religion of the masses for hundreds of years. It attacked Brahmanism on all sides as no religion had done before.[62]

Brahmanism was on the wane and if not on the wane, it was certainly on the defensive. As a result of the spread of Buddhism, the Brahmins had lost all power and prestige at the

Royal Court and among the people.⁶³ They were smarting under the defeat they had suffered at the hands of Buddhism and were making all possible efforts to regain their power and prestige. Buddhism had made so deep an impression on the minds of the masses and had taken such a hold of them that it was absolutely impossible for the Brahmins to fight the Buddhists except by accepting their ways and means and practising the Buddhist creed in its extreme form. After the death of Buddha his followers started setting up the images of the Buddha and building stupas. The Brahmins followed it. They, in their turn, built temples and installed in them images of Shiva, Vishnu and Ram and Krishna etc.—all with the object of drawing away the crowd that was attracted by the image worship of Buddha.⁶⁴ That is how temples and images which had no place in Brahmanism came into Hinduism.⁶⁵ The Buddhists rejected the Brahmanic religion which consisted of yajna and animal sacrifice, particularly of the cow. The objection to the sacrifice of the cow had taken a strong hold of the minds of the masses especially as they were an agricultural population and the cow was a very useful animal. The Brahmins in all probability had come to be hated as the killer of cows in the same way as the guest had come to be hated as Goghna, the killer of the cow by the householder, because whenever he came a cow had to be killed in his honour. That being the case, the Brahmins could do nothing to improve their position against the Buddhists except by giving up the Yajna as a form of worship and the sacrifice of the cow.

That the object of the Brahmins in giving up beef-eating was to snatch away from the Buddhist Bhikshus the supremacy they had acquired is evidenced by the adoption of vegetarianism by Brahmins. Why did the Brahmins become vegetarian? The answer is that without becoming vegetarian the Brahmins could not have recovered the ground they had lost to their rival namely Buddhism. In this connection it must be remembered that there was one aspect in which Brahmanism suffered in public esteem as compared to Buddhism. That was the practice of animal sacrifice which was the essence of Brahmanism and to which Buddhism was deadly opposed. That in an agricultural population there should be respect for Buddhism and revulsion against Brahmanism which involved slaughter of animals including cows and bullocks is only natural.[66] What could the Brahmins do to recover the lost ground? To go one better than the Buddhist Bhikshus not only to give up meat-eating but to become vegetarians—which they did. That this was the object of the Brahmins in becoming vegetarians can be proved in various ways.[67]

If the Brahmins had acted from conviction that animal sacrifice was bad, all that was necessary for them to do was to give up killing animals for sacrifice. It was unnecessary for them to be vegetarians. That they did go in for vegetarianism makes it obvious that their motive was far-reaching. Secondly, it was unnecessary for them to become vegetarians. For the Buddhist Bhikshus were not vegetarians. This statement might surprise many people owing to the popular belief that the connection between Ahimsa and Buddhism was immediate and essential. It is generally believed that the Buddhist Bhikshus eschewed animal food. This is an error. The fact is that the Buddhist Bhikshus were permitted to eat three kinds of flesh that were deemed pure. Later on they were extended to five classes. Yuan Chwang,[68] the Chinese traveller was aware of this and spoke of the pure kinds of flesh as *San-Ching*. The origin of this practice among the Bhikshus is explained by Mr Thomas Watters.[69]

According to the story told by him[70]—

> In the time of Buddha there was in Vaisali[71] a wealthy general named Siha who was a convert to Buddhism. He became a liberal supporter of the Brethren and kept them constantly supplied with good flesh-food. When it was noticed abroad that the Bhikshus were in the habit of eating such food specially provided for them, the Tirthikas made the practice a matter of angry reproach. Then the abstemious ascetic Brethren, learning this, reported the circumstances to the Master, who thereupon called the Brethren together. When they assembled, he announced to them the law that they were not to eat the flesh of any animal which they had seen put to death for them, or about which they had been told that it had been slain for them. But he permitted to the Brethern as 'pure' (that is, lawful) food the flesh of animals the slaughter of which had not been seen by the Bhikshus, not heard of by them, and not suspected by them to have been on their account. In the Pali and *Ssu-fen*[72] Vinaya it was after a breakfast given by Siha to the Buddha and some of the Brethren, for which the carcass of a large ox was procured that the Nirgranthas reviled the Bhikshus and Buddha instituted this new rule declaring fish and flesh 'pure' in the three conditions. The animal food now permitted to the Bhikshus came to be known as the 'three pures' or 'three pure kinds of flesh', and it was tersely described as 'unseen, unheard, unsuspected', or as the Chinese translations sometimes have it 'not seen, not heard nor suspected to be on my account'. Then two more kinds of animal food were declared lawful for the Brethren viz., the flesh of animals which had died a natural death, and that of animals which had been killed by a bird of prey or other savage creature. So there came to be five classes or descriptions of flesh which the professed Buddhist was at liberty to use as food. Then

the 'unseen, unheard, unsuspected' came to be treated as one class, and this together with the 'natural death' and 'bird killed' made a *san-ching*.

As the Buddhist Bhikshus did eat meat the Brahmins had no reason to give it up. Why then did the Brahmins give up meat-eating and become vegetarians? It was because they did not want to put themselves merely on the same footing in the eyes of the public as the Buddhist Bhikshus.

The giving up of the yajna system and abandonment of the sacrifice of the cow could have had only a limited effect. At the most it would have put the Brahmins on the same footing as the Buddhists. The same would have been the case if they had followed the rules observed by the Buddhist Bhikshus in the matter of meat-eating. It could not have given the Brahmins the means of achieving supremacy over the Buddhists which was their ambition. They wanted to oust the Buddhists from the place of honour and respect which they had acquired in the minds of the masses by their opposition to the killing of the cow for sacrificial purposes. To achieve their purpose the Brahmins had to adopt the usual tactics of a reckless adventurer. It is to beat extremism by extremism. It is the strategy which all rightists use to overcome the leftists. The only way to beat the Buddhists was to go a step further and be vegetarians.[73]

There is another reason which can be relied upon to support the thesis that the Brahmins started cow-worship, gave up beef-eating and became vegetarians in order to vanquish Buddhism. It is the date when cow-killing became a mortal sin. It is well-known that cow-killing was not made an offence by Asoka. Many people expect him to have come forward to prohibit the killing of the cow. Prof Vincent Smith regards it as surprising.[74] But there is nothing surprising in it.

Buddhism was against animal sacrifice in general. It had no particular affection for the cow. Asoka had therefore no particular reason to make a law to save the cow. What is more astonishing is the fact that cow-killing was made a Mahapataka,[75] a mortal sin or a capital offence by the Gupta Kings[76] who were champions of Hinduism which recognized and sanctioned the killing of the cow for sacrificial purposes. As pointed out by Mr D.R. Bhandarkar[77]—

> We have got the incontrovertible evidence of inscriptions to show that early in the 5th century AD killing a cow was looked upon as an offence of the deepest turpitude, turpitude as deep as that involved in murdering a Brahman. We have thus a copper-plate inscription dated 465 AD and referring itself to the reign of Skandagupta of the Imperial Gupta dynasty. It registers a grant and ends with a verse saying: 'Whosoever will transgress this grant that has been assigned (shall become as guilty as) the slayer of a cow, the slayer of a spiritual preceptor (or) the slayer of a Brahman. A still earlier record placing *go-hatya* on the same footing as *brahma hatya* is that of Chandragupta II, grandfather of Skandagupta just mentioned. It bears the Gupta date 93, which is equivalent to 412 AD It is engraved on the railing which surrounds the celebrated Buddhist stupa at Sanchi, in Central India. This also speaks of a benefaction made by an officer of Chandragupta and ends as follows: ... "Whosoever shall interfere with this arrangement... he shall become invested with (the guilt of) the slaughter of a cow or of a Brahman, and with (the guilt of) the five *anantarya*." Here the object of this statement is to threaten the resumer of the grant, be he a Brahminist or a Buddhist, with the sins regarded as mortal by each community. The *anantaryas* are the five *mahapatakas* according to Buddhist

theology. They are: matricide, patricide, killing an Arhant,[78] shedding the blood of a Buddha, and causing a split among the priesthood. The *mahapatakas* with which a Brahminist is here threatened are only two: viz., the killing of a cow and the murdering of a Brahman. The latter is obviously a *mahapataka* as it is mentioned as such in all the Smritis, but the former has been specified only [as] an upapataka by Apastamba, Manu, Yajnavalkya and so forth. But the very fact that it is here associated with *brahma-hatya* and both have been put on a par with the *anantaryas* of the Buddhists shows that in the beginning of the fifth century AD, it was raised to the category of *mahapatakas*. Thus *go-hatya* must have come to be considered a *mahapataka* at least one century earlier, i.e., about the commencement of the fourth century AD.

The question is why should a Hindu king have come forward to make a law against cow-killing, that is to say, against the Laws of Manu? The answer is that the Brahmins had to suspend or abrogate a requirement of their Vedic religion in order to overcome the supremacy of the Buddhist Bhikshus. If the analysis is correct then it is obvious that the worship of the cow is the result of the struggle between Buddhism and Brahminism. It was a means adopted by the Brahmins to regain their lost position.

Annotations

1   In a later text Ambedkar explicates precisely what he means by this 'another revolution'. The name he gives it is 'counter-revolution'. The text in question is the posthumously published incomplete manuscript "Revolution and Counter-Revolution" (Ambedkar 1989). In it, a clear formulation of a theory of revolution can be found. In many ways "Revolution and Counter-Revolution" sets out the generic procedures of Ambedkar's political method, so to speak. The book presents a close reading of the influential Hindu text, the Bhagavad Gita. Launching an attack on the Gita's idea of morality, Ambedkar sets forth how exactly it was a counter-revolutionary text which was produced in the wake of the true revolutionary break in society which came from Buddhism. Ambedkar through this text explicates a 'speculative' and 'partisan' understanding of the concept of revolution. The revolutionary nature of Buddhism or the counter-revolutionary nature of the Brahmanism that followed cannot be gleaned from a neutral position as observers of history. Rather, it comes when we become subjects of politics, where a certain universal truth, that of Dalit emancipation and fight for equality becomes self-evident and makes us its partisans. For a more engaged reading of Ambedkar's conception of revolution and counter-revolution read chapters "Caste and Debt" and "Ambedkar and Other Immortals: A Note on Comparative Politics and Incomparable Events" in Soumyabrata Choudhury (2018a), and the paper "The Ambiguous Debt of Counterrevolution to Revolution: Reply to a Vigilant Melancholic" (Choudhury 2018b). These papers expand on Ambedkar's use of the Bhagavad Gita to construct a cogent theory of the revolution. And yet Ambedkar's attitude towards the Gita has a meandering history which has been tracked by Aishwary Kumar (2015). In his early days, he used the figure of Arjuna to mobilize the Depressed Classes

into action, spurring them on using the concept of impersonal duty. However, Ambedkar, as Kumar shows, later became more acutely aware of the caste nature of this invocation. We see how the impersonality of the dharma which Krishna invokes is precisely guided by the dharma of a particular caste, that of the Kshatriya. And that Arjun is interpellated into the act of fratricide because his morality is overridden by the dharma of his caste. Ambedkar then goes on to demonstrate that one cannot simply do away with the caste nature of the dharma given in the text because that is precisely what is at its foundation. One cannot simply pick out the logic of the Gita and infuse it into the fight for Dalit emancipation, because the 'dharmic' reality to which it restricts its subjects is precisely the one defined by the station of one's birth. Here we see the unshakeable rigour of Ambedkar's thought, and how he wasn't simply a pragmatist (which is so often only deployed as a euphemism for opportunistic) but was constantly guided by the singular project of rendering the theory of equality consistent. Kumar also discusses how Ambedkar calls out the falseness of Gandhi's opposition to the Gita and the violent edifice on which Gandhian satyagraha and non-violence is built. Says Ambedkar: 'Violence meaning only killing is a very narrow approach to distinguish between violence and nonviolence. The meaning of violence includes hurt to the body or feelings of another person. Therefore, nonviolence means not to cause pain of any nature to any living being. If we apply this broader definition of nonviolence, then Mahatma Gandhi's nonviolence also is violence in a way. Because, according to his methods even though nobody is physically hurt, it hurts the sentiments of opposite parties. [...] In fact Satyagraha should adopt nonviolence as far as possible and may have to resort to violence in case of need [...] that would be a practical approach' (Kumar 2015, 147). The difference, to simplify Kumar's conclusion, would be that while Gandhi saw in people an essential 'unruliness' that had to be tamed, controlled and made to submit to an external (transcendental) will, Ambedkar saw the force of truth emerging from within the configurations occupied by a people. The possibility of newness was always immanent for him even as the way to this possibility (and even the possibility of this possibility) wasn't a given or 'essentially' fixed.

2 The *Satapatha* and *Aitareya Brahmanas* are two of the most important ones in the *Brahmana* stratum of Vedic literature. For more on the *Brahmanas*, see p. 166 note 10. The *Aitareya Brahmana* is linked to the *Rig Veda* and it acts as a manual of duties and explanation for the seven Hotri priests: Hotar, Maitravaruna (Prasastar), Brahmanachhamsi, Achhavaka, Potar, Nestar and Agnidhra. In particular, the *Brahmana* details how to carry out sacrifices which include those to Agni and Soma, the relation of the Hotri priests with the Kshatriyas, and distribution of meat after the performance of a sacrifice (Haug 1922, xl–xlviii). S.G. Sathaye (1969) juxtaposes the *Aitareya Brahmana* against Plato's *Republic* and concludes that while the latter was a text aimed towards social reform and rejection of existent organization of society, the former is a justification of society as it exists and tries to give religious grounds for practices and rituals. Sacrifices in the *Aitareya Brahmana* pertain to its own specific milieu. Firstly, caste was not as rigid as it became later. The most important aspect of life appeared to be the rituals and incantations themselves. So if a Kshatriya offered the appropriate materials to a Brahmin and if the Brahmin chose to accept them, the former could then adopt aspects of the Brahmin lifestyle and his progeny could be assimilated into the Brahmin fold. Nothing however is said about the Vaishya and Shudra castes. Questions of morality aren't dealt with in a philosophical sense, rather they are determined by sacrificial techniques and conformity to the laws relating to sacrifices. The

key formula of the text is 'What is appropriate at the sacrifice, that is successful.' Thus important questions of ethics and sociality are reduced to mechanistic repetition which has no life in thought: ironic since the Brahmins presumed to give themselves the monopoly of thought and learning (Sathaye 1969).

3 In his book *On Human Sacrifices in Ancient India* (1876), Rajendralala Mitra cites several instances in the *Aitareya Brahmana* that demonstrate the prevalence of human sacrifices, not to speak of those of animals. Similar sanctions are also found in *Satapatha* and *Taittiriya Brahmanas* as per Mitra's reading. Ambedkar writes in *Riddles in Hinduism* (Riddle No. 23): 'The religion of the Vedic Aryans was full of barbaric and obscene observances. Human sacrifice formed a part of their religion and was called Naramedha yagna' (Ambedkar 2016, 193–4). The *Rig Veda*'s Purusha Sukta hymn in which the deity Prajapati features (he is both the subject and object of sacrifice), acts as prototypical of the sacrifices that followed. The Purusha Sukta is also believed to be a later addition to the *Rig Veda*, after the varna system had taken definite shape (see Jamison and Brereton 2014, 58). The Prajapati sacrifice of the Purusha, the primordial being, spawns all creation including the four varnas. In the *Mahabharata*, the word Naramedha occurs four times. On regarding this as a self-sacrifice, see Heesterman 1987.

4 The Yupa is understood as a symbol of death and killing and is closely associated with the Vedic weapon vajra. It was the god Indra who wielded the vajra, a lightning bolt sword. When Indra smote Vrtra, the serpant/dragon Asura who symbolized drought, the vajra is said to have been sundered into four forms: a wooden sword (sphya) which is used to demarcate the area within which sacrifices are conducted, a Yupa, a chariot, and arrows (Hiltebeitel 1991). According to the *Aitareya Brahmana*,

the Yupa was the means by which the gods debarred humans from entering the celestial world. It was erected at the spot where the gods themselves had performed sacrifices to enter the sacred realm. Upon finding the Yupa, men and rishis dug it out, and turned it upside down to point to heavenwards. The sacred sacrifices were thus revealed to them and the celestial world was made known, equalizing the Brahmins with the gods (Haug 1863, 72–3).

5 [*Aitareya Brahmana* II, p. 72–74] The quotes from the *Aitareya Brahmana* that follow are taken from Martin Haug's 1863 translation. In his preface to the text, Haug clarifies his reliance on Sayana (a fourteenth century commentator of the *Aitareya Brahmana*) in order to interpret difficult sections of the text. He also writes about his search for living interpreters and practitioners of the Aitareya rituals, of which only few remained during his time. There was also a considerable taboo against sharing the sacred knowledge with a foreigner like him. Eventually, he got a Marathi-speaking Brahmin to open up after paying him a sum of money, and so Haug was able to witness how some of the key sacrifices mentioned in the text were performed (Haug 1922, iii–vi).

6 The Bilva tree is one of the most referenced ones in Brahmanical literature. It finds mention in the *Yajur Veda Samhita*, *Atharva Veda*, *Brahmanas*, *Kalpasutras*, *Puranas*, Panini, Patanjali and even in the *Ramayana* and the *Mahabharata*. The tree is closely associated with the worship of the deity Shiva. In the Brihat Stotra Ratnakara it is claimed that the mere sight of the tree is enough to absolve one's sins. Harshananda Swami's *A Concise Encyclopaedia of Hinduism* says that the tree is so sacred that not even its leaves can be broken (Dwivedi 2012).

7 In Sanskrit, Palasa means both 'leaf' and 'beauty'. Its trifoliate leaves are used to represent Brahma, Vishnu and Shiva in Hindu mythology. References to it can also be found in Buddhist texts.

Queen Mahamaya is said to have grabbed a Palasa branch immediately after giving birth to Siddhartha. A staff made out of Palasa wood is also wielded by a young Brahmin while undergoing the upanayana. The Bhattra, Muria and Pengu tribes, residents of the Bastar and Raipur regions in Central India, believe that the Palasa tree has its origin in forbidden love. When the chief Chaitu Bhattra's married daughter fell in love with a Muria boy, her husband, enraged on discovering the lovers, beat them to death with a stick. He dumped their corpses in the forest. The blood from the lovers' bodies flowed into each other, and from this stream grew the first Palasa tree with flame-like red flowers (Sood et al. 2005).

8   [*Aitareya Brahmana* (Martin Haug) II, p. 74–78.] Martin Haug (1827–1876) was a German scholar of the Orient who laid the foundation of Iranian studies in the West. He taught himself Sanskrit by reading Franz Bopp's 1919 translation of the Nala and Damyanti story from the *Mahabharata*. In 1859, he accepted the position of superintendent and professor of Sanskrit at the Government College of Poona, in order to acquaint himself in a deeper manner with the practices of Hindu and Zoroastrian priests. It was during this period that he produced his translation of the *Aitareya Brahmana*.

9   The Hotar is a Brahmin priest who specializes in the study and recitation of the *Rig Veda*. Hotar can also be translated as 'pourer (of ghee)' (Jamison and Witzel 1992, 35–7). Hermann Oldenberg (1993, 214) also contends that the Hotar corresponds with the old-Iranian Avestic Zaotar, who was the reciter of Gathas in Iranian Soma sacrifices.

10 A description of the animal to be sacrificed is also given: 'They say: the animal to be offered to Agni–Soma must be of two colours, because it belongs to two deities. But this (precept) is not to be attended to. A fat animal is to be sacrificed; because

animals are of a fat complexion, and the sacrifice (if compared with them) certainly lean. When the animal is fat, the sacrifice thrives through its marrow' (Haug 1863, 80). Next, the reader is asked to disregard any injunctions to abstain from meat-eating. This is done by way of Indra's example. In order to destroy the evil Vritra, he is said to have taken the help of Soma and Agni (the gods), who in turn demanded boons after the completion of the task, which was the meat of the animal that is sacrificed. Following their example, the *Brahmana* says, the sacrifice too mustn't abstain from meat (ibid.).

11 [*Aitareya Brahmana* (Martin Haug) II, p. 84–86]

12 The *Rig Veda* lists seven central sacrificial priests: The Hotar, the Adhvaryu, Agnidh, Prasastar, Potar, Nestar and the Brahman (see p. 230 note 16, to see how the same seven priests are referred to in the *Aitareya Brahmana*). While the Hotar is the reciter of the mantras during a sacrificial offering, the Adhvaryu is the one who tends the fire and performs the physical actions necessary for the ritual. He is the chief guardian of the fire and the straw and is responsible for the purification of the tools used. The Agnidh assists the Adhvaryu in tending to the fire and deals with all the duties that are connected to its kindling and maintenance. The Prasastar is only present during animal or soma-sacrifices, and not during minor rituals. He assists the Hotar by spurring on his flow of speech and is specially related to the gods Mitra and Varuna. The Potar (purifier) and Nestar (leader) are closely related to the purifying of the Soma. Oldenberg (1993) contends that the last type, the Brahman, became an important figure only in the later Vedic period. This priest supervises the entire ritual; he does not utter a word, but piously faces the fire with his palms joined. The Brahman is the 'physician of the sacrifice' and his presence corrects any mistakes made by the rest of the priests during the ritual. It is contended that the Rig Vedic Brahman does not conform in

stature with the priestly class who later came to be known as Brahmins (Oldenberg 1993).

13 [*Aitareya Brahmana* (Martin Haug) II, p. 86]

14 Sathaye (1969) claims that in the *Aitareya Brahmana* it is the Brahman (and not the lower order priests: Hotar, Adhvaryu etc) who gets the largest and choicest portions of the animal sacrificed.

15 [As a matter of fact the Brahmins took the whole carcass. Only one leg each was given to the sacrificer and his wife.]

16 In the later section of the Brahmana a total of eighteen priests are mentioned who get to partake in the sacrifice: Udgatar, Pratihartar, Hotar, Brahma, Maitravaruna (Prasastar), Brahmanachhamsi, Adhvaryu, Pratipashatar, Neshtar, Potar, Achhavaka, Agnidhara, Atreya, Sadasya, Brahmana, Gravastut, Unnetar, and Subrahmanya. The Atreya, though, has a right to a share of meat from the sacrifice, is not considered an officiating priest (Haug 1922, 301n3). The Grihapati (householder) and his wife are entitled to the backbone, the urinal bladder and the lips. If they offer the priests a feast at the end of the sacrifice, they are allotted the left and right legs of the cow.

17 [*Aitareya Brahmana* (Martin Haug) II, p. 86–87]

18 [*Aitareya Brahmana* (Martin Haug) II, p. 86-90]

19 The word 'Adhrigu' has been variously interpreted by scholars as: 'one who possesses cows shut in a mountain stronghold', 'one who does not go disgruntled', 'one whose cow is generous and doesn't hold her milk', 'one who is not poor', 'possessor of castrated bulls, and therefore wealthy'. Several scholars also attest the word to the Avestan 'drigu' which means poor, dependent or needy. Other interpretations of 'drigu' have been a meek follower of Zoroaster who is solely dependent on the god, a disciple, and a beggar, wanderer or ascetic of the Sufi

order. In certain Sogdian translations of Buddhist texts drigu indicates a bhikshu. In Vedic literature the usage of Adhrigu is limited to the *Rig Veda*, and it is likely that authors of the later texts were not privy to the meaning of the word. Apart from referring to obscure individuals the word also describes the following gods: Indra, Agni, the Maruts, the Asvins, and Soma; notably the Adityas, Mitra or Varuna are not associated with it (Thompson 2002).

20 Though the Sanskrit term 'apapa' may refer to sinless or virtuous, Haug points out the play on words here: 'apa' also means 'Away!' and in the mantra its repetition is used to signify the name of the slaughterer (Haug 1863, 89n18).

21 Japa is the practice of repetitive chanting of the name of a god. It is usually performed with rosary beads. Japa is usually used as a form of atonement and it can be done in three manners, each with increasing order of effectiveness: vacika (soft murmur which is audible), upamasu (mouthing inaudibly), and manasa (mental repetition). The japa is only meant to be performed by the dwija castes who have undergone Vedic training (Klostermaier 2007).

22 [*Aitareya Brahmana* (Martin Haug) II, p. 87]

23 Sacrifices in Vedic literature are said to be of two orders: haviryajna and soma. The difference lies mainly in the kinds of rites that are performed. In a harivyajna animal sacrifice (pasubandha), for instance, the Brahmin offers the sacrificer a part of the food according to rituals, and leads him to stride in water that has been poured out by the priest. The soma sacrifice does not contain these rites. The soma rite is performed (as is obvious) with soma, while haviryajna is a sacrifice of milk (Thite 1970; Lidova 1994).

24 [*Aitareya Brahmana* (Martin Haug) II, p. 93]

25 [Manota means the deity to whom the offering is dedicated.]
26 [*Aitareya Brahmana* (Martin Haug) II, p. 441–42]
27 Although the *Rig Veda* does not have a rhyming scheme, each section is written in a specific metre. Each stanza has a fixed number of quarter verses (pada), generally three or four, and each pada has a fixed number of syllables. Usually padas in a stanza are of equal length and conform to a particular metre, but on occasion a single stanza can contain two or more kinds of metres. The anustup metre, for instance, contains four padas, each of which contains eight syllables. A single line in the anustup metre consists of two padas. The Brihati metre mentioned here consists of four padas and a total of thirty-six syllables. The first, second and fourth line contain eight syllables each and the third line contains twelve syllables. In the *Aitareya Brahmana*, the Brihati metre is said to be useful if someone desires wealth and glory (Griffith 1896; Haug 1863).
28 Devabhaga is one of the brothers of Vasudeva, father of Krishna in the *Mahabharata*.
29 The *Aitareya Brahmana* tries to explain away the fact that it was the human who was at the centre at this ritualistic practice. In a section which follows the rituals listed by Ambedkar, it is explicitly mentioned that the gods demanded human sacrifice. However, the 'part' of man which was fit for sacrifice leaves him and enters a horse. What follows is a series of exits and entries of the nothingness that is the 'part fit for sacrifice', which flows from horse to ox to sheep to goat to earth, from which grew rice. It is further mentioned that 'might our animal sacrifice be performed with the sacrificial part (which is contained in the rice of the Purodasa)! Might our sacrificial part be provided with the whole sacrificial essence!' (Haug 1922, 62). This was probably a long-winded way for the priests to ask their clients, without losing face, for rice to go with the meat.

30 [*Aitareya Brahmana* (Martin Haug) II, p. 80]

31 In the eighth chapter (entitled "The Cow's Walk") of his book *The Arctic Home of the Vedas* (1903), Bal Gangadhar Tilak also closely studies the cow-related rituals in the *Aitareya* and *Taittiriya Brahmanas*. He brushes past all the invocations in the text which sanction beef-consumption and instead focuses on ascertaining what the length of a year was during the writing of the *Brahmanas*. He concludes that during the time a year was considered to be ten months long. Because the ancient Indians shared this practice with the ancient Romans, Tilak concludes that this was a remnant of an ancient custom that both the Aryan races shared when they lived together in the circumpolar region (Tilak 1903, 173–84).

32 The following extracts have been taken from Georg Bühler's translation, *The Laws of Manu* (1886, 173–7). In most of his works, including *Annihilation of Caste*, Ambedkar refers to Bühler's translation and commentary published in the *Sacred Books of the East* series edited by Max Müller. The ones here are all taken from Chapter V, which Bühler calls "Lawful and Forbidden Food". Ambedkar misses some of the other allowances made in the *Manusmriti* with regard to the consumption of meat: 'V.22. Beasts and birds recommended (for consumption) may be slain by Brahmanas for sacrifices, and in order to feed those whom they are bound to maintain; for Agastya did this of old. V.23. For in ancient (times) the sacrificial cakes were (made of the flesh) of eatable beasts and birds at the sacrifices offered by Brahmanas and Kshatriyas' (Bühler 1886, 172–3). This extract is of particular interest because here we see the writers acknowledge the earlier practice of meat-consumption.

33 Prajapati, in Vedic literature, refers to the creator of the universe. There are several accounts of the creation myth. The most important one is the Purusha Sukta, in which Prajapati is

described as the primordial man (purusha) who is sacrificed, and from whose parts the world arises. In later Hinduism 'Prajapati' was a moniker for Brahma (Lochtefeld 2002). Like the epithet 'Manu' refers to a plurality of persons, 'Prajapati' too has multiple points of reference. The *Puranic Encyclopaedia* (Mani 1975) entry under this head, citing the Shanti Parva of *Mahabharata*, pluralizes the term and says: 'Creators of the world. With a view to making creation easy Brahma at first created twenty-one Prajapatis (creators). They are Brahma, Rudra, Manu, Daksa, Bhrgu, Dharma, Tapa, Yama, Marici, Angiras, Atri, Pulastya, Pulaha, Kratu, Vasistha, Paramesthi, Surya, Candra, Kardama, Krodha and Vikrita. Jalalul Haq (1997) charts the varying functions of the figure of Brahma and shows how the slow demotion and disempowerment of the god took place in order to elevate the status of the Brahmin caste. Another attendant term is the hyphenated 'Visvakarma-Prajapati', regarded as the architect of the devas who has come to be regarded as the inventor of many handicrafts and ornaments. Since the nineteenth century census operations, many artisanal communities (blacksmiths, bronze smiths, goldsmiths, carpenters and stonemasons) respectably call their jati as Viswakarma across the subcontinent; some of them even wear the janeu thread. See George Varghese (2003) and Vijaya Ramaswamy (2004).

34 In the era that preceded the writing of the *Manusmriti* the practice of yajna was pre-eminent. The domain of sacrifice was itself a metaphor for the realm of society, reflecting a cosmogony of creation, hierarchy and Himsa (violence). It was within the domain of the yajna that the 'natural' order was enacted, extolled and enforced. This was reinforced in the time of Manu by envisioning a 'natural' order of Himsa most explicitly in the 'discourse concerning "food" and "eaters"' (Doniger and Smith 1991, 17). As evidenced in Manu V.29 that Ambedkar cites, those with the power to dominate and defeat the weaker, make

the latter their 'food'. In the system where the human was able to subjugate and domesticate the other animals, the consumption of their meat was the ultimate signal of their victory. That the yajna rightfully belonged to the Brahmin and that the Chandala was outcaste from the ceremony, proves that the hierarchical order in Brahmanical society was defined by the power of Himsa, such that the upper echelons essentially 'lived on' the lower. It was the perseverance and preservation of this order that guided the writing of the *Manusmriti*. Seen thus, Manu's exhortations against the killing of animals and use of the 'disgusting' flesh (see V.48) is itself a deviation from the order that had hitherto defined social relations. The ambivalent position of meat-eating in Manu—the exhortations against consuming flesh running parallel to the imperative position in the practice of yajna—reveals *Manusmriti* as a text representative of a shift from earlier customs, yet an embattled one that is not able to fully dissociate itself from animal sacrifice and consumption. The obvious intervening influence of Buddhism was one of the shifts in emphasis from bali (embodied in the yajna) to dana. Indeed, one of the reasons for the rise of multiple Sramana systems was the hugely exploitative system of sacrifices. The ethic of Buddhist dana, which was the acceptance of any offering without complaint, became the later bhiksha and offeratory aspects of the yajna.

35 One who has undergone the ritual samavartana, the rite that 'bathes one in knowledge', is known as a Snataka. The samavartana marks the end of studenthood and is a return to home. In direct contrast to the upanayana rites which are ascetic in nature, the samavartana thrusts the individual into a life of a householder (Toomey 1976, 40–5). In the *Dharma Sutras*, Snatakas are regarded with great respect and yet the exact meaning of the term remains unclear. In several instances Snatakas are accorded the role of householders. According to

the *Dharma Sutras*, a graduate Snataka was supposed to choose any given path after his studies: a householder, a permanent student, a hermit or a mendicant ascetic. However, the *Baudhayana Dharma Sutra* made it so that only the role of the householder was appropriate after completing one's studenthood. The rest of the ashramas (paths) were turned into stages of life for the Brahmin, to be taken up after fulfilling his duties as a householder (Lubin 2018, 114). In the *Manusmriti*, a Snataka is subsumed within the larger category of a householder; yet the particularity of their position in the *Mahabharata* and even in Asvaghosha's *Buddhacharita* (where both the Pandavas and the Buddha disguise themselves as Snatakas in order to enter a city without being questioned) point to the special status of Snataka as a particularly esteemed male principal in ancient Indian Brahmanical society (Lubin 2018, 113–24).

36 [Manu, 209] Ambedkar here mistakenly gives us the section number rather than the page number. The exact verse is as follows: (IV.209) 'Nor food at which a cow has smelt, nor particularly that which has been offered by an invitation to all comers, nor that (given) by a multitude or by harlots, nor that which is declared to be bad by a learned (man)' (Bühler 1886, 161). It is preceded and succeeded by injunctions against food at which a slayer of Brahmins has looked, touched by a menstruating woman, offered by a thief, musician, carpenter, usurer, performer of Srauta sacrifices, miser or one bound in fetters (ibid.). P.V. Kane (1941b, 775) cites V.128 from the *Manusmriti* which explicitly states that a cow is sacred in all its limbs except its mouth to explain the above injunction.

37 [Ibid., 38] Verse taken from (IV.38): 'Let him not step over a rope to which a calf is tied, let him not run when it rains, and let him not look at his own image in water; that is a settled rule' (Bühler 1886, 135).

38 [Ibid., 45] (IV.45): 'Let him not eat, dressed with one garment only; let him not bathe naked; let him not void urine on a road, on ashes, or in a cow-pen' (Bühler 1886, 136).

39 [Ibid., 48] (IV.48): 'Let him never void faeces or urine, facing the wind, or a fire, or looking towards a Brahmana, the sun, water, or cows' (Bühler 1886, 136).

40 [Ibid., 58] (IV.58): 'Let him keep his right arm uncovered in a place where a sacred fire is kept, in a cow-pen, in the presence of Brahmanas, during the private recitation of the Veda, and at meals' (Bühler 1886, 138).

41 [Ibid., 59] (IV.59): 'Let him not interrupt a cow who is suckling (her calf), nor tell anybody of it. A wise man, if he sees a rainbow in the sky, must not point it out to anybody' (Bühler 1886, 138).

42 [Ibid., 70] Ambedkar points to the wrong verse here. The above content is found at (IV.72): 'Let him not wrangle; let him not wear a garland over (his hair). To ride on the back of cows (or of oxen) is anyhow a blameable act' (Bühler 1886, 140). In the same page the following instruction for a Brahmin can be found, (IV.70): '...let him not do anything that is useless...'. A high achievement of subcontinental philosophy indeed.

43 [Ibid., 162] (IV.162): 'Let him never offend the teacher who initiated him, nor him who explained the Veda, nor his father and mother, nor (any other) Guru, nor cows, nor Brahmanas, nor any men performing austerities' (Bühler 1886, 154).

44 [Ibid., 142] (IV.142): 'A Brahmana who is impure must not touch with his hand a cow, a Brahmana, or fire; nor, being in good health, let him look at the luminaries in the sky, while he is impure' (Bühler 1886, 151).

45 On reading the original texts which Ambedkar paraphrases in the above guidelines for the Snataka, it is clear that the conclusion he draws here, that the cow was considered impure,

is a bit of a stretch. By this logic even water, fire and fellow Brahmins would have to be considered impure by a Snataka. At most, it can be said that the current understanding of 'purity' and 'impurity' could not be applied to the cow during the time of the conception of *Manusmriti*. Further, it seems unnecessary for Ambedkar to establish that cows were considered impure by Manu; the other evidence he gathers here points to the reactionary and uneasy relationship of Brahmanism with cows.

46   Ambedkar here renders the end of the extract (Bühler 1886, 75) as, 'present of a cow (the honey-mixture)', where as in the original it is given as, 'with (the present of) a cow (and the honey-mixture).' In the Doniger and Smith translation (1991, 43) the verse is given as: 'When he is recognized as one who has, by fulfilling his own duties, received the legacy of the Veda from his father, he should first be seated on a couch, adorned with garlands, and honoured with (an offering made from the milk of) a cow.' Given the differences in all three versions, it is difficult to see how beef is being offered to the honourable student. However, Smith and Doniger offer a commentary on the verse: 'The offering made from a cow is the madhuparka, the honey-mixture, referred to in 3.119–20.' In the verse 3.119–20, details about the contents of the Madhuparka aren't given and instead it is mentioned that the Madhuparka should be offered during the time of a sacrifice. Given the complex history of the contents of the Madhuparka (see p. 156–7), it is not easy to completely rule out that beef is being offered to the Snataka in the above verse; perhaps there is an element of translator's bias in ascertaining the contents of the Madhuparka.

47   From Bühler (1886, 172).

48   The verse that follows states: (V.19): 'A twice-born man who knowingly eats mushrooms, a village-pig, garlic, a village-cock, onions, or leeks, will become an outcast' (Bühler 1886, 172).

49 In Vedic Hinduism, mortal sins are known as a Mahapataka, whereas minor sins are called Upapataka. See p. 245–6 note 57. Sin is inextricably tied with the concept of dharma in Hinduism. In her paper, "The Dharma of Ethics, the Ethics of Dharma: Quizzing the Ideals of Hinduism", Aarti Dhand (2002) tries to extract an ethics which is common to all people irrespective of identity, in Hindu texts. Dhand concedes that most *Dharmasastra* texts, which are clearly texts of moral conduct, have no guidelines in a general sense but are aimed at policing behaviour specific to identities, including caste and gender. However, she claims that it is more valuable to look at myths—the figures presented in them and the ideals they represent—in order to glean the general moral outlook of a society. She fails to mention the incredibly casteist and misogynistic nature of these myths and how the 'Principles of Right' that can be extracted from them are by their nature embedded in caste superiority and Brahmanical patriarchy. Needless to say, the concept of 'sin' for a Hindu is tied to the non-fulfilment of one's dharma, which is necessarily dictated by one's caste and gender.

50 Bühler 1886, 441. A similar injunction is found in (IX.235–9): 'The slayer of a Brahmana, (a twice-born man) who drinks (the spirituous liquor called) Sura, he who steals (the gold of a Brahmana), and he who violates a Guru's bed, must each and all be considered as men who committed mortal sins (mahapataka)./ On those four even, if they do not perform a penance, let him inflict corporal punishment and fines in accordance with the law./ For violating a Guru's bed, (the mark of) a female part shall be (impressed on the forehead with a hot iron); for drinking (the spirituous liquor called) Sura, the sign of a tavern; for stealing (the gold of a Brahmana), a dog's foot; for murdering a Brahmana, a headless corpse./ Excluded from all fellowship at meals, excluded from all sacrifices, excluded from instruction and from matrimonial alliances, abject and excluded from

all religious duties, let them wander over (this) earth./ Such (persons) who have been branded with (indelible) marks must be cast off by their paternal and maternal relations, and receive neither compassion nor a salutation; that is the teaching of Manu' (Bühler 1886, 383–4).

51 Ambedkar slightly alters the verse here. In the Bühler original it reads: 'Slaying kine, sacrificing for those who are unworthy to sacrifice, adultery, selling oneself, casting off one's teacher, mother, father, or son, giving up the (daily) study of the Veda, and neglecting the (sacred domestic) fire' (Bühler 1886, 442). Bühler offers two interpretations of the 'selling oneself' in the verse; it could refer to the act of selling oneself for money into slavery, alternatively, it could mean 'the selling of forbidden merchandise' (ibid.).

52 Manu also offers penances suitable for minor sins which cause the loss of caste (IX.109–11): 'He who has committed a minor offence by slaying a cow (or bull) shall drink during (the first) month (a decoction of) barley-grains; having shaved all his hair, and covering himself with the hide (of the slain cow), he must live in a cow-house./ During the two (following) months he shall eat a small (quantity of food) without any factitious salt at every fourth meal-time, and shall bathe in the urine of cows, keeping his organs under control./ During the day he shall follow the cows and, standing upright, inhale the dust (raised by their hoofs); at night, after serving and worshipping them, he shall remain in the (posture, called) virasana./ Controlling himself and free from anger, he must stand when they stand, follow them when they walk, and seat himself when they lie down./ (When a cow is) sick, or is threatened by danger from thieves, tigers, and the like, or falls, or sticks in a morass, he must relieve her by all possible means:/ In heat, in rain, or in cold, or when the wind blows violently, he must not seek to shelter himself, without (first) sheltering the cows according to

his ability./ Let him not say (a word), if a cow eats (anything) in his own or another's house or field or on the threshing-floor, or if a calf drinks (milk)./ The slayer of a cow who serves cows in this manner, removes after three months the guilt which he incurred by killing a cow' (Bühler 1886, 453–4). Comparing this with the simple (though brutal) nature of the punishment meted out for mortal sins (p. 239 note 49) reveals the highly convoluted and bureaucratic nature of the punishment in question. It is bureaucratic in the sense that it resembles how one is bogged down by paperwork and procedures in modern society. It is worth considering whether this was to dissuade a populace, already habituated to cow-slaughter, by inconveniencing them from pursuing it; not through fear of consequences, but because of the very inconvenient and irritating nature of the punishments.

53 [Yaj. III. 227 and III 234.] It is unclear what in the *Yajnavalkya Smriti* Ambedkar is referring to here. The chapter he refers to here (Chapter III) mostly deals with guidelines pertaining to wedding rituals, with minimal references to the cow. In chapter VII we find the following: 'Yajnavalkya (CLXXX): That evildoer who slays beasts unlawfully shall dwell in horrible hell as many days as there are hairs on the body of the slain beast' (Vidyarnava 1918, 274). In chapter V, which details the duties of a householder, we find 'lawful' examples of meat consumption in two passages entitled "Beef-offering to the honoured guest" and "The Annual Feast on Beef". The first one goes: 'Let him show a learned Brahmana, a big bull or a big goat as well as good treatment, precedence, sweet food and kind speech' (Vidyarnava 1918, 229), and the second: 'Once a year Argha is to be given to the Snataka, the Acharya, the king, the friend and the son-in-law, again the Ritvija at each sacrifice' (ibid.). In the translation it appears 'sweet food' and 'Argha' are used as substitutes for Madhuparka. For the contentious nature of a Madhuparka offering see p. 156–7.

54 The *Vedanta Sutra* (or the *Brahma Sutra*), along with the *Upanishads* and Bhagavad Gita, is considered a canonical text of the Vedanta school of philosophy. The *Vedanta Sutra*, attributed to Badarayana, was written around 200 CE, to counter the dualistic interpretations of the *Upanishads*, promulgated by such Sankhya philosophers. It was also opposed to the adherence to and reduction of religion to the ritualistic pronouncements of the *Brahmanas* by such schools as the Purva Mimamsa. *Vedanta Sutra* was born of the necessity of systematizing contradictory views and philosophies that rose out of varying ritualistic interpretations of the *Vedas* and the contradictions inherent in the *Vedas* themselves. The result had been, for a long time, the flourishing of pragmatic decisions on practices that dealt with ambiguities as was most appropriate for particular situations (all, of course, united by the singular aim of upholding Brahmanical supremacy). Turning away from the centrality of karma (where no other higher being can be imagined as outside the karmic cycle), Vedanta philosophy puts the 'Brahman', the singular principal, at the centre of being. The most popular interpretation of this theory, that of Adi Sankara, takes this Brahman as the monotheistic being (Advaita) which permeates the universe and the multiplicity of appearances that we encounter as mere manifestations of this being in various forms. Later philosophers equated this supreme being (Brahman) with existent gods from Hindu mythology: Ramanuja and Madhava termed it as Vishnu while Srikantha referred to it as Shiva (Thibaut 1890; Hiriyanna 1993).

55 The section Ambedkar refers to here (II.1.28) does not explicitly deal with sacrifices. It is titled, "For thus it is in the (individual) Self also, and various (creations exist in gods &c.)" and it goes thus: 'Nor is there any reason to find fault with the doctrine that there can be a manifold creation in the one Self, without destroying its character. For Scripture teaches us that there exists a mul-

tiform creation in the one Self of a dreaming person, "There are no chariots in that state, no horses, no roads, but he himself creates chariots, horses, and roads" (Br. Up. IV, 3, 10). In ordinary life too multiform creations, elephants, horses, and the like are seen to exist in gods, &c., and magicians without interfering with the unity of their being. Thus a multiform creation may exist in Brahman also, one as it is, without divesting it of its character of unity' (Thibaut 1890, 352–3). A supplementary look at (I.1.4) makes Ambedkar's case stronger. In this passage it is first stated that: 'we [cannot] conclude the purport of these passages [which tell us of the nature of the Brahman] to be the intimation of the nature of agents, divinities, &c. (connected with acts of religious duty); for there are certain scriptural passages which preclude all actions, actors, and fruits' (Thibaut 1890, 22). This tells us that the descriptions of the Brahman cannot be found in those passages of the *Veda* which tell us about direct experiences of agents in the world, which include sacrifices. 'It is further known from Scripture that those only who perform sacrifices proceed, in consequence of the pre-eminence of their knowledge and meditation, on the northern path (of the sun)' (Thibaut 1890, 27). In effect, things that are termed as worldly experiences have a separation via concealment from the Brahman, even though the former is contained within the latter. The Sutra goes on to argue that the injunctive nature of the *Vedas* is what furnishes the reason for one to strive towards the knowledge of the Brahman; this injunctive nature is deduced from the fact that the *Vedas* also demand sacrificial action from their (Brahmin) subjects (Thibaut 1890, 23–4). Juxtaposing this against the passage Ambedkar picks out, it is clear that the *Vedanta Sutra* grants worldly actions their independence, and acts such as sacrifices which were demanded by the *Vedas* have no bearing on our existence as a part of the Brahman. One need not rely on the Vedanta edifice to justify sacrifices; rather one must (blindly) continue to perform them simply because that is what the *Vedas* demand.

56 [Kane's *Dharmasastras II. Part II.* p. 776] Kane, like Ambedkar, points to the strangeness of the fact that from being a commonplace thing cow-slaughter completely vanished from Brahmanical ideology after a time. He states: 'It appears that the causes that led on to the giving up of flesh at least by some people were many, the foremost being the metaphysical conception that one Supreme Entity pervades the whole universe, that all life was one, and that even the meanest insect was a manifestation of the divine Essence and that philosophical truths would not dawn upon the man who was not restrained, free from crude appetites and had not universal kindliness and sympathy' (Kane 1941b, 775–6). This is the section Ambedkar refers to above. Kane goes on to give more possible explanations for the move away from cow-slaughter. He says, 'Another motive for the insistence on ahimsa was probably the idea of defilement caused by eating flesh [...] Sahkha asks people to give up flesh, wine, onions and garlic because the body is built up on the food eaten' (ibid.). Why such defilement came to be tied with what was an important aspect of Hindu life is not offered. A weak line of argument he does provide is the fact that once the Aryans spread to Middle, East and South India climactic conditions made food plenty, resulting in no need for meat consumption. However, he categorically states that the 'notion that the eater of flesh would be devoured by the eaten in the next birth had nothing to do with the early stages of the doctrine of ahimsa, though by Manu and others that notion was later on exploited to emphasize its importance'(ibid.). He also provides reference to the *Brahadaranyaka Upanishad*, which contains both references to the transmigration of the soul and to cow-sacrifices, as does Ambedkar in the passage that follows.

57 The transmigration of the soul or metempsychosis is a thematic found within a variety of religious and spiritual traditions. In Vedic discourse—both philosophical and spiritual—time is considered to function cyclically, and it is governed by the conceptions of samsara, karma and moksha. It is believed that upon the death of a being, its soul does not cease to exist, but is transferred, after an appropriate time, to another entity. This is called samsara, and karma, the doings and experiences of one's life, is said to define the station—either low or high—of the next birth. The universe, caught in such an endless cycle, is understood as one characterized by suffering, liberation from which can only be achieved in the form of moksha, a complete salvation (exit) from this material world. The Buddha rejects the very existence of the soul. As Ambedkar explains in his *The Buddha and His Dhamma* (1956), for the Buddha, 'there is no such thing as a soul. That is why his theory of the soul is called Anatta, i.e., non-soul' (Ambedkar 1992b, 262). The notion of karma is central to caste society. Karma has three underlying features: 1) the notion of causality, 2) the ethical element (that actions have their allied effects, either good or bad), and 3) rebirth. The origin of belief in karma in connection to rebirth can be traced back to pre-Vedic tribal societies, though it is difficult to ascertain with surety. In the *Vedas*, sacrifices were known as 'karma'. The *Brahadaranyaka Upanishad* says pointedly that it is the karma which determines one's good or evil rebirth (Doniger 1980). In *The Buddha and His Dhamma*, Ambedkar produces his own interpretation of the Buddhist conception of karma. Unlike in Hinduism, one's actions do not produce an impress upon one's soul according to Buddhism. This is because the Buddha preached about the nonexistence of the soul. Unlike in Hinduism where sin is accrued to an individual's soul and where the individual is left to deal with this sin alone, Ambedkar produces a materialist and social reading of Buddha's notion

of transference of karma. The sin or suffering accrued from an action is the burden not of an individual's soul but of the situation as a whole. Parents who are sinful bring the child into an environment which is sinful and thus the burden of that sin, its suffering, is felt by the child too. Not because of divine jurisprudence, but because of the imbalanced nature of the life-world into which the child has been thrust. In this case, the Buddha positions the individual in the larger context of society, where he or she is not cut off from the shared nature of ethics (or the lack of it), he or she is not on a personal quest of deliverance in the postponed life-to-come, but rather is responsible for *this* life, of making the now free of sin. The individual is granted agency to act on his or her situation and is not made slave to the otherworldly 'past' of sin. Rather he or she is thrust into a situation, which is already in sin and then is forced to confront it (Ambedkar 2014, 337–44)

58 According to the *Brahadaranyaka Upanishad* the quality of reincarnation is contingent on the quality of deeds commited in the previous life. By general consensus, it is the oldest of the *Upanishads*. This is supported by at least four pieces of evidence: its length, its lack of organization, its archaic language, and its relationship to earlier Vedic texts. The opening passage gives an extended comparison between the world and the sacrificial horse, showing clear parallels with the earlier *Brahmana* literature. Moreover, by its very name (literally, 'great forest book'), the *Brahadaranyaka Upanishad* points to a transition from the *Aranyaka* ('forest books') literature, which followed *Brahmana* literature. This *Upanishad* first addresses many of the questions raised in later texts and is therefore an important source for the development of the tradition. Unlike most of the later *Upanishads*, it is written in prose rather than as poetry, with the instruction often in the form of dialogue between various speakers. See Olivelle 1998.

59 In VI.2, Svetaketa Aruneya, a recurring character throughout the *Upanishads* who represents a seeker of knowledge to whom wisdoms are bestowed, learns about the course of the soul and its reincarnations from Pravahana Jaibali, the king of Panchala. He compares the various worldly manifestations with the sacrificial fire. For instance, the rain-cloud is compared to the sacrificial fire, the year then is said to be its fuel, thundering clouds its smoke, lightning its flame, thunder-bolts its coals, and hailstones its sparks. In a similar vein the world, the seasons, the man and the woman too are compared to the sacrificial ritual. From the woman, purusa (man) arises and he lives and dies, and in the end is consumed by the sacrificial fire. From this flame light arises and man merges into day (which is made of light). From the day he becomes months and from there he enters the world of the gods... This cycle is shown to continue wherein man's connection with all the various facets of the world are revealed and his existence is shown to be cyclical. However only two kinds of people are said to be able to enter into such a wondrous cycle: those who possess the knowledge of this cycle and therefore truly worship with faith, such a man is freed from the cycle and can reside in Brahma forever. Then there are the ones who by 'sacrificial offering, charity, and austerity conquer the worlds' (Hume 1921, 163). Such people can re-enter the cycle of life as men. The rest 'know not these two ways, become crawling and flying insects and whatever there is here that bites' (Hume 1921, 160–3)

60 The above sacrifice can be found at (VI.4.18) in the *Brahadaranyaka Upanishad*. It says: 'Now, in case one wishes, "That a son, learned, famed, a frequenter of council-assemblies, a speaker of discourse desired to be heard, be born to me! That he be able to repeat all the Vedas! That he attain the full length of life!" they two should have rice boiled with meat and should eat it prepared with ghee. They two are likely to beget [him],

with meat, either veal or beef' (Hume 1921, 171). It is preceded by requirements to be fulfilled in order to attain a white son who is able to repeat one *Veda* and live a full life, a tawny son with reddish-brown eyes who can repeat two *Vedas* and live a full life, a swarthy son with red eyes who can repeat three *Vedas* and live a full life, and a learned daughter who may live a full life. For the conception of the last four kinds of offsprings the consumption of meat during the sacrifice is not required (VI.4.14–7, Hume 1921, 170–1).

61 In his essay "Revolution and Counter-Revolution", Ambedkar writes of 'Aryan society' being 'steeped in the worst kind of debauchery; social, religious, and spiritual' (Ambedkar 1987, 153), the revolution instituted by the emergent dhamma of Gautama Buddha, and the counter-revolution unleashed by the Brahmins in order to regain their position. After the Buddha's radical intervention turned the tide against Brahmanism, Emperor Asoka promulgated the Buddhist ethic of dhamma, and along these lines outlawed the killing of animals. The consequences for the Brahmanical practice of the yajna—since it revolved primarily around the ritual sacrifice of scores of animals—was dire. Ambedkar argues that the counter-revolution was instituted by Pushyamitra Sunga's (185–149 BCE) usurpation of the Maurya throne, after which he carried out the Ashvamedha yajna or horse sacrifice. Ambedkar writes: 'Indeed it is quite possible that the *Manusmriti* was composed at the command of Pushyamitra himself and forms the book of the philosophy of Brahmanism... the one and only object of Pushyamitra's revolution was to destroy Buddhism and re-establish Bramhanism' (Ambedkar 1987, 273). The *Smriti* was repurposed such that it divinely ordained regicide, but only by a Brahmin.

62 A point to remember is that society at the time was necessarily divided along feudal-class lines, and that hierarchy was a given. Under such conditions, in order to maintain power and ruler-

ship, it was natural that the monarchy sought out Brahmanical legitimation. Though Ambedkar labels Buddhism as revolutionary and Brahmanism as counter-revolutionary, he does not highlight the counter-revolutionary organization of ancient Indian society in general, which included the Buddhist element. Uma Chakravarti (1987) writes of the Buddha's attempt at creating an egalitarian social order, which was restricted to his monastic sangha, an organization over which he had total purview. The sangha had a heterodox representation as far as caste was concerned, and the hierarchy of the bhikkus who comprised it was set along the lines of seniority. This experimental organization did provide an alternative to the existent structures in society, but their effectiveness and legitimate challenge to power structures has been questioned by many. Chakravarti argues that the Buddhist conception of kula (divided along the lines of Brahamanas, Khattiyas and Gahapatis) did pose an opposition to the Brahmanical four-varna order. In the Buddhist schema the Khattiyas were even considered superior to the Brahmanas (see p. 178–81 note 45). However, it can be argued that the problem of the division of labour remained untackled, thus weakening the revolutionary potential of Buddhism. See p. 223–5 note 1 for an exegesis on Ambedkar's particular conception of revolution and counter-revolution.

63 Gail Omvedt's survey of the ancient subcontinental landscape finds that Buddhism was deeply rooted in the imperial traditions that emerged in the first millennium CE, and even earlier. In the kingdoms of Kosala and Magadha, the rulers Pasenadi, Bimbisara and Ajatasattu were all Buddhist 'sympathizers'. The region surrounding Magadha, long held to be the ancient imperial capital of the subcontinent, 'was considered by Brahmanic literature to be a *mlechha* (barbarian) land where Vedic sacrifices and Brahmanic rituals were not performed' (Omvedt 2003, 119). The first millennium CE, then, was an 'overwhelm-

ingly Buddhist' domain. The 'Buddhist vihars, stupas, caves including caitya halls and monasteries, statues' all predated the Brahmanic temples, which only first emerged in the time of the Guptas, the third century CE onwards (118).

64 According to Robert DeCaroli (2004), this adoption of image worship in Buddhism was a direct result of the loss of royal patronage which resulted in its having to ingratiate itself with a multiplicity of religious practices which did not fall within the pale of Brahmanism (see p. 135–6 note 23). This is surmised from archaeological evidences of statues of spirit deities: 'the visual and textual evidence for most types of spirit-deity worship points to a widespread set of practices that centered on images or altars (benches, thrones, etc.) set in fenced enclosures to which people turned in times of need or to mark important transitions (such as the birth of a child)' (DeCaroli 2004, 68). The influence of these diverse practices on present-day Hinduism is palpable: 'the wide-eyed gazes seen on all the images [of spirit-deity sculptures provided by DeCaroli] may suggest a link to modern Hindu *darsan* (ritually seeing and being seen by the deity), which would further confirm their function as objects of ritual devotion. This link with Hindu *darsan* is not totally unexpected. Coomaraswamy suggested years ago that Hindu bhakti practices found their origins in the worship of spirit-deities' (63). As Buddhism integrated itself into these religions, the role of such deities and yakshas was brought into subservience of the Buddha: they are often represented in sculptures and architectural structures as paying obeisance to the Buddha (see DeCaroli, Chapter 3: "Set in Stone", 59–86, for a comprehensive list of all such structures). Still it is to be remembered that 'portraying spirit-deities in sculptural form was by no means a Buddhist innovation. As we have seen, images of spirit-deities are among the oldest sculptural images found on the subcontinent. Yet by assembling these spirit-deities from across vast distances only

to represent them as impositions of secondary importance, the *samgha* was making a bold statement that challenged the very foundations of spirit-deity worship in India' (76).

65 Wendy Doniger (2010) claims that the first substantial cluster of Hindu temples were built around the sixth century CE under the rule of the Pallavas in Southern India. 'Building temples may have been, in part, a response to the widespread Buddhist practice of building stupas or to the Jaina and Buddhist veneration of statues of enlightened figures. Hindus vied with Buddhists in competitive fund-raising, and financing temples or stupas became a bone of contention' (2010, 345). This focus on temple-building led to the vision of the rulers becoming increasingly grand and ultimately culminating in temple towns and cities. It must also be noted that workers who sculpted the Buddhist Ajanta caves, emigrated southwards when the demand for Hindu architecture was high in the southern kingdoms (2010, 345).

66 Kancha Ilaiah elaborates on this point in *God as Political Philosopher: Buddha's Challenge to Brahminism* (2001) arguing that the mindless need to offer cattle to yajnas came to be slowly opposed by the Sudra and Vaishya communities that not only were influenced by the Buddha but also had an agricultural and economic interest in saving cattle. The burgeoning population meant that society had to move beyond shifting cultivation and this meant cattle were needed more for agriculture than for yajnas. 'Such a situation gave rise to conflict between the Brahmin class on the one hand and the Kshatriya and Vaisya classes on the other' (2001, 52).

67 Ilaiah likewise argues that the Buddha's 'limited non-violence and his opposition to killing cattle were used to convert the Brahmanical forces to vegetarianism and he himself was co-opted into one of the dasavataras, becoming merely a manifestation of Vishnu' (2001, 224).

68 Yuan Chwang, alternatively known as Hsuan Tsang and Xuan-zang, was a Buddhist monk who travelled from China to India in the seventh century. In his sixteen years of travel across the subcontinent, he recorded descriptions of the interaction between the separate forms of Buddhism practised in India and China (Watters 1904). For the import of his work in the present context, see p. 142–4 note 33.

69 Thomas Watters (1840–1901), served in many administrative positions in British China. Apart from producing a commentary and translation of Hsuan Tsang's travelogue, he also translated Lao Tzu, Confucius and several other Chinese texts.

70 [Yuan Chwang (1904) Vol. I p. 55] Thomas Watters' *On Yuan Chwang's Travels in India 629–645* was edited by T.W. Rhys Davids and S.W. Bushell and was only published after his passing in 1904.

71 Vaisali was the capital city of the Vajjian Confederacy of Mithila, one of the sixteen Mahajanapadas of the ancient Indian subcontinent (in the sixth to fourth centuries BCE). The Jain Tirthankara, Mahavira, is said to have been born and raised in Vaisali. It was also here that the Buddha delivered his last sermon in 483 BCE, and where, a hundred years thereafter, the Second Buddhist Council was convened (383 BCE). Vaisali is considered an important location in Jain and Buddhist traditions.

72 The *Ssu-fen-lu* or the *Shi-bun-ritsu* is a translation of the *Dharmagupta Vinaya* by Buddhayasas, a Sramana from present-day Kabul, and Choh-fo-nien in 405 CE. It was a central Vinaya text studied in China and Japan, and it gained prominence through its adoption by the Kai Ritsu school established by Dosen Risshi in eighth-century Japan (Petzold 1995). *Vinayas* are rulebooks based on the Buddha's teachings which are meant to be guides to live an ethical Buddhist life. The numerous splits and cultural differences owing to Buddhism's vast geographical reach led to

the creation of several *Vinaya* texts. The Dharmagupta school too arose from a split in the Mahasaka tradition; it was founded in the third century BCE by Dharmagupta who was a follower of the Buddha's disciple Maudgalyayana. The *Dharmagupta Vinaya* presently only exists in the form of Chinese translations (Heirman 2002).

73 Arguing how the world-renouncing Buddhist and Jain Sramanas challenged the 'fundamental assumptions of Vedism', Doniger and Smith write in their introduction to *The Laws of Manu* (1991): 'Vegetarianism was far more than an interesting new dietary custom. It was a focal point for what might be called a revaluation of all values in ancient India… at about the same time as the composition of Manu, the full extent of the reversal of Vedic ideals is striking' (xxxiii).

74 To corroborate, Smith (1909) writes: 'It is noteworthy that Asoka's rules do not forbid the slaughter of cows, which, apparently, continued to be lawful. The problem of the origin of the intense feeling of reverence for the cow, now felt by all Hindus, is a very curious one and still unsolved. The early brahmans did not share the sentiment' (58).

75 Mahapataka denotes one of the Four Great Crimes in the Vedic tradition. They are: murdering a Brahmin (brahmahatya), stealing a Brahmin's gold (steya), drinking liquor (surapana), or committing adultery with the wife of one's guru (gurutalpaga). Committing these crimes would result in the performer being ostracized or death due to the severity of the expiations (prayaschitta) (Klostermaier 2007, 141–2).

76 The Guptas were the imperial family of the Gupta dynasty, which ruled a large tract of the subcontinent from 240 CE to 590 CE. Its capital was at Pataliputra, today known as Patna, but was subsequently moved to Allahabad. The Indo-Gangetic basin formed the core of their territory and their rule is associ-

ated with a revival of Hinduism. The force of this revival lay in the state patronage provided to the Brahmanical order by the Gupta kings. They are characterized as devotees of the god Vishnu, and their efforts at temple construction and religious endowments point to a concerted effort of state patronage towards this religion. One of their court poets was Kalidasa, a master of the elite language, Sanskrit (Kosambi 2008, 192–8).

77 [Some Aspects of Ancient Indian Culture (1940), p. 78–79] Devadutta Ramkrishna Bhandarkar (1875–1950) was an epigraphist and archaeologist, and an academic of prominence. His father, Ramchandra Gopal Bhandarkar, was an important figure in the study of ancient Indian texts. The Bhandarkar Orient Research Institute was founded in 1917 after R.G. Bhandarkar donated a large collection of his books for public use. The institute encouraged several scholars, including P.V. Kane, to come out with their studies and translations of ancient Indian texts. R.G. Bhandarkar was a reformist Hindu affiliated with the Prarthana Samaj; the Samaj's stated goals included abolition of Untouchability and child marriage, and support for widow remarriage and women's education (Kane 1930; *Times of India*, 12 July 2003).

78 Arhant is used to denote a person who has achieved enlightenment. It also describes the highest stage of enlightenment in Mahayana Buddhism and is often used as by-word for the Buddha himself; several schools, however, separate an arhant from the Buddha (Warder 2004, 314). 'Arhant [is] used by the Buddhists for the 'perfected one' who has acquired enlightenment, attained extinction, in the Tipitaka [it is] usually synonymous with samyaksambuddha, 'perfectly enlightened', i.e. a title of the Buddha' (2004, 67).

Chapter XIV

Why should beef-eating make broken men Untouchable?

The stoppage of beef-eating by the Brahmins and the non-Brahmins and the continued use thereof by the Broken Men had produced a situation which was different from the old. This difference lay in the fact that while in the old situation everybody ate beef, in the new situation one section did not and another did. The difference was a glaring difference. Everybody could see it. It divided society as nothing else did before. All the same, this difference need not have given rise to such extreme division of society as is marked by Untouchability. It could have remained a social difference. There are many cases where different sections of the community differ in their foods. What one likes the other dislikes and yet this difference does not create a bar between the two.

There must therefore be some special reason why in India the difference between the Settled Community and the Broken Men in the matter of beef-eating created a bar between the two. What can that be? The answer is that if beef-eating had remained a secular affair—a mere matter of individual taste—such a bar between those who ate beef and those who did not wouldn't have arisen. Unfortunately beef-eating, instead of being treated as a purely secular matter, was made a matter of religion. This happened because the Brahmins made the cow a sacred animal. This made beef-eating a sacrilege. The Broken Men being guilty of sacrilege necessarily became beyond the pale of society.

The answer may not be quite clear to those who have no idea of the scope and function of religion in the life of the society. They may ask: Why should religion make such a difference? It will be clear if the following points regarding the scope and function of religion are borne in mind.

To begin with the definition[1] of religion. There is one universal feature which characterises all religions. This feature lies in religion being a unified system of beliefs and practices which (1) relate to sacred things and (2) which unite into one single community all those who adhere to them.[2] To put it slightly differently, there are two elements in every religion. One is that religion is inseparable from sacred things. The other is that religion is a collective thing inseparable from society.[3]

The first element in religion presupposes a classification of all things, real and ideal, which are the subject matter of man's thought, into two distinct classes which are generally designated by two distinct terms the *sacred* and the *profane*, popularly spoken of as secular.[4]

This defines the scope of religion. For understanding the function of religion the following points regarding things sacred should be noted:

> The first thing to note is that things sacred are not merely higher than or superior in dignity and status to those that are profane. They are just different. The sacred and the profane do not belong to the same class. There is a complete dichotomy between the two. As Prof Durkheim observes:[5]

> The traditional opposition of good and bad is nothing beside this; for the good and the bad are only two opposed species of the same class, namely, morals, just as sickness and health are two different aspects of the same order of facts, life, while the sacred and the profane have always and everywhere been conceived by the human mind as two distinct classes, as two worlds between which there is nothing in common.[6]

The curious may want to know what has led men to see in this world this dichotomy between the sacred and the profane. We must however refuse to enter into this discussion as it is unnecessary for the immediate purpose we have in mind.[7]

Confining ourselves to the issue the next thing to note is that the circle of sacred objects is not fixed. Its extent varies infinitely from religion to religion. Gods and spirits are not the only sacred things. A rock, a tree, an animal, a spring, a pebble, a piece of wood, a house, in a word anything can be sacred.

Things sacred are always associated with interdictions otherwise called *taboos*. To quote Prof. Durkheim again:[8]

> Sacred things are those which the interdictions protect and isolate; profane things, those to which these interdictions are applied and which must remain at a distance from the first.

Religious interdicts take multiple forms.[9] Most important of these is the interdiction on contact. The interdiction on contact rests upon the principle that the profane should never touch the sacred. Contact may be established in a variety of ways other than touch. A look is a means of contact. That is why the sight of sacred things is forbidden to the profane in certain cases. For instance, women are not allowed to see certain things which are regarded as sacred. The word (i.e., the breath which forms part of man and which spreads outside him) is another means of contact. That is why the profane is forbidden to address the sacred things or to utter them. For instance, the *Veda* must be uttered only by the Brahmin and not by the Shudra. An exceptionally intimate contact is the one resulting from the absorption of food. Hence comes the interdiction against eating the sacred animals or vegetables.[10]

The interdictions relating to the sacred are not open to discussion. They are beyond discussion and must be accepted without question. The sacred is 'untouchable' in the sense that it is beyond the pale of debate. All that one can do is to respect and obey.

Lastly the interdictions relating to the sacred are binding on all. They are not maxims. They are injunctions. They are obligatory but not in the ordinary sense of the word. They partake of the nature of a categorical imperative.[11] Their breach is more than a crime. It is a sacrilege.

The above summary should be enough for an understanding of the scope and function of religion. It is unnecessary to enlarge upon the subject further. The analysis of the working of the laws of the sacred which is the core of religion should enable any one to see that my answer to the question why beef-eating should make the Broken Men untouchables is the correct one. All that is necessary to reach the answer I have proposed is to read the analysis of the working of the laws of the sacred with the cow as the sacred object. It will be found that Untouchability is the result of the breach of the interdiction against the eating of the sacred animal, namely, the cow.

As has been said, the Brahmins made the cow a sacred animal. They did not stop to make a difference between a living cow and a dead cow. The cow was sacred, living or dead. Beef-eating was not merely a crime. If it was only a crime it would have involved nothing more than punishment. Beef-eating was made a sacrilege. Anyone who treated the cow as profane was guilty of sin and unfit for association.[12] The Broken Men who continued to eat beef became guilty of sacrilege.

Once the cow became sacred and the Broken Men continued to eat beef, there was no other fate left for the Broken Men except to be treated [as] unfit for association, i.e., as Untouchables.

Before closing the subject it may be desirable to dispose of possible objections to the thesis. Two such objections to the thesis appear obvious. One is what evidence is there that the Broken Men did eat the flesh of the dead cow. The second is why they did not give up beef-eating when the Brahmins and the non-Brahmins abandoned it. These questions have an important bearing upon the theory of the origin of Untouchability advanced in this book and must therefore be dealt with.

The first question is relevant as well as crucial. If the Broken Men were eating beef from the very beginning, then obviously the theory cannot stand. For, if they were eating beef from the very beginning and nonetheless were not treated as Untouchables, to say that the Broken Men became Untouchables because of beef-eating would be illogical if not senseless. The second question is relevant, if not crucial. If the Brahmins gave up beef-eating and the non-Brahmins imitated them why did the Broken Men not do the same? If the law made the killing of the cow a capital sin because the cow became a sacred animal to the Brahmins and non-Brahmins, why were the Broken Men not stopped from eating beef? If they had been stopped from eating beef there would have been no Untouchability.

The answer to the first question is that even during the period when beef-eating was common to both, the Settled Tribesmen and the Broken Men, a system had grown up whereby the Settled

Community ate fresh beef, while the Broken Men ate the flesh of the dead cow. We have no positive evidence to show that members of the Settled Community never ate the flesh of the dead cow. But we have negative evidence which shows that the dead cow had become an exclusive possession and perquisite of the Broken Men. The evidence consists of facts which relate to the Mahars[13] of the Maharashtra to whom reference has already been made. As has already been pointed out, the Mahars of the Maharashtra claim the right to take the dead animal. This right they claim against every Hindu in the village. This means that no Hindu can eat the flesh of his own animal when it dies. He has to surrender it to the Mahar. This is merely another way of stating that when eating beef was a common practice the Mahars ate dead beef and the Hindus ate fresh beef. The only questions that arise are: Whether what is true of the present is true of the ancient past? Can this fact which is true of the Maharashtra be taken as typical of the arrangement between the Settled Tribes and the Broken Men throughout India?

In this connection reference may be made to the tradition current among the Mahars according to which they claim that they were given 52 rights[14] against the Hindu villagers by the Muslim king of Bedar.[15] Assuming that they were given by the king of Bedar, the King obviously did not create them for the first time. They must have been in existence from the ancient past. What the king did was merely to confirm them. This means that the practice of the Broken Men eating dead meat and the Settled Tribes eating fresh meat must have grown in the ancient past. That such an arrangement should grow up is certainly most natural. The Settled Community was a wealthy community with agriculture and cattle as means of livelihood. The Broken Men were a community of paupers with no means of livelihood and entirely dependent upon the Settled Community. The principal item of food for both was beef. It was possible for the Settled Community to kill an animal for food because it was possessed of cattle. The Broken Men could not for they had none. Would it be unnatural in these circumstances for the Settled Community to have agreed to give to the Broken Men its dead animals as part of their wages of watch and ward? Surely not. It can therefore be taken for granted that in the ancient past when both the Settled Community and Broken Men did eat beef the former ate fresh beef and the latter of the dead cow and that this system represented a universal state of affairs throughout India and was not confined to the Maharashtra alone.

This disposes of the first objection. To turn to the second objection. The law made by the Gupta Emperors[16] was intended to prevent those who killed cows. It did not apply to the Broken Men. For they did not kill the cow. They only ate the dead cow. Their conduct did not contravene the law against cow-killing. The practice of eating the flesh of the dead cow therefore was allowed to continue. Nor did their conduct contravene the doctrine of Ahimsa assuming that it has anything to do with the abandonment of beef-eating by the Brahmins and the non-Brahmins. Killing the cow was Himsa. But eating the dead cow was not. The Broken Men had therefore no cause for feeling qualms of conscience in continuing to eat the dead cow. Neither the law nor the doctrine of Himsa could interdict what they were doing, for what they were doing was neither contrary to law nor to the doctrine.

As to why they did not imitate the Brahmins and the non-Brahmins the answer is two-fold. In the first place, imitation[17] was too costly. They could not afford it. The flesh of the dead cow was their principal sustenance. Without it they would starve. In the second place, carrying the dead cow had become an obligation[18] though originally it was a privilege. As they could not escape carrying the dead cow they did not mind using the flesh as food in the manner in which they were doing previously.

The objections therefore do not invalidate the thesis in any way.

Annotations

1 [This definition of religion is by Prof Emile Durkheim. See his *The Elementary Forms of the Religious Life*, p. 47. For the discussion that follows I have drawn upon the same authority.] Emile Durkheim (1858–1917) was one of the founders of sociology, who was concerned with establishing the discipline as a provider of an objective account of society, much like how the natural sciences studied the physical world objectively. He attempted to move away from generalizing social theories influenced by psychology that appeared more as philosophical meditations than science. In his last work, *The Elementary Forms of the Religious Life* (1912), he gives a functionalist definition of religion, according to which religious belief and practices are in effect the bond which hold society together. Durkheim's definition has since provided grounds for innumerable debates particularly for its totalizing and a priori view of society, in which all social practices, beliefs and rituals, are employed for its creation and maintenance. Besides failing to imagine society as embedded in history and constantly changing, this formulation also implies religious practitioners were deluded as to the true nature of their creed and only Western researchers have access to its true meaning. Yet, in the context of his contemporaries, he could be said to have taken religious life more seriously than they did. In *The Elementary Forms of the Religious Life*, Durkheim studies the totemic religion of a single aboriginal tribe in Australia, in order to draw out a general definition of religion and make claims about its origin. Much like Ambedkar had relied heavily on the historical experience of the Mahars to draw far-reaching conclusions about the origin and workings of Untouchability.

2 Criticisms against Ambedkar have been raised in the past for relying too heavily on Western sources, or for being

Eurocentric. An important inversion of this dynamic is made by Soumyabrata Choudhury in *Ambedkar and Other Immortals: An Untouchable Research Programme* (2018a) that hails Ambedkar as a Europeanist who was not simply displaying Europhilia by using a Western framework in his critique. Rather his was an engagement in the universal realm: that the articulation of the values of, say, 'liberty, equality, fraternity' found expression in the French Revolution was only a contingent occurrence. It was the *truth* of the articulation which was important. The essence of what Ambedkar says in the chapter "A Plea to the Foreigner", in *What Congress and Gandhi Have Done to the Untouchables* (1948), according to Choudhury is: 'Thought is nobody's monopoly.'

3 With reference to Durkheim's influence in the field of sociology, Bourdieu and Passeron (1967) argue that even the scholars who were opposed to him were caught within the coordinates set by his work: that being an assumption of a structural entity called 'society' and all analysis of this entity flowing from a pre-given notion of how humans operate and co-operate with each other within this structure. The thrust of their arguments situates Durkheim as an oppositional figure, who saw his self-given task as one of opening up a field of radical 'newness', of looking at the world from a new theoretical perspective. This was inevitably co-opted and tamed by University Discourse, resulting in wide streams of study which sat quite well within the material confines of the ruling ideology. On the other hand, it has also been argued that Durkheim was very much a part of the ruling French republican establishment. While he was opposed to the ancien régime represented by the Catholic Church, his was very much a pedagogical project of reining in the radical elements of society and standardizing a set of values and principles that would 'unite' the people of the nation through 'scientific' means (Allen and O'Boyle 2017). Durkheim's study of religion is

markedly different from the contemporary academic discipline known as 'world religions', which is more of a comparative field. Tomoko Masuzawa in *The Invention of World Religions: Or, How European Universalism Was Preserved in the Language of Pluralism* (2005) problematizes the entire Western framework within which the so-called 'world religions' are studied and underlines the simplistic outlook which defines the subject: a dichotomy between the 'venerable East on the one hand, and the progressive West on the other' (4). In her 1988 paper "The Sacred Difference in the Elementary Forms: On Durkheim's Last Quest", Masuzawa closely reads Durkheim's distinction between the sacred and the profane and brings to light how much more accommodative of difference these concepts are. Durkheim, she claims, was aware of the contingent nature of the emergence of these categories, and he also maintained that there was no fixed criterion that marked the difference between the sacred and the profane.

4 Ambedkar uses the term secular to mean that which does not have anything to do with the religious or the spiritual. In the West, the word is employed to assert the separation of church from state. In India, however, the word has come to imply something else altogether: i.e. the equidistance of state from all religions, a purported neutrality. This was a decision on the part of the postcolonial government to take a strong stance against communal polarization, especially in the wake of the bloodshed caused during the Partition. Shabnum Tejani (2013a) however explores the pre-independence history of Indian secularism and illustrates the importance of caste politics for its present mode of articulation. She contends that the notion of secularism as we know it arose in the context of the communal awards which were instituted through the constitutional reforms of 1919. These awards allowed for separate electorates for minority communities which included Muslims, Sikhs, Christians,

Anglo-Indians and the Depressed Classes. While the political elite, a majority of whom were Western-educated, privileged caste Hindus, accepted separation on communal lines for religious minorities, the representation of Depressed Classes as a separate element was vehemently opposed. It was seen as a colonial plot to weaken the 'Hindu' majority, and leaders like Ambedkar who demanded the separation were openly vilified. This conflict came to a head in the Poona Pact which forced Ambedkar to back down on his demands for separate representation. Before independence, Muslim representation was not as contested as Untouchable representation was. It was the Depressed Classes who were accused of trying to break up the integral whole that was presumed to be 'Hindu' (Tejani 2007b). This rhetoric of unity was transplanted wholesale in the post-Independence era under the moniker of secularism which sought to counterpose India against a decidedly communal Pakistan. The much-touted vision of a 'united' India was very much a repetition of the old tradition of glorifying a 'united Hinduism' which denied Dalits separate representation. Indian secularism from the beginning was a project which tried to wish away the contradictions of caste and of the experiences of minority communities in order to construct a united nationalist narrative.

5 [Prof Durkheim's *The Elementary Forms of the Religious Life*, p. 38] Another important scholar in this regard is the anthropologist Talal Asad, who has closely studied the notion of 'secularism' and how the West operates within its guise. Writes Asad: 'A secular state is not one characterized by religious indifference, irrational ethics or political toleration. It is a complex arrangement of legal reasoning, moral practice, and political authority. This arrangement is not the simple outcome of the struggle of secular reason against the despotism of religious authority. We do not understand the[se] arrangements

[...] if we begin with the common assumption that the essence of secularism is the protection of civil freedoms from the tyranny of religious discourse, that religious discourse seeks always to end discussion and secularism to create the conditions for its flourishing' (2003, 255).

6 In his introduction to the edited volume *The Sacred in a Secular Age: Toward Revision in the Scientific Study of Religion* (1985), Philip E. Hammond draws out the difference between the religious and the sacred. Drawing from Georg Simmel's conceptual framework, he suggests that the sacred need not always be tied with the religious, especially in the (purportedly) secular age in which we now find ourselves. 'Encounter with the sacred, or what Simmel calls "piety", is thus not necessarily religion, but "religion in a quasi-fluid state..." (1954:24), that is, not yet "objectified"' (1985, 3). This state of piety, or the distinction between the sacred and the profane, Hammond writes, are seen by Durkheim and Simmel not as intrinsic to humanity, but a necessary outcome of social organization. Hammond provides a helpful analogy to illustrate the difference between religion and the sacred: it is similar to the difference between marriage and love. While marriage is the institutional embodiment of love (or so goes the claim), it can be easily demonstrated that the two do not have a necessary relationship. Such an understanding of religion and the sacred is particularly reminiscent of the situation of caste in 'liberal–secular' discourse. Just because one disavows the formal structures which proscribe caste society (Hindu scriptures, *Manusmriti*, etc.) it does not imply that the 'sacredness' of that injunction and its material manifestations also vanish.

7 [The curious may refer to page 317 of the above book.] In a 1915 edition of the work that Ambedkar likely referred to, Durkheim writes on page 317: 'In one sense, it is logically implied in the very notion of sacredness. All that is sacred is the

object of respect, and every sentiment of respect is translated, in him who feels it, by movements of inhibition. In fact, a respected being is always expressed in the consciousness by a representation which, owing to the emotion it inspires, is charged with a high mental energy; consequently, it is armed in such a way as to reject to a distance every other representation which denies it in whole or in part.' This quote points towards Durkheim's position on the origin of religion in "the collective effervescence" that people living in the simplest societies experienced when they got together for collective acts such as harvests. When engaged together in collective action people became aware of something larger than themselves, which they interpreted as belonging to the spiritual realm. This way religion became a representation of society, which implies misrecognition. The Western scholars who drew from such a categorization of the sacred and the profane were interested in the social implications of religion—the social organization and dynamics of power that the existence of religion signals. Such perspectives have been critiqued for their faith in their own ability to successfully deduce what religion was about and their implication that practitioners of religion were somehow deluded.

8 [*The Elementary Forms of the Religious Life*, p 41. Interdictions which come from religion must be distinguished from those which proceed from magic. For a discussion of this subject see ibid., 300.] According to Durkheim, religious interdictions follow the structure of categorical imperatives, i.e. commandments that lie beyond the pale of reason (see p. 270–1 note 11). These interdictions are concerned with categorizing sacrilegious activities. Magical interdictions, however, have a secular structure and follow a certain reasoned discourse. Breaking such taboos do not offend opinion but rather have consequences that naturally follow from the actions. Durkheim

refers to them as 'utilitarian maxims' (1915, 300–301). They have a logic of hygiene behind them. There is nothing morally wrong with drinking contaminated water, but it follows that you may contract disease. Similarly, when one disregards magical interdictions, one does not undermine any sacred prescription but rather does oneself (or another) a kind of 'logical' harm.

9 Durkheim goes to quite some length about the interdictions made by religion (1915, 300–308 *passim*). On the subject of food, he draws out two categories: food forbidden to the profane on account of its sacredness and food forbidden to the sacred on account of its profanity. As Mary Douglas, a prominent scholar on the notion of the sacred and the profane, wrote in her book *Purity and Danger: An Analysis of the Concepts of Pollution and Taboo* (1984): 'A total opposition between sacred and profane seems to have been a necessary step in Durkheim's theory of social integration. It expressed the opposition between the individual and society. The social conscience was projected beyond and above the individual member of society onto something quite other, external and compellingly powerful. So we find Durkheim insisting that rules of separation are the distinguishing marks of the sacred, the polar opposite of the profane' (21–2). In the Brahmanical context, the cow is not consumed by the sacred (Brahmins) on account of its sacredness, whereas it is the profane (Untouchables) who consume the sacred animal's carcass. In the pre-Buddhist times, however, it was the Brahmins who had special access to sacrificial cow meat on account of its sacredness. In trying to understand these shifting dynamics, we can look to Mary Douglas' structuralist reading of pollution and dirt, substances and acts, the relationship of people to which will cause them to be cast out of society—a process that maintains social order. Since pollution and dirt are cause people to be cast out and made separate from the social structure, they are in a very

similar place to the sacred which is also separate. In this reading, the sacred is as dangerous as dirt; the sacredness of the cow is maintained through casting out those that dare to touch it.

10 Durkheim dedicates several pages to discuss the various ways in which the profane is excommunicated from the sacred. He does this from a seemingly neutral perspective, from a position that is *outside* of the system. These discussions for him build towards the conclusion that such interdictions are necessary for the maintenance of religious sanctity: '[R]eligious life and profane life cannot coexist in the same place. If the former is to develop, a special [place] must be placed at its disposition, from which the second is excluded' (1915, 308). He uses this conclusion to underline the necessity of the division between the sacred and the profane. It is Ambedkar who radicalizes this finding by situating himself *within* the ideology of religion. For Ambedkar these were deeply political concepts that were existentially charged. His very being was marked as 'profane' by Brahmanical society. One can thus see how Ambedkar builds on Durkheim's conclusions to develop his thesis of the rejection of Hinduism altogether in order to annihilate caste, in order to render meaningless this dichotomy of the sacred and the profane.

11 The concept of categorical imperatives lies at the centre of Kantian ethics. It was developed by Immanuel Kant in *Groundwork in The Metaphysics of Morals* (1785). For Kant, moral duties were categorical imperatives, i.e. that which we have to follow unconditionally even though we have the freedom to not do so. There are three categorical imperatives that govern all moral duties according to Kant: 1) all our moral actions must be such that they are universalizable, i.e. they must be followed whatever the situation, e.g. if we take the universal law to be 'never tell a lie', then we must follow it unconditionally even if it means telling a lie might save someone's life; 2) we

must always treat humanity, in ourselves or in others, as an end in itself and not as a means; 3) our ethical acts and decisions must be such that they derive and rest solely on principles and must not arise from external influences, further we must act such that these principles may be accepted by society at large where the society must always be presumed to be composed of agents who are free and possess rational capacity (Johnson and Cuerton 2018). In his undelivered speech *Annihilation of Caste* (1936), Ambedkar develops an ethic which has Kantian echoes: '[The] difference between rules and principles makes the acts done in pursuit of them different in quality and in content. Doing what is said to be good by virtue of a rule, and doing good in the light of a principle, are two different things. The principle may be wrong, but the act is conscious and responsible. The rule may be right, but the act is mechanical. A religious act may not be a correct act, but must at least be a responsible act. To permit of this responsibility, Religion must mainly be a matter of principles only. It cannot be a matter of rules. The moment it degenerates into rules, it ceases to be Religion, as it kills the responsibility which is the essence of a truly religious act' (Ambedkar 2014, 304–5).

12 The terms 'association' and 'associated life' have a special significance for Ambedkar. He borrows it from Deweyan philosophy, wherein democracy is seen not merely as a political tool, but an essential aspect of social life in all its quarters: education, personal relationships and so on. Soumyabrata Choudhury (2018a) develops an Ambedkarite reading of a 'collective life of association'. It is a life of 'common feelings' and fraternity which grants the 'freedom to encounter others in their strangeness' (28).

13 Mahar is an Untouchable caste in western India that was forced to offer baluta or compulsory unfree service to the caste Hindus of the village. For this, Mahars received no wage but a share in the village produce—the prerogative of disposing of dead cattle

(finding a use for everything 'from the tip of the horn to the end of the tail', as Daya Pawar notes in *Baluta*), the privilege of skinning cows, guarding the village perimeter, announcing the births and deaths in Savarna households that held them vassal—52 such impositions that passed for rights. Under the colonial government, several Mahars found employment as soldiers in British regiments. Ambedkar himself was the son of a subedar in the British Indian Army. (For an account of the 'Mahar army tradition' to which Ambedkar belonged, see Zelliot [2013, 45–52].) Many key arguments in this text are drawn from the particular experience of the Mahar caste; so much so that his essay "The Mahars: Who Were They and How They Became Untouchables" (Ambedkar 2003, 137–50) is identical in its arguments and conclusions to the present volume. In the essay, he also argues that the Mahars in particular, in addition to being Broken Men, were also Kshatriyas who were later cast out of the in-group. Which begs the question, can the experience of a single caste in a particular region be used to conceive a generalized theory of how Untouchability arose? Ambedkar was often dubbed as a 'Mahar leader' and most organizations he floated had an overwhelmingly Mahar base. Jaffrelot (2005) notes, 'Indeed Ambedkar met with many difficulties attracting the support of Chambhars or Mangs who considered him to be a Mahar leader' (76–7).

14 The Untouchables were traditionally not allowed to join martial ranks. However, under the Muslim rulers of the second millennium several 'outcastes' were recruited as soldiers and they grew to be quite influential. One such soldier was Amritnak, in the employ of the king of Bedar. He managed to convince the king to pass a 'Charter of 52 Rights' for the Mahars. These included the right to collect baluta, a small sum in lieu of the services that the Mahars provided in the villages. This, R.K. Kshirsagar notes, proved to be detrimental to the Mahars: even

though they now had a few petty rights, it was expected of them to carry out all the 'dirty' and hazardous tasks. Their conditions further worsened under the rule of the Brahmin peshwas who imposed severe restrictions on them and intensified their degradation (Kshirsagar 1994). When exactly the 52 rights were granted is unclear. Kshirsagar states the year to be 1129 CE. However, Bedar was under Chalukya and Kakatiya rule in the eleventh and twelfth centuries (Yazdani 1995). It was only in 1322 that Muslim rule was established, when prince Ulugh Khan (Muhammad bin Tughluq) captured it. The following list can be found in a document which dates back to the year 1738, unearthed by Paswan and Jaideva (2004), in which the upper-caste members of Lalgun village in Satara deliberated about the compulsory duties of the Mahar caste:

1. Mahars should be engaged in miscellaneous labour for Patil.
2. Mahars should be engaged in miscellaneous labour for the Government (*Divan*), etc.
3. Mahar should offer a bundle of firewood (to village headman) on each festival day (*Sana*).
4. Mahar should remove the skin of dead cattle of the headman's, accountant's and assistant headman's families, and submit it to its respective owner' (Paswan and Jaideva 2004, 34).

Another document from the 1700s reveals the different kinds of bonded labour which was extracted in Maharashtra. This practice was called 'Vethbegar', derived from the Sanskrit word, 'visti' meaning compulsory work, and the Urdu word 'begar' which also meant the same thing. Seven kinds of vethbegars are said to have been common in the era: construction and repair (of forts, police stations, houses of bureaucrats and dams), porterage of goods including crops and timber, cutting fodder from government land, miscellaneous labour in government offices, handling extraneous work in stables, keeping guard of chowkis and marketplaces, and construction and porterage services in an inamdar's (those who have been given special grants by the government) house (37).

15 Muslim rule began in Bedar after its conquest by Muhammad bin Tughlaq in 1322. As the dynasty of the Tughlaqs began to decline, several regents in the Deccan rebelled against the king and established independent states. One of these was Amir Hasan Gangu who went on to found the Bahmani dynasty. The Bahmanids were in constant animus with the Warangal and Vijayanagar empires to their south. In 1425 Warangal was annexed by Ahmad Shah I. Towards the end of the fifteenth century as the Bahmani dynasty began to crumble, several regional officials declared independence. Of these, the Barid Shahis of Bedar established the Bedar dynasty in 1489. Their rule too came to an end when in 1619 Bedar was annexed by Bijapur, which was soon felled by the Mughal armies of Aurangzeb (Bosworth 1996).

16 The zeal for cow-protection was only one of the several ways in which Brahmanism gained in strength under the Guptas. Rejecting the homegrown art which flourished under Buddhist influence and was mostly created by those who were lower in the social order, they embraced the Hellenist-inspired Gandhara style. Several attempts to rewrite old religious texts to make them more palatable to the ruling ideology were also undertaken. These would include Kalidasa's expansive rendering of Shakuntala's story from the *Mahabharata* and also the rewriting of the Bhagavad Gita. Reinterpretations of the multifarious puranas and the writing of *Dharmasastras* were taken up. With the reach of the empire being so wide, several non-Brahmin mendicants tried to become chroniclers and bards to sneak in their own ideas into the Brahmanical fold. This was allowed for, but attempts were also made to 'Puranicize' the

plural ideas and make them palatable to the conservative tastes of the ruling ideology. The cult of Vaishnavism also became the phenomenon that it is, thanks to the patronage of the Gupta kings (Doniger 2010). See also p. 253–4 note 76 on the Guptas.

17 Imitation was an important concept which Ambedkar deployed in his 1916 paper delivered in New York City, "Castes in India: Their Genesis, Mechanism and Development", in which he tried to map the conceptual logic of the emergence of caste. He begins the paper by first fixing the definition of caste: it is an enclosed class in which exogamy is superposed on endogamy, that is to say though marriages appear to occur only outside one's gotra, it is still limited to marriage within caste. These, he claimed, were practices which emerged from one caste: the one at the top of the hierarchy which existed in a theocratic society like India: the Brahmins. In order to explain how this dynamic of caste proliferates, Ambedkar borrows the concept of 'imitation' from Walter Bagehot and Gabriel Tarde. Bagehot was an English businessman who was closely allied with state historians; his 1872 work, *Physics and Politics*, dedicates an entire chapter to explain how imitation works between groups. He makes it clear that such imitation need not be voluntary or even conscious. Rather, it stems from that part of human nature which causes belief and therefore creates hierarchies. Tarde, a French sociologist, develops these ideas further in order to explain the formation and flow of culture between different classes in a society (also see p. 197–8 note 16). Essentially, the practices of those higher up the hierarchy were imitated by those lower down the ladder. As one moves lower in a hierarchy, imitation gets diluted and becomes an imperfect copy of the original. Ambedkar explains that caste is such that it necessarily proliferates once its logic enters a society. Once the Brahmins have declared themselves to be separate and refuse to inter-marry with the outgroup, the non-Brahmins are

automatically made into a caste, without any say in the matter. And this leads to a necessary imitation: non-Brahmins now can only intermarry among themselves, which leads to further compartmentalization of society because of the now implanted imitative urge. Ambedkar's theory is often seen as closely related to M.N. Srinivas's theory of Sanskritization, according to which those that occupy lower rungs in the caste hierarchy feel the need to imitate and change their practices to suit those of the ones higher up. However, a crucial difference between Ambedkar and Srinivas is the position of their critiques: Srinivas already takes for granted the existence of caste and theorizes about the imitation after the fact, whereas Ambedkar is examining the origins of caste and how it came to be. Further, Ambedkar's theory of excommunication is an important counter-point to the Sanskritization thesis: he claims that some groups find themselves excommunicated from the in-group in the first place precisely because of their non-imitative urges. Ambedkar terms it 'innovation': Whenever a segment of the population (in caste society) 'innovates', they find themselves thrown out of the caste order, precisely because the innovation acts as a threat to the existence of the social reality as construed by caste-logic (see Ambedkar 2013, 77–108). Mary Douglas (1984) also puts forward a similar account of excommunication.

18 [Owing to the reform movement among the Mahars the position has become just the reverse. The Mahars refuse to take the dead animal while the Hindu villagers force them to take it.]

Part VI
Untouchability and the date of its birth

Chapter XV

The impure and the Untouchables

I

WHEN did Untouchability come into existence? The orthodox Hindus insist that it is very ancient in its origin. In support of their contention reliance is placed on the fact that the observance of Untouchability is enjoined not merely by the *Smritis* which are of a later date but it is also enjoined by the *Dharma Sutras* which are much earlier and which, according to certain authors, date some centuries before BC.[1]

In a study devoted to exploring the origin of Untouchability the question one must begin with is: Is Untouchability as old as is suggested to be?

For an answer to this question one has to examine the *Dharma Sutras* in order to ascertain what they mean when they refer to Untouchability and to the Untouchables. Do they mean by Untouchability what we understand by it today? Do [Are] the class, to which they refer, Untouchables in the sense in which we use the term Untouchables today?

To begin with the first question. An examination of the *Dharma Sutras*[2] no doubt shows that they speak of a class whom they call Asprashya. There is also no doubt that the term Asprashya does mean Untouchables. The question however remains whether the Asprashya of the *Dharma Sutras* are the same as the Asprashya of modern India. This question becomes important when it is realized that the *Dharma Sutras* also use a variety of other terms such as Antya, Antyaja, Antyavasin and Bahya. These terms are also used by the later *Smritis*. It might be well to have some idea of the use of these terms by the different *Sutras* and *Smritis*. The following table is intended to serve that purpose:

I. Asprashya

Dharma Sutra	Smriti
1. Vishnu V.104[3]	1. Katyayana verses 433, 783[4]

II. Antya

Dharma Sutra	Smriti
1. Vasistha (16.30)[5]	1. Manu IV.79;[6] VIII. 68[7]
2. Apastamba (III.I)[8]	2. Yajnavalkya I.148, 197[9]
	3. Atri 25.4; Likhita 92[10]

III. Bahya

Dharma Sutra	Smriti
1. Apastamba 1.2.39.18[11]	Manu 28[12]
2. Vishnu 16.14[13]	Narada I.155[14]

IV. Antyavasin

Dharma Sutra	Smriti
1. Gautama XXXI; XXIII 32[15]	1. Manu IV.79; X.39[16]
2. Vasistha XVIII. 3[17]	2. Shanti Parva, Mahabharata 141: 29–32[18]
	3. Madhyamangiras (quoted in Mitakshara on Yaj. 3.280)[19]

V. Antyaja

Dharma Sutra	Smriti
1. Vishnu 36.7[20]	1. Manu IV.61; VIII.279[21]
	2. Yajnavalkya 1.273[22]
	3. Brihadyanya Smriti (quoted by Mitakshara on Yajnavalkya III. 260)[23]
	4. Atri. 199[24]5. Veda Vyas I.12–13[25]

The next question is whether the classes indicated by the terms Antya, Antyaja, Antyavasin and Bahya are the same as those indicated by the term Asprashya which etymologically means an Untouchable. In other words are they only different names for the same class of people?[26]

It is an unfortunate fact that the *Dharma Sutras* do not enable us to answer this question. The term *Asprashya* occurs in two places (once in one Sutra and twice in one *Smriti*). But not one gives an enumeration of the classes included in it. The same is the case with the term *Antya*. Although the word *Antya* occurs in six places (in two Sutras and four *Smritis*) not one enumerates who they are. Similarly, the word *Bahya* occurs in four places (in two *Sutras* and two *Smritis*), but none of them mentions what communities are included under this term. The only exception is with regard to the terms Antyavasin and Antyajas. Here again no *Dharma Sutra* enumerates them. But there is an enumeration of them in the *Smritis*.[27] The enumeration of the Antyavasin occurs in the *Smriti* known as *Madhyamangiras* and that of the Antyajas in the *Atri Smriti* and *Veda Vyas Smriti*.[28] Who they are, will be apparent from the following table:

ANTYAVASIN	ANTYAJA	
Madhyamangiras	Atri	Veda Vyas
1. Chandala	1. Nata	1. Chandala

2. Shvapaka	2. Meda	2. Shvapaka
3. Kshatta	3. Bhilla	3. Nata
4. Suta	4. Rajaka	4. Meda
5. Vaidehika	5. Charmakar	5. Bhilla
6. Magadha	6. Buruda	6. Rajaka
7. Ayogava	7. Kayavarta	7. Charmakar
		8. Virat
		9. Dasa
		10. Bhatt
		11. Kolika
		12. Pushkar

From this table it is quite clear that there is neither precision nor agreement with regard to the use of the terms Antyavasin and Antyaja.[29] For instance Chandala and Shvapaka fall in both the categories Antyavasin and Antyaja according to *Madhyamangiras* and *Veda Vyas*. But when one compares *Madhyamangiras* with *Atri* they fall in different categories. The same is true with regard to the term Antyaja. For example while (1) Chandala and (2) Shvapaka are Antyajas according to Veda Vyas, according to Atri they are not. Again according to Atri (1) Buruda and (2) Kayavarta are Antyajas while according to Veda Vyas they are not. Again (1) Virat (2) Dasa (3) Bhatt (4) Kolika and (5) Pushkar are Antyaja according to Veda Vyas but according to Atri they are not.

To sum up the position reached so far: neither the *Dharma Sutras* nor the *Smritis* help us to ascertain who were included in the category of Asprashya. Equally useless are the *Dharma Sutras* and the *Smritis* to enable us to ascertain whether the classes spoken of as Antyavasin, Antyaja and Bahya were the same as Asprashya. Is there any other way of ascertaining whether any of these formed into the category of Asprashya or Untouchables?

It would be better to collect together whatever information is available about each of these classes.[30]

What about the Bahyas? Who are they? What are they? Are they Untouchables? They are mentioned by Manu. To understand their position, it is necessary to refer to Manu's scheme of social classification. Manu divides the people into various categories. He first[31] makes a broad division between (1) Vaidikas and (2) Dasyus. He then proceeds to divide the Vaidikas into four sub-divisions: (1) Those inside Chaturvarnya (2) Those outside Chaturvarnya (3) Vratya and (4) Patitas or outcastes.

Whether a person was inside Chaturvarnya or outside, was a question to be determined by the Varna of the parents. If he was born of the parents of the same Varnas, he was inside the Chaturvarnya. If, on the other hand, he was born of parents of different Varnas i.e., he was the progeny of mixed marriages or what Manu calls *Varna Samkara*, then he was outside the Chaturvarnya. Those outside Chaturvarnya are further sub-divided by Manu into two classes. (1) Anulomas and (2) Pratilomas. Anulomas[32] were those whose fathers were of a higher Varna and mothers of a lower Varna. Pratilomas, on the other hand, were those whose fathers were of a lower Varna and the mothers of a higher Varna. Though both the Anulomas and Pratilomas were alike for the reason that they were outside the Chaturvarnya, Manu proceeds to make a distinction between them. The Anulomas, he calls *Varna Bahya* or shortly *Bahyas*, while Pratilomas he calls *Hinas*.[33] The Hinas are lower than the Bahyas. But neither the Bahyas nor the Hinas does Manu regard as Untouchables.

Antya as a class is mentioned in Manu IV.79.[34] Manu however does not enumerate them. Medhatithi[35] in his commentary suggests that Antya means Mleccha, such as Meda, etc.[36] Bühler translates Antya as a low-caste man.[37]

There is thus nothing to indicate that the Antyas were Untouchables. In all probability, it is the name given to those people who were living in the outskirts or *end* (Anta) of the village. The reason why they came to be regarded as low is to be found in the story narrated in the *Brahadaranyaka Upanishad* (1.3) to which reference is made by Mr Kane.[38] The story is that:

> Gods and Asuras had a strife and the gods thought that they might rise superior to the Asuras by the Udgitha. In this vidya occurs the passage, 'this devata (Prana) throwing aside the sin that was death to these devatas (vak, etc.) sent it to ends of these devatas there; therefore one should not go to the people (outside the Aryan pale) nor to the ends [*disam anta*] (of the quarters) thinking, otherwise I may fall in with *papman* i.e., death.

The meaning of Antya turns on the connotation of the phrase 'disam anta' which occurs in the passage quoted above. If the phrase 'ends of the quarters' can be translated as meaning the end of the periphery of the village, without its being called a far-fetched translation, we have here an explanation of what Antya originally meant. It does not suggest that the Antyas were Untouchables. It only meant that they were living on the outskirts of the village.[39]

As to the Antyajas, what we know about them is enough to refute the view that they were Untouchables. Attention may be drawn to the following facts:[40]

In the Shanti Parvan (109.19) of the Mahabharat there is a reference to Antyajas who are spoken of as soldiers in the army.[41] According to *Sarasvativilasa*,[42] Pitamaha speaks of the seven cases of Rajakas included in the term Antyaja as Prakritis. That Prakritis mean trade guilds such as of washermen and others is quite clear from the Sangamner Plate of Bhillama II dated Saka

922[43] which records the grant of a village to eighteen Prakritis. *Viramitrodaya*[44] says that Srenis mean the eighteen castes such as the Rajaka, etc., which are collectively called Antyajas. In view of these facts how could the Antyajas be said to have been regarded as the Untouchables?[45]

Coming to the Antyavasin, who were they? Were they Untouchables? The term Antyavasin has been used in two different senses. In one sense it was applied to a Brahmachari living in the house of the guru during his term of studentship. A Brahmachari was referred to as Antyavasin.[46] It probably meant one who was served last. Whatever the reason for calling a Brahmachari Antyavasin it is beyond dispute that the word in that connection could not connote Untouchability. How could it when only Brahmins, Kshatriyas and Vaishyas could become Brahmacharis. In another sense they refer to a body of people. But even in this sense it is doubtful if it means Untouchables.

According to Vas.Dh.Sutra (18.3)[47] they are the offspring of a Sudra father and Vaishya mother. But according to Manu (V.39)[48] they are the offspring of a Chandala father and a Nishad mother. As to the class to which they belong, the *Mitakshara* says they are a sub-group of the Antyajas which means that the Antyavasin were not different from the Antyajas. What is therefore true of the Antyajas may also be taken as true of the Antyavasin.

III

Stopping here to take stock of the situation as it emerges from such information as we have regarding the social condition of the people called Antyavasin, Antya, Antyaja, as is available from ancient literature, obviously it is not open to say that these classes were Untouchables in the modern sense of the term.

However, for the satisfaction of those who may still have some doubt, the matter may be further examined from another point of view. Granting that they were described as Asprashya, we may proceed to inquire as to what was the connotation of the term in the days of the *Dharma Sutras*.

For this purpose we must ascertain the rules of atonement prescribed by the Shastras. From the study of these rules we will be able to see whether the term Asprashya had the same connotation in the times of the *Dharma Sutras* as it has now.

Let us take the case of the Chandalas as an illustration of the class called Asprashya. In the first place, it should be remembered that the word Chandala does not denote one single homogenous class of people. It is one word for many classes of people, all different from one another. There are altogether five different classes of Chandalas who are referred to in the Shastras.[49] They are (i) the offspring of a Shudra father and a Brahmin mother,[50] (ii) the offspring of an unmarried woman,[51] (iii) the offspring of union with a sagotra woman,[52] (iv) the offspring of a person who after becoming an ascetic turns back to the householder's life[53] and (v) the offspring of a barber father and a Brahmin mother.[54]

It is difficult to say which Chandala calls for purification. We shall assume that purification is necessary in the case of all the Chandalas. What is the rule of purification prescribed by the Shastras?

Gautama in his *Dharma Sutra* (Chapter XIV, Verse 30)[55] also refers to it in the following terms:

> On touching an outcaste, a Chandala, a woman impure on account of her confinement, a woman in her courses, or a corpse and on touching persons who have touched them, he shall purify himself by bathing dressed in his clothes.

Below is the text of the rule given by the *Vasistha Dharma Sutra* (Chapter IV, Verse 37):[56]

> When he has touched a sacrificial post, a pyre, a burial ground, a menstruating or a lately confined woman, impure men or Chandalas and so forth, he shall bathe, submerging both his body and his head.

Baudhayana agrees with Vasistha for he too in his *Dharma Sutra* (Prasna 1, Adhyaya 5, Khanda 6, Verse 5) says:

> On touching a tree standing on a sacred spot, a funeral pyre, a sacrificial post, a Chandala or a person who sells the Veda, a Brahmin shall bathe dressed in his clothes.[57]

The following are the rules contained in Manu:[58]

> V.85: When he (the Brahmin) has touched a Chandala, a menstruating woman, an outcaste, a woman in childbed, a corpse, or one who has touched a (corpse), he becomes pure by bathing.
>
> V.131: Manu has declared that the flesh of an animal killed by dogs is pure, likewise (that) of a (beast) slain by carnivorous (animals) or by men of low caste (Dasya) such as Chandalas.
>
> V.143: He who, while carrying anything in any manner, is touched by an impure (person or thing), shall become pure, if he performs an ablution, without pulling down that object.

From these texts drawn from the *Dharma Sutras* as well as Manu, the following points are clear:

(1) That the pollution by the touch of the Chandala was observed by the Brahmin only.

(2) That the pollution was probably observed on ceremonial occasions only.[59]

IV

If these conclusions are right then this is a case of Impurity as distinguished from Untouchability. The distinction between the Impure and the Untouchable is very clear. The Untouchable pollutes all while the Impure pollutes only the Brahmin. The touch of the Impure causes pollution only on a ceremonial occasion. The touch of the Untouchable causes pollution at all times.

There is another argument to which so far no reference has been made which completely disproves the theory that the communities mentioned in the *Dharma Sutras* were Untouchables. That argument emerges out of a comparison of the list of communities given in the Order-in-Council (which is reproduced in Chapter II) with the list given in this chapter prepared from the *Smritis*.[60] What does the comparison show? As anyone can see, it shows:

> *Firstly:* The maximum number of communities mentioned in the *Smritis* is only twelve,[61] while the number of communities mentioned in the Order-in-Council comes to 429.[62]
>
> *Secondly:* There are communities which find a place in the Order-in-Council but which do not find a place in the *Smritis*. Out of the total of 429 there are nearly 427 which are unknown to the *Smritis*.
>
> *Thirdly:* There are communities mentioned in the *Smritis* which do not find a place in the Order-in-Council at all.
>
> *Fourthly:* There is only one community which finds a place in both. It is the Charmakar community.

Those who do not admit that the Impure are different from the Untouchables do not seem to be aware of these facts. But they will have to reckon with them. These facts are so significant and so telling that they cannot but force the conclusion that the two are different.

1. Out of the 429 communities mentioned in the Order-in-Council, there are only three which are to be found in the list given by the *Smritis*.
2. There are also two other communities mentioned in both lists (1) Nata and (2) Rajaka. But according to the Order-in-Council they are Untouchables in some parts of the country only. The Chamar is Untouchable throughout India.

Take the first fact. It raises a very important question.

If the two lists refer to one and the same class of people, why do they differ, and differ so widely? How is it that the communities mentioned in the Shastras do not appear in the list given in the Order-in-Council? Contrarywise, how is it that the communities mentioned in the Order-in-Council are not to be found in the list given by the Shastras? This is the first difficulty we have to face.

On the assumption that they refer to the same class of people, the question, assumes a serious character. If they refer to the same class of people then obviously Untouchability which was originally confined to twelve communities came to be extended to 429 communities! What has led to this vast extension of the Empire of Untouchability? If these 429 communities belong to the same class as the twelve mentioned by the Shastras why none of the Shastras mention them? It cannot be that none of the 429 communities were not in existence at the time when the Shastras were written. If all of them were not in existence at least some of them must have been. Why even such as did exist find no mention?

On the footing that both the lists belong to the same class of people, it is difficult to give any satisfactory answer to these questions. If, on the other hand, it is assumed that these lists refer to two different classes of people, all these questions disappear. The two lists are different because the list contained in the Shastras is a list of the Impure and the list contained in the Order-in-Council is a list of the Untouchables. This is the reason why the two lists differ. The divergence in the two lists merely emphasizes what has been urged on other grounds, namely, that the classes mentioned in Shastras are only Impure and it is a mistake to confound them with the Untouchables of the present day.

Now, turn to the second. If the Impure are the same as the Untouchables, why is it as many as 427 out of 429 should be unknown to the *Smritis*?[63] As communities, they must have been in existence at the time of the *Smritis*. If they are Untouchables now, they must have been Untouchables then. Why then did the *Smritis* fail to mention them?

What about the third? If the Impure and the Untouchables are one and the same, why those communities which find a place in the *Smritis* do not find a place in the list given in the Order-in-Council? There are only two answers to this question. One is that though Untouchables at one time, they ceased to be Untouchables subsequently.[64] The other is that the two lists contain names of communities who fall in altogether different categories. The first answer is untenable. For, Untouchability is permanent. Time cannot erase it or cleanse it. The only possible conclusion is the second.

Take the fourth. Why should Chamar alone find a place in the lists? The answer is not that the two lists include the same class of people. If it was the true answer, then not only the Chamar but all others included in the list given by the *Smritis* should appear in both the lists. But they do not. The true answer is that the two lists contain two different classes of people. The reason why some of those in the list of the Impure appear in the list of the Untouchables is that the Impure at one time became Untouchables. That the Chamar appears in both is far from being evidence to support the view that there is no difference between the Impure and the Untouchables. It proves that the Chamar who was at one time an Impure, subsequently became an Untouchable and had therefore to be included in both the lists. Of the twelve communities mentioned in the *Smritis* as Impure communities, only the Chamar should have been degraded to the status of an Untouchable is not difficult to explain. What has made the difference between the Chamar and the other impure communities is the fact of beef-eating. It is only those among the Impure who were eating beef that became Untouchables, when the cow became sacred and beef-eating became a sin.[65] The Chamar is the only beef-eating community. That is why it alone appears in both the lists.[66] The answer to the question relating to the Chamars is decisive on two points. It is conclusive on the point that the Impure are different from the Untouchables. It is also decisive on the point that it is beef-eating which is the root of Untouchability and which divides the Impure and the Untouchables.

The conclusion that Untouchability is not the same as Impurity has an important bearing on the determination of the date of birth of Untouchability. Without it any attempt at fixing the date would be missing the mark.

Annotations

1. Current scholarship affirms Ambedkar. Olivelle (1999, xxiv) says that a large number of works dealing with dharma—composed in an aphoristic style known as *Sutra*—were likely composed in the centuries immediately prior to the common era, and that they 'belong to the same literary tradition that produced the works comprising the scriptural corpus of the Veda' (xxv). Most *Dharma Sutras* are lost and only four—of *Apastamba, Gautama, Vasishtha* and *Baudhayana*—have survived. The *Smritis*—attributed to Manu, Yajnavalkya, Narada and so on—are regarded as *Dharmasastra* texts. Ancient Brahmanic texts are divided into two kinds—*Smriti* (passed through memory, tradition) and shruti (transmitted orally via hearing, revelation). C.J. Fuller (2003, 484) notes that the British administrators depended on *Dharmasastras* such as the *Manusmriti* to develop a legal system for India, thus subjecting the Hindu population as a whole to a Brahmanical legal code. For the most authoritative, exhaustively annotated edition (1,131 pages) of the *Manusmriti*, see Olivelle (2005).

2. For a definitive modern edition of the *Dharma Sutras* see Olivelle's *Dharmasutras: The Law Codes of Apastamba, Gautama, Baudhayana, and Vasistha* (1999). Ambedkar often cited from Bühler's various translations but in what ensues he refers primarily to Kane (1941a).

3. Ambedkar's secondary source for the table reproduced here is Kane's chapter on "Untouchability" in *History of Dharmasastra (Ancient and Medieval Religious and Civil Law)* Vol. II, Part I that details references to ideas of Untouchables/Untouchability since the Rig Vedic period. Says Kane, 'Among the earliest occurrences of the word asprsya (as meaning untouchables in general) is that in Visnu Dh. S. V.104; Kātyāyana also uses the

word in that sense. [A footnote here in Kane's text references Kātyāyana 433 and 783.] It will have been seen from the quotations above that candalas, mlecchas and Parasikas are placed on the same level as regards being asprsya' (1941a, 172–3). Julius Jolly's edition of the *Vishnu Smriti, The Institutes of Vishnu* (1880, x), says: 'The Vishnu-smriti or Vaishnava Dharma-sastra or Vishnusutra is in the main a collection of ancient aphorisms on the sacred laws of India, and as such it ranks with the other ancient works of this class which have come down to our time.' V.104 reads: 'If one who (being a member of the *Kandâlas* or some other low caste) *must not be touched*, intentionally defiles by his touch one who (as a member of a twice-born caste) may be touched (by other twice-born persons only), he shall be put to death' (1880, 33–4, emphases added).

4 Olivelle and Davis say: 'A few lost Dharmasastras have been reconstituted by collecting medieval citations. The two most prominent ones are the texts of Brhaspati and Katyayana, both great jurists dealing with legal procedure' (2018, 29) The *Katyayana Smriti,* said to be the first *Smriti* to use the term 'Asprashya'—literally untouchable—is regarded as among 'the four major legal texts produced during or shortly after the Gupta period, that is, between the fifth and seventh centuries CE' (2018, 292) along with the *Smritis* of Yajnavalkya, Narada and Brihaspati. It was reconstructed by P.V. Kane and published in 1933 as *Katyayanasmrti on Vyavahara (Law and Procedure)* providing the full Sanskrit version along with an English translation and commentary. Kane cites internal and external evidence to date Katyayana later than Kautilya, Yajnvalkya, Narada and Brihaspati (1933, xv). He renders verse 433, which does use the word *asprashya* along with *mleccha* (55), as follows: 'But in the case of the Untouchables, the lowest castes, slaves, mlecchas, and those who are the offspring of mixed

unions in the reverse order of castes [Pratiloma], when guilty of sins, the determination (by the above named ordeals) should not be done by the king. He should indicate such ordeals as are well known among them in case of doubt (about their guilt)' (1933, 201). As the previous verses state, punishments to other communities are directly meted out by the king but the outcastes and slaves do not merit an audience with him—even as they are punished, they must remain unseen and untouched. Verse 783 reads: 'The punishment for untouchables, gamblers, slaves, for mlecchas, for persistent sinners, and for those who are born of unions in the reverse order of castes is beating (whipping) and not in money' (281).Notwithstanding the gross injustices pronounced in the text, Kane in his preface says Katyayana on vyavahara (law and procedure) 'represents the high water-mark of smriti literature' (1933, i), a feeling contemporary Indological scholars share. Both Ambedkar and Aktor cite Kane (1941a), yet we find that Ambedkar's 1948 work (or any of his other writings on Brahmanic Hinduism) is rarely referred to among both historians and Indological scholars working on ancient India, caste and such. When Vivekanand Jha and his mentor R.S. Sharma do engage with Ambedkar, they are dismissive of what they call his tall, untenable claims (see p. 308–9 note 33 and p. 321–2 note 66). Ambedkar admittedly does not approach Untouchability in a cold academic tone, but treats it as an aspect of history that irreparably affects him and condemns a wide swathe of population to an unequal life. The academic Untouchability Ambedkar is condemned to by the *learned* becomes all the more stark when modern scholars (D.N. Jha in *The Myth of the Holy Cow* or Mikael Aktor in his many essays on Untouchability), with the necessary institutional support and access, often citing the exact same verses through the same secondary sources, arrive often at the near-same deductions as Ambedkar. Except, the questions they ask and the conclusions they draw tend to be at odds. Significantly, the why, how and wherefore of untouchability cause Ambedkar to explore the connection between beef-eating and Untouchability, questions that do not concern either D.N. Jha, V. Jha, Sharma or Aktor; a clear material disjunction is palpable while 'scholars of note' assiduously trawl through Brahmanical paperwork, Ambedkar turns to a material point of memory—beef—which was consequential in his and his community's life and infuses it with theoretical life.

5 Says Kane in an entry under Antya: 'According to Vas. Dh. S. 16.30, Manu IV. 79, VIII. 68, Yaj. I. 148, 197, Atri 251, Likhita 92, verse Apastamba (III.1) this word is a generic appellation for all lowest castes like the candala... The word 'Bahya' has the same sense. Ap. Dh. S. I. 3. 9.18 says that there is a cessation of Vedic study on the day on which Bahyas enter a village; vide also Narada (155), Visnu Dh. S. 16.14' (1941a, 69–70). Olivelle (1999, xxvi): 'Gautama and Vasistha... are ancient seers. They could not have been the historical authors of the texts ascribed to them. These texts represent some of the earliest evidence for a phenomenon that became common in the versified *Smritis*, namely the emergence of eponymous literature, that is, the ascription of treatises to eminent persons of the mythical past.' Olivelle renders 16.30, which is part of a discussion on who may serve as witnesses: 'For women, he should get women to act as witnesses; for twice-born men, twice-born men of equal standing; for Sudras, Sudras; and for the lowest caste people, men of the lowest birth' (1999, 291).

6 Chapter IV of the *Manusmriti* deals with how a Brahmana must live in this world. Bühler renders IV.79 as: 'Let him not stay together with outcasts, nor with Kandalas, nor with Pukkasas, nor with fools, nor with overbearing men, nor with low-caste men, nor with Antyavasayins' (1886, 141). Doniger and Smith (1991, 81): 'He should not live with people who have fallen,

nor with "Fierce" Untouchables, "Tribals", fools, arrogant men, men of the lowest castes, and "Those Who End Up at the Bottom".' Historian R.S. Sharma offers evidence of how several Pali and Buddhist texts and *Jataka* stories held views that echoed the Brahmanic texts: 'Several despised jatis of the Buddhist texts roughly correspond to the untouchable sections of Brahmanical society. According to the Buddhist and Jain texts the candalas and the pukkusas were not included in the Sudra varna' (1990, 125). In the third revised edition of his 1958 study *Sudras in Ancient India*, he says (337): 'Antyavasayins, though defined as a separate mixed caste in Vasistha and Manu, seems to have been an omnibus term applied to all the untouchables.' In his classic work *Buddhist India*, T.W. Rhys Davids, a scholar Ambedkar consults often, concurs (1903, 55): 'We hear in both Jain and Buddhist books of aboriginal tribes, Chandalas and Pukkusas, who were more despised even than these low tribes and trades.' Rhys Davids says that while 'the fact of frequent intermarriage is undoubted', 'the great chasm between the proudest Kshatriya on the one hand and the lowest Chandala on the other was bridged over by a number of almost imperceptible stages, and the boundaries between these stages were constantly being overstepped, still there were also real obstacles to unequal unions. Though the lines of demarcation were not yet drawn hard and fast, we still have to suppose, not a state of society where there were no lines of demarcation at all, but a constant struggle between attracting and repelling forces' (1903, 60).

7 Bühler (1886, 266): 'Women should give evidence for women, and for twice-born men twice-born men (of the) same (kind), virtuous sudras for sudras, and men of the lowest castes for the lowest.' Doniger and Smith, who say Bühler's translation is unreadable for its bad English and interpolation of commentaries into the text, render it, quite similarly, as: 'Women should be

witnesses for women, and twice-born men for twice-born men who are like them; good servants for servants, and men born of the lowest castes for men of the lowest castes' (1991, 68).

8   The *Apastamba Dharma Sutra* has only two books. Kane lists III.1 as featuring the term Antya and following him Ambedkar lists the same, but Olivelle's edition of the four major *Dharma Sutras* including Apastamba does not feature a Book 3.

9   Olivelle and Davis (2018, 26): 'Yajñavalkya was the most influential writer after Manu in terms of his effect on the later tradition. The text was composed probably in the fourth or fifth century CE in Eastern India during the rule of the Guptas.' I.148, which pertains to the duties of a Snataka Brahmin, reads: '[the study of *Vedas* should be stopped when interrupted by] the voice of a dog, a jackal, an ass, an owl, a Sâma (chanting), a bamboo, or one in distress (is heard). In the neighbourhood of impurities, a corpse, a Sudra, an Antyaja, a cemetery or an outcast' (in Vidyarnava 1918, 253). According to the Monier-Williams dictionary, Snataka is a Brahmin who, after performing the ceremonial lustrations required on his finishing his studentship as a Brahmacharin under a religious teacher, returns home and begins the second period of his life, as a Grihastha. There are three kinds of Snataka—*vidya*, a *vrata* [who has completed the vows, such as fasting, continence etc., without the *Vedas*], and a *vidya-vrata* or *ubhaya snataka* [who has completed both *Vedas* and vows], the last being the highest. I.197, part of chapter 7 that lists methods of purification for a Brahmin, reads: 'The mud and waters of the road if touched by out-castes (Antya) and dogs and crows become pure by the wind alone so also houses built of burnt brick' (Vidyarnava 1918, 291). See also p. 235–6 note 35.

10 Ambedkar lists this vide Kane 1941a, 70 (see p. 291–2 note 3 above). There are no scholarly editions of *Atri Smriti* or *Likhita*

Smriti that could be referred to. Atri is a Rig Vedic ancestor; Mandala V of the *Rig Veda* is attributed to him and known as the Atri Mandala, though Jamison and Brereton say he was not the author of all the verses in the Mandala but his gotra-clan, the Atris, sang most of them (2014, 659). The *Atri Smriti* takes his antiquated name merely as a legitimacy-seeking exercise, just like many shastraic texts claim mythic rishis as authors.

11 Both Ambedkar (1948, 132) and the BAWS edition list this erroneously as '1.2.39.18' via his source Kane (1941a, 70) who lists it as '1.3.9.18'. Kane likely referred to George Bühler who, in 1868, during his term as professor of Oriental languages at Elphinstone College in Bombay (where Ambedkar would study), collated five different extant handwritten manuscript editions of the work (two each from Pune and Nashik and one from Madras) and published it in Sanskrit with the subtitle 'Aphorisms of the Sacred Law of the Hindus'. In 1879, Bühler published an extensively annotated translation of the *Apastamba Dharma Sutra* along with *Gautama Dharma Sutra* as the second volume of the *Sacred Books of the East* edited by Max Müller and he went on to do the *Sutras* of Vasistha and Baudhayana (with Olivelle to follow in his footsteps in 1999) and did an edition of *Manusmriti* as well. The *Apastamba Dharma Sutra* is written in lines of aphoristic prose and not in the sloka/verse format. The line that corresponds (with the reference to Bahya) occurs in Bühler under 1.3.9.18 as part of a list of injunctions for a Brahmin about Vedic recitation and its suspension, where it appears that at the trigger of flimsy and whimsical excuses (regarded as 'inauspicious'), a Brahmin must desist from reciting the Veda: '14. (He shall not study in a village) in which a corpse lies; 15. Nor in such a one where Kandalas live. 16. He shall not study whilst corpses are being carried to the boundary of the village, 17. Nor in a forest, if (a corpse of a Kandala) is within sight. 18. And if outcasts have entered the village, he

shall not study on that day, 19. Nor if good men (have come). 20. If it thunders in the evening, (he shall not study) during the night...' (Bühler 1898 I, 34–5; see also Olivelle 1999, 17). Crucially, Bühler, who renders Bahya as outcast, has this footnote: 'Haradatta [a commentator] explains Bāhya, 'outcasts', by 'robbers, such as Ugras and Nishadas'. But, I think, it means simply such outcasts as live in the forest or outside the village in the Vâdî, like the Dhers, Mahârs, Mângs of the present day. Most of these tribes, however, are or were given to thieving' (1898, 34n18). That Bühler speculatively relates present-day Dhers, Mahars and Mangs (all Untouchables) to Bāhyas—in Hindi and Marathi, literally that which exists outside or is external/extrinsic, or that which has been externed, cast out—falls in line with Ambedkar's own speculative exercise of regarding present-day Untouchable as Broken Men (Buddhists), except that for Sanskrit-leaning Indologists and historians (such as Bühler, Kane, Olivelle and Aktor) the Buddhism/Buddhist linkage is not a concern nor is it tenable (R.S. Sharma 1990; V. Jha 2018). See also R.C. Dhere's reading of Marathi bhakti poetry (1984, trans. Feldhaus 2011) from the twelfth to seventeenth centuries around the cult of Vitthal of Pandharpur and its possible Buddhist origins (Dhere 2011, 186–8), a speculative conclusion Ambedkar too arrives at hoping (in 1954) to write at length about it (see Keer 1954/2001, 482).

12 This seems to be an error since the required details of Manu are not given; also Kane (1941a, 70) does not list Manu as one of the sources of Bahya; the references to *Vishnu Dharma Sutra* and *Narada Smriti* that follow via Kane do tally.

13 Says 16.14 (in Jolly 1880, 67): 'Kandalas must live out of the town, and their clothes must be the mantles of the deceased. In this their condition is different (from, and lower than, that of the other mixed castes)'. However, the term Bāhya (as per Kane cited by Ambedkar) does not occur in the said instance (only

Chandala does). Bāhya does occur in *Vishnu Dharma Sutra* later at 54.15: 'An atheist, one who leads the life of a member of the Kandala or of other low castes that dwell outside the village (Bāhyas), an ungrateful man, one who buys or sells with false weights, and one who deprives Brahmanas of their livelihood (by robbing them of a grant made to them by the king or private persons, or by other bad practices), all those persons must subsist upon alms for a year.'

14 Kane gives this as 155, and in Ambedkar (1948, 132) and BAWS (1990a) it is I.155; however, nothing tallies with the first ever English translation of *Narada Smriti* by Julius Jolly (1876); the use of Bāhya could not be established in the entire text though the term 'outcast' occurs in five instances in Jolly's English.

15 The reference given here for the *Gautama Dharma Sutra* doesn't appear to make sense; it's likely a typo or an oversight. The text of *Gautama Dharma Sutra* is divided into 28 chapters and each chapter is further subdivided into numbered verses. So references would have to be given as '28.4', for example. In Patrick Olivelle's translation, no reference to the term 'Antyavasin' can be found.

16 IV.79 in Bühler (1886, 141): 'Let him not stay together with outcasts, nor with Kandalas, nor with Pukkasas, nor with fools, nor with overbearing men, nor with low-caste men, nor with Antyavasayins'; in Doniger and Smith (1991, 81): 'He should not live with people who have fallen, nor with "Fierce" Untouchables, "Tribals", fools, arrogant men, men of the lowest castes, and "Those Who End Up at the Bottom".' X.39 Bühler (1886, 141): 'A Nishada woman bears to a Kandala a son (called) Antyavasayin, employed in burial-grounds, and despised even by those excluded (from the Aryan community). Doniger and Smith (1991, 240): 'A "Hunter" woman bears to a "Fierce" Untouchable man a son "Who Ends Up at the Bottom", who haunts the cremation-grounds and is despised even by the excluded

castes.' On the Antyavasayin, Kane draws our attention to a Sanskrit work of the post-Sultanate period written by a Brahmin scholar about the possible linkage between Antyavasis and the community we know as Doms of the present day (often cremation and burial ground workers): 'Some modern works like the *Jativiveka* (D.0. Ms.No.347 of 1887–91) say that Dom in modern times is the antyavasayin of the smrtis' (1941a, 71). There is little work on Gopīnātha's *Jātiviveka* ('Discernment of *Jātis*') save for Rosalind O'Hanlon et al.'s commentary (2015) on this 'modern' Sanskrit manual which they say was written by a Saivite Brahmin from Ahmadnagar (of present-day Maharashtra) at a time of 'the decline of Hindu royal power in western India'. This 'defence of varnasramadharma against the degenerated social condition of varnasamkara, 'confusion of varnas', a state to be expected in the fallen age of the Kaliyuga, and portending great harm to dharma in the world' was composed 'sometime between the middle of the fourteenth century and the later fifteenth' (103). Working within the caste categories of Manu and Yajñavalkya, demonstrating 'a marked hostility to bhakti religion' (111), *Jātiviveka* 'listed the parentage, proper occupation and ritual entitlements of some 85 local jati communities' (103–4). O'Hanlon et al. note that this successor to Brahmanic *Smriti* literature espoused 'a social order consisting really only of two varnas. There were Brahman like himself, and a great mass of mixed people... Gopinatha's was a world, therefore, in which there were few people of worth, apart from Brahman' (104, 111). Unsurprisingly, the work holds the Muslim 'Turuska' rulers of the Deccan really low. '[Even] a Candala is better than him. He is merciless and cruel. In the west, there is Mleccha land. They kill cows. One should not speak the Mleccha language at any rate. He earns his living by cruelty' (111). Gopinatha's text, at the receiving end of which were also scribal (Kayastha) and various artisanal castes, may seem obscure but this work of restating Brahmanism for the times, we are told, 'continued to exercise influence in the nineteenth century, shaping both social reform debates and the emerging politics of non-Brahmanism', so much that when 'the Sonar community of goldsmiths petitioned the Bombay government in defence of their rights, as high-born Rathakaras [literally chariot-makers but also craftspersons who worked on temple sculptures], to Vedic ritual, the *Jativiveka* was one of the works cited by H.H. Wilson, Secretary to the Committee of Public Instruction, and William Chaplin, Commissioner of the Deccan, against their case' (116). Wilson was the author of the six-volume *Rig-Veda Sanhita* that Ambedkar often consulted; see p. 163 note 2.

17 Chapter XVIII of *Vasistha Dharma Sutra* deals with varnasamkara, the consequences of intermixture of varnas. In Bühler's translation it reads, verse 3: '(That of a Sudra and) of a female of the Vaishya caste, an Antyavasayin' (1882, 94).

18 Kane (1941a, 71): 'Santi (141: 29–32) gives a graphic description of a hamlet of candalas and calls them 'Antyavasaya' (verse 41)'. *Mahabharata*'s longest section is the Shanti Parva, and 141 is part of what is called Apad Dharma Anushasana Parva, which speaks of what's to be done when one's dharma faces a crisis. The section sees a dialogue between Yudhistira and Bhishma, with Bhishma recounting the story of how the sage Viswamitra once finds himself without food or fire for days and sneaks into a Chandalas' quarters, along a forest, and tries to steal a haunch of dog's meat in desperation. Part of the description Kane has in mind, of a bewildering wilderness and desolation, here in K.M. Ganguli's translation: 'One day he [Viswamitra] came upon a hamlet, in the midst of a forest, inhabited by cruel hunters addicted to the slaughter of living creatures. The little hamlet abounded with broken jars and pots made of earth. Dog-skins were spread here and there. Bones and skulls, gathered in heaps, of boars and asses, lay in different places. Cloths [stripped] from

the dead lay here and there, and the huts were adorned with garlands of used up flowers' (Ganguli 1883–1896, Vol 8, 338). But Viswamitra is caught in the act by an elderly Chandala man, and a long dialogue ensues with Viswamitra arguing that he be allowed to sate his hunger. While the Chandala says, 'The dog is certainly an unclean food to members of the regenerate classes', Viswamitra insists: 'Any other kind of meat is not to be easily had during a famine like this. Besides, O Chandala, I have no wealth (wherewith to buy food). I am exceedingly hungry. I cannot move any longer. I am utterly hopeless. I think that all the six kinds of taste are to be found in that piece of dog's meat' (Ganguli, 339). Despite the Chandala's protestations and rather peculiar defence of varna-dharma, Viswamitra does take away the haunch of the dog's meat, cooks it with his wife and eats it, but owing to ascetic powers and the practice of the required rituals, he does not lose caste. Most Brahmanic rules are framed such that the Brahmin, at least the exemplary Brahmin, remains one despite transgressions (even if Viswamitra in this case is an ironic example offered by Bhishma and the *Mahabharata*: born a Kshatriya he becomes a super-Brahmin after much self-denial and struggle). In this light, though the bone of contention seems to be the question of who gets to remain a Brahmin forever, the worse idea is that there forever must be a Brahmin. The persistence of the figure of the Brahmin generates the need of several people imagined to be untouchable—from the menstruating woman within the Brahmin household to the Sudra/ Chandala/ Antyaja/ Avarna, sometimes even the Brahmin male who trespasses tabooed boundaries—graded, shaded in ever-shifting degrees. Without this the justification of the position of the Brahmin, held as superior, becomes fraught. Once a fictive purity is imagined, a million ways of getting polluted become necessary. If the world were filled only with Brahmins, they would lose their mind and reason for existence, for they would have no one to defend their purity against. Anyone reading the *Smritis* and *Shastras* would come out feeling that the Brahmin is forever in a crisis, forever swearing by inherent inequality, guarding his turf and afraid of the radical equality that the very idea of Dalit-ness poses.

19 *Madhyamangiras* appears to be another ghost text cited by Ambedkar and is not listed in Kane's *History of Dhamasastra* (1941a). Vivekanand Jha: 'Vijnanesvara in his Mitaksara commentary on a verse of the *Yajnavalkya Smriti*, quotes Madhyamangiras to differentiate between antyavasayins represented by the Candala, Svapaca, Ksatr, Magadha, Suta, Vaidehaka and Ayogava and the seven Antyajas occuring in Atri and Yama and including the leather worker...' (1979, 103).

20 36.7 is part of a set of injunctions which proscribe sexual intercourse with specific types of women: 'And with a sister's female friend (or with one's own female friend), with a woman of one's own race, with a woman belonging to the Brahmana caste, with a (Brahmana) maiden (who is not yet betrothed to a man), with a low-caste woman, with a woman in her courses, with a woman come for protection, with a female ascetic, and with a woman entrusted to one's own care' (in Jolly 1880, 134).

21 Manu IV.61: 'Let him not dwell in a country where the rulers are Sudras, nor in one which is surrounded by unrighteous men, nor in one which has become subject to heretics, nor in one swarming with men of the lowest castes' (in Bühler 1886, 138). Chapter VIII of Manu deals with punishments to be meted out to Sudras and outcastes for transgressions, imagined hence real, against the 'twice-born'. VIII.279 reads: 'With whatever limb a man of a low caste does hurt to (a man of the three) highest (castes), even that limb shall be cut off; that is the teaching of Manu' (303). To give some context for this system of 'caste justice', here's VIII.271: 'If he [Sudra] mentions the names and

castes (jati) of the (twice-born) with contumely, an iron nail, ten fingers long, shall be thrust red-hot into his mouth' (301).

22 This is from Chapter 9 that speaks of the worship of the elephant-headed god Ganapati known also as Vinayaka, 'the remover of obstacles'. In 1.273, Yajnavalkya says a good Brahmin must not even dream of an Antyaja: 'Or dreams of persons wearing red garments, or dreams that he mounts on carnivorous animals or he dreams that he is in the company of low-caste [Antyaja] people or surrounded by asses and camels' (Vidyarnava 1918, 367).

23 It has not been possible to establish this in Mitakshara's commentary even via Kane (1941a).

24 See p. 296–7 note 10 above on the ghost text of *Atri Smriti*.

25 It has not (yet) been possible to access a reliable edition of the *Vyasa Smriti* attributed to Vyasa (see p. 152 note 3) though it is much cited via secondary sources by several scholars from Kane and Ambedkar to D.N. Jha. A right-wing online repository, Hindu Online (http://hinduonline.co), features a PDF in Sanskrit uploaded by 'Maharishi University of Management: Vedic Literature Collection' sans any authentication or provenance. In it, I.12–13 does have a reference to the term Antyaja. Earlier in this book, along notes 51–2, Ambedkar cites the *Veda Vyasa Smriti* and offers I.12–13 via Kane (1941a, 71) although this is I:11 in the online text of dubious provenance.

26 Surveying literary narratives, sastraic literature and Buddhist texts, Aktor (2018, 87–117) identifies three types of Chandalas depending on topography: those that live in the wilderness/forest, further than even the outskirts of the village, whom he calls 'tribe Chandala'; those that live at the edge of the village or sometimes even inside it (Chandalas connected with work such as cremation) and are referred to as 'sons' in *Dharmasastraic* literature: they are not seen as ethnically different, and are

expected to wear certain visible marks of clothing to indicate their lowness; and lastly, the 'adultery Chandala', born of wrong sexual relations, varnasamkara (typically the Pratiloma progeny of Brahmin women and Sudra men). Aktor concludes, almost using Ambedkar's language: 'Since these early dharmasastras did not distinguish clearly between 'caste Chandalas' and 'adultery Chandalas', both being referred to as "sons". This is a *riddle* inherent in the very notion of varnasamkara' (2018, 92, emphasis added). Aktor's use of 'tribe Chandala' harks back to D.D. Kosambi's observation that in ancient India, 'the Candala is of tribal origin, as are innumerable other castes actually found today in India—mostly sudras, but some risen by vocation in economic and therefore social status, to a place among the three higher caste-classes' (1985, 193). The accompanying footnote explicates: 'The Candalas had their own settlements and their own separate language according to Jatakas 497 (*Matanga-pandita*) and 498 (*Citta-shmbhutta*); however, they were even then so despised that brahmin girls washed out their eyes after having gazed by accident upon the untouchable. On the other hand, clever Candalas could manage to pass themselves off as brahmins, according to these tales' (193).

27 Mikael Aktor says of this proliferation of terms and lack of consensus on what each meant: 'It has often been argued that these classifications were speculative manoeuvres, which did not reflect actual practices of caste formation but were applied as a means of recognizing a relative and differentiated inclusion of indigenous and foreign people in the interaction with the people of the four varnas' (2018, 93).

28 Citing the work of the Indological scholar Horst Brinkhaus from the German, Aktor says, 'these classifications made it possible to integrate indigenous groups while at the same time establishing a clear demarcation between these and the varnas. The varnasamkara groups were linked to the varnas

without forming a fifth varna beyond the scheme authorized in the Purushasukta. Thus, when it is denied in Manavadharmasastra [Manu] 10.4 that such a fifth varna exists, this is not an attempt to deny social facts, as it has been understood by [Louis] Dumont and [Vivekanand] Jha, but a matter of controlling these facts in a manner which respects the tradition' (2008, 94). Echoing Ambedkar's thesis in *Castes in India* (1989a) (but not citing him), historian Uma Chakravarti (1987) explains that the Brahmanic varnasamkara theories came in 'to explain the proliferation of the number of occupational groups which resulted from the expansion of the economy' and sees this as 'probably one way in which many tribal groups were being assimilated into society.' She adds: 'Since the Brahmanical system of stratification was a hierarchical or linear order, every new group or occupation had to be fitted into the scheme of the social order in relation to the total system. This empirical reality of assimilation had to be given a conceptual formulation which was provided by the vamasamkara theory' (29). Furthermore, R.S. Sharma in the revised edition of his *Sudras in Ancient India* (1990, 332–45), in an Appendix chapter, examines the proliferation of servile and peasant castes by citing epigraphic evidence to show both Brahmana priests and Buddhist monks from c. 200 BCE to 500 CE coming up with mechanisms to 'absorb the tribals'. While Buddhist monks appointed by emperor Asoka played a key role in propagating Buddhist social ethics among tribals in central and western India, between the second and seventh centuries CE, Brahmins were granted large swathes of land in modern-day Andhra Pradesh, Maharashtra, Madhya Pradesh, Orissa, Bengal, Assam, Himachal and Nepal, in order to convert the people in these regions into the varna ideology, thus facilitating governance and administration. Sharma contends (1990, 341): 'This is the reason why the lists of Manu and of the later

Puranas disclose a large number of mixed castes, all Sudras, whose tribal origins can be detected without difficulty.'

29 The exposé mode here is similar to the one Ambedkar was to later use in *Riddles in Hinduism*, written in 1954–55 (Anand 2016, 11) which was posthumously published. The extensive tabular exposition of the many contradictions between *Smritis* and *Shastras* is especially used in Riddle No. 18, "Manu's Madness or the Brahmanic Explanation of the Origin of the Mixed Castes", where lamenting the 'wholesale bastardisation of huge communities', Ambedkar (2016, 152) asks (with an exasperation conventional scholars do not betray): 'If these different Smritikaras are dealing with facts about the origin and genesis of mixed castes mentioned above, how can such a wide difference of opinion exist among them?' (2016, 149). Trying to understand 'this madness on their part', he concludes: 'It is possible that Manu had realized that *chaturvarna* had failed and that the existence of a large number of castes— which could neither be described as Brahmans, Kshatriyas, Vaishyas or Shudras—was the best proof of the breakdown of the *chaturvarna* and that he was therefore called upon to explain how these castes who were outside the *chaturvarna* came into existence notwithstanding the rule of *chaturvarna*' (153). Sharma's explanation on this proliferation is outlined in the preceding note.

30 Following unwittingly in Ambedkar's footsteps, Aktor writes in another paper (2002, 244): 'Ancient and medieval texts frequently refer to what looks like *proto-untouchable* groups, such as Candalas, Pulkasas, and Svapacas. But these texts are literary sources in which direct evidence of the actual historical, economic, and social conditions of these groups is very limited. Even the law literature, the *Dharmasastra*, in which we find the most systematic account of the phenomenon, is not a source for the history of the untouchables but, at most, a source

for Brahmanical attitudes that to some extent have been influential in forming the later observed social practices.' Arguing that Brahmanical literature aimed at 'both interaction and segregation at the same time' (246, emphasis added), he says that segregation of untouchable groups was not absolute but negotiable. 'The concern was with safeguarding and regulating a necessary interaction and not with prohibiting it altogether. In this sense, the untouchables were in an ambiguous position. They did not stand outside the community of the four varnas but at its margins' (247).

31 [See Manu I.45]. Both Ambedkar (1948) and BAWS edition (1990a) cite Manu wrongly. It is Chapter X that discusses 'mixed castes' at length and the matching reference to Dasyus appears in X.45: 'All those tribes in this world, which are excluded from (the community of) those born from the mouth, the arms, the thighs, and the feet (of Brahman), are called Dasyus, whether they speak the language of the Mlekkhas (barbarians) or that of the Aryans' (Bühler 1886, 413).

32 [Ibid.] The use of Bahya, spelt Vâhya in Bühler's text, occurs at X.28: 'As a (Brahmana) begets on (females of) two out of the three (twice-born castes a son similar to) himself, (but inferior) on account of the lower degree (of the mother), and (one equal to himself) on a female of his own race, even so is the order in the case of the excluded (races, vâhya)' (Bühler 1886, 408). X.31 refers to both Vâhya and Hina: 'But men excluded (by the Aryans, vâhya), who approach females of higher rank, beget races (vâhya) still more worthy to be excluded, low men (hina) still lower races, even fifteen (in number)' (409).

33 Hina as a generic reference to 'low' castes is found in contemporaneous and pre-Mauryan Buddhist texts as well. Many scholars, including Chakravarti (1987, 101) point to how in Buddhist texts, '[a] basic opposition between high and low appears

in the context of jati, kula, kamma (work) and sippa (craft); thus there are high jatis and low jatis... Thus ukkatta [high] jati is defined as khattiya [Pali for kshatriya] and brahmana, while hina jati is defined as candala, vena, nesada, ratthakara, and pukkusa. The latter categories are conventionally translated as low caste-man, bamboo worker or basket maker, hunter, cartwright, and flower sweeper or scavenger, by Buddhist scholars. The same division is repeated exactly in the same form further on in the *Vinaya Pitaka*.' Ambedkar, as such, can be faulted for bias and for bypassing Buddhist texts in his surveys and this has been pointed to by scholars such as R.S. Sharma (1990) and Vivekanand Jha (2018). With specific reference to Ambedkar's case that untouchables were formerly Buddhists who continued to eat beef, Sharma says: 'It has been suggested that in the majority of instances the origin of untouchables took place as a result of complete isolation and loss of tradition of the Buddhist communities. But such a view is untenable, for this social phenomenon appears in the pre-Mauryan period, which witnessed the rise and growth of Buddhism. It has been contended that those who continued beef-eating were condemned as untouchables. This may have swelled the ranks of the untouchables in later times, but cannot be taken as an explanation of their origin, for except for a late reference in the *Gautama Dharma Sutra*, there is nothing which may imply that beef-eating was prohibited in brahmanical society during this period' (Sharma 1990, 131). However, Ambedkar's main contention—how beef-eating and a ghetto existence define Untouchability in the modern sense—has not been addressed by scholars who are quick to cite the Buddhist embrace of caste distinctions to dismiss him.

34 IV.79: 'Let him not stay together with outcasts, nor with Kandalas, nor with Pukkasas, nor with fools, nor with overbearing men, nor with low-caste men, nor with Antyavasayins' (Bühler 1886, 141).

35 Medhatithi's *Manubhashya* is one of the most cited commentaries on the *Manusmriti*. With no biographical facts available about its mysterious author—whether he was a Brahmin from the north or the south of the subcontinent—scholars have speculated that he lived in Kashmir or Nepal. Using textual evidence from the works that Medhatithi cites, Kane infers he must have lived between 820 CE and before 1050 CE and gives *Manubhashya*'s date as c.900 CE (Kane 1941a, xi).

36 Ambedkar is likely citing from Bühler's notes where he summarizes the commentaries of all his predecessors and often offers his own take, quite like Kane and other Indologists up to Doniger and Olivelle do. Bühler (1886, 411): 'Thus according to Medh. [Medhatithi] and Kull. [Kulluca]. But Gov. [Govindaraja] and Ragh. [Raghavananda] understand in the second line with "from a Vaidehaka", the words "by women of the Vaideha caste." Nar. [Narayana], who in the preceding verse takes the words *ete trayah*, "those three," in the sense of "the following three other races," assumes of course that the mothers of Karavaras, Medas, and Andhras are Ayogava females. The latter two "castes" are the well-known nations inhabiting Mevad/(Medapata) in south-eastern Rajputana, and the eastern Dekkan.'

37 On the contrary, Bühler is rather careful in making the distinction between Antya (its attendant suffixes) and low-caste, though often these two terms are used almost interchangeably by commentators. At IV.79 cited above in note 34, low-caste men and Antyavasayins are both listed. In fact, unlike Doniger and Smith (1991) or Olivelle (2005), Bühler, by translating less, allows space for a wide array of jati terms that Manu coins and uses (many of them obsolete and some that may never have existed) instead of resolving the confusion in a language (English) that does not have the vocabulary for so many ways of being unequal. Crucially, Bühler in his 1886 translation of

Manu nowhere uses the term Untouchable, whereas Doniger and Smith choose to translate the word Chandala as 'Fierce-Untouchable' and do not always alert us to the different ways in which the idea of Untouchability figures in the text. For further problems on this, see p. 339–40 note 11.

38 [Kane,*History of Dharmasastras* II. Part I. p. 167]. Kane begins his chapter on Untouchability (1941a, 165–179) with a curious statement that while the contemporary world may make much of the existence of Untouchables in India, similar problems and conditions are obtained globally, and cites the various forms of 'discrimination against Negroes' prevalent in the southern states of the United States, and the experiences of Gandhi and other Indians in South Africa. Arguing, like Ambedkar, that the Vedic and Upanishadic periods did not recognize anyone as untouchable as such, he says there's only evidence of how some 'castes' were held in contempt: the 'Paulkasa lived in such a way as to cause disgust and the Candala lived in the wind (i.e. probably in the open or in a cemetery)' (166).

39 In the same passage that Ambedkar cites, Kane enforces this view with further commentary: 'Sankara explains that by "end of the quarters" are meant regions where people opposed to Vedic culture dwell. This description can only apply to people like the mlecchas and not to candalas who are not opposed to Vedic knowledge (but who have no adhikara to learn it). Besides candalas might stay outside the village, but they do not stay at the end of the quarters (or at the end of the Arya territory). Hence this passage does not help in establishing the theory of untouchability for Vedic times' (1941a, 167). Why the Chandalas would not be opposed to Vedic knowledge merely because the Brahmin books say they have no adhikara to learn it, is not clear. That there was an antagonism between the Antyas and the Brahmins has variously been asserted by anti-caste radicals, including Ambedkar. As we have shown earlier, the Holeyas

were opposed to the Brahmins entering their cheris and considered them inauspicious (see p. 132–3 note 18). Ambedkar's key point is that those who became Untouchables were not simply barred from Vedic learning, but rather that they were opposed to it and actively militated against it from the beginning.

40 [Kane, *History of Dharmasastras*. Vol. II. part I. p. 70] In the ensuing paragraph, Ambedkar paraphrases Kane.

41 Kane, Ambedkar's source, adds: 'Nilakantha explains that they were the kaivartas and bhillas of the border regions.' When Kane and Ambedkar wrote, the 1958 Bhandarkar Oriental Research Institute's critical edition of the *Mahabharata* had not been prepared. In K.M. Ganguli's edition, a match for 109:19 in Shanti Parva could not be found. In the matching verse in the BORI Critical Edtion, the terms Antyaja does figure, but at 102.19: 'tyaktaatmaanah sarva ete *antyajaa* hyanivartinah/ puraskaaryaah sadaa sainye hanyante ghnanti chaapi te'. This, according to Bibek Debroy, means: 'All of them are ready to give up their lives. They dwell in the frontier regions and do not retreat. They place themselves ahead of the soldiers and kill or are killed.' The context is Bhishma is describing (to Yudhishtira) warriors who dwell in the extremities of the kingdom.

42 The reference in Kane pertains to *Saraswativilasa*, a digest on 'ancient Hindu Law' written by Prataprudradeva (1497–1540 CE), a king of the Gajapati dynasty in Orissa. *Saraswativilasa* has come to be considered a part of *Dharmasastra* commentarial literature. It was published by the University of Mysore in a Sanskrit edition in 1927 by the scholar Rudrapatna Shama Sastry, who in 1905 also re-discovered and published the *Arthashastra* attributed to Kautilya (see Ellis 1833; Sastry 1927).

43 Bhillama II was a king of the dynasty known as Seuna or Sevuna Yadavas of Devagiri that ruled the Deccan after starting as feudatories of the Chalukyas.Bhillama II ruled from c. 985–1005

CE (Sen 1988, 403).

44 *Viramitrodaya* is a vyavahara text (a law digest) written in the early seventeenth century by Mitra Misra of the 'Benares School' on the *Dharmasastra*. The translated edition in circulation is Golapchandra Sarkar's *The Law of Inheritance as in the Viramitrodaya of Mitra Misra* first published in 1879. Sarkar was a lawyer in the Calcutta high court, and the *Viramitrodaya* was often cited and consulted in legal judgements in British-ruled India.

45 Kane further adds: 'This shows that these low castes had risen in social status in the medieval ages by their organization and wealth' (1941a, 70).

46 [Amarkosh II Kanda Brahmabarga Verse II.] The reference is to *Amarakosha*, also known as *Namalinganushasana*, a Sanskrit lexicon written in metrical poetry in the fourth century CE by Amarasimha. A 1913 edition from Poona by Krishnaji Govind Oka opens with these lines: 'Amarasimha's lexicon, well-known to every Sanskrit student, is the oldest work of the kind now extant. It is of great interest to note that, though the production of a Buddhist, it has been universally accepted as an authority by the Brahmans and the Jainas alike' (1913, 3). It is not clear which edition Ambedkar used or if he is citing this from a secondary source. But *Amarakosha* does list Antyevasin (not Antyavasin as is rendered in romanized versions by most scholars) in the sloka numbered 2|7|11|1|2: Chatr*antavesin*au sishye shaikshah praathamakalpikah ekabrahmarvataachara mithah sabrahmacharinah. However, since words have multiple meanings, Amarakosha also has the following sloka (2|10|20|1|3), nishaada-shvapachav-antevasi-chandala-pukkasaah/ bhedah kiraata-shabara-pulindaa-mlechha-jaatayah, which lists that castes that may be called Mlechha jaati: to wit, Nishada, Svapacha, Antevasi, Chandala, Pukkasa, Bheda, Kirata, Shabara,

Pulinda are the mleccha jati. The scholar Bibek Debroy, who led us to this, glosses the two terms: etymologically, in the word *antevasin*, the verb root is to reside, to reside outside inner quarters. So it means 'those who dwell outside inner habitations'. *Antyaja* means 'those cast aside from inner habitations'. Ambedkar was absolutely right—neither has anything to do with untouchability.

47 Chapter 16 of *Vasistha Dharma Sutra* lists the jati names of those born of mixed marriages. Verses 1 to 3 with the third mentioning the Antyavasayin read: '1. They declare that the offspring of a Sudra and of a female of the Brahmana caste becomes a Kandala, 2. (That of a Sudra and) of a female of the Kshatriya caste, a Vaina, 3. (That of a Sudra and) of a female of the Vaishya caste, an Antyavasayin' (Bühler 1882, 94).

48 It is erroneously printed as V.39 in Ambedkar (1948, 137) and BAWS (1990a); the right reference is the already discussed X.39 on p. 299–301 note 16.

49 In his *History of Dharmasastra* Kane devotes over a page (1941a, 81–2) to the many valencies and occurrences of the term Chandala from the Vedic period to Fa-Hian's descriptions up to the use of the term in the 1931 census. Ambedkar derives his ensuing list from Kane. See p. 345–6 notes 20–1 where Fa-Hian's description of Chandalas is cited by Ambedkar, who says the Chinese traveller's description of the Chandala does not fully indicate Untouchability: 'The Chandala is not a good case to determine the existence or non-existence of Untouchability. The Brahmins have regarded the Chandalas as their hereditary enemies and are prone to attribute to them abominable conduct; hurl at them low epithets and manufacture towards them a mode of behaviour which is utterly artificial to suit their venom against them. Whatever, therefore, is said against the Chandalas must be taken with considerable reservations.'

50 [According to all *Dharma Sutras* and *Smritis* including *Manusmriti*.]

51 [According to *Veda Vyas Smriti* (1.910)] It has not been possible to establish the provenance of this reference, but the same is cited in Kane. Even the dubious online source cited earlier on p. 304 note 25 does not feature 1.910; and often with different editions, the romanization and chapterization modes also vary.

52 [According to *Veda Vyas Smriti* (1.910)]

53 [According to Yama quoted in Parasura Madhavya] Parasara Madhaviya (spelt as Parasura Madhavya in Ambedkar 1948, 138, and 1990a, 366) was authored in the thirteenth century by Madhavacarya who cites from the *Yama Smriti*, a text often cited in other commentaries but a reliable edition of which has not been found.

54 [Anusasan Parva (29.17). He is also called Matanga.] See p. 347–8 note 25 for a discussion of the term 'Matanga'.

55 Ambedkar is citing from Bühler (1898, 253).

56 Bühler (1882, 30).

57 Bühler (1882, 171).

58 Manu V.85: Bülher (1886, 183), V.131 (192), V.143 (194).

59 In making this seemingly fraught and persistent point, and in arguing a little earlier that those classed as 'Antyavasin, Antya, Antyaja' (or even slapped with the generic 'Chandala') in ancient literature need not have been 'Untouchables in the *modern* sense of the term', Ambedkar is asking us to turn and return to the *radical* meaning of such terms that have their root in Vedic Brahmanic ritual: how a word in itself, say antevasya, contained a range of meanings: a celibate Brahmachari Brahmin at one end and the ones who live at the end of the village, the outcaste, at the other end. Contempt and inequality surely undergirded the very premise of caste even within the varna

fold, and Ambedkar himself in "Castes in India" (1916) says that caste never exists in singular, is always plural and works as a *system*. But here Ambedkar wagers much in saying that this cannot be taken to mean the wholesale rejection of an Antyaja or Chandala from all forms of sociality (despite the evidence of Fa-Hian or *Kadambari* or Brahmanic texts), the way it has come to be in the 'modern' sense where Untouchability is *hereditary*, where an Untouchable is an object of permanent derision and exclusion, not just for the ritual-minded Brahmin but to most non-Brahmin non-Dalits as well as sometimes to Adivasis. To state it more politically, like the modern Dalit movement puts it, the presence of the Untouchable-Dalit is resisted in our times both by Brahmanic temples as well as faculties of such universities as Jawaharlal Nehru University. A university founded in Ambedkar's name, Ambedkar University, Delhi, can institute an annual Ambedkar Memorial Lecture and not invite a single Dalit to deliver a talk over nine years (see Dalit Bahujan Adivasi Collective's "An Open Letter to the Vice Chancellor, Ambedkar University, Delhi" 2016). Any 'progressive, leftist' Brahmin and the Sankaracharya or any anti-reservationist will gleefully point out how there's Untouchability observed amongst 'SCs' themselves (say the Chamar who looks down on a Musahar who looks down on a Dom and so on, with each resisting connubiality and commensality)—the endless mathematical reproduction of both caste and its consequence, Untouchability, such that there is always someone more Untouchable than one Untouchable—owes of course to the sheer Brahmanic cunning invested in sustaining the thought of inequality as attested to by the range of Brahmanic literature Ambedkar surveys here. This is the perverse unreflective comfort derived in saying, 'But it is not just I who practises Untouchability, everybody does.'

60 In our concern for producing an annotated edition of manageable length, Chapter 2 (called "Untouchability among Hindus"

in Ambedkar 1990a, 256-67) was one of the portions that we had to forego. Here, Ambedkar discusses at length Brahmanic notions of ritual pollution, purity and defilement as defined in *Manusmriti* and such texts, and compares them to the taboos that exist among 'primitive and ancient peoples'. Examining how birth, death and menstruation were seen as sources of defilement by Manu and others, he says even the Brahmin was not 'ever pure'. But Ambedkar's concern here is what he called 'hereditary Untouchability' (1990a, 259) and he adduces a list prepared by the British Government of India in 1935 and 'attached to the Orders-in-Council issued under the Government of India Act of 1935'. Ambedkar offers the list of nine sections across six pages that, he says, 'may be taken to be both exhaustive and authentic' so as 'to give an idea of the vast number of communities which are regarded as hereditary Untouchables by the Hindus' (259). At the end of the list he makes in 1948, he writes: 'This is a very terrifying list. It includes 429 communities. Reduced to numbers it means that today there exist in India 50-60 millions of people whose mere touch causes pollution to the Hindus. Surely, the phenomenon of Untouchability among primitive and ancient society pales into insignificance before this phenomenon of hereditary Untouchability for so many millions of people which we find in India. This type of Untouchability among Hindus stands in a class by itself. It has no parallel in the history of the world' (265). He then concludes that 'defilement as observed by the Primitive Society was of a temporary duration', for 'after the period of defilement was over and after the purificatory ceremonies were performed the defilement vanished and the individual became pure and associable. But the impurity of the 50-60 millions of the Untouchables of India, quite unlike the impurity arising from birth, death, etc., is permanent' (266). Unlike pollution-related taboos of tribal and primitive societies, Ambedkar says

'Hindu society insists on segregation of the Untouchables. The Hindu will not live in the quarters of the Untouchables and will not allow the Untouchables to live inside Hindu quarters. This is a fundamental feature of Untouchability as it is practised by the Hindus. It is not a case of social separation, a mere stoppage of social intercourse for a temporary period. It is a case of territorial segregation and of a *cordon sanitaire* putting the impure people inside a barbed wire into a sort of a cage. Every Hindu village has a ghetto. The Hindus live in the village and the Untouchables in the ghetto' (266). To explain this 'unique phenomenon, unknown to humanity in other parts of the world', Ambedkar comes up with the Broken Men theory.

61 See the list of twelve in the table by Ambedkar on p. 280–1 under Antyaja and Antyavasin.

62 Ambedkar places much premium on this colonial census-driven 'Scheduled Castes' list, calling it 'exhaustive and authentic'. For a critique of how colonialism and Census freeze-dried communities into castes and how colonialism and Orientalism shaped the caste system in the modern sense, see p. 121–2 note 1 where Ambedkar calls the Census a 'wealth of information'.

63 Here Ambedkar makes an exaggerated claim in bemoaning the difference in the communities or jatis listed in the *Dharmasastra* texts and a colonial-era post-Census list. It is likely that much has changed over time. After all, the status of any caste, even those listed as Brahmin, is often contested and open to negotiation with shifting power centres over time, as is clear from how a Brahmanic text like *Jativiveka* in the sixteenth century sets down afresh who is Sudra and who is Savarna, and their relative positions in the hierarchy (see p. 299–301 note 16 above on *Jativiveka*). If varnasamkara (intermixture of caste) is inevitable, and if the nature of caste is that of proliferation under all circumstances—historical, social, geographic and

economic—then new names and mechanisms of inequality have to constantly be invented, and Untouchability necessarily follows. During the colonial moment, caste and Untouchability were permanently defined and any change to the 'Schedule'—getting into or out of it—involved (and continue to do so) protracted legal battles that were often untenable. The Pallars of present-day Tamil Nadu (see p. 132 note 17) are embroiled in a struggle to get out of the Schedule while the Mauryas (also known variously as Sakhya, Saini and Binds) of Uttar Pradesh and Haryana (currently listed as an Other Backward Class) are involved in a struggle to get on to the Schedule as an Untouchable caste. Whether it is the Rathakaras or Sonars in the nineteenth century contesting the validity of *Jativiveka* or Pallars and Mauryas today, these definitions of who does and who does not belong are always contested. In Bihar, Nitish Kumar as chief minister in 2007 established the State Mahadalit Commission enlisting eighteen jatis (subsequently expanded to twenty-one) under the Mahadalit category, arguing that only a few jatis had cornered the benefits of reservation as SCs (see Teltumbde 2018, 70–1). Getting in or out of the Schedule list—originally notified in 1950—needs a bill in parliament to be passed followed by a presidential notification. As on date, only six such Presidential Orders have been issued between 1950 and 1978.

64 History provides several instances of those who face Untouchability moving out of this pale but over centuries. While the category Untouchable remains, those classed as so can change. See p. 283–4 above where Ambedkar via Kane draws our attention to Rajakas whom the Shastras define as Antyaja but who, by the tenth century, had no stigma of Untouchability. According to historian Irfan Habib, the Jats (or Jatts) who are today demanding Other Backward Class (OBC) status were, until the eighth century, regarded as Chandala, an Untouchable jati in

the Sindh and Punjab regions. By the eleventh century they had attained Sudra status; after the Jat rebellion of the seventeenth century, a segment of the Jats aspiring to be zamindars sought Rajput (Kshatriya) status (see Habib 1976).

65   Ambedkar takes an important argumentative risk here. This dissonance between the two lists (in the *Smritis* and the colonial censuses) is explained through their common term: the Chamar caste. The consumption of beef by this community becomes the crucial fact on which the origin of untouchability is pegged. For 'objective' academia, which isn't moved by the urgency of Ambedkarite politics, this might seem absurd and untenable. But Ambedkar's gesture is worth exploring: beef-eating takes on two roles. It is the remnant of the practices of the Buddhist faithful before the onslaught of the Brahminic counter-revolution. Beef-eating also functions as a symptom: a revolutionary violation even as the counter-revolution keeps growing stronger. And this is what Ambedkar reminds us: beef itself is largely unimportant. It is its position in the schema of caste society that is consequential. Such symptomal objects can differ depending on the contingencies of politics. In the present, we latch on to what these incisional objects, like beef, reveal about the truth of the conditions of certain subjects caught in a system that appears 'normal'. With beef, Ambedkar captures the body of the Untouchable subject, in a time when they weren't untouchable, and infuses their position with revolutionary potential by locating them in an anonymous scene of historical battle—a battle whose memory has been erased, but we continue to remember it anyway because of our faith in equality.

66   Vivekanand Jha takes further his mentor R.S. Sharma's accusation that Ambedkar got it wrong in connecting beef-eating with Untouchability and defeated Buddhists. There is cold comfort in Jha and Sharma at least reckoning with Ambedkar and arguing their differences unlike others who tactically do

not even acknowledge his work. In the collection of his various essays on Untouchability, revised and published in 2018, Jha chides Ambedkar for 'lacking the discipline of a historian' and 'prizing his imagination' to arrive at 'wild generalisations' and concludes that 'his survey of the origin, development and expansion of untouchability is full of subjective impressions' especially given that he 'idealized and lionized the role of Buddhism' (2018, 66–7). In his essay "Stages in the History of Untouchables", he concludes: 'It is amusing to see Ambedkar deny the very being of the Candala in his bid to push ahead the date of the beginning of untouchability in this country' (67). As we have seen, Ambedkar treats the Chandala or the Antyavasin as a generic category and not exactly an Untouchable, and in this he is merely following the scholar P.V. Kane (and the Indologist Mikael Aktor follows in their path). But Kane, a Brahmin scholar who knows his Sanskrit, never comes in for such rebuffs. While Jha accuses Ambedkar—who tried learning Sanskrit in India, was denied, and then tried picking it up at Bonn University in three months (see Bellwinkel-Schempp 2003)—of not having 'thorough first-hand knowledge of wide-ranging original sources dispersed over a long period,' often Jha himself depends on secondary and tertiary sources (like several contemporary scholars) that he cherry-picks, a tactic used by any writer who is a subjective subject. Jha prizes 'objectivity' and 'hard evidence' only to often succumb to subjective conclusions. Meanwhile, as we have shown, Ambedkar contends with the presence of caste in Buddhism and the contempt for proto-Untouchable groups in Buddhist texts, and attempts to extract the Buddha's 'original teachings' from their historical appropriations and distortions. Jha, on the other hand, over-reaches in expressing his love for the Bhagvad Gita ("Social Content of the Bhagvadgīta: Idealized Notion of Caste sans Untouchability" 119–70), a text he deliberately misreads 'as one that [is] meant for all classes of people in equal measure' (120). This is pointed out, with dissent, by fellow-historian Suvira Jaiswal in her preface to his book (xiii). The late Jha also displays unabashed and subjective love for Gandhi, another defender of varnashrama and the Gita, and says that Ambedkar 'took an uncharitable view of Mahatma Gandhi's vigorous championship of their [untouchables'] cause and even dubbed him a "humbug"' (45). How Ambedkar anticipates such attacks as Jha's is explained in the first endnote (p. 92–3 note 1) of this edition.

Chapter XVI

When did broken men become Untouchable?

The foregoing researches and discussions have proved that there was a time when the village in India consisted of a Settled Community and Broken Men and that though both lived apart, the former inside the village and the latter outside it, there was no bar to social intercourse between the members of the Settled Community and the Broken Men. When the cow became sacred and beef-eating became taboo, society became divided into two—the Settled Community became a touchable community and Broken Men became an untouchable community. When did the Broken Men come to be regarded as Untouchables? That is the last question that remains to be considered. There are obvious difficulties in the way of fixing a precise date for the birth of Untouchability. Untouchability is an aspect of social psychology. It is a sort of social nausea of one group against another group. Being an outgrowth of social psychology[1] which must have taken some time to acquire form and shape, nobody can venture to fix a precise date to a phenomenon which probably began as a cloud no bigger than man's hand and grew till it took its final all-pervading shape as we know it today. When could the seed of Untouchability be said to have been sown? If it is not possible to fix an exact date, is it possible to fix an approximate date?

An exact date is not possible. But it is possible to give an approximate date. For this the first thing to do is to begin by fixing the upper time-limit at which Untouchability did not exist and the lower time-limit at which it had come into operation.

To begin with the question of fixing the upper limit the first thing to note is that those who are called Antyajas are mentioned in the *Vedas*. But they were not only not regarded as Untouchables but they were not even regarded as Impure. The following extract from Kane may be quoted in support of this conclusion. Says Kane:[2]

> In the early Vedic literature several of the names of castes that are spoken of in the Smritis as Antyajas occur. We have Carmamna[3] (a tanner of hides) in the Rig Veda (VIII.5.38)[4] the Chandala and Paulkasa occur in Vaj. S., the Vapa or Vapta[5] (barber) even in the Rig., the Vidalakara or Bidalakar[6] (corresponding to the Buruda[7] of the Smritis) occurs in the Vaj.S. and the Tai.Br. Vasahpalpuli[8] (washer woman) corresponding to the Rajakas[9] of the Smritis in Vaj.S. But there is no indication in these passages whether they, even if they formed castes, were at all Untouchables.

Thus in Vedic times there was no Untouchability. As to the period of the *Dharma Sutras*, we have seen that there was Impurity but there was no Untouchability.

Was there Untouchability in the time of Manu? This question cannot be answered offhand. There is a passage[10] in which he says that there are only four varnas and that there is no fifth varna. The passage is enigmatical. It is difficult to make out what it means. Quite obviously the statement by Manu is an attempt by him to settle a controversy that must have been going on at the time he wrote. Quite obviously the controversy was about the status of a certain class in relation to the system of Chaturvarna. Equally obvious is the point which was the centre of the controversy. To put briefly, the point was whether this class was to be deemed to be included within the Chaturvarna or whether it was to be a fifth varna quite distinct from the original four varnas. All this is quite clear. What is, however, not clear is the class to which it refers. This is because Manu makes no specific mention of the class involved in the controversy.

The verse is also enigmatical because of the ambiguity in the decision given by Manu. Manu's decision is that there is no fifth varna. As a general proposition it has a meaning which everybody can understand. But what does this decision mean in the concrete application to the class whose status was the subject matter of controversy. Obviously it is capable of two interpretations. It may mean that as according to the scheme of Chaturvarna there is no fifth varna the class in question must be deemed to belong to one of the four recognized varnas. But it may also mean that as in the original Varna System there is no provision for a fifth varna the class in question must be deemed to be outside the Varna System altogether.

The traditional interpretation adopted by the orthodox Hindu is that the statement in Manu refers to the Untouchables, that it was the Untouchables whose status was in controversy and that it was their status which is the subject-matter of Manu's decision. This interpretation is so firmly established that it has given rise to a division of Hindus into two classes called by different names, Savarnas or Hindus (those included in the Chaturvarna) and Avarnas or Untouchables (those excluded from the Chaturvarna). The question is, is this view correct? To whom does the text refer? Does it refer to the Untouchables?[11] A discussion of this question may appear to be out of place and remote from the question under consideration. But it is not so. For if the text does refer to the Untouchables then it follows that Untouchability did exist in the time of Manu—a conclusion which touches the very heart of the question under consideration. The matter must, therefore, be thrashed out.

I am sure this interpretation is wrong. I hold that the passage does not refer to the Untouchables at all.[12] Manu does not say which was the fifth class whose status was in controversy and about whose status he has given a decision in this passage. Was it the class of Untouchables or was it some other class? In support of my conclusion that the passage does not refer to Untouchables at all I rely on two circumstances. In the first place, there was no Untouchability in the time of Manu. There was only Impurity. Even the Chandala for whom Manu has nothing but contempt is only an impure person. That being so, this passage cannot possibly have any 'reference to Untouchables'. In the second place, there is evidence to support the view that this passage has reference to slaves and not to Untouchables. This view is based on the language of the passage quoted from the *Narada Smriti* in the chapter on the Occupational Theory of Untouchability.[13] It will be noticed that the *Narada Smriti* speaks of the slaves as the fifth class. If the expression fifth class in the *Narada Smriti* refers to slaves, I see no reason why the expression fifth class in *Manusmriti* should not be taken to have reference to slaves. If this reasoning is correct, it cuts at the very root of the contention that Untouchability existed in the time of Manu and that Manu was not prepared to include them as part of the Varna System. For the reasons stated, the passage does not refer to Untouchability and there is, therefore, no reason to conclude that there was Untouchability in the time of Manu.[14]

Thus we can be sure of fixing the upper limit for the date of the birth of Untouchability. We can definitely say that *Manusmriti* did not enjoin Untouchability. There, however, remains one important question. What is the date of *Manusmriti*? Without an answer to this question it would not be possible for the average to relate the existence or non-existence of Untouchability to any particular point in time. There is no unanimity among savants regarding the date of *Manusmriti*. Some regard it as very ancient and some regard it as very recent. After taking all facts into consideration Prof Bühler has fixed a date which appears to strike the truth. According to Bühler, *Manusmriti* in the shape in which it exists now, came into existence in the Second Century AD.[15] In assigning so recent a date to the *Manusmriti* Prof Bühler is not quite alone. Mr Daphtary[16] has also come to the same conclusion. According to him *Manusmriti* came into being after the year 185 BC and not before. The reason given by Mr Daphtary is that *Manusmriti* has a close connection with the murder of the Buddhist Emperor Brihadratha of the Maurya dynasty by his Brahmin Commander-in-Chief Pushyamitra Sunga and as even that took place in 185 BC, he concludes that *Manusmriti* must have been written after 185 BC. To give support to so important a conclusion it is necessary to establish a nexus between the murder of Brihadratha Maurya by Pushyamitra and the writing of *Manusmriti* by strong and convincing evidence. Mr Daphatry has unfortunately omitted to do so. Consequently his conclusion appears to hang in the air. The establishment of such a nexus is absolutely essential. Fortunately there is no want of evidence for the purpose.

The murder of Brihadratha Maurya[17] by Pushyamitra[18] has unfortunately passed unnoticed. At any rate it has not received the attention it deserves. It is treated by historians as an ordinary incident between two individuals as though its origin lay in some personal quarrel between the two. Having regard to its consequences it was an epoch-making event. Its significance cannot be measured by treating it as a change of dynasty—the Sungas succeeding the Mauryas. It was a political revolution as great as the French Revolution, if not greater. It was a revolution—a bloody revolution—engineered by the Brahmins to overthrow the rule of the Buddhist Kings. That is what the murder of Brihadratha by Pushyamitra means.[19]

This triumphant Brahmanism was in need of many things. It of course needed to make Chaturvarna the law of the land the validity of which was denied by the Buddhists. It needed to make animal sacrifice, which was abolished by the Buddhists, legal. But it needed more than this. Brahmanism in bringing about this revolution against the rule of the Buddhist Kings had transgressed two rules of the customary law of the land which were accepted by all as sacrosanct and inviolable. The first rule made it a sin for a Brahmin even to touch a weapon. The second made the King's person sacred and regicide a sin. Triumphant Brahmanism wanted a sacred text, infallible in its authority, to justify their transgressions. A striking feature of the *Manusmriti* is that it not only makes Chaturvarna the law of the land, it not only makes animal sacrifice legal but it goes to state when a Brahmin could justifiably resort to arms and when he could justifiably kill the King. In this the *Manusmriti* has done what no prior *Smriti* has done. It is a complete departure. It is a new thesis. Why should the *Manusmriti* do this? The only answer is, it had to strengthen the revolutionary deeds committed by Pushyamitra by propounding philosophic justification. This interconnection between Pushyamitra and the new thesis propounded by Manu shows that the *Manusmriti* came into being sometime after 185 BC, a date not far removed from the date assigned by Prof

Bühler. Having got the date of the *Manusmriti* we can say that in the Second Century AD, there was no Untouchability.

Now to turn to the possibility of determining the lower limit to the birth of Untouchability. For this we must go to the Chinese travellers who are known to have visited India and placed on record what they saw of the modes and manners of the Indian people. Of these Chinese travellers Fa-Hian[20] has something very interesting to say. He came to India in 400 AD. In the course of his observations occurs the following passage:[21]

> Southward from this [Mathura] is the so-called middle-country (Madhyadesa). The climate of this country is warm and equable, without frost or snow. The people are very well off, without poll-tax or official restrictions. Only those who till the royal lands return a portion of profit of the land. If they desire to go, they go; if they like to stop they stop. The kings govern without corporal punishment; criminals are fined, according to circumstances, lightly or heavily. Even in cases of repeated rebellion they only cut off the right hand. The King's personal attendants, who guard him on the right and left, have fixed salaries. Throughout the country the people kill no living thing nor drink wine, nor do they eat garlic or onion, with the exception of Chandalas only. The Chandalas are named 'evil men' and dwell apart from others; if they enter a town or market, they sound a piece of wood in order to separate themselves; then, men knowing they are [near], avoid coming in contact with them. In this country they do not keep swine nor fowls, and do not deal in cattle; they have no shambles or wine shops in their market-places. In selling they use cowrie shells. The Chandalas only hunt and sell flesh.

Can this passage be taken as evidence of the prevalence of Untouchability at the time of Fa-Hian? Certain parts of his description of the treatment given to the Chandalas do seem to lend support to the conclusion, that is, a case of Untouchability.

There is, however, one difficulty in the way of accepting this conclusion. The difficulty arises because the facts relate to the Chandalas. The Chandala is not a good case to determine the existence or non-existence of Untouchability. The Brahmins have regarded the Chandalas as their hereditary enemies and are prone to attribute to them abominable conduct; hurl at them low epithets and manufacture towards them a mode of behaviour which is utterly artificial to suit their venom against them. Whatever, therefore, is said against the Chandalas must be taken with considerable reservations.

This argument is not based on mere speculation. Those who doubt its cogency may consider the evidence of Bana's[22] *Kadambari*[23] for a different description of the treatment accorded to the Chandalas.

The story of Kadambari is a very complex one and we are really not concerned with it. It is enough for our purpose to note that the story is told to king Shudraka by a parrot named Vaishampayana who was the pet of a Chandala girl. The following passages from the Kadambari are important for our purpose. It is better to begin with Bana's description of a Chandala settlement. It is in the following terms:[24]

> I beheld the barbarian settlement, a very market-place of evil deeds. It was surrounded on all sides by boys engaged in the chase, unleashing their hounds, teaching their falcons, mending snares, carrying weapons, and fishing, horrible in their attire, like demoniacs. Here and there the entrance to their dwellings, hidden by thick bamboo forests, was to be inferred, from the rising of smoke of orpiment. On all sides the enclosures were made with skulls; (627) the dust-heaps

on the roads were filled with bones; the yards of the huts were miry with blood, fat, and meat chopped up. The life there consisted of hunting; the food, of flesh; the ointment, of fat; the garments, of coarse silk; the couches, of dried skins; the household attendants, of dogs; the animals for riding, of cows; the men's employment, of wine and women; the oblation to the gods, of blood; the sacrifice, of cattle. The place was the image of all hells.

It is from such a settlement that the Chandala girl starts with her parrot to the palace of king Shudraka. King Shudraka is sitting in the Hall of Audience with his Chieftains... The king and the Chieftains did not at first take notice of her. To attract attention she struck a bamboo on the mosaic floor to arouse the King. Bana then proceeds to describe her personal appearance.

> Then the king, with the words, 'Look yonder' to his suite, gazed steadily upon the Candala maiden, as she was pointed out by the portress; Before her went a man, whose hair was hoary with age, whose eyes were the colour of the red lotus, whose joints, despite the loss of youth, were firm from incessant labour, whose form, though that of Matanga,[25] was not to be despised, and who wore the white raiment meet for a court. Behind her went a Candala boy, with locks falling on either shoulder, bearing a cage, the bars of which, though of gold, shone like emerald from the reflection of the parrot's plumage. She herself seemed by the darkness of her hue to imitate Krishna when he guilefully assumed a woman's attire to take away the amrita seized by the demons. She was, as it were, a doll of sapphire walking alone; and over the blue garment, which reached to her ankle, there fell a veil of red silk, like evening sunshine falling on blue lotuses. The circle of her cheek was whitened by the ear-ring that hung

from one ear, like the face of night inlaid with the rays of the rising moon; she had a tawny tilaka of gorocana, as if it were a third eye, like Parvati in mountaineer's attire, after the fashion of the garb of Siva.

She was like Sri darkened by the sapphire glory of Narayana reflected on the robe on her breast; or like Rati, stained by smoke which rose as Madana was burnt by the fire of wrathful Civa; or like Yamuna, fleeing in fear of being drawn along by the ploughshare of wild Balarama; or, from the rich lac that turned her lotus feet into budding shoots, like Durga, with her feet crimsoned by the blood of the Asura Mahisha she had just trampled upon.

Her nails were rosy from the pink glow of her fingers; the mosaic pavement seemed too hard for her touch, and she came forward, placing her feet like tender twigs upon the ground....[26]

... And the king was amazed; and the thought arose in his mind, 'Ill-placed was the labour of the Creator in producing this beauty! For if she has been created as though in mockery of her Candala form, such that all the world's wealth of loveliness is laughed to scorn by her own, why was she born in a race with which none can mate? Surely by thought alone did Prajapati create her, fearing the penalties of contact with the Matanga race, else whence this unsullied radiance, a grace that belongs not to limbs sullied by touch? Moreover, though fair in form, by the basenness of her birth, whereby she, like a Lakshmi of the lower world, is a perpetual reproach to the gods, she, lovely as she is, causes fear in Brahma, the maker of so strange a union.'...

On reading this description of a Chandala girl many questions arise. Firstly, how different it is from the description given by Fa-Hian?[27] Secondly Bana is a Vatsyayana Brahmin.[28]

This Vatsyayana Brahmin, after giving a description of the Chandala settlement, finds no compunction in using such eloquent and gorgeous language to describe the Chandala girl. Is this description compatible with the sentiments of utter scorn and contempt associated with Untouchability? If the Chandalas were Untouchables how could an Untouchable girl enter the King's palace? How could an Untouchable be described in the superb terms used by Bana? Far from being degraded, the Chandalas of Bana's period had Ruling Families among them. For Bana speaks of the Chandala girl as a Chandala princess[29] Bana wrote some time about 600 AD, and by 600 AD the Chandalas had not come to be regarded as Untouchables. It is, therefore, quite possible that the conditions described by Fa-Hian, though bordering on Untouchability, may not be taken as amounting to Untouchability. It may only be extreme form of impurity practised by the Brahmins who are always in the habit of indulging in overdoing their part in sacerdotalism. This becomes more than plausible if we remember that when Fa-Hian came to India it was the reign of the Gupta Kings. The Gupta Kings were patrons of Brahmanism. It was a period of the triumph and revival of Brahmanism. It is quite possible that what Fa-Hian describes is not Untouchability but an extremity to which the Brahmins were prepared to carry the ceremonial impurity which had become attached to some community, particularly to the Chandalas.

The next Chinese traveller who came into India was Yuan Chwang. He came to India in 629 AD. He stayed in India for 16 years and has left most accurate records of journeys up and down the country and of the manners and customs of the people. In the course of his description of general characters of the cities and buildings of India, he says:[30]

> As to their inhabited towns and cities the quadrangular walls of the cities (or according to one text, of the various regions) are broad and high, while the thoroughfares arc narrow tortuous passages. The shops are on the highways and booths (or, inns) line the roads. Butchers, fishermen, public performers, executioners, and scavengers have their habitations marked by a distinguishing sign. They are forced to live outside the city and they sneak along on the left when going about in the hamlets.

The above passage is too short and too brief for founding a definite conclusion thereon. There is, however, one point about it which is worthy of note. Fa-Hian's description refers to the Chandalas only while the description given by Yuan Chwang applies to communities other than the Chandalas. This is a point of great importance. No such argument can be levelled against the acceptance of a description since it applies to communities other than the Chandalas. It is, therefore, just possible that when Yuan Chwang came to India, Untouchability had emerged.

On the basis of what has been said above we can conclude that while Untouchability did not exist in 200 AD, it had emerged by 600 AD.

These are the two limits, upper and lower, for determining the birth of Untouchability. Can we fix an approximate date for the birth of Untouchability? I think we can, if we take beef-eating, which is the root of Untouchability, as the point to start from. Taking the ban on beef-eating as a point to reconnoitre from, it follows that the date of the birth of Untouchability must be intimately connected with the ban on cow-killing and on eating beef. If we can answer when cow-killing became an offence and beef-eating became a sin, we can fix an approximate date for the birth of Untouchability.

When did cow-killing become an offence?

We know that Manu did not prohibit the eating of beef nor did he make cow-killing an offence. When did it become an offence? As has been shown by Dr D.R. Bhandarkar, cow killing was made a capital offence by the Gupta kings sometime in the 4th Century AD.

We can, therefore, say with some confidence that Untouchability was born some time about 400 AD. It is born out of the struggle for supremacy between Buddhism and Brahmanism which has so completely moulded the history of India and the study of which is so woefully neglected by students of Indian history.

Annotations

1 Freud's *Civilization and Its Discontents* (1930) bears mentioning in the context of social psychology. In this work, he argues that any construction of an overarching social reality causes a feeling of discontentment in any subject who sees herself as belonging to that society. This, Freud said, was a result of the repression of certain primal desires that is necessitated by having to live in a community. For Lacan, this desire is non-sensical, it does not arise out of any innate or primal truth which is hidden in us, but is a contingent manifestation of particular signifiers that tie us to the communal life-world. He reads most performative acts of opposing societal systems as those which are already conditioned by the system itself, and the true radical act as that which rejects all interpellation to the system (Cho 2006). When Ambedkar maps out a genealogy of Untouchability in the proceeding section, he doesn't attribute the logic of inequality of caste to any innate or primal tendency in humans, but deals with them as contingent appearances which are not necessary in themselves, and therefore as structures which can be rejected and overturned.

2 [*Dharmasastras Vol. II Part I.* p. 165]

3 Vivekanand Jha maps out the difference in social prestige faced by those involved in tanning as an occupation across different periods of time. In the Vedic period, for instance, there was a particular caste identity which could be applied to the particular group of people working with animal hides. They seemed to have been very much a part of Aryan society. Jha goes on to hypothesize that even with the rise of urban centres and consolidation of the Varna system, Carmamnas did not become ritually impure. However, as the powerful castes moved away from physical labour, increasingly considered undignified, the tanning community lost its position as a Vaishya

caste. There was a pronounced difference in the economic strength of tanners in urban and rural areas, the former holding more wealth and power. Further, in the *Brahmanas* tanners are mentioned as separate from Sudras, and therefore it is hypothesized that they were not looked down upon as a caste but rather the occupation itself had stigma attached to it. It is only in the *Manusmriti* that one finds references to tanning communities as castes unto themselves; however, it is difficult to ascertain whether they were considered Untouchables as yet. References continue in the *Anusana Parva* and *Amarakosa* and also the *Vinaya Pitaka*. It is only after the Gupta era that the Carmamnas or Carmakaras begin to be referred to as Antyajas (Jha 1979).

4   VIII.5 is the longest hymn to the Asvins in the *Rig Veda*. It has little mythological material and no mention of the exploits of the Asvins. Rather the hymn is an exhortation to perform sacrifices and a prayer to the gods to fulfil desires of supplicants. The verse mentioned above is as follows; in it Kasu, the lord of the Cedis, is being praised for his generosity: 'He who (previously) bestowed on me a king's ten (horses?) of golden appearance—/ beneath the feet of the lord of the Cedis are (all) the communities, the "hide-tanning" men all around' (Jamison and Brereton 2014, 1037).

5   In the *Rig Veda* only one reference to a barber is made. It can be found at X.143.4. The hymn X.143 is dedicated to Agni and it speaks of the dangerous nature of fire. The verse is as follows: 'When you travel to the heights and the depths, snapping, you go in all directions, like an army in greedy pursuit./ When the wind fans your flame, like a barber a beard you shave the ground' (Jamison and Brereton 2014, 1628). In H.H. Wilson's translation of the *Rig Veda*, another instance of the appearance of the word 'barber' can be found, in the Sixth Ahyaya of the First Ashataka. The hymn in which it is found is in praise of the

Ushas (Dawn): 'Ushas cuts off the accumulated (glooms); as a barber (cuts off hair): she bares her bosom; as a cow yields her udder (to the milker) ...' (Wilson 1866, 237). He provides an alternative translation of the reference to the barber as like a dancing girl; the original Sanskrit includes the terms *nritue iva* and *pesansi vapate* which could refer to both the performance of a dance and the actions of a barber (ibid.).

6   Vidalakara or Bidalakara refers to bamboo-workers and basket makers. In the *Vajasaneyi Samhita* and the *Taittiriya Brahmana* they are among the 148 victims listed for human sacrifice (purushamedha). In this sacrifice, the Bidalkaras are dedicated to the pisacas, a class of deities that are in the same class as asuras and raksasas; Vivekanand Jha (1978) surmises that this fact points to the aboriginal origin of the caste. The name for the Bidalkaras becomes 'Vena' in the post-Vedic age, and several references to them as hina jatis (lesser castes) can be found in Pali texts. Jha also cites the *Kusa Jataka* in which an enraged queen uses the terms 'Vena' and 'Candali' to address her daughter-in-law. In the same text, however, we see a prince apprenticing under the court basket-maker, which shows that they were not considered Untouchable at this point in time (Jha 1978).

7   Buruda is a basket-weaving caste from Maharashtra and Telangana (Russell 1916, 209).

8   In the *Atharva Veda*, Vasahpalpuli is the word used to refer to a female washer of clothes. References to the handling of clothes in this *Veda* do not seem to have a derisory tone as can be expected thanks to the later prevalent caste-nature of the work: night and day are personified as twin sisters weaving themselves into existence. However, Pesakaris, or embroiders of intricate designs of gold into cloth, are listed as victims of purshamedha in the *Vajasaneyi Samhita* and the *Taittiriya*

Brahmana (Verman 2013). In the later Vedic age (1000–500 BCE) with material progress, increased urbanization and a proliferation of several occupations, Vivekanand Jha postulates, the specific job of washing clothes was formalized. The two categories of this profession were based on gender: Malaga corresponding to men and Vasahpalpuli to women. Women were especially predominant in occupations that pertained to clothing and weaving, with professional categories like Vayitri, Rajayitri, Pesakari, Bidalakari and Kantakikar emerging, which dealt with weaving, dyeing, embroidery, basket making and thorn working [what is this?] respectively (Jha 1991).

9 Rajaka refers to communities involved in the washing of clothes in Andhra Pradesh, Telangana and Sri Lanka. The caste is also referred to as Vannan, Vannar (in Tamil) and Chakali (Telugu). References to the community can be found in the *Ramayana* in which it is a Rajaka who questions Sita's chastity upon her return to Ayodhya with Rama, and also in the Basavapuranam, an epic which charts the life and philosophy of Basavanna, a Shaivite social reformer of the twelfth century and founder of Lingayatism (Thirupathi 2016). In Sri Lanka, the Rajakas are called Radas and are part of the Sinhalese caste society. For an overview of caste distribution in Sri Lanka, see Silva et al. (2009).

10 [Manu X.4] Bühler renders X.4 as: 'The Brahmana, the Kshatriya, and the Vaishya castes (varna) are the twice-born ones, but the fourth, the Sudra, has one birth only; there is no fifth (caste)' (1886, 402).

11 While Ambedkar rightly makes much of this passage the non-use of the term Untouchable and the possibilities this gives rise to, the term Chandala—often used derogatorily for Untouchables even today—is repeatedly used in *Manusmriti* besides other terms that connote Untouchability. That logical consistency

is not a virtue of *Manusmriti* or other Brahmanic texts, often written by a collective and collated over a period of time, is something Ambedkar himself draws our attention to repeatedly (see especially *Riddles in Hinduism*, 2016, especially Riddle No. 18, "Manu's Madness or the Brahmanic Explanation of the Origin of the Mixed Castes", 139–54). Bühler leaves Chandala as is in III.239 and does not use the term 'untouchable' even once in his work though he often uses the term 'outcast/s': 'A Kandala, a village pig, a cock, a dog, a menstruating woman, and a eunuch must not look at the Brahmanas while they eat' (1886, 119). However, Doniger and Smith consistently translate Chandala as '"Fierce" Untouchable, saying that the Chandala is 'the paradigmatic Untouchable', 'often used as the generic term for any Untouchable' (1991, 234), quite like the Chinese traveller Fa-Hian does, as we shall see. Also, outcast and Chandala are listed one after another in the *Manusmriti*, making them distinct and separate categories of exclusion, thus adding to the confusion. Doniger and Smith (1991) in their introduction argue that *Manusmriti*, written when Brahmanism was pushed into a crisis by the emergent Sramana critiques, 'attempts to extend its reach to all people as well as all situations—the king as well as the ritual priest; the Untouchable as well as the priest; the householder as well as the world-renouncer; women as well as men' (xxxvi). Yet Ambedkar with great conviction argues that there was likely no Untouchability recognized by *Manusmriti* and that the outcasts who lived outside the village were 'Broken Men' who became untouchable later, after they embraced Buddhism and continued eating the dead cow.

12 Ambedkar offers a contradictory reading of this passage from Manu in his posthumously published essay entitled "The House the Hindus Have Built". This essay was meant for foreign readers unfamiliar with Indian society, but the contradiction is striking: 'What Manu meant was there were originally four

Varnas and four they must remain. He was not going to admit the Untouchables into the House the ancient Hindus had built by enlarging the Varna System to consist of five Varnas. That is what he meant when he said that there is not to be a fifth Varna. That he wanted the Untouchables to remain out of the Hindu social structure is clear from the name by which he describes the Untouchables. He speaks of them as Varna–Bahyas (those outside the Varna System). That is the difference between the Primitive and Criminal Castes and the Untouchables. There being no positive injunction against their admission in Hindu Society, they may in course of time become members of it. At present they are linked to Hindu Society and hereafter they may become integrated into it and become part of it. But the case of the Untouchables is different. There is positive injunction against their incorporation in Hindu Society. There is no room for reform. They must remain separate and segregated without being a part of the Hindu Society. The Untouchables are not a part of the Hindu Society. And if they are a part they are a part but not of the whole. The idea showing the connection between the Hindus and the Untouchables was accurately expressed by Ainapure Shastri the leader of the orthodox Hindus at a Conference held in Bombay. He said that the Untouchables were related to the Hindus as a man is to his shoe. A man wears a shoe. In that sense it is attached to man and may be said to be a part of the man. But it is not part of the whole for two things that can be attached and detached can't be said to form parts of one whole. The analogy though is none the less accurate' (1989b, 169).

13 The *Narada Smriti* comprises of eighteen laws that concern legal and economic proceedings. In a chapter entitled 'Head of Dispute', under the subhead 'Breach of Promised Obedience' one can find discussions on existent slavery. Five kinds of labourers are listed, of which four are proclaimed to be free (a

pupil, an apprentice, a hired servant and an agent) and they can be of any caste. The fifth kind, the slave, is said to be of fifteen kinds and they are declared as impure. The jobs assigned to them are: 'Clearing the house, the gateway, the convenience, and the road from rubbish, rubbing the secret limbs, and gathering and removing impurities, especially urine and faeces' (Jolly 1876, 61–2). 'Attending to the master's pleasure' is also said to be an impure task. The fifteen kinds of slaves are: 'One born in the house, one bought, one received by donation, one got by inheritance, one maintained in a famine, one pledged by a former master, one relieved from a great debt, one made prisoner in a war, one obtained through a wager, one who has offered himself, saying, "I am thine", an apostate from religious mendicity, a slave for a fixed period, one maintained in reward of the work performed by him, a slave for the sake of his wife, and one self-sold' (Jolly 1876, 63–4). The service of the first of four of these are said to be hereditary.

14 All the same, Ambedkar ceremonially burnt a copy of the *Manusmriti* on 25 December 1927 at Mahad following the effort by Brahmins to purify Chavadar Tank after the Dalits, led by Ambedkar, drank water from it on 20 March 1927. By the twentieth century, the *Manusmriti*, first translated by William Jones, came to symbolize Brahmanism and its excessive defence of caste ideology. While Ambedkar holds the work in contempt, he is here willing to grant that technically the terms untouchable or untouchability were not deployed in this text. Besides, in *Who Were the Shudras?* (1946) Ambedkar says he undertook a study for fifteen years, that is from 1930 onwards, of relevant shastraic literature in translation. It could be argued that till 1932, till the gains of separate electorates for Untouchables at the Round Table Conferences, which were stymied by Gandhi and the Hindu Mahasabha with the 1932 Poona Pact, Ambedkar held the hope that Hinduism could be reformed and

repaired. It is after the Poona Pact was signed owing to Gandhi's blackmail that Ambedkar undertakes his extensive study of caste and Untouchability.

15 [Bühler, *Laws of Manu* (S.B.E.) Vol. XXV. Int. CXIVI.] In the mentioned source, Bühler tries to fix the date of *Manusmriti*'s authorship. The difficulty of fixing such a date is discussed at length by Bühler. The main reason given for this is the continuity within which the *Manusmriti* was produced. Without a doubt, it draws on several *Sutras*, but the problem then becomes whether the *Sutras* came first or the *Manusmriti*. Furthermore, the contradictory nature of injunctions contained in the *Sutras* and the *Manumriti* make it even more complicated, for it becomes unclear which tract is trying to improve on the imperfections of which one. By comparing Manu's injunctions to texts across the Brahmanical fold, Bühler provides comparative studies of different values held in different times and the different valencies and usages of words in different texts to place its authorship at around the second century CE. In their introduction to *The Laws of Manu* (1991), Doniger and Smith state that the text was composed around the same time (xvii). Patrick Olivelle (2005) draws on the *Manusmriti*'s relationship with the *Mahabharata*, the older sutra texts, similarity to lines in the *Arthasastra* and references in texts like the *Kamasutra*, *Mrichhakatika* and *Vajrasuchi* to fix its date of composition to somewhere between the second and third centuries CE (22–5).

16 Chander Kishan Daphtary was an Indian lawyer and bureaucrat. He was appointed India's first solicitor general, and was, between 1963 and 1968, the attorney general of India. From 1972 to 1978 he held office in the Rajya Sabha.

17 After the reign of Asoka (269–232 BCE), the Mauryan Empire devolved into a state of instability. This culminated in the revolt carried out by the military general Pushyamitra who assassi-

nated the king Brihadratha and established the Sunga dynasty in 184 BCE. The Sungas are chiefly credited with reviving the Vedic practice of the yajna. It was during the time of Pushyamitra's rule that Patanjali's Sanskrit grammar and prose books were written (Kosambi 2008, 187–8).

18 Pushyamitra is said to have had strong anti-Buddhist convictions. It is claimed that he destroyed Buddhist monasteries and persecuted monks throughout his empire which stretched from Pataliputra to Sakala. Buddhist texts Divyavadana and Manjusrimulakalpa ascribe several conflicts to Pushyamitra in which he invaded several Buddhist kingdoms, one of which was the conquest of Sakala. The claim these texts make is that Pushyamitra died ingloriously while fighting one such battle in the vicinity of his Sakala territory. The Sungas after Pushyamitra were a weak succession of kings, and inroads into their kingdom were made by the Greeks, Satavahanas and tribal chiefs like Kharavela. However, Ujjain remained under Sunga rule for the length of their existence. It was during this period that Krishna was raised from a tribal deity of the Yadus to a more prominent position with the Greek ambassador Heliodoros proclaiming his devotion to the god; however, he was not as yet made into the powerful figure as a Vishnu-avatar which he was to become later. D.D. Kosambi tells about the Sungas that despite their symbolic importance, as in the case of the revivial of the yajna, 'their success lay more on the parade ground and in fields of culture than in battle' (2008, 188). However, the memory of the dynasty persisted in the Brahmin imagination as can be gleaned from Gupta-era poet and playwright Kalidasa's *Malavika and Agnimitra*, a romantic play about Pushyamitra's son. The tenth and last Sunga king, Devabhuti, was assassinated by his Kanvayana Brahmin minister, Vasudeva, to establish the Kanva dynasty (Sen 1949; Kosambi 2008, 187–8). See also p. 248 note 61 earlier.

19 Ambedkar elaborates on the significance of this moment in subcontinental history in his ambitious but unfinished book-length manuscript "Revolution and Counter-Revolution in Ancient India" (1987, 149–440) where he is largely concerned with the 'decline and fall of Buddhism' and argues that 'the object of the Regicide by Pushyamitra was to destroy Buddhism as a state religion and to make the Brahmins the sovereign rulers of India' (269). Devoting a chapter to the 'Literature of Brahmanism' that was deployed after Pushyamitra's rise, he says though 'most Hindus, whether orthodox or not, learned or not, have an inerradicable belief that their sacred literature is a very old one in point of time.' It is a fact that '(1) Manusmriti (2) Gita (3) Shankaracharya's Vedant (4) Mahabharat (5) Ramayana and (6) the Puranas' were written in the wake of Pushyamitra's putsch (1987, 239). Throughout this chapter, Ambedkar uses an array of sources and internal evidence from the texts to arrive at possible dates of various *Puranas*, *Smritis*, *Sutras* and epics—just as he is keen in *The Untouchables* to establish a date for the emergence of Untouchability or the banning of the sacrifice of the cow and the consumption of beef.

20 With the spread of Buddhism in China, after the first century CE, several monks, guided by their devotion, felt the need to travel back to the land of Buddha particularly to visit the Bodhi tree. Several names of such travellers have been discovered on inscriptions from the second and third century, such as Chi-I and Ho-Yun. It is also possible that many pilgrims have been lost to history and their time in India went unrecorded. Fa-Hian (CE 399–414), also known as Faxian, was one such Buddhist pilgrim. Having concerned himself with this religious pursuit, he travelled from China to India, and visited monasteries in what is now Xinjiang, Pakistan, India, Nepal, Bangladesh, and Sri Lanka. Like Hsuan Tsang, he recorded a survey of 'Buddhistic Kingdoms'. His travel writings were translated into the

English by James Legge as *A Record of Buddhistic Kingdoms* (1886).

21 [*Buddhist Records in Western India* by Beal. Introduction p. xxxvii–xxxviii.] The following quote is taken from Samuel Beal's Introduction to his translation of Hsuan Tsang's writings, *Buddhist Records in Western India, Vol. I* (1884). This introduction includes a section which is a translation of Fa-Hian's writings, entitled "The Travels of Fa-Hian: Buddhist Country Records". The above text is part of the sixteenth chapter of Fa-Hian's work, and in another translation, done by James Legge, it is titled as "On to Mathura or Muttra. Condition and customs of Central India; of the monks, viharas, and monasteries". When the term 'Chandala' occurs in Legge's translation for the first time, he provides the following reference from Ernest J. Eitel's *Hand-Book of Chinese Buddhism, being A Sanskrit-Chinese Dictionary with Vocabularies of Buddhist Terms*: 'The name Chandalas is explained as "butchers," "wicked men," and those who carry "the awful flag," to warn off their betters;— the lowest and most despised caste of India, members of which, however, when converted, were admitted even into the ranks of priesthood' (Legge 1886, 43). Legge slightly alters the origin definition given by Eitel, changing its language and structure, and most noticeably its spelling: from 'Tchhandala' (see Eitel 1904, 175).

22 Also known as Banabhatta, Bana was a Brahmin poet and author in the seventh CE. He was a member of the court of king Harsha of the Vardhana dynasty. Bana is considered one of the greatest Sanskrit writers. His two most famous works are *Harshacharita* and *Kadambari*. *Harshacharita* is a book of praise which lists the great deeds of king Harsha. In addition, it also traces the illustrious history of Bana's family, and connects them to the goddess Saraswati and the sage Dadhica (Lochtefeld 2002; Sharma 1968).

23 *Kadamabari* is considered one of the first novels in world literature (though the 11th century Japanese work, *The Tale of Genji*, stakes a greater claim since it uses only prose). It is a romance that broke the tyranny of fixed metres and is set in free verse. Historian D.D. Kosambai says, '*Kadambari* has compound words that go at times to several lines each in printed editions. But his skill was such that the very name of the book, actually the name of its heroine, has now come to mean a 'novel' or 'romance' in Indian languages' (2008, 203). The love story between the main characters, a princess named Kadambari and a prince named Chandripida, is but one element of the book's complex plot. *Kadambari* was left unfinished at Bana's death and is said to have been completed by his son Bhusanabhatta (Sharma 1968).

24 [*Kadambari* (Ridding's Translation), p. 204] Ambedkar is citing from *The Kadambari of Bana* translated by C.M. Ridding and published in 1896 by the Royal Asiatic Society. Unlike modern translations (such as Padmini Rajappa 2010), Ridding's work is closer to the poetic temper of Bana's work.

25 Matanga: there are many Matangas, at least four, in Vedic mythology and Puranic lore. One of them becomes a knowledgeable sage by his deeds despite his low place in the Varna hierarchy and figures in the Buddhist tradition as well. Says Omvedt in *Buddhism in India: Challenging Brahmanism and Caste*: 'Another sutta in the *Sutta Nipata*, the *Vasalasutta*, makes the same point that whether a person is a 'wastrel' is also determined by action, not birth; and in doing so it uses the example of Matanga, the son of a Chandala, who wins glory, fame and paradise by his actions and in the process draws masses of Brahmans and Khattiyas to serve him' (2003, 77). Omvedt also discusses another real (not mythical) Kasyapa Matanga, a Buddhist missionary who 'left for China in 65 CE' through the treacherous Karakoram route, whose name owes to the 'semi-

legendary Candala hero Matanga' (123–4). Speaking of how this could well be the 'earliest mention of a Dalit in any Indian literature' she cites from the *Sutta Nipata*, #136–41: 'Birth does not make an outcaste, birth does not a Brahman make;/ action makes a person low, action makes him great./ To prove my case I give just one example here/ –the Sopaka Matanga, Candala's son, of fame./ This Matanga attained renown so high and rare/ that masses of Brahmans and Khattiyas to serve him were drawn near' (281). Kosambi looks at a range of literary and living examples to argue that the name Kasyapa (Kassapa in Pali) attests to an aboriginal tribal root since the Vedic period (since some of the Soma hymns are attributed to a sage Kasyapa). 'The Kasyapas have clear connection with aborigines through the prajapati myths and also the tortoise totem which their name indicates. It is very well known that a good many of the spurious Brahmins claim the Kasyapa gotra' and that the Kasyapa genus is 'a residuary for all doubtful Brahmins. Census enumerators used to report that highly improbable claimants to Brahminhood in the hinterland generally offered the Kasyapa gotra.' He also pertinently delineates the Chandala–Kasyapa connection: '...if a child be born of a marriage between forbidden degrees, one rule would make it an outcaste Candala while the other, seemingly more generous, says that it should be assigned to the gens Kasyapa. This discrepancy is not so great as it seems, for the Candalas were a tribe (or several tribes) that became a low caste, due to stubborn persistence in breaking tabus kept by good Aryans; the Kasyapas, on the other hand, rose slowly from their ambiguous position' (1985, 160).

26 [Ibid., p. 8–10] Ambedkar provides a 1100-word excerpt from *Kadambari* where Bana, in his own narrative voice and in that of the emperor's, describes the celestial beauty of the Chandala maiden in epic terms. We have retained the key passages here, but the curious may consult BAWS 7 (1990b, 376–7) to

read it in full. Given the nature of *Kadambari*'s florid prose-poetry, there's a great deal of fictive excess and exaggeration in describing everything. An example, which we have dropped from Ambedkar's main text, has been retained in this endnote as illustration. Before the king sets his eyes on the Chandala woman, the king is described thus: 'And she entered and beheld the king in the midst of a thousand chiefs, like golden-peaked Meru in the midst of the noble mountains crouching together in fear of Indra's thunderbolt; or, in that the brightness of the jewels scattered on his dress almost concealed his form, like a day of storm, whereon the eight quarters of the globe are covered by Indra's thousand bows. He was sitting on a couch studded with moon-stones, beneath a small silken canopy, white as the foam of the rivers of heaven, with its four jewel-encrusted pillars joined by golden chains, and enwroathed with a rope of large pearls' (Ridding 1896, 6).

27 Ambedkar's comparison of Fa-Hian's non-fictional documentary effort with Bana's fictional poetic fantastic excess appears untenable. Besides, Bana's narrative makes it clear that the Chandala woman—who is never named—is an exception and that her birth into such a station is unfortunate. The earlier passage from *Kadambari* is clear about the Chandala quarter is a 'market-place of evil deeds'. Also, Brahmanic mythologies abound in instances of liaisons between Kshatriya and Brahmin men with Shudra and outcaste women and the other way around (although Anuloma or hypergamy where a 'superior' male took an 'inferior' female was countenanced and instanced in Puranic lore than Pratiloma or hypogamy). In the *Mahabharata*, the Kuru king Shantanu falls in love with the fisherwoman Satyavati and marries her, and soon a story about her high origins is concocted. See also Ambedkar's own Riddle No. 18, "Manu's Madness or the Brahmanic Explanation of the Origin of the Mixed Castes" about how common mixed caste

affairs were and how the multitude of names (given by various Brahmanic texts) for the progeny of such miscegenation boggle the mind. See also p. 347–8 note 25 on Kasyapa and Matanga.

28 A gotra of the North Indian Saraswat Brahmin caste, it is also known as 'Vatsa' and claims its lineage from the sage Bhrigu. Another famous member of the gotra is the philosopher Vatsyayana who composed the Kama Sutra. His original name was Malla-naga but after the recognition he received for his work, he chose to go by his gotra name (Datta 1989; Somasundaram 1986).

29 [Kadambari (Ridding's Translation), p. 204]

30 [Watters-Yuan Chwang Vol. I. p. 147] See p. 252 notes 68 through 70 for more information about the cited volume. The rest of the passage describes the houses of richer folks in the town he visited. The longest descriptions, and the only ones about the interior of a structure, are of monasteries and houses of the Buddhist laity. And by laity, he refers to the ruling elite and the gentry: he notes the comforts and opulence, and the lack of rigid form in the interior design of such houses (Watters 1904, 147–8).

The Broken Men Theory: Beginnings of a Reading

Alex George and S. Anand

In the following pages we will present a reading of one of the more difficult aspects of Ambedkarite thought—the Broken Men theory. This reading is indebted to developments in contemporary philosophy, specifically the speculative realist movement which is ascendant in our time, and even more specifically, the speculative materialist philosopher, Quentin Meillassoux. We have refrained from discussing the specifics of Meillassoux's theories (2009, 2012) or how we have used them for our particular purpose. In their lieu, we begin with the acknowledgement of this influence. Without citing the specifics of speculative materialism, we have tried to concentrate on Ambedkar's own theory to uncover what appears to us to be a singular philosophical pronouncement on our historical subjectivity. In this spirit, our hope is that this essay is a modest addition to both the Ambedkarite and the speculative materialist movements. Whether it is right to bring together these divergent disciplines is a fair question that has been asked by readers of an earlier draft of this essay which is forever contingent. And yet, it seems our justifications can only be made retrospectively. If the ideas developed here hold true and raise further fruitful encounters, then alone would we have been justified. Else this would have indeed been a fool's errand. With this uncertainty, which is perhaps the uncertainty intrinsic to any philosophical work, we begin.

Readings

First, we must confront the difficulty embedded at the very inception of this project, the difficulty of reading. In reading intensely political thinkers like Ambedkar, who write with resolute conviction, one cannot help but feel a sense of suspicion. Not so much a suspicion with the words which these thinkers present to us, but rather with oneself, and with one's capacity to grasp the 'fullness', the entire truth of what one reads. Now, of course, none of us can be perfect readers, just as no text can in itself be perfect. Often, we lack knowledge, we lack the idiom, we lack the motivation—however it is we would like to name it, it is something we lack that mars our approach towards a text. The text appears an inaccessible alien, which we then must pretend to understand. This becomes more pronounced when we read from within systems. The various social, political, economic categories within which we are held, act as formidable barriers, always distracting us from the thing that is to be read. Always making us feel small, inadequate. In militating against such barriers, one cannot help but feel dwarfed, impotent; that nothing one does will ever be enough to be 'accepted' by those who seem to be on the other side, by those who seem to 'understand', who are in on the joke. Living in caste society, one feels compelled to be suspicious of everything, even oneself. How much has my caste-reality affected my ability to read? Will I ever be able to escape this? Will I ever be able to read 'normally'? What distortions may a Brahmin translator bring to a Dalit text, what further distortions a Brahmin reader? What ruptures does the very word Dalit unleash in those not Dalit? Is all that we are left with just a reading?

What all these questions both shroud and reveal is the necessity of lack. What if the problem isn't that some of us lack a certain unnameable something, which must be (re)gained, but that lack is embedded into ontology itself? What if the problem with the systems which interpellate us is that they pretend as if they aren't cut through with this sense of lack, that they pretend to have a total, incontrovertible view of the universe? Perhaps, the point of emancipatory politics is to unleash this sense of lack. To make the universe confront its own incompleteness. Whenever Brahmanical ideology operates to totalize the world, anti-caste icons emerge and disrupt this completeness, militate against 'assimilation'. Perhaps the world which any radical thought envisions is one with the freedom to work with and mobilize this essentially displaced relation, and the world's own uneasy relation with itself. To mould, innovate and restructure beyond the tyranny of norms.

As we work (perhaps tragically) towards this possibility, we are caught in the stranglehold of a present that seems endless. The ruling ideology seeps through everything, infects every thought, infiltrates every reading. Against this we must be ever vigilant. The most important tenet to be upheld, beyond every nicety of good grace, is to constantly ask, how does the ruling ideology want me to see reality? The task is to constantly read against the grain. To embrace the suspicion that is engendered by our position. We must always ask, how does caste society want me to read Ambedkar? In what manner does it want me to defang him, render him banal and powerless, make him lose the urgency of his politics? This is the primary responsibility of any reader who is a subject of politics. In this wariness, in this need for constant innovation when faced with a seemingly undefeatable enemy, a thousand readings must bloom.

The Thing-in-Itself

The Broken Men theory in *The Untouchables: Who Were They and Why They Became Untouchables?* (1948) is Ambedkar's unique solution to the problem of the origin of Untouchability. No historian or scholar has been able to produce a valid thesis for how this system of oppression was established. One sees much analysis of historical material and text, but never a definitive explanation of its singular conception. While the latest cross-disciplinary efforts that combine genome and DNA studies with archaeology and linguistics (Reich 2018, Joseph 2018) proffer near-accurate dates for the Harappan era, for 'Aryan' migration and for the likely onset of the caste system, they do not have an answer yet for the when and how of Untouchability.

Ambedkar proceeds by locating disparate object-occurrences in history and speculates their concatenation in the context of caste society. He begins with the fact that Untouchable communities are relegated to living outside the village. Here he identifies two possibilities: either Untouchability came first and then the ousting of Untouchables from inside the village, or vice versa. He affirms the latter. To institute Untouchability first and then undertake the massive operation of ousting people from villages across the subcontinent is an absurd and improbable task. Therefore, one can assume that certain communities were already living outside the village. Why this happened, he demonstrates by looking at the organization of primitive societies. The evolution of society from primitive to modern began with the transformation of nomadic communities into settled ones. As evidence for this he provides the example of

English pre-history. During the transformation, settled communities had no way of defending themselves against nomadic ones who attacked them for their cattle and, more importantly, their agricultural produce which the nomads couldn't produce themselves. This left several settled communities ravaged, and because early tribal societies were based on blood relations, such settled tribes couldn't simply assimilate into other tribes. Survivors of tribal warfare were therefore Broken Men, who floated around looking for subsistence in constant danger.

They were to find employment in established settled communities in need of guards to protect themselves from unexpected attacks. But because the Broken Men couldn't be a part of tribal blood-associations they were relegated to live outside the village. For their services, they were provided with the surplus food (in the caste context, mostly leftovers) that the village produced, including animal carcasses. Here, Ambedkar directly references the experiences and position of his own caste, the Mahars of western India, whose traditional role (among other duties thrust upon them) was the policing of the village periphery. The existence of such communities of Broken Men is evidenced by citing the examples of Fuidhirs (strangers, refugees or migrants, placing themselves under the protection of a chief and becoming his tenant) in primitive Ireland and the Alltudes (those banished and exiled) in Wales. How the subcontinental Broken Men became Untouchables is explained by the emergence of Buddhism and its popularity among the Broken Men and the subsequent Brahmanical backlash against the Sramanic religion. Once the shape-shifting Brahmanism moved away from the consumption of beef and condemned the act as sacrilegious, its continued consumption by the Broken Men rendered them impure, Untouchable, even as they were expected to dispose of the carcasses provided by the settled communities by law.

Terrains

What we must extract from Ambedkar's theory is its defiant materialism. Here Ambedkar is not taking on a critical posture or reducing existence to discursivity. He posits a cold hard materiality via speculation. This has been the case for several radical anti-caste thinkers from Phule to Iyothee Thass to Kancha Ilaiah, all construct an alternate reality which is defiantly material—'this is how it is', they proclaim, much to the discomfort of those accustomed to governing mores.

At this point we will need to develop, or define, two philosophical concepts: materialism and speculation. Materialism, to put it simply, is to think of reality as independent of thought and subjectivity (human or divine). By speculation we mean the thinking of possibilities or hypotheticals in a specific philosophical sense—it is the ability to think of an 'absolute' (a function or essential feature of reality) without acceding to dogmatic metaphysics; it is concerned with the non-factual existence of facticity as such (Meillassoux 2012).

> [Speculation] by contrast with the repetitive continental focus on texts, discourse, social practices, and human finitude, [thinks of] the nature of reality independently of thought and of humanity more generally. This activity of 'speculation' may be cause for concern amongst some readers, for it might suggest a return to pre-critical philosophy, with its dogmatic belief in the powers of pure reason. The speculative turn, however, is not an outright rejection of these critical advances; instead, it comes from a recognition of their inherent limitations. Speculation in this sense aims

at something 'beyond' the critical and linguistic turns. As such, it recuperates the pre-critical sense of 'speculation' as a concern with the Absolute, while also taking into account the undeniable progress that is due to the labour of critique' (Bryant et al. 2011, 3)

Speculation and materialism are inseparably connected, if one is to render a consistent theory of reality. What quantum physics has taught us is the universe's own contradictory and incomplete nature. Materialism must therefore contend with the chaotic, unstable and divided nature of the universe itself—of its being and nothingness both as positive 'materials'. Speculation therefore is the philosophical position which asserts the necessity of contingency—that is, the Absolute 'component' of the universe is contingency itself. Natural laws and material reality have no necessity, but are only contingent appearances. And this contingency—a contingency that lends itself as proximate to empirical scrutiny and demands reappraisals of all theories of reality asserted as necessary—itself is the necessary principle of reality. When we are unable to grasp the totality of the universe, it is not merely because we lack this knowledge or that it is inaccessible to us, but because reality itself is an incomplete field, riven by a void (Žižek 2011). With the various figures of anti-caste thought, chief among them Ambedkar, indulging in both speculation and materialism, we must now develop their singularity, especially in the context of their uncanny proximity to contemporary philosophers of speculative materialism.

Remembrance/History

Let us return to history, that sanctified concept against which Ambedkar militates with his Broken Men theory. What is the function of history? It gathers data from the past and reconstructs a temporality of which we become subjects. Historians scrupulously work to verify evidence, to study archaeological material, that give us glimpses into a lost time. In its register as a myth-creating discipline, history generates causalities. There are of course those historians who challenge these causalities, pose alternatives, and offer corrections, but there is a problematic at the heart of the discipline itself.

No history can be complete. And yet history offers us a certain kind of completion. Of an unbroken line, no matter how much it zigs and zags, which converges onto our present. But we do not live in history. We live in the present. To be able to read history necessarily requires that we be outside of it. There are things in history which have a material continuity with the present, the caste system or Untouchability, for example. But the assertion of this continuity discounts the necessary difference between the past and the present—Untouchability was different (not better or worse, but different) in the past from what it is now.

The simple question is: what does history tell us about reality? We wager that it doesn't tell us why things are the way they are, but offers us a myth of its journey. To ask why are things the way they are is a properly philosophical question, and its answer cannot be found in history. It must be thought and deduced in the here and now. If we look for answers in the past all we get are the repetition of habits, and any radical assertion, any breakthrough in understanding, is also a break with past habits.

What is constructed as history is necessarily retroactively posited. Why did caste arise? Why are Brahmins considered superior? Such naïve and simple questions are explained away via discursive fabulation that do not go to the contingency that is at their heart. That is to say, Brahmins are considered superior for no reason, caste arose for no reason. More precisely, whatever the contingent events that led to these results, they aren't necessary truths. That is to say there is nothing essential in the nature of reality that led to the emergence of caste or Brahmins or Untouchability. Materialism shows us that reality emerges without underlying laws or reason. Therefore, the way in which society was shaped in history also has no reason—various contingent factors led to its being a certain way, and it could very well have not been this way. History could have gone one way or another.

This contingency of the past is of course true for the present too. That the past could have been different, and was the way it was for no necessary reason, means that our present also has no underlying necessity for being maintained in the way it is.

There is a register of the past which does help us in this regard—memory. Memory is fickle, it remembers what it requires and discards the rest, it carries forward pain and the dream of emancipation. Memory is aware of its own fallibility. Often history is overpowered, overshadowed by the power of collective memory, no matter how false it may be.

Ambedkar's speculation

To speculate of a history, where none can be found, while admitting the speculative nature of this history, is an Ambedkarite affirmation of the truth. The truth is none other than that of equality. Indeed, many Western scholars, anthropologists, historians, of his time were given to speculation. But the singularity of the Broken Men theory is to be found in the truth of the memory of this equality that is wagered onto the past.

Ambedkar through this particular case then mobilized history itself to be in service of the future-oriented goal: the annihilation of caste. He does this because he 'remembers' an egalitarian past, its memory haunts him. Of course, Ambedkar's memory might be false, as many university historians gloat in claiming. But it is permeated by the truth of equality—Ambedkar's body and the physico-political body of Untouchables, hitherto made invisible and reduced to automatons by 'official history', in its existence as a subject of equality, is proof that this memory is *real*.

In Ambedkar's speculation of the Broken Men theory two registers of contingency can be sensed: one, is that history is a mere emergence of contingencies (annotations, even) which must be read and scrupulously deployed to establish the norm of equality. Second, the future is also contingent; no matter how improbable it may seem, things have no inherent necessity to remain the way they are, and it is just as possible to change it as it is difficult.

Wagers

This speculative position Ambedkar occupies is of course not produced in a vacuum. There are reasons to consider the historical development of his theories. Especially in the light of our own speculative work in this essay, in which we have attributed later philosophical developments of 'speculation', 'materialism' and 'contingency' back to Ambedkar. He certainly did not hold these words in the same valency as we explicate here. Can the correspondence developed here then be valid?

Before answering this we must first examine the milieu in which Ambedkar's work developed, how it was received, what position it occupied, and the current of anti-caste thought it conversed with. First, let us take the case of how Ambedkar's Broken Men theory was received by subsequent scholarship.

For decades, the few establishment scholars who read him dismissed Ambedkar's thesis; the dismissal was offered often in footnotes, as an aside. Vivekanand Jha in his essay "Candala and the Origin of Untouchability"—first published in the *Indian Historical Review* in 1986—conducts his own independent inquiry into the questions that concerned Ambedkar. In the revised edition of this essay, Jha (2018) makes several less than charitable remarks about Ambedkar's threading together of Buddhism, beef and Broken Men (see p. 321–2 note 66). Jha does offer important counter-evidence when it comes to the attitude of Buddhists towards the 'hinajatis' which weakens Ambedkar's claim that Buddhism was a succour for the oppressed masses. But what doesn't bother Jha, and he prides himself on this 'objectivity', is the sheer virulence with which some sections of the society were treated, and the singularity of this oppression. It becomes too easy for him to conclude that it was class difference which led to such ousting as was meted out to various groups across the subcontinent.

For Ambedkar such an answer is not satisfactory; it does not hold. The system of class difference included the Shudras too; in fact, to the Brahmin no one is or was equal. Yet, what made some sections so deplorable that their existence itself became despised? The problem with such inquiries as Jha's, an embodiment of University Discourse, is that they can only refer to texts that survive to look for clues, and the texts that survive—even Buddhist ones—belong necessarily to the ruling classes of different times. The task in the present is to try and suture the gaps in history which such texts produce. Unfortunately, University Discourse cannot withstand the melancholy of loss intrinsic to such gaps, of forever being out of touch with a time and a system of being, of having to contend with loss and *embrace* this loss. The University tries to cover this up by hypothesizing from *within* the evidence that is up to standard. So the suturing that occurs is one that necessarily inhabits the dominant worldview, for one is already accepting the terms of existence, thought and sociality that the ideology provides in its texts.

The rejection of this blackmail is primary for Ambedkar. Sure, he refers to several scholarly texts, like any university scholar would, but his readings always function against the grain of the texts themselves. He reads knowing full well that his political endeavour is diametrically opposed to the ideology of what he reads. And so, he reads the Manusmriti, the Dharma Sutras, all that is available to read, in order to extract the specific things needed for the political purposes that come from his ideological standpoint. He carefully reads and cites 'Mahamahopadhyay' Pandurang Vaman Kane (1880–1972), the archetypal Brahmin scholar figure, but in the Constitution Assembly he argues against the state bestowing such titles. He reads from the standpoint of the present, not as a subject of history. Ambedkar exits the reality of the ruling ideology, and in doing so he *returns* agency to the enforced silence of broken historical subjects. The people who were made outcasts were not silent witnesses to their own degradation. Ambedkar makes them active bodies in conflict with their colonizers. This agency itself comes from the present. The people who suffer now at the hands of an unjust system are not silent either. Their struggles and memory of egalitarianism, is transposed back to their anonymous ancestors. The ideology of equality is made transhistorical. In this sense, even Buddhism which was for a time an official state religion, is returned to the silenced parts of history.

In *The Untouchables*, while Ambedkar does not elaborate on the how and why of outcastes embracing Buddhism, he does say elsewhere that Buddhism, even if it had no love lost for Untouchables, provided an egalitarian thrust that was, in principle, attractive. Vedism and Brahmanism offer no such scope. The Buddhist sangha was the first organized religion in the subcontinent that both theoretically and institutionally opened itself up to Shudras, Untouchables and women even if the rest of society remained watchful of such moves, even if the Brahmin converts and the mercantile classes appear to have had a greater say in the annals as historians tell us. It appears the non-elite sections negotiated their way with Buddhism on their own terms (as Decaroli 2004 argues by looking beyond what he calls the 'seeming disjuncture between textual Buddhism and early Buddhist art'). Ambedkar had reason to believe that people written out of history would still have had reasons to be part of it. Reflecting on how the Marathi 'bhakti' poets from the twelfth to seventeenth centuries emerged in the vacuum created by the eviction of Buddhism from the subcontinent, Ambedkar in a speech in 1954 in Poona alludes to this. His biographer Dhananjay Keer says, Ambedkar

> told the gathering of 20,000 men and women that he was writing a book on Buddhism explaining its tenets in simple language to the common man. A year might be needed to complete the book: on its completion he would embrace Buddhism. Ambedkar also told his audience that the image of the god Vithoba at Pandharpur was in reality the image of the Buddha. He *intended writing* a thesis on the subject, and after completing it, he would read it before the Bharatiya Itihas Sanshodhan Mandal at Poona. The name of the god Pandurang, he observed, was derived from Pundalik. Pundalik meant lotus, and a lotus was called Pandurang in Pali. So Pandurang was none other than the Buddha. (Keer 1954/2001, 482)

Vitthal or Vithoba of Pandharpur in Maharashtra's Solapur district, who likely began as a pastoral pre-Vedic cult of nomadic shepherds, is eventually Buddhisized and then Vishnuized as Pandurang. By the fifteenth century, the Vitthal temple in Pandharpur that starts its journey as a wood and brick 'primitive' statue, comes to be a major site of pilgrimage for not just caste Hindus but many Untouchables as well, even if the Untouchables were not allowed into the temple and had to sing their prayers at the gates along the outcast shrine for the Untouchable poet-saint Chokhamela to whom Ambedkar dedicates his book. The scholar Ramchandra Chintaman Dhere's *Sri Vitthal: Ek Mahasamnvay* (Lord Vitthal: A Great Confluence or Syncretization, 1984 in Marathi), says till the twelfth century what's today Maharashtra was largely Buddhist (like much of the subcontinent had once been) and the Varkari cult grew around the time when Namdev, Jnandev, Chokhamela, Janabai and their cohort of saint-poets would have seen the Buddhist caves being emptied out of monks who were persecuted by a resurgent Brahmanism. Dhere's work, translated in 2011 by Anne Feldhaus, has this passage that fills the gap that seems to appear in Ambedkar's *The Untouchables*:

> We must not forget that in Indian traditions nothing ever gets destroyed: it only gets transformed, taking on different names and forms. Followers of the Buddha were spread throughout Maharashtra continuously for a thousand or fifteen hundred years, until just before the time of Jnandev and Namdev. There is not a single mountain range in Maharashtra where Buddhists did not carve out caves. From within these hundreds of caves in the sides of the Sahyadri Mountains, the cries of Buddhist monks continually resounded: Buddham saranam gacchami, "I take refuge

in the Buddha." The great mantra of non-violence and compassion echoed from each granule of Marathi soil. Still today, inscriptions show that the whole society, from kings to agricultural laborers, was prepared to renounce the world in order to serve these dispassionate monks. Monks (bhikshus) had become objects of respect, as indicated by the common use of the name Bhikoba for men and Bhikubai for women in village after village. It is historically inconsistent to think that a philosopher who took pride in the Vedic religion [by this Dhere means Sankara of Kalady, the arch Brahmin revivalist] would have had the power to completely erase ten or fifteen centuries of this profound influence on the folk mind. Indeed, that influence was strong enough that such a philosopher was cursed as a "Buddhist in disguise" (187).

Ambedkar considers this vacuum, these emptied-out Buddhist caves, and the effusive songs and poetry that make Vitthal sacred, and tells us what may have possibly happened before a people were made untouchable in and by history. Buddhism, through the Ambedkarite gesture, is shown to not merely belong to the royal courts where annals are produced, but in the invisible life-worlds of labouring classes as a consciousness towards freedom, both physical and metaphysical. Buddhism therefore becomes the name of this consciousness of freedom in an unknown time that Ambedkar speculates.

Now how do we mean that Ambedkar speculates an egalitarian Buddhist past? How does Ambedkar 'choose' Buddhism, so to speak? Is it a blind devotional decision made in transcendental ecstasy? No. He undertakes a close reading of the defining principles of Buddhism, and in studying it, 'learns' of its equalizing core, even if as a potentiality. We must remember how careful he was in making his own decision to convert. It was a decision made after thorough examination of the principles of the religion and its suitability for the future sociality of the members of his community and indeed the rest of the subcontinent. Having thus isolated its principles, and becoming convinced of its truth, he is able to map this core principle back into history. This is the act of speculation. In history, Buddhism emerged as the contingent name for the egalitarian uprising against the excesses of Vedic Brahmanism. Having emerged along this axis of opposing inequality, Buddhism then can be speculated about as historical object that turns around its egalitarian core. Had the religion emerged under different conditions, under a different name, and yet with the same core of egalitarianism, Ambedkar would have been equally satisfied with adopting it in this different form. This gesture of making us subjects capable of thinking of the principles of various objects and making decisions on the basis of its truth and validity, especially in the realm of politics where all thought is foreclosed by ruling ideology, is what grants Ambedkar a proximity to a certain kind of speculative materialism.

Broken, and made whole

The most impressive of Ambedkar's speculative breaks is of course that of the invisible subjectivity he christens as 'Broken Men'. What does Ambedkar tell us about the Broken Men? That they were part of different nomadic tribes that were defeated in battle. That is all. In this minimal description of the origin of Untouchability, we are also provided an essential lesson of what we are as subjects. In the primordial scene of battle, we are equal subjects. In this sense this originary battle is an egalitarian one, in the sense that in it humans fought as equals and not as a part of the caste system. The Broken Men all came from different tribes in different places, who in the contingencies of history, found themselves on the losing side. That is all we are: victims of a contingent unfolding of history, with no particular reason for being in the current state of subjugation we are held in.

In the egalitarian battle which produces Broken Men, there is no hierarchy of merit, nor divine cycle of karma and gunas, only two warring factions fighting for survival. It is the caste-society, which followed this battle, that wants us to believe in our essential separation and difference from each other as subjects. It is caste-society that segregates and makes some people axiomatically higher than the others. This society tries to maintain that its system of values is timeless and primordial, when in fact society has always been tumultuous, always going through shifts and imbalances. Often, history tends to ascertain a purity in the past, even when it studies oppression and communities that are oppressed, it tends to essentialize a sense of an original idyll—be it in the form of Matanga, Buddha or even Ambedkar—which was then disturbed. But this notion of purity must absolutely be rejected.

The various Brahmanic manuals that Ambedkar carefully examines that describe and classify the proliferation of jatis with the will-to-govern—where someone is always placed lower than the lowest, ad infinitum, to wit Manu X.39, 'A 'Hunter' woman [Nishada] bears to a 'Fierce' Untouchable man [Chandala] a son 'Who Ends Up at the Bottom' [Antyavasayin], who haunts the cremation-grounds and is despised even by the excluded castes'—unwittingly reveal that there was never (and never will be) the 'pure' of Time when the intermixture of varnas and jatis would not have happened. Scholars say even the early 'Aryans' who produced the Rig Veda were migrants who did not bring along enough women and they cohabited with the indigenous population and invented new lineages. Smritis and sastras hold forth against the unnaturalness of Pratiloma (hypogamy) relations (which occur but naturally), and force upon us the imagined naturalness of caste, while asking us to think of equality as abnormal, as if we are cursed to live inside a self-perpetuating nightmare with no wake in sight.

To illustrate, as we prepared this note, an ordinary piece of feature writing in a newspaper's 'culture' pages ("Friday Review", *The Hindu*) paraded Brahmanic purity imagined in a man bearing a Muslim name, opening with these lines:

> On a concert stage, with his Brahminical looks accentuated by his tall, slim, fair frame, broad forehead, back-brushed and pony-tailed long hair and thoughtful eyes, Rudraveena maestro Mohi Bahauddin Dagar seems to belong to the era of sages (Banerjee 2018).

This strain of thought, this base desire for the pure of the imagined essence of caste—always the Übermensch–Brahman, never the Chandala—causes few eyebrows to arch, let alone triggers outrage. But this essence of caste does not exist, it is an ideological construction which can be and must be annihilated. When the historicity of particular habits becomes the only reason for their repetition, which is the case for so many oppressive practices, history is upheld as pure. When the contingency of history is asserted, on the other hand, we grant the past the playfulness of impurity. Decisions and structures of the past were constructed on the back of an interplay of so many permutations of human imagination, and we are allowed to speculate the possibilities and impossibilities that are entailed by the boundlessness of this imagination in the past, the present and the future.

For the purposes of politics in the present, no precedence in history is consequential. No particular subject position is essential, no decision is eternal, no sequences of arrangement are permanent. We are faced with a future that holds no promises, but towards which we work from the present through our fidelity to principles we hold as universal. The past persists only out of habit, a habit whose rules are self-defined. The hard work of the present is to lay bare the non-essentiality of the rules of old. And to wilfully propose the new rules (the new constitution, a new dhamma even). The bringing forth of such a 'new' requires the acceptance of absolute (terrifying) freedom even as all of history conspires to lull you into the security of given narratives and unfree thoughtlessness. In 1936, in *Annihilation of Caste*, defiantly published as the "Speech Prepared... but Not Delivered", Ambedkar declares to the Hindus who invited him but refused to let him speak: 'I am sorry, I will not be with you. I have decided to change.' He goes on to say:

> It means conversion; but if you do not like the word, I will say it means new life. But a new life cannot enter a body that is dead. New life can enter only into a new body. The old body must die before a new body can come into existence and a new life can enter into it. To put it simply: the old must cease to be operative before the new can begin to enliven and to pulsate. This is what I meant when I said you must discard the authority of the shastras, and destroy the religion of the shastras (2014, 311).

Mathematics

Another consequential aspect of Ambedkar's speculation is how he employs a mathematical method to solve a problem in history—mathematical in the sense of that which is infinitely repeatable. The square-root of minus one will remain the square-root of minus one throughout time and space; it is endlessly repeatable. Ambedkar identifies specific yet geographically and culturally far-removed occurrences from the past that, unlike what Untouchability entails till date, do not preoccupy anyone any longer—in English primitive society, the existence of the Fuidhirs in Ireland and the Alltudes in Wales—and universalizes them. He then *repeats* them within the particularity of caste-society. The implication of this universalization and repetition is interesting. Universality always pertains to principles; it subsumes within itself all particular relations of specificities in all their modes. More importantly universality is imposed, and it is so imposed from a particular position within a specific relation. From his singular (factional) position which enunciates the axiom of equality, Ambedkar thus gives a universal principle of history. Insofar as equality is a relation every subject holds with another, time is the axis on which this relationship must necessarily exist. That is to say, it is not that suddenly equality appeared on the scene and from this point forward we will act as if it is real, and that before this point all were unequal (Choudhury 2018a). Rather, people were always equal but contingent structures forbade the realisation of this principle. So a Greek philosopher, an African slave being smuggled into the New World, the Untouchable who was persecuted under the Peshwas, all, we can now recognize, were equals—in capacities, in thought, as subjects. This opens up the space of comparability, of ideas and existence in different points in history. The principle of equality commissions a near-quantitative relation between subjects on the axis of time.

That is not to say one can replace subjects like one does numbers when one mechanically repeats them. However, the quantization is the work of thought: thought can permeate history. One can *think* history equally. One participates in the same temporal field, albeit in severally articulated modes of being. And yet comprehensibility is never forbidden. The enunciation of such a comprehension of course must not be exaggerated, for no comprehension is total. At the same time, it must be recognized that the world that one tries to comprehend is not a totality itself: it is ridden with holes which it tries to cover up. This incompleteness of any given 'world' is not an ununderstandable core, but rather an opening which allows us to think, to touch that which is forbidden. In this sense, Ambedkar's is a project of invitation. He invites us to touch all that was deemed true and ancient and primordial and holy, to not fearfully hide it away from thought as if it was ununderstandable, but to play with it, mould it and think it as if it was any other object. To carve together the bits of matter we find in history into the weapon that will free us from our con-temporary chains.

The Banishment of Untouchability

Now comes the question of truth, especially in the context of right-wing politics distorting facts of history for their own purposes. One would say, isn't this exactly the thing Ambedkar would prescribe? Aren't they also constructing a narrative that 'does not exist' in order to maintain and build power? The obvious answer to this is that there is no deified position 'we' hold where we are neutral observers of history reporting what are merely facts. Such a position is always-already ideologically charged. Any position of neutrality is already beholden to a certain worldview. The point isn't that the right-wingers are distorting history, but why they are doing it and what principles underlie such a distortion—the project of equality is surely not one they are invested in. Thus, defeating the enemy is not a question of protecting (our) history (as if it exists) but an ideological struggle played out in the present. What must be universalized is the conviction that drives us to look at the past, the present and the future in a certain way. This is the banishment of Untouchability, the abolishment of inequality from all of time for all people. It is not the sequestering of hallowed spaces from the rampages of some unthinking horde. Uncovering of archaeological evidence, discovery of documents, engaging with these documents, mapping ancient DNA, radiocarbon dating... all must and will go on. But the position historians occupy in the present is determined by a decision of subjectivity. And any construal of a narrative or breaking down of narratives is performed from this necessarily decisional agency of the historian-subject. It cannot be escaped. Such a subjective decision orients future politics. It contributes to the construction of the new or to the persistence of the old. The right-wingers and 'apolitical' subjects of an old history, in a sense, perform the same task: affirming an old continuity. But a historian like Ambedkar, who is a subject of equality, must speculate the new in the future and in the past.

Historical being, for Ambedkar, is therefore the realm of universal participation. It is completely comprehensible, analyzable, open to participation. That is to say, the particularities within history are not separate or wholly other, but linked by a subjectivity of equality. This is his revolutionary hypothesis. We no longer participate in disparate worlds of becoming which are forever other to the outside. On the contrary, there is no outside. History as mathematized in its notional repeatability, makes our particularities touchable; there is no 'untouchable' if we are subjects of Ambedkarite history.

If the all-but-forgotten Fuidhirs and Alltudes existed in history, and we can *think* of their existence, why can we not also think of a repetition of their mode of existence in a situation elsewhere? The Fuidhirs and Alltudes aren't wholly unto themselves, but are also *ours* in thought. Their touchability allows us to transpose them into a new situation, the situation of caste.

The mathematical imposition of the case of the Fuidhirs and the Alltudes on to the Untouchables in India, then begs the question of what subjectivity itself is. Does the fact that disparate cases can be superimposed onto another subject also point to the contingent becoming of the subject itself? As subjects that participate in a contingent reality, we must confront our own contingency, we too have no necessary identity or essence that makes us who we are. We too are the void that is superimposed by the various narratives of power. This knowledge then gives us one thing: choice, freedom.

The Difficulty of Freedom

To be free is to not be caught in discourses that give us the comfort of necessity. To be free is to embrace the contingency of reality and to reject all easy answers. To be free is the rejection of the old: syntax and time. Radical politics is hard work, and becoming free is a painful process. In the state of freedom, a subject knows that they cannot rely on any given narratives and dogmas of hope, and makes a choice without knowing where it would lead. True moments of freedom are difficult to come by, caught as we are in our struggles to survive, to fulfil our desires. It is difficult to accept one's own incompleteness and contingency. But when we look at Ambedkar, when he writes his fearless historical-political treatises, when he drinks water from Chavadar Tank, when he calls for the annihilation of caste, we know true moments of freedom are possible.

References

Aktor, Mikael. 2018. "Untouchability". In *Brill's Encyclopedia of Hinduism*. Edited by Knut A. Jacobsen, Helene Basu, Angelika Malinar, Vasudha Narayanan. Consulted online on 22 October 2018, http://dx.doi.org/10.1163/2212-5019_beh_COM_000261. First published online: 2012

———. 2002. "Rules of untouchability in ancient and medieval law books: Householders, competence, and inauspiciousness". *International Journal of Hindu Studies*. Vol. 6, No. 3. Copenhagen: Museum Tusculanum Press. 243–74.

Aktor, Mikael and Robert Deliège (eds). 2010. *From Stigma to Assertion: Untouchability, Identity and Politics in Early and Modern India*. Copenhagen: Museum Tusculanum Press.

Allen, Charles. 2012. *Ashoka: The Search for India's Lost Emperor*. London: Abacus.

Allen, Kieran and Brian O'Boyle. 2017. *Durkheim: A Critical Introduction*. London: Pluto Press.

Alsdorf, Ludwig. 2010. *The History of Vegetarianism and Cow-Veneration in India*. Translated by Bal Patil. Abingdon: Routledge.

Ambedkar, B.R. 1948. *The Untouchables: Who Were They and Why They Became Untouchables?* New Delhi: Amrit Book Depot.

———. 1987. "Revolution and Counter-Revolution." In *BAWS 3*. Edited by Vasant Moon. Bombay: Education Department, Government of Maharashtra. 151–437.

———. 1987a. "The Decline and Fall of Buddhism." In *BAWS 3*. Edited by Vasant Moon. Bombay: Education Department, Government of Maharashtra. 229–38.

———. 1989a. "States and Minorities." In *BAWS 1*. Edited by Vasant Moon. Bombay: Education Department, Government of Maharashtra. 381–449.

———. 1989b. "The House the Hindus Have Built." In *BAWS* 5. Edited by Vasant Moon. Bombay: Education Department, Government of Maharashtra. 145–169.

———.1990a. *The Untouchables: Who Were They and Why They Became Untouchables?* In *BAWS* 7. Edited by Vasant Moon. Bombay: Education Department, Government of Maharashtra. 229–382.

———.1990b. *Who Were The Shudras? How they came to be the Fourth Varna in the Indo–Aryan Society.* In *BAWS* 7. Edited by Vasant Moon. Bombay: Education Department, Government of Maharashtra. 1–227.

———. 1990c. *Pakistan or the Partition of India.* In *BAWS* 8. Edited by Vasant Moon. Bombay: Education Department, Government of Maharashtra.

———. 1991. *What Congress and Gandhi have done to the Untouchables.* In *BAWS* 9. Edited by Vasant Moon. Bombay: Education Department, Government of Maharashtra.

———. 1992a. "Dr Ambedkar's Speech at Mahad." *Poisoned Bread: Modern Marathi Dalit Literature.* Edited by Arjun Dangle. Hyderabad: Orient Longman. 223–33.

———. 1992b. *The Buddha and his Dhamma. BAWS 11.* Edited by Vasant Moon. Bombay: Education Department, Government of Maharashtra.

———. 2003. "The Mahars: Who were they and how they became the Untouchables." In *BAWS 17, Part II.* Edited by Hari Narake, M.L. Kasare, N.G. Kamble, Ashok Godghate. Bombay: Education Department, Government of Maharashtra. 137–50.

———. 2013. "Castes in India: Their Mechanism, Genesis and Development." In *Against the Madness of Manu.* Edited by Sharmila Rege. New Delhi: Navayana. 77–108.

———. 2014. *Annihilation of Caste: The Annotated Critical Edition.* Edited by S. Anand. New Delhi: Navayana.

———. 2016. *Riddles in Hinduism: An Exposition to Enlighten the Masses.*

The Annotated Critical Selection. New Delhi: Navayana.

Anand, S. 2016. "Preface" to B.R. Ambedkar. *Riddles in Hindusim: An Exposition to Enlighten the Masses: The Annotated Critical Selection*. New Delhi: Navayana.

Appadurai, Arjun. 1993. "The Number in the Colonial Imagination." In *Orientalism and the Postcolonial Predicament: Perspectives on South Asia*. Edited by Carol A. Breckenridge and Peter van der Veer. Philadelphia: University of Pennsylvania Press.

Asad, Talal. 2003. *Formations of the Secular: Christianity, Islam, modernity*. Stanford: Stanford University Press.

Badiou, Alain. 2009. *Theory of the Subject*. Translated by Bruno Bosteels. London: Bloomsbury.

Bajrange, Dakxin, Sarah Gandee, William Gould. 2018. "Settling the citizen, settling the nomad: 'Habitual offenders', rebellion and civic consciousness in western India, 1938–1952." *White Rose Research Online*. Cambridge: Cambridge University Press.

Bamford, P.C. 1974. *Histories of the Non-Co-operation and Khilafat Movement*. Delhi: Deep Publications.

Banaji, Jairus. 2003. "The Fictions of Free Labour: Contract, Coercion, and So-Called Unfree Labour." *Historical Materialism: Research in Critical Marxist Theory*. Vol 11, Issue 3. Leiden: Brill Publishing. 69–95.

Banerjee, Meena. 2018. "Veena is like an elephant: Ustad Mohi Bahauddin Dagar" (12 October). Friday Review, *The Hindu*. https://www.thehindu.com/entertainment/music/veena-is-like-an-elephant-ustad-mohi-bahauddin-dagar/article25202737.ece. Accessed 24 November 2018.

Bates, Crispin. 1995. "Race, Caste and Tribe in Central India: The Early Origins of Indian Anthropometry." *The Concept of Race in South Asia*. Edited by Peter Robb. New Delhi: Oxford University Press. 219–59.

Bauer, Laurie. 1983. *English Word-Formation*. Cambridge: Cambridge

University Press.

Bayly, C.A. 1988. *Indian Society and the Making of the British Empire.* *Cambridge*: Cambridge University Press.

Bayly, Susan. 1999. *Caste, Society and Politics in India from the Eighteenth Century to the Modern Age.* Cambridge: Cambridge University Press.

Beal, Samuel. 1884. *Si-Yu-Ki: Buddhist Records of the Western World, Translated from the Chinese of Hieun Tsiang, Vol I.* London: Trübner & Co.

Bellwinkel-Schempp, Maren. 2003. "Ambedkar Studies at Heidelberg," South Asia Institute Report, Summer, 2003.

Bhagat, R.D. 2013. "Census enumeration, religious identity and communal polarization in India." *Asian Ethnicity.* Vol. 14, No. 4. Abingdon: Routledge. 434–48.

Bharti, Kanwal. 2017. "Holi: Celebrating the immolation of an Asur woman." *Forwardpress.in.* March 8. https://www.forwardpress.in/2017/03/holi-celebrating-the-immolation-of-an-asur-woman/

Bhattacherje, S. B. 2008. *Encyclopaedia of Indian Events & Dates.* New Delhi: Sterling Publishers.

Bosworth, Clifford Edmund. 1996. *The New Islamic Dynasties: A Chronological and Genealogical Manual.* Edinburgh: Edinburgh University Press.

Bourdieu, Pierre and Jean-Claude Passeron 1967. "Sociology and Philosophy in France since 1945: Death and Resurrection of a Philosophy without Subject." *Social Research.* Vol. 34, No. 1. Baltimore: The Johns Hopkins University Press. 162–212.

Brass, Paul R. 2000. "Elite groups, symbol manipulation and ethnic identity among the Muslims of South Asia." *Nationalism: Critical Concepts in Political Science, Volume III.* Edited by John Hutchinson and Anthony D. Smith. New York: Routledge. 879–911.

Briggs, G.W. 1920. *The Chamars.* Calcutta: Oxford University Press.

Bühler, George. 1882. Trans. *The Sacred Laws of The Aryas: Apastamba,*

Gautama, Vasistha and Baudhayana. Part 2: Vasistha and Baudhayana. Oxford: The Clarendon Press.

———. 1886. *The Laws of Manu*. Sacred Books of the East 25. Oxford: Clarendon Press.

———. 1898. Trans. *The Sacred Laws of The Aryas: Apastamba, Gautama, Vasistha and Baudhayana. Part 1: Apastamba and Gautama*. New York: The Christian Literature Company.

Burnouf, Eugène. 2010. *Introduction to the History of Indian Buddhism*. Translated by Katia Buffetrille and Donald S. Lopez Jr. Chicago: University of Chicago Press. (from *Introduction à l'histoire du Buddhisme indien* published in 1844 in French.)

Bryant, Levi, Nick Srnicek and Graham Harman. 2011. "Towards a Speculative Philosophy." *The Speculative Turn: Continental Materialism and Realism*. Edited by Levi Bryant, Nick Srnicek and Graham Harman Melbourne: re:press. 1–18.

Candea, Matei. 2010. *The Social after Gabriel Tarde: Debates and Assessments*. New York: Routledge.

Cardona, G. 1999. *Recent Research in Paninian Studies*. Delhi: Motilal Banarsidass.

Carri, Sebastian J. 2000. *Gavesanam: Or, On the Track of the Cow; And, In Search of the Mysterious Word; And, In Search of the Hidden Light*. Wiesbaden: Otto Harrassowitz Verlag.

Chakravarti, Mahadev. 1979. "Beef-Eating in Ancient India." *Social Scientist*. Vol. 7, No. 11. New Delhi: Indian Council of Historical Research. 51–5.

Chakravarti, Uma. 1987. *Social Dimensions of Early Buddhism*. New Delhi: Munshiram Manoharlal.

Charsley, Simon. 2004. "Interpreting Untouchability The Performance of Caste in Andhra Pradesh, South India". *Asian Folklore Studies*. Vol. 63. Nagoya: Nanzan University. 267–290.

Chinmayananda, Swami. 2013. *Taittiriya Upanishad*. Mumbai: Chinmaya Prakshan.

Cho, Daniel. 2006. "Thanatos and Civilization: Lacan, Marcuse, and the death drive." *Policy Futures in Education*. Vol. 4, No. 1. SAGE Publications. 18–30.

Choudhury, Soumyabrata. 2018a. *Ambedkar and Other Immortals: An Untouchable Research Programme*. New Delhi: Navayana.

————.2018b. "The Ambiguous Debt of Counterrevolution to Revolution: Reply to a Vigilant Melancholic." *Cultural Critique*, Vol. 98. Minneapolis: University of Minnesota Press.

Cohn, Bernard. 1987. *An Anthropologist Among the Historians and Other Essays*. Oxford: Oxford University Press.

————.1996. *Colonialism and Its Forms of Knowledge*. Princeton: Princeton University Press.

Coomaraswamy, Ananda. 1919. "Notes on the Epics II—Mahabharata: Bhagavat Gita." *Young India*. Vol. 2, No. 1. New York: India Home Rule League of America. 12–4.

Cotton, J.S. 1911. *Mountstuart Elphinstone, and the Making of Southwestern India*. Oxford: Clarendon Press.

Cross, Stephen. 2013. *Schopenhauer's Encounter with Indian Thought Representation and Will and Their Indian Parallels*. Hawai'i: University of Hawai'i Press.

Cush, Denise, Robinson, Catherine and York, Michael. 2008. *Encyclopedia of Hinduism*. Abingdon: Routledge.

Dalal, Roshen. 2010. *Hinduism: An Alphabetical Guide*. New Delhi: Penguin.

————. 2014. *The Vedas: An Introduction to Hinduism's Sacred Texts*. New Delhi: Penguin Books India.

Dalit Bahujan Adivasi Collective. 2016. "An Open Letter to the Vice Chancellor, Ambedkar University, Delhi, to Reconsider Decision to Invite Prof. Romila Thapar for Ambedkar Memorial Lecture, 2016." *Roundtableindia.co.in*. 5 April. roundtableindia.co.in/index.php?option=com_content&view=article&id=8560:open-letter-to-vc-ambedkar-university-reconsider-invitation-to-prof-romila-thapar-for-ambedkar-memorial-lecture&catid=129:events-and-

activism&Itemid=195. Accessed on 29 November 2018.

Datta, Swati. 1989. *Migrant Brahmanas in Northern India: Their Settlement and General Impact c. A. D. 475–1030*. Delhi: Motilal Banarsidass Indological Publishers and Booksellers.

Davis, John R. 2007. *The Victorians and Germany*. Bern: Peter Lang AG.

DeCaroli, Robert. 2004. *Haunting the Buddha: Indian Popular Religions and the Formation of Buddhism*. New York: Oxford University Press.

Desai, Ashwin and Goolam Vahed. 2015. *The South African Gandhi: Stretcher-Bearer of Empire*. New Delhi: Navayana.

Devji, Faisal. 2013. *Muslim Zion: Pakistan as a Political Idea*. Massachusetts: Harvard University Press.

Deshpande, G.P. (ed.) 2002. *Selected Writings of Jotirao Phule*. New Delhi: LeftWord.

Deshpande, Satish and John, Mary E. 2010. "The Politics of Not Counting Caste". *Economic & Political Weekly*. June 19. Mumbai: Sameeksha Trust. 39–42.

Dhand, Arti. 2002. "The Dharma of Ethics, the Ethics of Dharma: Quizzing the Ideals of Hinduism." *The Journal of Religious Ethics*. Vol. 30, No. 3. New Jersey: Wiley. 347–72.

Dhere, Ramchandra Chintaman. 1984/2011. *Rise of a Folk God: Vitthal of Pandharpur*. Ranikhet: Permanent Black. Translated by Anne Feldhaus of *Sri Vitthal: Ek Mahasamnvay*.

Dhulipala, Venkat. 2015. *Creating a New Medina: State Power, Islam, and the Quest for Pakistan in Late Colonial North India*. Delhi: Cambridge University Press.

Dirks, Nicholas B. 1996. "Reading Culture: Anthropology and the Textualization of India." *Culture/Contexture: Exploration in Anthropology and Literary Studies*. Edited by E. Valentine Daniel and Jeffrey M. Peck. Berkeley: University of California Press. 275–95.

———. 2001. *Castes of Mind: Colonialism and the Making of Modern India*. New Delhi: Permanent Black.

———. 2015. *Autobiography of an Archive: A Scholar's Passage to India.* New York: Columbia University Press.

Doniger, Wendy. 1980. "Introduction." *Karma and Rebirth in Classical Indian Traditions.* London: University of California Press. ix–xxv.

———. 2010. *The Hindus: An Alternative History.* Oxford: Oxford University Press.

———. 2015. "Hinduism." *Norton Anthology of World Religions, Vol. 1.* New York: W.W. Norton & Company, Inc. 53–722.

Doniger, Wendy and Smith, Brian K. 1991. *The Laws of Manu.* London: Penguin Books.

Douglas, Mary. 1984. *Purity and Danger: An Analysis of the Concepts of Pollution and Taboo.* New York: Routledge.

Dubois, Abbé J.A. 2002. *Hindu Manners, Customs and Ceremonies: The Classic First Hand Account of India in the Early Nineteenth Century.* Translated, Edited and Annotated by Henry K. Beauchamp. Mineola: Dover Publications.

Duncan, Ian. 2005. "Ambedkar, Ambedkarites and the Adivasi: The Dog that Didn't Bark in the Night." Paper delivered at the *International Conference on Reinterpreting Adivasi Movements In South Asia.* Sussex: University of Sussex.

Durkheim, Emile. 1915. *The Elementary Forms of the Religious Life.* Translated by Joseph Ward Swain. London: George Allen & Unwin Ltd.

Dwivedi, Dhananjay Vasudeo. 2012. "Bilva in Indian Tradition." *Indian Journal of History of Science.* New Delhi: Indian National Science Academy.

Eggeling, Julius. 1882. *The Satapatha-Brahmana: According to the text of fhe Madhyandina School, Vol. 1.* Sacred Books of the East Vol. 12. Oxford: The Clarendon Press.

———. 1885. *The Satapatha-Brahmana, Vol 2.* Sacred Books of the East, Vol. 26. Oxford: The Clarendon Press.

Eitel, Ernest J. 1904. *Hand-book of Chinese Buddhism, being a Sanskrit-*

Chinese Dictionary with Vocabularies of Buddhist Terms in Pali, Singhalese, Siamese, Burmese, Tibetan, Mongolian and Japanese. Tokyo: Sanshusha.

Elliot, Walter. 1869. "On the Characteristics of the Population of Central and Southern India." *The Journal of the Ethnological Society of London. Vol 1*. London: Ethnological Society of London.

Ellis, F.W. 1833. "Sources of Hindu Law". *The Law Magazine: Or, Quarterly Review of Jurisprudence*. Vol. 9. Feb–May. London: Saunders and Benning.

Elphinstone, Mountstuart. 1843. *The History of India*. London: John Murray.

Figueira, Dorothy. 2002/ 2015. *Aryans, Jews, Brahmins: Theorizing Authority through Myths of Identity*. New York: SUNY Press/New Delhi: Navayana.

Freud, Sigmund. 1930/2018. *Civilisation and its Discontents*. New Delhi: General Press.

Fuller, C.J. 2003. *The Renewal of the Priesthood: Modernity and Traditionalism in a South Indian Temple*. Princeton: Princeton University Press.

Ganguli, K.M. 1883–1896. *The Mahabharata of Krishna-Dwaipayana Vyasa Translated into English Prose. Vol VIII. Santi Parva (Part I)*. Calcutta: Pratap Chandra Roy.

Ghosa, Pratapachandra. 1871. *Durga Puja: With Notes and Illustrations*. Calcutta: Hindoo Patriot Press.

Ghose, Jogendra Chunder. 1917. *The Principles of Hindu Law—Volume I*. Third Edition. Calcutta: S. C. Auddy & Co., Booksellers and Publishers.

Ghosh, Jayati. 2015. "How poor is poor?" *Frontline*. August 21. Print Edition.

Gopalan, V. 1992. *A Critical Study of the Kausika Sutra*. PhD Thesis submitted to the Department of Sanskrit. Dharwad: Karnatak University.

Gordon, David. 2014. *The Yoga Sutra of Patanjali: A Biography*. Princeton: Princeton University Press.

Gorky, Maxim. 1982. *On Literature. Collected Works, Volume X.* Moscow: Progress Publishers.

Griffin, Nicholas. 1984. "Bertrand Russell's Crisis of Faith". *Russell: The Journal of Bertrand Russell Studies.* Ontario: McMaster University. 101–22

Griffith, Ralph T. B. 1896/2003. *Rig Veda—Book 10.* Benares: E. J. Lazarus and Co.

———. 1892/2003. *The Vedas: With Illustrative Extracts.* San Diego: The Boom Tree.

Guha, Sumit. 2017. *Beyond Caste: Identity and Power in South Asia, Past and Present.* New Delhi: Permanent Black.

Guha, Ramachandra. 2016. "Which Ambedkar?". *Indian Express.* 21 April. https://indianexpress.com/article/opinion/columns/br-ambedkar-2762688/ Accessed 1 September 2018.

Habib, Irfan. 1976. "Jatts of Punjab and Sind". *Punjab Past and Present: Essays in Honour of Dr Ganda Singh.* Edited by Harbans Singh and N. Gerald Barrier. Patiala: Punjabi University. 92–103.

Hammond, Phillip E. 1985. "Introduction." *The Sacred in a Secular Age.* Edited by Phillip E. Hammond. Berkeley: University of California Press. 1–6.

Harvey, David Allen. 2012. *The French Enlightenment and its Others: The Mandarin, the Savage, and the Invention of Human Sciences.* New York: Palgrave Macmillan.

Haug, Martin. 1863. *The Aitareya Brahmanam of the Rigveda, Volume 2.* Edited, Translated and Explained by Martin Haug. Bombay: Government Central Book Depot.

———. 1922. *The Aitareya Brahmanam of the Rigveda.* Allahabad: The Panini Office.

Haq, Jalalul. 1997. *The Shudra: A Philosophical Narrative of Indian Superhumanism.* New Delhi: Institute of Objective Studies.

Heestermen, J.C. 1987. "Self–Sacrifice in Vedic Ritual." *Gilgul: Essays on Transformation, Revolution and Permanence in the History of Religions.* Edited by Guy G. Stroumsa, Shaul Shaked and David Shulman. Leiden: E. J. Brill. 91–106.

Heirman, Ann. 2002. "Can We Trace the Early Dharmaguptakas?" *T'oung Pao Second Series.* Vol. 88, Fasc. 4/5. Leiden: E. J. Brill. 396–429.

Hiltebeitel, Alf. 1991. *The Cult of Draupadi, Volume 2: On Hindu Ritual and the Goddess.* Chicago: The Chicago University Press.

Hintze, Almut. 2003. "Haug, Martin." *Encyclopaedia Iranica.* Vol. 12, Fasc. 1. New York: Columbia University. 61–3.

Hiriyanna, M. 1993. *Outlines of Indian Philosophy.* Delhi: Motilal Banarsidass Publications.

Hoefe, Rosanne. 2017. *Do leather workers matter? Violating Labour Rights and Environmental Norms in India's Leather Production: A report by ICN—March 2017.* Utrecht: India Committee of the Netherlands.

Hultzsch, E. 1925. *Inscriptions of Asoka.* Corpus Inscriptionum Indicarum, Vol. 1. Oxford: Clarendon Press.

Hume, Robert Ernest. 1921. *The Thirteen Principal Upanishads.* London: Oxford University Press.

Ilaiah, Kancha. 2001. *God as Political Philosopher: Buddha's Challenge to Brahminism.* Calcutta: Samya.

Jaaware, Aniket. 2019. *Practicing Caste: On Touching and Not Touching.* Hyderabad: Orient BlackSwan.

Jaffrelot, Christophe. 2002. *Pakistan: Nationalism Without A Nation.* New Delhi: Manohar Publishers and Distributors.

———. 2005. *Dr Ambedkar and Untouchability: Analysing and Fighting Caste.* London: Hurst and Co.

Jaiswal, Suvira. 1998. *Caste: Origin, Function and Dimensions of Change.* New Delhi: Manohar.

Jalal, Ayesha. 1985. *The Sole Spokesman: Jinnah, the Muslim League and the Demand for Pakistan.* Cambridge: Cambridge University Press.

Jamison, Stephanie .W. and Michael Witzel. (trans.) 1992. *Vedic Hinduism.* Unpublished Manuscript. https://sites.fas.harvard.edu/~witzel/vedica.pdf.

Jamison, Stephanie and Joel Brereton. 2014. *The Rigveda: The Earliest Religious Poetry of India, Vol. I, 2 and 3.* New York: Oxford University Press.

Jamnadas, K. "Holi—A Festival to Commemorate Bahujan Burning." *Ambedkar.org.* http://www.ambedkar.org/jamanadas/Holi.htm. Accessed 1 November 2018.

Jha, D. N. 2009. *The Myth of the Holy Cow.* New Delhi: Navayana.

Jha, Vivekanand. 1978. "Position and status of bamboo-workers and basket-makers in ancient and early medieval times." *Proceedings of the Indian History Congress.* Vol. 39, No. I. Srinagar: Kashmir University. 230–40

———. 1979. "Leather Workers in Ancient and Early Medieval India." *Proceedings of the Indian History Congress.* Vol. 40. Srinagar: Kashmir University. 99–108.

———. 1991. "Social Stratification in Ancient India: Some Reflections." *Social Scientist.* Vol. 19, No. ¾. New Delhi: Indian Council of Historical Research. 19–40.

———. 2018. *Candala: Untouchability and Caste in Early India.* New Delhi: Primus Books.

Johnson, Robert and Adam Cureton. 2018. "Kant's Moral Philosophy", *The Stanford Encyclopedia of Philosophy* https://plato.stanford.edu/archives/spr2018/entries/kant-moral/.

Jolly, Julius. 1876. *Naradiya Dharmasastra or The Institutes of Narada.* London: Trübner and Co.

———. 1880. Trans. *The Institutes of Vishnu.* Oxford: Clarendon Press.

———. 2010. "Georg Bühler (1837–1898)." *Annals of the Bhandarkar Oriental Research Institute.* Vol. 91. Translated by G. U. Thite. Pune: BORI. 155–86.

Joseph, Tony. 2018. *Ancient Indians: The Story of Our Ancestors and Where*

We Came From. New Delhi: Juggernaut.

Kalyana Rao, G. 2000. *Antarani Vasantam*. Hyderabad: Virasam.

———. 2010. *Untouchable Spring*. Translated by Alladi Uma and M. Sridhar. Hyderabad: Orient BlackSwan.

Kane, P.V. 1926. "Introduction, Notes and Appendices." *The Vyavaharamayukha of Bhatta Nilakantha*. Bombay: Nirnaya-sagar Press.

———. 1930. *History of Dharmasastras (Ancient and Medieval Religious and Civil Law) Vol 1*. Poona: Bhandarkar Oriental Research Institute.

———. 1933. *Kātyāyanasmriti on Vyavahāra (Law and Procedure)*. Poona: Oriental Book Agency.

———. 1941a. *History of Dharmasastras (Ancient and Medieval Religious and Civil Law) Vol II, Part I*. Poona: Bhandarkar Oriental Research Institute.

———. 1941b. *History of Dharmasastras (Ancient and Medieval Religious and Civil Law) Vol II, Part II*. Poona: Bhandarkar Oriental Research Institute.

Keer, Dhananjay. 1954/2001. *Dr. Ambedkar: Life and Mission*. Mumbai: Popular Prakashan.

Keith, Arthur Berriedale. 1920. *Rigveda Brahmanas: The Aitareya and Kausitaki Brahmanas of the Rigveda*. Harvard Oriental Series, Vol. 25. Cambridge: Harvard University Press.

Kimball, David et al (ed.). 1845. "Ante–Roman Races of Italy." *Southern Quarterly Review*. Vol. 7. University of Michigan: Humanities Text Initiative. 261–300.

Kinnunen, Jussi. 1996. "Gabriel Tarde as a Founding Father of Innovation Diffusion Research." *Acta Sociologica*. Vol. 39, No. 4. Mexico City: Center for Sociological Studies of the Faculty of Political and Social Science, Universidad Nacional Autónoma de México. 431–42.

Kittel, Ferdinand. 1872. *A Tract on Sacrifice (Yajnasudhānidhi)*. Mangalore: Stolz & Reuther.

Klostermaier, Klaus K. 2007. *A Survey of Hinduism: Third Edition*. Albany: State University of New York Press.

Kosambi, D.D. 2008. *The Culture and Civilisation of Ancient India in Historical Outline*. Delhi: UBSPD.

———. 1985. *D.D. Kosambi on History and Society: Problems of Interpretation*. Edited by A.J. Sayed. Bombay: University of Bombay, Dept. of History.

Kotani, Hiroyuki. 1997a. "Conflict and Controversy over the Mahar Vatan in the Nineteenth- Twentieth Century Bombay Presidency". In *Caste System, Untouchability and the Depressed*. Edited by H. Kotani. New Delhi: Manohar. 55–78.

———. 1997b. "Ati Sūdra Castes in the Medieval Deccan ". In *Caste System, Untouchability and the Depressed*. Edited by H. Kotani. New Delhi: Manohar. 105–32.

Krishan, Y. 1986. "Buddhism and the Caste System" in *Journal of the International Association of Buddhist Studies*. Vol 9. No. 1. Lausanne: Lausanne University. 71–84.

Krishnasamy, K. 2018. "Devendra Kula Vellalars were wetland farmers, not untouchables, says Krishnasamy." *The Hindu*. 6 May. Interviewed by Udhav Nag. https://www.thehindu.com/news/national/tamil-nadu/devendra-kula-vellalars-were-wetland-farmers-not-untouchables-says-krishnasamy/article23788595.ece. Accessed 20 November 2018.

Kshirsagar, R. K. 1994. *Dalit Movement in India and Its Leaders, 1857–1956*. New Delhi: MD Publications Pvt Ltd.

Kumar, Aishwary. 2015. *Radical Equality: Ambedkar, Gandhi and the Risk of Democracy*. Stanford: Stanford University Press.

Lahiri, Nayanjot. 2015. *Ashoka in Ancient India*. New Delhi: Permanent Black.

Legge, James. 1886. *A Record of Buddhistic Kingdoms; Being an Account by the Chinese Monk Fa-Hien of his Travels in India and Ceylon, A.D. 399–414*. Oxford: Clarendon Press.

Lidova, Natalia. 1994. *Drama and Ritual of Early Hinduism*. Delhi:

Motilal Banarsidass.

Lochtefeld, James G. 2002. *The Illustrated Encyclopaedia of Hinduism*. New York: The Rosen Publishing Group, Inc.

Lubin, Timothy. 2018. "The Vedic Graduate: snataka." *Hindu Law: A New History of Dharmasastra*. Edited by Patrick Olivelle and Donald R. Davis, Jr. Oxford: Oxford University Press. 113–24.

Mackenzie, J.S.F. 1874. "The Village Feast." *The Indian Antiquary, Vol III*. Bombay: Thacker, Vining & Co. 6–9.

Macnaghten, William Hay. 1860. *Principles of Hindu and Mohammadan Law*. Edited by H.H. Wilson. London: Williams and Norgate.

Malkovsky, Bradley. 1997. "The Personhood of Sankara's "Para Brahman"." *The Journal of Religion*. Vol. 77, No. 4. Chicago: The University of Chicago Press. 541–62.

Mander, W.J. 2011. *British Idealism: A History*. New York: Oxford University Press.

Mani, Vettam. 1975. *Puranic Encyclopaedia: A Comprehensive Dictionary with Special Reference to the Epic and Puranic Literature*. Delhi: Motilal Banarsidass Indological Publishers and Booksellers.

Masuzawa, Tomoko. 1988. "The Sacred Difference in the Elementary Forms: On Durkheim's Last Quest." *Representations*. No. 23. Berkeley: University of California Press. 25–50.

———. 2005. *The Invention of World Religions: Or, How European Universalism Was Preserved in the Language of Pluralism*. Chicago: The Chicago University Press.

McAufille, Jane Dammen. 2015. "Islam." *Norton Anthology of World Religions, Vol. 2*. New York: W.W. Norton & Company, Inc. 1375–544.

Meillassoux, Quentin. 2009. *After Finitude: An Essay on the Necessity of Contingency*. Translated by Ray Brassier. London: Continuum.

———. 2012. "Iteration, Reiteration, Repetition: A Speculative Analysis of the Meaningless Sign." Paper delivered at the Freie Universität, Berlin on 20 April. Translated by Robin Mackay.

Minault, Gail. 1982. *The Khilafat Movement: Religious Symbolism and Political Mobilization in India*. New York: Columbia University Press.

Mitra, Rajendralala. 1876. *On Human Sacrifices in Ancient India*. Calcutta: Asiatic Society of Bengal.

Mitra, Trailokyanath. 1881. *The Law Relating to the Hindu Widow*. Calcutta: Thacker, Spinck and Co.

Mohan, Jyoti. 2004. "British and French Ethnographies of India: Dubois and His English Commentators." *French Colonial History* Vol. 5. Michigan: Michigan State University Press. 229–46.

Mookerji, Radhakumud. 1928. *Asoka (Gaekwad Lectures)*. London: MacMillan and Co. Ltd.

Nanda, B.R. 1977. *Gokhale: The Indian Moderates and The British Raj*. New Jersey: Princeton University Press.

Neal, Dawn. 2014. "The Life and Contributions of CAF Rhys Davids." *The Sati Journal—Women's Contributions to Buddhism: Selective Perspectives Volume II*. Redwood City: Sati Press. 15–31.

O'Hanlon, Rosalind. 1985. *Caste, Conflict and Ideology: Mahatma Jotirao Phule and Low-Caste Protest in Nineteenth-Century Western India*. Cambridge: Cambridge University Press.

———. 2007. "Cultural pluralism, empire and the state in early modern South Asia—A review essay." *The Indian Economic & Social History Review*. Vol. 44, No. 3. New Delhi: SAGE. 363–81.

———. 2013. "Contested Conjunctures: Brahman Communities and "Early Modernity" in India." *The American Historical Review*. Vol. 118, No. 3. Bloomington: Oxford University Press. 765–87.

O'Hanlon, Rosalind, Gergely Hidas & Csaba Kiss. 2015. "Discourses of caste over the longue durée: Gopīnātha and social classification in India, ca. 1400–1900." *South Asian History and Culture*. Vol. 6, No. 1. London: Routledge. 102–29.

Oka, Krishnaj Govind. 1913. *The Namalinganushasana or Amarakosha of Amarsimha*. Poona: Law Printing Press.

Oldenberg, Hermann. 1886. *The Grihya-sûtras, rules of Vedic domestic ceremonies*. Translated by Max Müller. Oxford: The Clarendon Press.

———. 1993. *The Religion of the Veda*. Translated by Shridhar B. Shrotri. First published in 1894. Delhi: Motilal Banarsidass Publishers.

Olivelle, Patrick. 1998. *The Early Upanishads: Annotated Text and Translation*. New York: Oxford University Press.

———. 1999. *Dharmasutras: The Law Codes of Ancient India*. New York: Oxford Univeresity Press.

———. 2005. *Manu's Code of Law: A Critical Edition and Translation of the Manava-Dharmasastra*. New York: Oxford University Press.

Olivelle, Patrick and Donald R. Davis, Jr.. Ed. 2018. The Oxford History of Hinduism Hindu Law: *A New History of Dharmaśāstra*. London: OUP

Omvedt, Gail. 2003. *Buddhism in India: Challenging Brahmanism and Caste*. New Delhi: Sage Publications.

Pande, G.C. 1974. *Studies in the Origin of Buddhism*. New Delhi: Motilal Banarsidass.

Pandey, Gyanendra. 1990. *The Construction of Communalism in Colonial North India*. Delhi: Oxford University Press.

Paswan, Sanjay and Pramanshi Jaideva. 2004. *Encyclopaedia of Dalits in India, Volume 7: Social Justice*. Delhi: Kalpaz Publications.

Patil, Prachi. 2016. "Understanding sexual violence as a form of caste violence." *Journal of Social Inclusion*. Vol. 7, No. 1. Meadowbrook: Griffith University. 59–71.

Pawar, Daya. 2015. *Baluta*. Translated by Jerry Pinto. New Delhi: Speaking Tiger.

Petzold, Bruno. 1995. *The Classification of Buddhism Bukkyo Kyohan: Comprising The Classification of Buddhist Doctrines in India, China and Japan*. In collaboration with Shinsho Hanayama, edited by Shohei Ichimura. Wiesbaden: Harrassowitz Verlag.

Philip, Kavita. 2004. *Civilizing Natures: Race, Resources and Modernity in Colonial South India*. New Jersey: Rutgers University Press.

Plutarch. 2017. *The Rise of Rome*. London: Penguin UK.

Poliakov, Leon. 2003. *The History of Anti-Semitism, Vol. 3: From Voltaire to Wagner.* Philadelphia: University of Pennsylvania Press.

Potter, Karl H. 1998. *Encyclopaedia of Indian Philosophies, Volume 3*. Delhi: Motilal Banarsidass.

Purcell, Nicholas. 1994. "Women and Wine in Ancient Rome." *Gender, Drink and Drugs*. Edited by Maryon McDonald. Oxford: Berg Publishers. 191–208.

Raj, Richa. 2015. "A Pamphlet and its (Dis)contents: A Case Study of *Rangila Rasul* and the Controversy Surrounding it in Colonial Punjab,1923–29." *History and Sociology of South Asia*. Vol. 9, No. 2. New Delhi: SAGE Publications. 146–62.

Rajagopalachari, C. 1946. *Ambedkar Refuted*. Bombay: Hind Kitab Publishers.

Rajah, M.C. 1925/2005. *The Oppressed Hindus*. New Delhi: Critical Quest.

Ramaswamy, Vijaya. 2004. "Vishwakarma Craftsmen in Early Medieval Peninsular India." *Journal of the Economic and Social History of the Orient*. Vol. 47, No. 4. Leiden: Brill. 548–82.

Ramdas, Ravindranath Vaman. 1986. "Glimpses of Apararka— Tika of Aparaditya the King of the Shilahara Dynasty of North Konkan (1127–1148 A. D.) which was presented to the court of Jayasimha the King of Kashmir." *Proceedings of the Indian History Congress—Volume I*. Vol 47. Srinagar: Kashmir University. 122–7.

Randeria, Shalini. 1989. "Carrion and corpses: conflict in categorizing untouchability in Gujarat". *European Journal of Sociology*. Vol. 30, No. 2. Cambridge: Cambridge University Press. 171–91.

Reich, David. 2018. *Who We Are and How We Got Here*. New Delhi: Oxford University Press.

Rhys Davids, Caroline Foley. 1901. "Notes on Early Economic

Conditions in Northern India." *The Journal of the Royal Asiatic Society of Great Britain and Ireland.* Cambridge: Cambridge University Press. 859–88.

———. 1917. *The Book of the Kindred Sayings (Sanyutta Nikaya) or Grouped Suttas, Part I.* Pali Text Society Translation Series, No. 7. London: Oxford University Press.

Rhys Davids, T.W. 1899. *Dialogues of the Buddha.* Sacred Books of the East, Vol. 11. London: Oxford University Press.

———. 1903. *Buddhist India.* New York: G.P. Putnam's Sons.

Ridding, C.M. 1896. *The Kadambari of Bana.* London: Royal Asiatic Society.

Risley, H. H. and E.A. Gait. 1901. *Census of India, 1901 Volume I: India: Part I—Report.* Calcutta: Government of India Central Printing Office.

Robinson, Francis. 1974. *Separatism Among Indian Muslims: The Politics of the United Provinces' Muslims, 1860–1923.* Cambridge: Cambridge University Press.

Rocher, Ludo. 1986. *A History of Indian Literature: The Puranas Volume II.* Edited by Jan Gonda. Wiesbaden: Otto Harrassowitz Verlag.

Russell, R.V. 1916. *The Tribes and Castes of the Central Provinces of India, Vol II.* London: Macmillan and Co.

Ryder, Arthur William. (trans.) 1905. *The Little Clay Cart (Mrcchakatika) attributed to King Shudraka.* Cambridge: Harvard University Press.

Sabrang. 2002. 'Appendix F—Adivasi vs Vanvasi: The Hinduization of Tribals in India.' *The Foreign Exchange of Hate: IDRF and the American Funding of Hindutva.* Mumbai: Sabrang Communications Private Limited, and France: The South Asia Citizens Web.

Sastri, Ramakrishna Harshaji. 1926. *Manavagrhyasutra of the Maitrayaniya Sakha with the Commentary of Astavakra.* Baroda: Baroda College.

Sastry, R. Sharma. 1927. *The Saraswati Vilasa of Prataparudramahadeva Maharaja (Vyavaharakanda).* Mysore: University of Mysore.

Sathaye, S.G. 1969. "The Aitareya Brahmana and the Republic."

Philosophy East and West. Vol. 19, No. 4. Hawai'i: University of Hawai'i Press. 435–41.

Saunders, Bailey. 1906. *The Maxims and Reflections of Goethe.* New York: The Macmillan Co.

Schwarz, Henry. 2010. *Constructing the Criminal Tribe of Colonial India: Acting Like a Thief.* Oxford: Wiley–Blackwell.

Sen, Benoy Chandra. 1949. "The Extent of The Rule of The Sunga Dynasty." *Proceedings of the Indian History Congress.* Vol. 12. Srinagar: Kashmir University. 54–62.

Sen, Sailendra Nath. 1988. *Ancient Indian History and Civilization.* New Delhi: New Age International.

Shank, J.B. 2015. "Voltaire." *The Stanford Encyclopedia of Philosophy.* https://plato.stanford.edu/archives/fall2015/entries/voltaire/. Accessed on 20 November 2018.

Sharma, Neeta. 1968. *Banabhatta: A Literary Study.* Delhi: Munshiram Manoharlal; Oriental Publishers.

Sharma, R.S. 1958/1990. *Sudras in Ancient India.* Delhi: Motilal Banarsidass.

Silva, Kalinga Tudor, P.P. Sivapragasam and Paramsothy Thanges. 2009. "Caste Discrimination and Social Justice in Sri Lanka: An Overview." *Working Paper Series.* Vol. 3, No. 6. New Delhi: Indian Institute of Dalit Studies.

Smith, Brian K. 1990. "Eaters, Food, and Social Hierarchy in Ancient India: A Dietary Guide to a Revolution of Values". *Journal of the American Academy of Religion.* Vol. 58, No. 2. Indianapolis: Indiana University–Purdue University. 177–205.

Smith, Michael E. 2009. "V. Gordon Childe and the Urban Revolution: a historical perspective on a revolution in urban studies." *Town Planning Review.* Vol. 80, No. 1. Liverpool: Liverpool University Press. 3–29.

Smith, Vincent A. 1909. *Asoka: The Buddhist Emperor Of India.* Oxford: Clarendon Press.

Solomon, Robert C. 1983. *In the Spirit of Hegel*. New York: Oxford University Press.

Somasundaram, Ottilangam. 1986. "Sexuality in the Kama Sutra of Vatsyayana". *Indian Journal of Psychiatry*. Vol. 28, No. 2. Mumbai: Medknow Publications. 103–8.

Sood, S.K., Thakur, T.N Vandana Lakhanpal. 2005. *Sacred and Magico-Religious Plants of India*. Jodhpur: Scientific Publishers.

Sullivan, Bruce M. 1990. *Krisna Dvaipayana Vyasa and the Mahabharata: A New Interpretation*. Leiden: E. J. Brill.

Sundar, Nandini. 2002. '"Indigenise, nationalise and spiritualise" – an agenda for education?' *International Social Science Journal*. Vol. 54, No. 173. September 1. 373–83.

Tejani, Shabnum. 2007a. "Reconsidering Chronologies of Nationalism and Communalism: The Khilafat Movement in Sind and its Aftermath, 1919–1927." *South Asia Research*. Vol. 27, Issue 3. London: SAGE Publications. 249–69.

———. 2007b. "Reflections on the Categories of Secularism in India: Gandhi, Ambedkar and the Ethics of Communal Representation, c. 1931." *The Crisis of Secularism in India*. Edited by Anuradha Dingwaney Needham and Rajeswari Sunder Rajan. London: Duke University Press. 45–65.

———. 2013a. "Defining Secularism in the Particular: Caste and Citizenship in India. 1909–1950." *Politics and Religion*. Vol. 6, Issue 4. Cambridge; Cambridge University Press. 1–27.

———. 2013b. "The Necessary Conditions for Democracy: B. R. Ambedkar on Nationalism, Minorities and Pakistan." *Economic and Political Weekly*. Vol. 48, No. 50. December 14. Mumbai: Sameeksha Trust. 111–9.

Teltumbde, Anand. 2015. "The Holy Cow." *Economic and Political Weekly*. Vol 1, No 14. April 4. Mumbai: Sameeksha Trust. 10–1.

———. 2018. *Republic of Caste: Thinking Equality in the Time of Neoliberal Hindutva*. New Delhi: Navayana.

Thapar, Romila. 2009. "Ashoka—A Retrospective". *Economic and Political Weekly*. Vol. 44, No. 45. November 7–13. Mumbai: Sameeksha Trust. 31–7.

Thibaut, George. 1890. *The Vedanta-Sutra: with the commentary by Sankarakarya, Part I*. Oxford: Clarendon Press.

Thirupathi, G. 2016. "Caste, Occupation and Identity: An Ethnographic Study of Rajaka caste in Telangana State." *International Journal of Arts, Humanities and Management Studies*. Vol. 2, No. 4. Bhopal: Orbit Publication. 27–32.

Thite, Ganesh Umakant. 1970. "Animal-Sacrifice in the Brahmana texts." *Numen*. Vol. 17, Fasc. 2. Tokyo: International Association for the History of Religions. 143–58.

Thompson, George. 2002. "Adhrigu and drigu: On the Semantics of an Old Indo-Iranian Word." *Journal of the American Oriental Society*. Vol. 122, No. 2. Ann Arbor: American Oriental Society.

Thursby, Gene R. 1975. *Hindu–Muslim Relations in British India: A Study of Controversy, Conflict, and Communal Movements in Northern India, 1923–1928*. Leiden: E. J. Brill.

Thurston, Edgar and K. Rangachari. 1909. *Castes and Tribes of Southern India Volume I—A and B*. Madras: Government Press.

———. 1909. *Castes and Tribes of Southern India Volume II—C to J*. Madras: Government Press.

Tikhonov, Nikolay. 1946. "Gorky and Soviet Literature." *The Slavonic and East-European Review*. Vol. 25, No.64. London: UCL. 28–38.

Tilak, Lokmanya Bal Gangadhar. 1903. *The Arctic Home in the Vedas: Being Also a New Key to the Interpretation of Many Vedic Texts and Legends*. Poona: Tilak Bros.

Times of India. 2003. "Ramkrishna Gopal Bhandarkar—orientalist par excellence." *The Times of India*. 12 July. https://timesofindia.indiatimes.com/Ramkrishna-Gopal-Bhandarkar-orientalist-par-excellence/articleshow/72430.cms. Accessed 1 September 2018.

Toomey, Paul M. 1976. "The Upanayana and Samavartana Rites: A

Paradox of Two 'Dharmas'." *Indian Anthropologist*. Vol. 6, No. 1. Delhi: Indian Anthropological Association.

Trigger, Bruce. 1994. "Childe's Relevance to the 1990s". *The Archaeology of V. Gordon Childe: Contemporary Perspectives*. Edited by David R. Harris. London: UCL Press. 9–34.

Valhe, Vijaya. 2015. "Madhuparka: A Comparative Study (From Agnistomasaptahautraprayoga & Asvalayanagrihyasutra)." *Bulletin of the Deccan College Research Institute*. Vol. 75. Pune: Deccan College.

Varadpande, M. L. 2005. *History of Indian Theatre: Classical Theatre*. New Delhi: Abhinav Publications.

Varghese K, George. 2003. "Globalisation Traumas and New Social Imaginary: Visvakarma Community of Kerala." *Economic and Political Weekly*. Vol. 38, No. 45. November 8. Mumbai: Sameeksha Trust. 4794–802.

Veda Vyasa Smriti. http://www.hinduonline.co/vedicreserve/smriti/02Vyasa_Smriti.pdf. Accessed 20 October 2018.

Verman, Sanghamitra Rai. 2013. "Women and Their Role in Ancient Indian Textile Craft." Journal of Eurasian Studies. Vol. 5, No. 4. Seoul: Hanyang University. 11–21.

Vidyarnava, Rai Bahadur. 1918. *Yajnavalkya Smriti: with the commentary of Vijnanesvara called The Mitaksara and note from the gloss of Balambhatta*. Allahabad: The Panini Office.

Vishwanath, Rupa. 2014. *The Pariah Problem*. New Delhi: Navayana.

Walshe, Maurice. 1987. *The Long Discourses of the Buddha: A Translation of the Digha Nikaya*. Boston: Wisdom Publications.

Warder, A.K. 2004. *Indian Buddhism*. Delhi: Motilal Banarsidass Publishers.

Watters, Thomas. 1904. *On Yuan Chwang's Yravels in India, 629–645 A.D*. London: Royal Asiatic Society.

Weber, Albrecht. 1882. *The History of Indian Literature*. Translated by

John Mann and Theodor Zachariae. London: Trübner & Co.

Wilson, H.H. 1866. *Rig Veda Samhita, Book I*. London: Trübner & Co.

White, David Gordon. 2014. *The Yoga Sutra of Patanjali: A Biography*. Princeton: Princeton University Press.

Yazdani, Ghulam. 1995. *Bidar, Its History and Monuments*. Delhi: Motilal Banarsidass.

Zelliot, Eleanor. 2013. *Ambedkar's World: The Making of Babasaheb and the Dalit Movement*. New Delhi: Navayana.

Žižek, Slavoj. 2008. *The Sublime Object of Ideology*. London: Verso.

———. 2011. "Interview with Ben Woodward." *The Speculative Turn: Continental Materialism and Realism*. Edited by Levi Bryant, Nick Srnicek and Graham Harman Melbourne: re:press. 406–15.

Acknowledgments

This volume wouldn't have been possible without the help we received as we waded through uncertain terrains of inquiry. The incisive and critical feedback, and guidance to further readings, we received from Uma Chakravarti, Vaibhav Abnave, V. Geetha, Aishwary Kumar, Soumyabrata Choudhury, Shiraz Iqbal and Anupama Rao were crucial. From them we learnt the blind spots of our exercise and the right questions we should ask ourselves. Their advice forced us to re-evaluate and strengthen our nascent ideas. The consistent and unstinting support we received from Wendy Lochner of Columbia University Press helped us push through the long months that went into the book's creation. We were also helped along by interns Purvi Rajpuria, Asad Dhaumya, Arjun Banerjee and Ishan Bhattacharya, who brought wisdom beyond their years to this project. Bibek Debroy, as always, helped us with unpacking some of the Sanskrit verses. Shiva Shankar and Hoshang Merchant kept us afloat in times of scarcity. The immense contribution of Juli Perczel, who edited this book for us, pointed out our theoretical blunders, and cut down our excesses, cannot be overstated. We thank Shyama Haldar for her keen proof-reading. For the exhaustive and meticulous Index, we thank Aatika Singh.

The charged and much-needed partisan critiques of our annotated edition of *Annihilation of Caste* (2014) kept us on our toes—the exercise here, we hope, is nourished by such lessons firmly dealt out; its intrinsic lacks, its own. Lastly, our gratitude to Kancha Ilaiah Shepherd for lending his voice to this book, for bringing his years of experience and knowledge, to contextualize the import of this project in the present.

Index

Abbé Dubois, 116, 130–1n16
Aboriginal, Aborigine: 77, 87, 98–9n3, 263n1, 295n6, 338n6, 348n25; Aboriginal Tribes, 295; Durkheim on, 263; origins of society, 98–9
Adi Sankara: 142n33, 190n1, 242n54, 311n39; and Brahmanical revivalism, 180, 142n33, 333; and Vedanta, 176n41, 215, 242–3n54
Adivasi(s): 11, 12, 14–37, 50; and Brahmanism, 58n2, 99n3, 114–6; and Dalits, 57–8n2, 316n59; and Ian Duncan on Ambedkar's views, 100n3; and food rights, 18–9, 24–5; and the RSS, 129–30n13; in universities, 67, 316n59. *See also* Tribes, Tribals, tribal
Advaita: 176n41; and Adi Sankara, 242n54; and animal killing, 159–60, 215. *See also* Adi Sankara, Vedanta, Yajnavalkya
Aga Khan III: 113, 126n5n6; and the Simla deputation, 126n5
Aghnya: 153–4; and the cow, 153–4, 168n16; linguistic origins, 168n16
Agra: 53, 127; leather industry, 53–4
Ahimsa: 218; and Buddhism, 23, 142–4n33, 218–9; and the cow, 23, 244n56, 26; and defilement, 244n56; Hindu appropriation, 23. *See also* Himsa, non-violence, violence

Aitareya Brahmana: 166n10, 202, 204–9, 226n3, 227n5, 228n8, 229n11n12, 230n13n14n17n18, 231n22n24, 232n26n27n29, 233n30; on animal sacrifices, 200–5; Brahmins and the rights of flesh, 207, 209; and the Brihati metre, 208–9, 232n27; how to conduct a sacrifice, 200–5; human sacrifices, 226n3; and the Madhuparka, 172n28; and Plato, 225n2; sacrifice of kine in honour of guests, 172n28n30; on the sacrificial essence, 167n12; sacrificial meat and its division, 168n14; and B.G. Tilak, 233n31; translation and interpretation, 230n19; on the Yupa, 200–2, 226–7n4
Akhil Bharatiya Vidyarthi Parishad (ABVP), 12–3
Akhlaq, Mohammed, 29, 38, 55
Aktor, Mikael: origin of Untouchability, 307n30; proliferation of caste names, 305n26; similarity with Ambedkar, 293–4n4, 298n11; "Stereotypes and Proliferations", 305n27; types of Chandalas, 304–5n26n27n28, 307n30, 321n66
Allen, Charles, 192n3
Alltudes, 70, 355, 370, 373
Alsdorf, Ludwig: on the word 'Aghnya', 168n16
Amarakosha, 313n46
Ambedkar, B.R.: method, 74–5, 78–81, 106–7n11, 132n18, 141n30, 162–3n1, 180n45, 223–5n1, 263–4n2, 275–6n17, 294n4, 298n11, 315–8n60, 320n65,

354–6, 359–74; *Annihilation of Caste*, 32, 35, 70, 72, 126n4, 233n32, 271n11, 36; "Buddha or Karl Marx", 70; "Castes in India: Their Genesis, Mechanism and Development", 275n17, 306n28, 316n59; "The Decline and Fall of Buddhism", 142–3n33, 345n19; "The Mahars: Who Were They and How They Became Untouchable?", 272n13; "Racial Difference as the Origin of Untouchability", 124n4; "Revolution and Counter-Revolution in Ancient India", 70, 76, 223n1, 248n61, 345n19; *Riddles in Hinduism*, 66, 70, 76, 123n2, 226n3, 307n29, 340n11, 350n27; *The Shudras—Who they were and How they came to be the Fourth Varna of the Indo; Aryan Society*, 65, 81, 82, 87, 96–7n1, 342n14; "States and Minorities", 100n3; *What Congress and Gandhi Have Done to the Untouchables*, 103n6, 264n2
Ambedkar Students' Association (ASA), 13, 15
Ambedkar–Periyar Study Circle (APSC), 22
Ambedkarite: 75, 79, 271n12, 359, 365, 373; Broken Men Theory, 107, 351; Constitution, 68; Ian Duncan, 100n3; Neelam Cultural Centre, 21; politics, 15, 320n65; thought, 75, 351
Ambedkar University, Delhi, 316n59
Andhra Pradesh, 39, 125n4, 151n2, 306n28, 339n9
Anguttara Nikaya, 177n43

Animists, animism: distinction in the Census, 129n10; and Hinduism, 112–5, 122–3n2
Anthony, Frank, 26
Antya: 75, 284, 294n5, 296n8n9, 311n39, 315n59; in the *Brahadaranyaka Upanishad*, 283; connection with the term 'Asprashya', 75, 278–80; in *Manusmriti*, 282, 294n5; usage in *Sutras* and *Smritis*, 279–81; translation by Bühler, 282, 310n37. *See also* Antyaja, Antyavasin, Asparshya, Bahya
Antyaja: 75, 283–4, 296n9, 302n18, 303n19, 304n22, 313n46, 318n61, 319n64; castes regarded as Antyaja in *Atri Smriti* and *Veda Vyas Smriti*, 280–1, 304n25, 312n41; connection with the term 'Asprashya', 280–1; and the cow, 150n1; Vivekanand Jha on, 336n3; in P.V. Kane 1941, 152n4; in the *Mahabharata*, 283; in the *Mitakshara*, 284; usage in *Sutras* and *Smritis*, 279–81; in the *Veda Vyas Smriti*, 147–8; in Vedic literature, 315–6n59, 324. *See also* Antya, Antyavasin, Asparshya, Bahya
Antyavasin: 75, 284, 299n15, 313n46, 315n59, 321; as a Brahmachari, 284; castes regarded as Antyavasin in *Madhyamangirs*, 281; connection with the term 'Asparshya', 280; in *Manusmriti*, 294n6; in the *Mitakshara*, 284; usage in *Sutras* and *Smritis*, 279–81; translations, 301n17. *See also* Antya, Antyaja, Asprashya, Bahya

Anuloma, 282, 349n27. *See also* Pratiloma
Anusasana Parva, 301n18, 315n54, 337n3
Apararka, Aparaditya, 74, 118, 137–8n26
Apastamba: 167n13, 222, 291n1n2, 294n5; *Apastamba Dharma Sutra*, 154–5, 157, 159, 168n15, 175n40, 195n13, 279, 296n8, 297n11; *Apastamba Grihya Sutra*, 173n32, 175n39; disposal of the dead, 157; editions, 296n8; and the Madhuparka, 156, 173n32; on meat eating, 154–6, 159, 167–8n14n15, 171n27; on sins, 118. *See also Dharma Sutras*
Aranyakas (in general), 166n10, 170n24, 246n58
archaeology, archaeologist, 41, 94, 100n4, 101n4, 135n23, 192n3, 195n13, 250n64, 254n77, 354, 358, 372
Aryan(s): 41–2, 43–4, 70–3, 77, 140, 156, 226n3, 283, 299n16, 308n31, 308n32, 336n3, 348n25, 354, 367; and ancient Romans, 233n31; Aryan invasion theory, 41, 124–5n4; B.R. Ambedkar on Aryan society, 65, 70–2, 87, 96n1, 248n61; as cow-killers, 153–5, 159–60, 244n56; sacrificial customs, 156; in South India, 191n2
Asad, Talal, 266n5
Asoka: 193n10, 194n11, 195n14, 196–7n15, 220–1, 253n74, 306, 343n17; and Buddhism, 191–2n3, 248n61; comparison with Manu, 184, 186–9, 210; on cow-slaughter, 187–9; non-violence,
187–9; Pillar Edicts, 184–6, 192–3n5; Rock Edicts, 184–6, 192n4
Asvaghosha: 236n35; *Buddhacharita*, 236n35
Asprashya, 75, 278–81, 285, 292n4. *See also* Antya, Antyaja, Antyavasin, Bahya
Asura, 44, 136n23, 207, 226n4, 283, 332, 338n6
Asvalayana, *Asvalayana Grihya Sutra*, 157–9, 172n31, 175n38n39
Atri, *Atri Smriti*, 234n33, 279–81, 294n5, 296–7n10, 303n19, 304n24
Ayodhya, 339n9
Ayyankali, 14
Ayyathurai, Gajendran, 79

Bagehot, Walter, 275n17
Bahmani dynasty, 274n15
Bahujan, 12–4, 18, 26, 43–4, 57n1, 58n2, 100n3, 316n59
Bahujan Samaj Party, 14, 57n1
Bahya: 294n5, 341n12; in *Apastamba Dharma Sutra*, 297n11; Bühler's translation, 297–8n11, 308n32; connection with the term 'Asparshya', 280–1; in *Manusmriti*, 282; in *Narada Smriti*, 299n14; usage in *Sutras* and *Smritis*, 279–81; in *Vishnu Dharma Sutra*, 298n12n13. *See also* Antya, Antyaja, Antyavasin, Asparshya
Bajrange, Dakxin, 98n2
baluta: 19, 130n14, 272n13; Amritnak, 272n14
Bana, Banabhatta: 332; on Chandala settlements, 330; description of the Chandala girl, 331–3, 348n26; *Harshacharita*, 346n22; *Kadambari*,

330, 346n22, 347n23n24; poetry, 349n27
Basavanna, 339n9
Basham, A.L., 141n31
Baudhayana Dharma Sutra, 236n35, 286, 291n1n2, 297n11
Bauer, Laurie, 162n1
Bayly, Christopher, 122n1
Bayly, Susan, 122n1
Bedar dynasty: 274n15; special rights of Mahars, 260, 272n14
beef: 146–61 *passim*, 183–9 *passim*, 238n46, 241n53, 248n60, 255–62 *passim*; beefarian(ism), 41; Beef Anthem, 21; beef-eating as sacrilege, 135n22, 256, 258–9, 355; beef-eating in mythology, 150n2; Beef Song, 19, 21; why Brahmins gave up beef-eating, 149, 153–4, 159–61, 189, 199–210, 213–33; in Buddhist literature, 47, 160, 361; differences and similarities in modern scholarship, 23–4, 196n15; festival, 11–8, 21–2, 34, 55–6; fresh meat and carcasses, 20–1, 23, 29, 35–6, 67, 150–1n2, 260–1, 269n9; origin of Untouchability, 24, 66–7, 77, 91, 114, 146–8, 150n2, 255–61, 290, 294n4, 309n33, 320n65n66, 323, 334, 345n19, 355; philosophical justification, 328; beef-eating in Hindu society, 32, 155, 159–61, 169n17, 175n40, 189
begar, Vethbegar, 273n14
Beteille, Andre, 33
Bhagat, R.D, 128n10
Bhagavad Gita: 242n54, 274n16, 321–2n66, 345n19; as counter-revolutionary, 223–4n1

bhakti: emergence, 190n1, 250n64, 300n16; poetry, 298n11, 363
Bhandarkar Orient Research Institute: 254n77; Critical Editions, 312n41
Bhandarkar, Devadutta Ramkrishna, 254n77
Bhandarkar, Ramchandra Gopal, 254n77
Bharatiya Janata Party (BJP), 11–4, 17–8, 28–30, 43, 45, 48, 51, 55, 70, 77
Bhattra tribe, 228n7
Bhavabhuti: *Malati-Madhava*, 139n29
Bhikshus/bhikkus: 23, 217–20, 222, 249n62, 365; and meat-eating, 218–20
Bhillas, 147, 281, 312n41
Bhillama II, 283, 312n43
Bhishma, 301–2n18, 312n41
Bidalkara/Bidalkari, 338n6
Bilva tree, 200–1, 227n6
Blacks: discrimination, 54, 102n5, 311n38
Bodhisatta, bodhisattva, 179–80n45
Bombay, 30, 49, 69, 105n9, 137n25, 150n1, 169n17, 195n13, 297n11, 301n16, 341n12
Bonn University: Ambedkar at, 321n66
Bourdieu, Pierre, 264n3
Bosworth, Clifford Edmund, 274n15
Brahadaranyaka Upanishad: 245n57, 246n58; on Antyas, 283; and sacrifices, 244n56, 247n60; and the transmigration of the soul, 215, 244n56
Bradley, F.H., 123n2
Brahma (god), 211, 226n3, 233–

4n33, 247n59, 332, 348n25
Brahmachari, Brahmacharin,
 174n35, 284, 296n9, 313n46,
 315n59
Brahman (universal principle in
 Advaita), 176n41, 242–4n55
Brahmanas, 154–60, 166n10,
 170n24, 181n45, 212, 225n2,
 226n3, 227n6, 233n31n32,
 237n40n43, 242n54, 249n62,
 299n13, 337n3, 340n11
Brahmin, Brahmanic(al): 12, 18,
 19, 22, 26, 27, 28, 33, 35, 37, 38,
 39, 79, 81, 96n1, 114–5, 123n2,
 136n24, 143–4n33, 152n3,
 234n33, 236n35, 237–8n45,
 239n49, 251n66, 275n17,
 300–1n16, 302–3n18, 307–8n30,
 314n49, 316n59, 342n14;
 appropriation of Sramanic
 systems, 23, 99n3, 142n33,
 194n12, 195n15; assimilation
 by colonisers, 71, 121, 131n16;
 contempt for Buddhism, 118–20,
 148, 328; assimilating into
 Brahmanism, 107n11, 142n33,
 189, 225n2, 251n67, 274n16, 275–
 6n17; things Brahmins should
 avoid, 239n39n40n41n42n43n44,
 238n48, 239–40n50, 286, 294–
 5n6, 302–3n18, 303n20, 304n22,
 340n11; in Buddhist texts, 160–1,
 177–8n44, 179–81n45, 249n62,
 347–8n25; considered as inferior,
 116–7, 120, 132n18, 311–2n35;
 culture, 15, 16, 30–1, 39–40,
 43–4; decline, 190n1; genetic
 questions, 44, 72, 73, 124–6n4;
 Kanvayana, 345n18; Kayastha,
 32, 301n16; killing a Brahmin,
 137n25, 141n30, 142n32,
214, 221–2, 236n36, 253n75;
 land-grab, 306n28; and linear
 hierarchies, 318–9n63; monopoly
 on flesh, 165n8, 175n40, 176n42,
 206–9, 211–2, 269n9, 297n11;
 obsession with obscurantist
 rules, 35, 165n6, 291n1, 294n4,
 317n60; Pancha Dravida and
 Pancha Gauda, 190–1n2; regicide,
 248n61, 327, 328; revival, 66,
 80, 181n3, 254n76; Saraswat,
 191n2, 350n28; as scholars but
 not intellectuals, 24, 66–7, 76,
 88–90, 129n10; as slaughterers,
 32, 44, 154–60, 200–6, 231n23;
 Tamil, 103n6; and tribal culture,
 99n3, 250n64, 306n28, 348n25;
 triumph over Buddhism, 66, 120,
 133n25, 216–20, 248n61, 328,
 344n18; Tulu, 133n21; turning
 vegetarian, 36, 91, 153, 184,
 199–222, 244n56, 251n67, 259,
 261; under the Guptas, 138n26,
 221–2, 254n76, 274–5n16, 296n9,
 333, 344n18; Vatsyayana, 332–3
Brahmin priests: 182n47, 228n9,
 229n12; Achhavaka, 203, 225n2;
 Adhvaryu, 154, 166n10, 201, 202,
 207, 209, 229n12, 230n14n16;
 Agnidhara/Agnidh, 208, 225n2,
 229n12, 230n16; Atreya, 208,
 230n16; Brahma, 230n16;
 Brahman, 229n12, 230n14;
 Brahmanachhamsi, 208, 225n2;
 Gravastut, 208, 230n16; Hotar,
 165n8, 166n10, 201–8, 225n2,
 228n9, 229n12, 230n14n16;
 Maitravaruna (Prasastar), 208,
 225n2, 229n12, 230n16; Neshtar/
 Nestar, 208, 225n2, 229n12,
 230n16; Potar, 208, 225n2,

229n12, 230n16; Pratihartar, 208, 230n16; Pratipashatar, 208, 230n16; Sadasya, 208, 230n16; Subrahmanya, 208, 230n16; Udgatar, 208, 230n16; Unnetar, 208, 230n16
Brereton, Joel P., 99, 163n2n3n4n5, 164n6, 165n8, 166n9, 169n20n21n22, 226n3, 297n10, 337n4n5
Briggs, G.W., *The Chamars*: 151n2
Britain, British, 70–1, 79, 89, 97n2, 105n9n10, 121n1, 123n2, 126n5, 128n10, 131n16, 167n13, 193n6, 252n69, 272n13, 291n1, 313n44, 317n60. *See also* colonial
Broken Men: 23, 70, 91, 106n11, 117, 255–62 *passim*, 272n13, 323–35 *passim*, 351–74 *passim*, 361, 366–7; becoming Untouchable, 66, 91, 118, 120, 148, 256, 258, 323, 340n11, 355; as beef-eaters, 91, 146, 148, 255, 259–61, 323; the Broken Men theory, 24, 73, 78, 107n11, 134–5n22, 318n60, 351–74 *passim*; as Buddhists, 23, 66, 91, 106n11, 118, 120, 148; not considered untouchable or impure, 91, 117–8, 340n11; opposition to Brahmins, 91, 117–8, 120, 355; similar communities, 70, 355, 370, 373; as speculation, 78, 79, 135, 147, 354, 298n11, 356–7, 359–60, 365–6, 369
Buddhism, Buddhist:19, 23, 36, 39–41, 120–20 *passim*, 252n68, 295n6, 306n28, 344n18, 355, 361–3; against animal sacrifice, 160, 221–2; Ambedkar's interpretation, 66, 77, 140–1n30, 180n45, 223n,
245–6n57, 248–9n61, 320n65, 321n66; appropriation of local gods and customs, 135n23; Arhant, 254n78; Buddhist kings, 182n47, 191n3, 196n14, 210; Buddhist monks in Brahmanical literature, 138n26, 139n29, 142n32; and caste, 179–81n45, 308–9n33; contempt for, 74, 91, 118–20; Divyavadana and Manjusrimulakalpa, 344n18; kulas, 181n45; *Lalitavistara Sutra*, 180n45; Mahasaka tradition, 253n72; Mahayana Buddhism, 180n45; and non-vegetarianism, 47, 148, 218–9; reasons for rise and fall, 136n23, 142–4n33, 250n64, 345n19, 364–5; opposition to yajna, 235n34; pilgrims to India, 193n5, 345n20; religion of the majority, 216–7; Second Buddhist Council, 252n71; outside the Indian subcontinent, 345n20; stratification of the Buddhist canon, 176–7n43; strife with Brahmanism, 216–8, 220, 251n65, 328, 335, 366; Theravada, 178n45; translation of texts, 231n19
Buddhist architecture: 136n23; Ajanta caves, 251n65; Fifth pillar edict (Pillar Edict No. V), 184–5, 188, 192n5, 193n8; Girnar rock, 192n4; as revolutionary, 136n23, 250–1n64; Rock Edict No. 1, 184, 192n4; Sanchi stupa, 221; Sangamner Plate, 283; survival among the people, 135–6n23
buffalo, 18, 24, 32, 36, 41–8, 171n27, 175n40

Bühler, Johann Georg: 195n13, 236n36; origin of *Manusmriti*, 327–9, 343n15; criticism of Bühler's translation, 194n13, 294n6, 295n7, 299n16, 340n11; *Laws of Manu*, 194n13, 233n32; specifics of Bühler's translations, 236n36n37, 237n38n39n40n41n42n43n44, 238n46n47n48, 239n50, 240n51, 241n52, 291n2, 297–8n11, 301n17, 309n34, 310n36, 314n47, 315n55n56n57n58; translation of Antya, 282, 310n37
Burnouf, Eugène, 179n45
Buruda (caste), 281, 324, 338n7

capitalism, 31
Carmakaras or Carmamnas, 337n3
The Casteless Collective, 21
Catholic Church, Catholicism, 88–9, 264n3
Census: 97n2, 112, 121n1, 128–9n10n11, 146, 233n33, 318n62n63, 320n65, 348n25; 1872, 129n12; 1901, 133n21; 1910, 112–6, 122n2; 1911, 123n2, 129n12, 130n15; 1931, 75, 123n3, 314n49; 2001, 123n3; 2007 Livestock Census, 42; 2011, 123n3
Census Act 1948, 123n3
central India, 191n2, 221, 228n7, 306n28, 346n21
Central University of Hyderabad, 12
chaanya, 19
Chaityabhoomi, 130n14
Chakkiliyar, 116, 132n17
Chakravarti, Uma: on assimilation of tribal groups into Brahmanical society, 306n28; on Buddha's egalitarianism, 181n45, 249n62; on caste-organization in Buddhist society, 181n45
Chalukya, 273n13, 312n43
Chamar: 72, 151n2, 288, 316n59, 320n65; appearing on both colonial lists and ancient *Smritis*, 289–90
Chambhars, 35, 272n13
Chandala, Candala, Kandala: 75, 140–1n30, 148, 235n34, 284–6, 303n19, 315n59, 321n66, 347n25, 361, 367–8; adultery Chandala, 305n26; in Buddhist literature, 179n45, 295n6, 304n26; caste Chandala, 305n26; Fa-Hian on, 314n49, 329–30, 334, 346n21; as impure but not untouchable, 313n46, 324, 326; in *Kadambari*, 330–3, 348n26, 349n27; in the *Mahabharata*, 301–2n18; purification, 285–6; relation to the term Asparshya, 285, 292n3; usage in the *Smritis*, 280–1; translation by Bühler, 340n11; translation by Doniger and Smith, 311n37, 340n11; translation by P.V. Kane, 294n5, 301n18, 311n39, 319n64; tribe Chandala, 295n6, 305n26; in *Vishnu Dharma Sutra*, 292n3, 299n13
Chandran, Ravi, 17
Charsley, Simon, 151n2
Chavadar Tank, 34, 342n14, 374
Chemudugunta, Seshu, 13
cheri, 132n18, 312n39
Childe, V. Gordon, 100–1n4. *See also* civilization, civilized
China, Chinese, 43, 218–9, 252n68n69n72, 314n49, 329, 333,

340n11, 345n20, 346n21, 347n25
Choudhury, Soumyabrata: 271n12, 223n1, 264n2; on Ambedkar as a Europeanist, 264n2; on the Bhagavad Gita, 223n1
Christian, Christianity, 16, 40, 50, 69, 112, 123n2, 130n13, 131n16, 265n4
civilization, civilized: 42, 79, 131n16, 191n2; Hindu Civilization, 67, 87–90; definition, 74, 100–1n4
Cohn, Bernard, 121n1
colonial, colonialism, colonised: 15, 22, 24, 28, 51, 66, 71, 76, 78, 99n3, 128n10, 131n16, 132n17, 133n20, 134n21, 142n33, 196n15, 265n4, 266n4, 318n63, 320n65, 362; consolidation of caste identity, 121–2n1, 318n62; and 'Criminal Tribes', 78, 97n2; Mahar soldiers, 150n1, 272n13; ethnography, 121n1; penchant for Census taking, 121n1; use of the term 'aborigine', 98n3
communal: 16, 39, 336n1; division, polarisation, 128n9n10, 265–6n4
Communist Party of India (Marxist), 38
Congress (Indian National), 18, 27–8, 43, 55, 103n6, 126n5, 264n2
cow: and Asoka, 187–9, 195–6n14, 196n15, 210, 220–1, 253n74; belt, 42; and B.G. Tilak, 233n31; in the Census, 42, 146; consuming the dead cow, 23, 66–7, 150n1n2, 259–61, 340n11; cow-killing as a sin, 25, 29, 221, 259; cow-protectors, 25–8, 48, 55, 69–70, 165–6n8, 188, 197n15, 274n16;

dung, 50, 132n18, 137n25; giving up cow-killing, 25, 218–22, 335; and guests, 157, 172n30, 174–5n37, 217, 241n53; indiscriminate killing, 159–60; in the Madhuparka, 156–7, 174n35, 238n46; in the *Manusmriti*, 194n12, 211–13; in mythology, 151–2n2; reverence for, 115, 148, 235n74; as sacred in the Vedas, 154–5; sacrifice, 23, 44, 154, 165n6, 166n8, 168n15n16, 194n12, 220; in the *Satapatha Brahmana* and the *Apastamba Dharma Sutra*, 154, 158–60, 167–8n14; smugglers, 22, 30, 46; Untouchable tasks in relation with the cow, 21, 23, 29, 35–6, 67, 146, 148
Criminal Tribes: 87; and Ambedkar, 100n3, 341n12; Criminal Tribes Act, 1871, 97–8n2. *See also* Adivasis, Tribes, Tribals, tribal

Dadri (lynching), 29
Dalit: 21, 24, 26, 28–30, 33, 35–7, 39, 41–4, 46–7, 50, 53, 55–6, 57n1n2, 65, 70, 80, 98n2, 100n3, 266n4, 342n14, 348n25, 352–3; emancipation, 223–4n1; Christians, 40; Dalitization, 33–4, 40; Dalit-ness, 303n18; Gods, 44–5, 151n2; movement, 316n59; subjectivity, 162n1; Tamil Nadu, 132n17, 151n2 ; University politics, 11–6, 18–9, 22, 34
Dalit Adivasi Bahujan Minority Students' Association (DABMSA), 12, 58n2
Dalit-Bahujan, 13, 26, 43–4, 57n1, 58n2, 100n3, 316n59

Damodaran, Harish, 42
Dandekar, V.M., 31
Dange, S.A., 81
Daphtary, Chander Kishan, 327, 343n16
darsan, 250n64
Dasa, 147, 281
Dasyus, 282, 308n31
Datta, Swati, 191n2, 350n28,
Dattatreya, Bandaru, 13
Davis, Donald R., 123n2, 138n26, 176n42, 292n4, 296n9
DeCaroli, Robert: *Haunting the Buddha: Indian Popular Religions and Formation of Buddhism*, 135n23; and image-worship, 250n64; incorporation of existent customs, 144n33; persistence of Buddhism, 250n64. *See also* Buddhism, Buddhist
Deccan, 195n13, 274n15, 300n16, 312n43
defilement, 117, 244n56, 317n60
Delhi: 14, 18, 26, 27, 29, 30, 37, 44, 46, 134n21, 316n59; Delhi Agricultural Cattle Preservation Act, 1994, 17; Delhi High Court, 17; Delhi-Topra pillar, 192–3n5
Deliège, Robert, 67
Denotified Tribes (DNTs), 97n2. *See also* Criminal Tribes
Deobandi Ulema, 127n9
Depressed Classes, 103n6, 112, 223n1, 266n4
Desai, Ashwin, 32, 49–51, 71
Deweyan philosophy, 271n12
dhamma: 70, 178n44, 180n45, 245n57, 248n61, 369; and Asoka, 191–2n3
Dhand, Aarti, 239n49
dharma, 167n13, 171n27, 224n1, 234n33, 239n49, 300n16, 301n18,
Dharma Sutras: 92, 138n26, 139n28, 154–5, 157, 159, 167n13n14, 168n15, 171n27, 175n40, 195n13, 235n35, 278–81, 285–6, 287, 291n1n2, 296n8, 297n11, 301n17, 314n47, 315n50, 324, 362; on Untouchability, 280, 284–90, 294n5, 301n117, 309n33, 314n47; terms denoting impure subject, 279–81
Dhere, R.C., 298n11, 364–5
Dhulipala, Venkat: creation of Pakistan, 127–8n9
Dirks, Nicholas B., caste and colonialism, 121n1, 134n21
Doniger, Wendy: appropriation of folk myths, 190n1; on Bühler's translation, 238n46, 295n7, 299n16, 310n36n37; Gupta patronage of Hinduism, 275n16; on karma, 245n57; *Laws of Manu*, 194n12n13, 253n73, 343n15; on the Madhuparka, 238n46; Sramanic challenge to Brahmanism, 340n11; on temple-worship, 251n65; *The Hindus: An Alternative History*, 18; translation issues, 295n7; translation of *Manusmriti*, 194n12, 294n6, 340n11; on violence, 234n34
Dravidian, 42, 70–2, 124n4
Dumont, Louis: 306n28; *Homo Hierarchicus*, 73
Durga, 44–5, 99n3, 332
Durkheim, Emile: 197n16; influence, 264n3; interdictions, 268n8, 269n9, 270n10; origin of religion, 263n1, 268n7; on taboos, 257; *The Elementary Forms of the Religious Life*, 263n1, 266n5;

170n22, 172n30; as a tribal text, 99n3
right-wing, 11–3, 28, 51, 70, 77, 132n17, 304n25, 371–2
Rights of the Child, 1990, 51
rishi(s), 160, 170n24, 209, 227n4, 297n10
Risley, H.H.: 133n21; on animism, 122–3n2; definition of Hinduism, 123n2; ethnographic methods, 134n21
Rome, Romans, 98n3, 233n31
Round Table Conference, 1932, 34
Roundtable India, 45
Rudra, 154–5, 166n9, 171n25, 234n33
Ryder, Arthur William: 141n30, 141n31; translation of *Mrichhakatika*, 140n30

sacred: 134n21, 184–5, 201, 204, 214–5, 227n4n5n6, 269n8, 286, 292n3, 297n11, 328, 345n19, 365; cow as, 23, 153, 155–6, 168n16, 174n35, 213, 236n36, 256, 258–9, 290, 323; fire, 237n40, 240n51; objects, 257; as opposed to the profane, 34, 36–7, 54, 256–8, 265n3, 267n6, 268n7, 269n9, 270n10; and the religious, 256, 267n6, 268n7, 270n10; rituals and rites, 172n29, 195n14, 212
Sacred Books of the East (SBE) series, 195n13, 233n32, 297n11
sacrifice: 20, 142n33, 156–7, 169n18, 170n23, 212, 226–7n4, 227n5, 229n12, 234n34, 238n46, 239n50, 240n51, 241n53, 242n55, 247n59n60, 286, 337n4; to Agni, 155, 225n2, 228n10; animal, 23, 44, 69, 154, 161, 165n6, 168n14n15n16, 170n22, 171n26n27, 194n12, 195n14, 199–210, 214–5, 217–8, 220, 228–9n10, 233n32, 244n56, 245n57, 246n58, 248n61, 269n9, 328, 331, 345n19; Asoka on, 184, 188, 195–6n14; Buddha on, 160, 177–8n44, 181n47; in Buddhist literature, 138n26, 221, 249n63; division of sacrificial meat, 156, 166n8, 175n40, 230n14n15n16; exclusion from, 209–10; human, 209–10, 226n3, 232n29, 234n33, 338n6; implements, 157–9, 200, 203; ingredients recommended by the *Apastamba Dharma Sutra*, 157–9, 175n40; sacrificial essence, 167n12; Soma sacrifices, 163n2, 172n28, 208, 225n2, 228n9, 228n10, 231n23; Srauta sacrifices, 172n28, 236n36; to Vishnu, 155
Said, Edward W., 128n10
Saivite(s), 183, 190n1, 300n16
Sakhya (clan), 182n47, 319n63
sangha, samgha, 180–1n45, 249n62, 251n64, 363
Samhitas, 166n10, 169n18, 170n24
samsara, 245n57
Samskara, 172n29
Sangh parivar, 17
Sankhya, 242n54
Sanskrit: 40–1, 44, 124n4, 152n4, 344n17; Ambedkar's ability in, 76, 82, 96n1; Buddhist plays, 118, 139n29; modern editions of literature in Sanskrit, 300n16; scholars, 137n25, 168n16n17, 174n37, 195n13, 228n8, 254n76, 321n66, 346n22; translations, 227n7, 231n20, 273n14, 292n4, 297n11, 304n25, 312n42, 313n46, 338n5

Sanskritization: 33, 39–40, 276n17; Sanskritized Victorian values, 130n13
Saraswati, 346n22
Saraswativilasa, 312n42
Satapatha Brahmana: 155, 166n10, 172n28, 225n2, 226n3; on cow-killing, 154, 159–60
Satavahana dynasty, 192n4, 344n18
Sathaye, S.G., 225n2, 226n2, 230n14
Savarna, 150n1, 179n45, 272n13, 318n63, 325
Scheduled Castes: 33, 38, 57n1, 98n2, 103n6, 132n17, 318n62; getting into the schedule, 123n3
Scheduled Tribes, 99n3, 123n3
Schwarz, Henry, 98n2
scientific inquiry, 94, 105n11
secular: 18, 24, 27, 38, 41, 55–6, 255–6, 268n8; difference with the sacred, 256, 267n6; in the Indian subcontinent, 265–6n4; in Western society, 265–6n4, 266–7n5
Settled communities: conflict with Nomadic communities, 135n22, 354–6; creation of Broken Men, 255, 259–61, 323. *See also* Broken Men Theory, Nomadic Tribes
Shaikh, Ghulamuddin, 46
Shakahari, 183
shakhas, 170n24, 191n2
Shanti Parva: 234n33, 279, 283, 312n41; on facing a crisis in dharma, 301n18
Sharma, R.S.: 346n22, 347n23; 'absorption of tribals', 306n28; commonality between Buddhist and Brahmanic texts, 295n6; engagement with Ambedkar, 293–4n4, 298n11, 307n29, 309n33, 320n66; *Sudras in Ancient India*, 306n28
Shastras: 147, 152n4, 288–9, 297n10, 303n18, 307n29, 319n64, 342n14, 369; five classes of Chandalas, 285
Shatrugna, Veena, 30–1, 37
Simla, 126n5
Shiva: 227n6n7, 242n54; spread Shiva worship, 142–4n33, 190n1, 217; tribal origin, 99n3
Shudra: 11, 14, 19, 24, 37, 39–40, 44, 47, 55, 56, 57n1n2, 87, 225n2, 258, 285, 307n29, 349n27, 361, 363; interdictions related to, 96n1, 258; origin of the caste, 42, 96n1
Shudraka: 330–1; *Padmaprabhrutakam*, 139n29
Simmel, Georg: on piety, 267n6
sin: 14, 74, 118, 137n25, 227n6, 283, 293n4, 328; as caste-dharma, 239n49; cow-killing as, 25, 29, 221, 259; Buddhist notion of, 245–6n57; meat-eating as, 211; minor sin, 214, 239n49, 240n52; mortal sin, 214, 239n49n50, 241n52
Smith, Brian K.: on Bühler's translation of the *Manumriti*, 294n6, 295n7, 299n16, 310–11n37, 340n11; date of origin of the *Manusmriti*, 343n15; natural order and violence in *Manusmriti*, 194n12; on Madhuparka, 238n46; meat-eating in *Manusmriti*, 194n12, 253n73; on sacrifices, 194n12; translation issues, 195n13n14, 238n46; on vegetarianism, 253n73
Smith, Vincent: 193n6n7n8,

196n14; on Asoka's prohibition of cow-killing, 187–8, 197n15, 220; Snataka: 235–6n35, 237–8n45, 238n46, 241n53, 296n9; and the Madhuparka, 156; rules for the, 213
socialist, 28
Socio Economic Caste Census (SECC), 123n3
Soma: 164n4, 172n30; god, 231n19; hymns, 163n2, 348n25; sacrifice, 172n28, 206, 208, 210, 225n2, 228n9n10, 229n12, 231n23
South Asia, 99n3, 122n1, 191n3
southern India, South India, 42, 44, 131n16, 133n20, 171n24, 191n2, 244n56, 251n65
speculation: 106–7n11, 147, 166n10, 305n27, 330; and Ambedkar, 78–81, 93, 135n22, 223n1, 298n11, 356, 359–60, 366, 369; definition, 108n13, 356–7
Speculative Materialism, 351, 356–7, 366
Speculative Realism, 81
spirit-deities: 250–1n64; asuras, 136n23; bhutanis, 136n23; bhutas, 135n23; gandharvas, 136n23; kimpurusas, 135n23; kinnaras, 135n23; mahoragas, 136n23; nagas, 136n23; pisacas, 135n23; raksasas, 135n23; suvarnas, 136n23; vidyuts, 136n23; yaksas, 135n23
Sramana, Sramanic, 138n26, 144n33, 235n34, 252n72, 253n73, 340n11, 355
Srauta rituals and sacrifices, 172n28, 236n36
Sri Lanka: 345n20; and caste, 339n9; Vattagamini, 176n43

Srinivas, M.N.: difference with Ambedkar, 276n17; Sanskritization, 33
sruti, 138n26, 172n28, 174n35
Ssu-fen-lu (Shi-bun-ritsu), 219, 252n72
State Mahadalit Commission, 319n63
Suds, 46
Sufi, 230n19
Sunga dynasty: 136n23, 248n61, 327–8, 343–4n17; in literature, 344n18; overthrowing the Mauryas, 248n61, 327–8, 344n18; Vedic counter-revolution, 344n17
Supreme Court of India, 30, 32, 49–51
Sura, 214, 239n50
Surya, 165n6, 171n25, 234n33
Suttas, Sutta Pitaka: 177n43, 181n47, 347n25; *Kutadanta Sutta*, 160, 177n43n44; *Sutta Nipata*, 348n25; *Vasalasutta*, 347n25
svapaca, 75, 303n19, 307n30
Swaminathan, M.S., 31

Taittiriya Brahmana: 170n23, 226n3; caste descriptions in, 338n8; on human sacrifices, 338n6; origin, 170n24; B.G. Tilak on, 233n31; sacrifice of oxen and cows, 155, 171n25
Tamil, Tamil Nadu, 20, 22, 27, 51, 53, 79, 103n6, 132n17, 151n2, 191n2, 319n63, 339n9
Tanjore, 116, 132n18
Tarde, Gabriel: contemporary influence, 197n16; and the law of imitation, 189, 198n16, 275n17; social interaction theory, 197n16
Tejani, Shabnum: on Ambedkar's conception of nationalism,

128n9; on the meaning of secularism in India, 265–6n4
Telangana, 338n7, 339n9
Telangana Students' Association, 12
Teltumbde, Anand, 319n63
Telugu, 14, 20, 40, 132n17, 151n2, 339n9
Thapar, Romila, 192n3
Thass, Iyothee, 79, 356
Therigatha, 178n45
Thibaut, George, 242n54, 243n55
Thite, Ganesh Umakant, 231n23
Thurston, Edgar: biased and racist methods, 134n21; on types of Brahmins, 190n2; *Castes and Tribes of Southern India*, 133n21; work on the Census, 133n21
Tilak, B.G.: *The Arctic Home in the Vedas*, 73, 233n31
Tipitaka: 254n78; *Abhidhamma Pitaka*, 176n43; *Sutta Pitaka*, 176n43; *Vinaya Pitaka*, 176n43
Tishya, 186, 194n11
Touchable: 153, 323; linguistic analysis, 72, 124n4, 162n1, 354
Transmigration of the Soul: 215–6, 244n56; and the Buddha, 245n57
Tribes, Tribals, tribal: 19, 54, 57n1n2, 123n3, 259–60, 295n6, 298n11, 299n16, 348n25, 355; Ambedkar's attitude, 77, 87, 99n3, 308n31, 366–7; assimilation, 98n3, 306n28; Australian, 263n1; colonial characterisation of, 97–8n2; difference from Hindus, 91, 112, 114–5, 123n2, 129n10; gods and their appropriation, 99n3, 144n33; kings, 182n47, 344n18; languages, 130n13; myths, 228n7, 245n57; origin of society, 42; primitive, 135n22, 317n60; and the RSS, 130n13; texts, 304–5n26

Tsang, Hsuan/Yuan Chwang: 218–20, 252n69n70, 333–4, 350n30, 345n20; descriptions of houses, 333–4, 350n30; on pure flesh, 218; on violence against Buddhists, 143n33; also Yuan Chwang and Xuanzang, 252n68
Tughlaq dynasty: 193n5; Muhammad bin Tughlaq, 273n14, 274n15
Turkey, Turkish, Turk (Turuska), 42, 89, 127n9, 134n21, 142n33, 300n16

Ugras, 298n11
Ujjain, 344n18
Una, 29, 35, 65
Union Human Resource Development Minister, 13
United Kingdom, 128n10
United Nations' Food and Agriculture Organisation (FAO), 43
United Nations' World Conference against Racism, 2001, 56
United Provinces, Uttar Pradesh, 100n3, 127n9, 193n6
upanayana, 96n1, 167n13, 173–4n35, 228n7, 235n35
Upanishads: 215–6, 242n54, 244n56, 245n57, 246n58, 247n59n60, 283, 311n38; reinterpretations of, 242n54; style, 246n58; as part of the *Vedas*, 166n10, 170n24
Upapataka, 222, 239n49. *See also* Mahapataka
Upapuranas, 152n3

Vahed, Goolam, 71
Vaideha, Vaidehika, Vaidehaka, 281,

GPSR Authorized Representative: Easy Access System Europe, Mustamäe tee
50, 10621 Tallinn, Estonia, gpsr.requests@easproject.com